LEGAL MEDICINE 1985

LEGAL MEDICINE 1985

CYRIL H. WECHT,
M.D., J.D., Series Editor

Former coroner, Allegheny County (Pittsburgh), Pa.; Clinical Associate of Pittsburgh Schools of Medicine and Dental Medicine; Adjunct Associate Professor of Epidemiology, University of Pittsburgh Graduate School of Public Health; Adjunct Professor of Pathology, Duquesne University School of Pharmacy; Adjunct Professor of Law, Duquesne University School of Law; Director, Pittsburgh Institute of Legal Medicine; Past President, American Academy of Forensic Sciences; Past President, American College of Legal Medicine.

PRAEGER

PRAEGER SPECIAL STUDIES • PRAEGER SCIENTIFIC

New York • Philadelphia • Eastbourne, UK
Toronto • Hong Kong • Tokyo • Sydney

ISSN 978-0-275-90182-0
Library of Congress Catalogue Card No. 80-647751

While care has been taken to maintain the accuracy of the information contained in this volume, the authors, editors, and publisher cannot accept any legal responsibility for errors or omissions, or for consequences arising from the use of the information contained herein and make no warranty, express or implied, with respect to the materials presented in this volume.

Published in 1985 by Praeger Publishers
CBS Educational and Professional Publishing, a Division of CBS Inc.
521 Fifth Avenue, New York, NY 10175 USA

56789 052 987654321

INTERNATIONAL OFFICES

Orders from outside the United States should be sent to the appropriate address listed below. Orders from areas not listed below should be placed through CBS International Publishing, 383 Madison Ave., New York, NY 10175 USA

Australia, New Zealand
Holt Saunders, Pty, Ltd., 9 Waltham St., Artarmon, N.S.W. 2064, Sydney, Australia

Canada
Holt, Rinehart & Winston of Canada, 55 Horner Ave., Toronto, Ontario, Canada M8Z 4X6

Europe, the Middle East, & Africa
Holt Saunders, Ltd., 1 St. Anne's Road, Eastbourne, East Sussex, England BN21 3UN

Japan
Holt Saunders, Ltd., Ichibancho Central Building, 22-1 Ichibancho, 3rd Floor, Chiyodaku, Tokyo, Japan

Hong Kong, Southeast Asia
Holt Saunders Asia, Ltd., 10 Fl, Intercontinental Plaza, 94 Granville Road, Tsim Sha Tsui East, Kowloon, Hong Kong

Manuscript submissions should be sent to the Editorial Director, Praeger Publishers, 521 Fifth Avenue, New York, NY 10175 USA

Preface

Medical technology has made significant advancements in recent years, and there has been a concomitant increase in the number and variety of legal complications arising from and associated with these exciting scientific achievements. To complicate the medico-legal scene even further, the federal government has instituted several new programs which have mandated dramatic changes not only in the economics of medicine, but also in the substantive practice of medicine. These innovative concepts will undoubtedly create additional legal concerns for physicians, hospitals, and other groups involved in the health care delivery system in the near future.

Various court decisions in civil and criminal lawsuits, as well as a fascinating panorama of other cases dealing with such issues as the determination of life and death, mental patients' right to treatment and right to refuse treatment, abortions and test-tube babies, and many other controversies involving ethical, moral, and theological principles, have also expanded horizons and complicated the fields of legal medicine and forensic science. Societal problems such as drug and alcohol abuse, industrial toxins, drug and vaccine reactions, and chemical and environmental carcinogens, along with many others, continue unabated.

This edition of *Legal Medicine* includes chapters by outstanding authorities dealing with several of these topics. As in past years, our major purpose is to add to the medico-legal knowledge of physicians, forensic scientists, and civil and criminal attorneys, thereby enhancing their professional expertise.

I should like to express my gratitude and appreciation to all the contributing authors, and to my personal secretary, Maribeth Groff, for her extensive assistance.

Cyril H. Wecht

Contributors

MARK E. BATTISTA, M.D., J.D. Attending physician at the Maine Medical Center/Mercy Hospital Family Practice Center; consultant to the Health Care Financing Administration; faculty member, the New England College of Osteopathic Medicine

FRANK MITCHELL CORSO, ESQUIRE. Trial attorney and senior partner, Frank Mitchell Corso, P.C., Westbury, New York

DAVID A. CROWN. Examiner of Questioned Documents in private practice in Fairfax, Virginia

FRANCIS M. ESPOSITO, M.S. Toxiocology Manager, Department of Laboratories, Allegheny County; Lecturer of Toxicology, Duquesne University School of Pharmacy, Pittsburgh, Pennsylvania

BERNARD J. FICARRA, M.D. Director of Medical Legal Research, Ficarra Foundation, Oyster Bay, New York

TERRANCE G. FURLOW, M.D., J.D. Private Practice, Internal Medicine, Lexington, Kentucky; Fellow, American College of Legal Medicine

HAROLD L. HIRSH, M.D., J.D., F.C.L.M. Adjunct Professor, Catholic, George Washington, and American Universities and Montgomery College; Editor-in-Chief, *Legal Aspects of Medical Practice;* Editor, *Medical Trial Technique Quarterly* and *Medicine and Law*

DAVID S. KAUFER. Associate Professor of English, Carnegie-Mellon University

BERNARD KNIGHT, M.D., B. Ch., F.R.C. Path, D.M.J. (Path), Barrister-at-Law. Professor of Forensic Pathology, Welsh National School of Medicine, University of Wales, Cardiff, Wales

REBECCA LEVINE, ESQUIRE. New York City-based attorney in private practice

ELIZABETH A. PRINCIPI, J.D., LL.M. Special Assistant for Medical-Legal Affairs, Naval Medical Command, Washington, D.C.

LORI G. RUSSELL, Ph.D. Psychological Service of Pittsburgh, Pittsburgh, Pennsylvania

ARNOLD SCHAM, M.D. Medical Director, Northwest Bergen Hospice Program and The Raymond E. Banta Valley Center; The Valley Hospital, Ridgewood, New Jersey

MARLENE SCHAM, M.A. Health Educator, Discussion Group Leader, Northwest Bergen Hospice Volunteer Training Program

NATHANIEL SHAFER, M.D. Associate Professor, New York Medical College

ROBERT SHAFER, M.D. Medical Resident, Lenox Hill Hospital, New York City

EDWIN R. STEINBERG, Ph.D. Thomas S. Baker Professor of English and Interdisciplinary Studies, Carnegie-Mellon University

SHEILA TAUB, J.D. Professor of Law, University of Bridgeport School of Law, Bridgeport, Conn.

SARAH D. TONEY, M.A. Teacher, Shady Side Academy, Pittsburgh, Pennsylvania

ROBERT M. WETTSTEIN, M.D. Assistant Professor, Department of Psychiatry, University of Pittsburgh School of Medicine

CHARLES WINEK, Ph.D. Director of Laboratories and Chief Toxicologist, Allegheny County; Professor of Toxicology, Duquesne University School of Pharmacy; Adjunct Professor of Toxicology, University of Pittsburgh School of Medicine

JERRY ZASLOW, M.D., J.D. Associate Professor of Surgery (Clinical), Temple University Medical School; Lecturer in Law, Temple University Law School; Instructor in Legal Medicine, Medical College of Pennsylvania; Professor of Forensic Podiatry, Pennsylvania College of Podiatric Medicine; Senior Surgeon, Rolling Hill Hospital, Elkins Park, Pennsylvania; Senior Surgeon, John F. Kennedy Hospital, Philadelphia, Pennsylvania; Att. Surgeon, Albert Einstein Medical Center & Frankford Hospital

Contents

The Examination of Skeletal Remains

Bernard Knight, MD, B.Ch., F.R.C.Path, D.M.J.(Path), Barrister-at-Law

INTRODUCTION

The forensic pathologist is frequently asked to examine remains that are—or are thought to be—human skeletal remains. The circumstances in which this request is made vary widely, from the discovery of an isolated bone to the late results of some mass disaster. Probably the majority of such examinations arise from the chance finding of skeletal remains during building, demolition work, or historical excavations.

The finds come to the notice of the pathologist because of the possibility of some criminal element in the death or, more often, because the legal system requires some medico-legal investigation to be made before final disposal of the matter.

The first thing to be emphasized is that where weighty legal issues may rest upon the outcome of the examination, expert advice sometimes from several different sources, is mandatory. The expertise of an anatomist, a forensic odontologist, a radiologist, an archeologist, a serologist, and sometimes a veterinarian or chemist, may be needed in certain circumstances.

This short survey of the problem is intended only to map out the most effective routine for pathologists to follow. Where the issues are obviously superficial—such as the finding of a few very ancient bones of unknown historical provenance—pathologists might be able to handle the whole situation without recourse to any more specialized colleagues. This also applies when they act as screeners for suspect remains and find them to be non-human. In other circumstances, their own expert appreciation of various facets of the problem will allow pathologists to choose the correct specialists, thereby facilitating the investigation without waste of time or resources. Where important matters of identification or dating hang upon the examination, especially if there are potential criminal aspects, then the pathologist initially consulted would be ill-advised to "go it alone" and not call in specialist help.

The doctor presented with skeletal remains—which may vary in quantity from a single shattered fragment to several sackfuls liberally coated with earth—needs to employ some rational system of examination in order to offer the best possible opinion.

THE PROBLEM

In the author's experience, admittedly in the crowded and history-ridden Britain, the examination of alleged skeletal remains is almost a monthly occurrence. The usual mode of presentation is the staggering of a police officer into the office with a large carton or plastic bag containing earth, sand, stone, and bones. These have been brought to the attention of the police by excavations on building sites, by demolition workers, by builders during renovation of old houses, or by cave enthusiasts, and quite often from shifting sand on dunes and beaches. Some are unearthed in known archeological sites, though most of these are dealt with by the archeologists themselves, since the date of the bones is usually well known enough to remove them from the interest of the coroner and law enforcement authorities.

The number of such discoveries have increased in Britain in the past few decades because of the large program of urban demolition and rebuilding, both from blitz-damaged city sites and the gradual replacement of defunct Victorian buildings.

THE FIRST STEPS

On receipt of the bones, it is essential to obtain as much background information as possible. Due to the paucity of information often gained from the bones themselves, especially with regard to date, every scrap of history is useful. Local antiquarians may be of considerable help, by being able to date the erection of some building or to relate that some plague-pit or old cemetery once lay on the site of the finds. Very often the police know very little of the background, but contacts in the city authorities, public records office or municipal library may be mines of information.

Another practical necessity is to make sure that the remains are well-labelled and securely boxed, for after a year or two, an examination room, laboratory or store cupboard may come to resemble a boneyard with a confusion of scattered remains, poorly identified with soiled and faded labels.

The next stage depends upon the condition of the remains. Often they are wet and mud-coated, and sometimes odorous. They should be spread out on a plastic sheet on a bench and allowed to dry.

A general survey should then be made, and any bones removed from obvious debris such as earth, sand, gravel, or stones. The debris should not be discarded until the case is completed; neither should it be separated without a close examination, because small objects like teeth and metal, or other artifacts like buttons, may be of more help than the actual bones themselves. At this stage the bones should not be cleaned, other than to remove gross soiling, such as accretions of mud.

Are the Remains Bones?

Though this might seem a rather facetious question, it is very relevant; police officers and members of the public, through excessive zeal and the hope of having discovered a homicide, may be mistaken in their idea of what constitutes a bone.

The police once presented the author with a human left clavicle, which seemed sinister until an almost intuitive suspicion about its weight led to the revelation that it was made from plaster-of-Paris coated with some plastic resin—obviously the remnant of a student's synthetic skeleton. On other occasions, even stones may be brought into the laboratory because they bear some fancied resemblance to a bone; to be fair, however, some very ancient fossil bones are identical to stone in all but configuration.

Are the Bones Human?

Once the remains are identified as bone, then the next stage in the screening process is to decide upon the species, or at least to decide whether they are human or animal in the broad sense. If any appreciable amount is present, then even a rudimentary knowledge of anatomy will usually solve the problem. However, one cannot always depend upon the anatomical knowledge possessed by many doctors, let alone the lay public or police officers. In a number of instances, the remains have previously been taken to a local physician near the scene of discovery, and quite a high proportion of such cases have been referred to the forensic department with a diagnosis of human remains, only to be rejected on the most cursory examination. For example, a bone was recently submitted to the author by the police, after having been shown to a general physician who suggested that it was a human femur. It was, in fact, a tibia of such proportions that it could only have come from a bovine beast! It is probably better for the local doctor to exercise caution than for truly human remains to be discarded before being seen by more experienced eyes.

Thus, the first stage of species recognition is made on gross anatomical grounds. It is often sufficient to distinguish between human or non-human rather than to go the lengths of distinguishing the actual animal. However, this might be important in some cases, more often when some crime of theft, rustling, or even hoaxing, has occurred. The recognition of animal species from the anatomical features may well be beyond most pathologists, but much depends on the country and area involved. In Britain, the most common animal bones presented are sheep, pigs, foxes, and cattle, though the size of the latter, unless fragmented, is usually obvious to the police. However, it is common for human and animal bones to be mixed, so one never can safely discard a whole caché because some of the remains are patently bovine. Where broken bones or small bones such as phalanges, carpal or tarsal elements are found, anatomical differences may be slight, though a doctor should be able to pick out most human bones. In countries where bears or primates are common the differences may be minimal, and if the issues are really important, the services of a suitable anatomist or even a veterinary surgeon may be needed. It should be appreciated that these days all academic anatomists are by no means interested in, or expert in, osteology.

When the bones are so fragmented or so scanty in amount that anatomical features are of no help, the only recourse is a forensic serologist, who might be able to detect species-specific protein. This will only be successful if the death took place within a few years—or even months—prior to the examination. The length of time varies, especially if environmental conditions have hastened decay. There is often no serological activity after a period of two to five years, unless the bones have been in freezing conditions or mummified in a warm, dry climate. The rotting damp of many temperate climates soon alters the protein structure, but if the matter is important, it is always worth an attempt. Recently, even tissue typing was successfully carried out in Scandinavia on the remains of Greenland Eskimos who were frozen to death during an ice cave-in in the fifteenth century.

Species testing on bone is performed by elution-extraction of bone powder into buffered saline; after concentration this is run by crossover electrophoresis against a variety of immune sera, prepared by repeated *in vivo* injections into rabbits of different animal sera. An antigen-antibody reaction will become visible if the titre of the bone extract is high enough; there may be some cross-reactions between closely-related species.

How Many Persons Are Present?

Once the bones have been identified as human (this may necessitate sorting them from admixed animal material and non-bony debris) the next problem is to estimate how many individuals are represented. This again is a purely anatomical exercise, with the pathologist identifying as many bones and bone fragments as possible, deciding whether each bone is from the left or right side, and if from a bilateral structure. Finally, the pathologist must calculate whether there are too many items to fit into one individual and, if so, how many are present.

Where any appreciable part of the skeleton(s) is recovered, the best procedure is to place the pieces in the correct anatomical relationship. Where more than one individual is present, it may be a difficult or impossible task to assign various bones and recognizable fragments to the correct skeleton; it is here that an accurate knowledge of the position of the remains at the time of discovery is invaluable.

Unfortunately, except in properly-conducted archeological digs, this position is frequently unknown. Even good site photographs cannot replace the careful plotting and labelling carried out by expert excavators. This emphasizes the value of the pathologist's being called to the scene of an incident, but usually the discovery of bones is a rather casual affair, often handled initially by lay persons or police officers without the backup of the scenes-of-crime team that is usually associated with the discovery of more recent suspicious deaths.

There is a tendency for police and coroner's officers, unless some unusually suspicious circumstances exist, to gather up all the bones and dump them in a plastic sack, so that no topographical distinction can be made in the laboratory. Circumstances may make careful recording impossible, as when most of a skeleton or hoard of bones is unexpectedly scooped up in the bucket of a mechanical digger on an excavation or building site.

Returning to the enumeration of individuals present, the best possible anatomical reconstruction must be made. Sometimes a quick preliminary forecast can be made by a cursory count of femoral heads, where an obviously multiple burial has been found. These can be assigned almost instantaneously to right or left, and so a rapid count of persons can be made. Naturally, some femoral heads might be missing, but they tend to be fairly resistant, even in damp, crumbly, ancient material. The definitive count depends entirely on a careful reassembly, and it may be that the assistance of an expert osteologist is needed where much fragmentation has occurred.

General and Individual Identification

Once the presence of bone and its human origin has been confirmed and the enumeration and assignation of bones and fragments made, two basic procedures must be followed. First, the general characteristics of sex, age, race, and stature must be evaluated. Following this, any particular features that will further distinguish the identity of the remains must be attempted.

Determination of Sex

For the first phase of the general identification, the primary need is to determine the sex of the remains. This is done on purely anatomical grounds, and the success rate is directly proportional to the number and variety of bones present. If the whole skeleton is available, then sexing can be carried out with almost complete certainty, assuming it is post-pubertal. Sexual differentiation in children is much more difficult and may be impossible if the pelvis is absent.

In adult material, the skull and the pelvis both give a success rate in excess of 90 percent, unless some intersex condition is present. Other bones are progressively less useful, though the femur and, to a lesser extent, other long limb bones, may give some indication. The actual anatomical criteria that reveal sex are to be found in standard works on the subject, foremost among which is Wilton Krogman's *The Human Skeleton in Forensic Medicine.*

The skull of the female tends to be rounder and more smooth, with a high forehead and low supraorbital ridges. The mastoid process is smaller than that of the male, and the posterior prolongation of the zygoma fails to extend behind the external auditory meatus. There are differences in the shape of the orbits and their margins, as well as in the shape of the dental arch and the bony palate. Caution must be used, however, when the remains are not Caucasian, because sexual differences in the skeletons of persons from the Indian subcontinent are very much less marked.

Sexual differences in the pelvis are well known: the most useful criteria are the general shape, the configuration of the pelvis inlet, the width of the subpubic arch, the greater sciatic notch and obdurator foramen. Recent anatomical research has developed most objective tests, such as the ratio of pubis length to ischium length. The shape of the sacrum is also characteristic, as is the size of the acetabulum, and hence the size of the femoral head. Apart from the femoral head, the femur differs in the two sexes, in that the wider pelvis in the male makes the angle of the condyles at the knee less vertical; the popliteal length is a different proportion of the total length.

Racial differences are much less reliable and, apart from some unreliable variation in negroid long-bone lengths as a fraction of the total height, most criteria are confined to the skull. A subjective opinion made by an experienced osteologist may be more reliable than attempts at indexes based on measurements. The orbits and nasal apertures, the zygomatic arches, the degree of prognathism and other subjective impressions may lead to assumptions about negroid or mongoloid origins, even though actual measurements may not be significantly outside the limits for any skull. The teeth may have more specific features, such as the "shovel-shaped incisors" of mongoloid races, but here the opinion of a forensic odontologist is necessary.

Stature can be measured directly if the whole skeleton is available, though the loss of cartilage and fibrous tissue from the intervertebral discs and the large joints makes an approximation inevitable. Even if a recent skeleton with some articulation and joint tissues still present is available, the stature obtained by direct measurement may not be exactly that during life. The error can be a few centimeters either way, the dead body usually slightly taller than the living height.

Whether the whole skeleton is present or not, the stature is usually measured or checked from calculations based on the measurements of long bones, the femur, tibia, and humerus, respectively, being most useful. Care must be taken to measure the bones in exactly the way used by the compilers of the various tables available in most textbooks. This should be done on an osteological board, but various makeshift devices can be used to arrive at a length accurate to within a few millimeters of the optimum.

Tables such as that of Trotter and Gleser may be employed, but it must always be appreciated that even if sex and race are known, there is always a margin of error. Where all limb bones are available, all should be measured and a mean stature calculated. Sometimes this act of measurement exposes the probability that the bones available did not, in fact, originate from the same skeleton.

The age of the individual (not to be confused with the "age" or, more accurately, the date of the inhumation of the body) is the most complicated determination of all, depending upon the age range in which the remains lay. In fetal and infant material, age can often be estimated to within weeks, or even days, in very young skeletons; the odontologist contributes most at this period. In childhood and adolescence, the dentist again reigns supreme, due to the mass of dates to be gained from examination (including radiology) of the teeth and jaws.

In addition, the appearances of ossification centers, and the dates of fusion of epiphyses with diaphyses, provide information that is reasonably accurate until the third decade. However, the range of uncertainty must be appreciated; the earlier maturity of females and those living in tropical climates can cause variations of up to several years in the second decade.

This is an area in which forensic odontology comes into maximum usefulness, and the details must be sought in the appropriate textbooks, although wherever possible the aid of dental experts might be enlisted. The estimation of age from bone growth markers also requires the help of a radiologist and an osteologist, unless the issues at stake are relatively unimportant, as with obviously ancient material with no archeological interest attached.

After the middle of the third decade, when all teeth and epiphyses have ceased activity, ageing is a much more difficult and inexact part of the examination. Skull sutures as an index of age have been largely discarded, except in most general terms. The use of the opposing surfaces of the pubic symphysis is a trustworthy, but difficult, technique. It is not an examination to be taken up for the first time when an identity problem comes along. Forensic pathologists are advised to make a collection of pubic bones from a series of bodies of known age and to study them with the original publications of Todd and of McKern & Stewart, and to retain them as a reference collection against the time when a practical problem arises. It is claimed that in middle age the true age can be determined to within half a decade; much depends on the expertise of the examiner, and a margin of a decade is more realistic for the nonspecialist.

Other nondental techniques available are the translucency of the scapula, the remodeling of the cancellous bone in the marrow cavity of the head of the femur, and the upward encroachment of the marrow cavity into the upper part of the humerus. These are mainly radiological procedures and need the cooperation of an experienced radiologist with knowledge of, and an interest in, osteological appearances.

The details of these techniques are fully described in the major legal medicine textbooks and in the specialist texts such as Krogman, so no attempt is made here to compress the technicalities into this short review, which merely aims to set out the plan of campaign.

Personal Identification

When as much information as possible has been gained about the species—sex, stature, race and age of the skeletal remains—attention is then directed to their individuality. In many cases, probably the majority, this utterly fails, because the finds are often ancient, in terms of potential law enforcement consequences. There is an arbitrary time threshold of about 50 to 70 years, beyond which the human bones can be of no practical importance in the legal medicine sense; even if they were the result of a homicide, the culprit would almost certainly also be dead.

For example, a young female skeleton was discovered in 1961 in a cave in South Wales, sawn into three segments, through the upper chest and arms and across the lower thighs. From the dating of artifacts such as hallmarked rings and mouldering clothing, the remains were identified as those of a woman who had vanished in suspicious circumstances in 1920. Her lover was suspected of her murder, but no body could be discovered. When the skeleton was found 41 years later, the police immediately sought the old suspect. They found him—six feet down in a cemetery where he had been deposited three years before after a natural death from heart disease!

There is, therefore, a cut-off point at around half a century, beyond which the examination may be of no interest to the police other than for administrative tidiness. Usually historians and archeologists are the only ones concerned if the remains are very old and have some topographical relevance to ancient buildings or settlements. For example, bones from several bodies found in yet another cave in Wales were originally thought to be Roman, but close examination not only brought their date into the nineteenth century, but revealed multiple sword wounds. They were almost certainly the victims of cavalry attacks upon rioting Chartist workers in 1849.

The pathologist, then, has the task of trying to identify and date the remains. The latter problem will be dealt with later, but a scheme of examination is needed to attempt the personal naming of the deceased, where this is at all possible.

The central requirement in attaching an individual identity to a skeleton is that there be one or more potential matches available. This is self-evident, but sometimes overlooked in the enthusiasm of "the chase." This applies equally well to dental identification; although there are now numerous techniques available, these are all useless unless the dental characteristics of a relatively short list of prospective individuals is available.

The pathologist and his team may know, for instance, that some unidentified remains are those of a Caucasian woman of 160 cm stature and about 23 years of age, with a certain number of dental fillings. However, unless the investigators can turn up a short list of persons missing in a time-band consistent with the pathologist's estimate of dating, then all the work is in vain.

In this respect the dating is important, for the chances of finding the true identity are naturally greater in the recent past, when record keeping was better and more accessible and the memories of witnesses and informants fresher. Bones from deaths 30, 50 or 100 years ago are progressively less likely to be identified for these reasons, unless associated with some newsworthy or dramatic event, such as an old homicide or transport disaster.

Because of the loss of the soft tissue, singular identifying criteria are rare on skeletal remains. Such identifying characteristics as hair color, eyes, skin pigmentation, tattoos, surgical or wound scars, and industrial stigmata will all be destroyed. Only lesions affecting the bony structures are of any use.

Old healing fractures. Where a fracture has occurred some weeks before death, it is likely that new bone (callus) will have formed at the site of union. This may be comparable either with a medical history or even with written medical records, as far as the position and an approximate date are concerned. Radiology may be a particular help here, especially if radiographs from the time of treatment of the fracture are recovered.

Very recent fractures and very old fractures are of limited or no value. If the fracture occurred very soon before death, there may have been no time for callus to form—it is frequently delayed for weeks or even months. The finding of a newly-fractured bone is almost impossible to distinguish from the very frequent postmortem damage to bones that occurs either during burial or concealment or, more often, during discovery and transit. There is very little way in which a postmortem fracture can be distinguished from an antemortem one sustained at or soon before death. Possible exceptions are some characteristic skull fractures, such as basal ring fracture or a "pond fracture," or some wedge fractures of the spine. Almost any other break in the bone can be simulated by damage after death.

Many an archeologist and journalist has been misled by reporting a skull fracture that was interpreted as some sign of a fight, assault, or battle. The fragile skull, especially in ancient brittle remains, is very vulnerable to shovels and even the passive pressure of stones and rocks in the ground.

Similarly, a very old fracture may heal almost completely and leave virtually no signs in the bone unless untreated or poorly treated, in which case there may be angulation, misalignment, overriding, residual callus, or even a pseudo-arthrosis. These are rare in material of forensic data, but badly-aligned fracture healing is relatively common in archeological material, for obvious reasons. Where good union has taken place, there may still be radiological evidence of an old fracture.

The author recently saw a skeleton with tags of soft tissue surviving, suggesting that it was less than a year since death. This was supported by the extent of vegetation growing up through the bones. From the sex, age and stature, the police eventually produced a short list of about four missing persons from that area in the past year. The skeleton had a series of healing rib fractures with callus still present. One potential "identitee" had had a road accident six months before with chest injuries. The hospital was traced, and radiographs and notes confirmed beyond doubt that the number and position of the rib fractures corresponded exactly with the skeletal lesions.

Deformities and anomalies. Skeletal defects due to congenital or acquired causes may be of great use, since they are usually known about by lay persons such as relatives, neighbors or other witnesses. Severe lameness, club foot, congenital hip defects, hunchback, spastic asymmetry, rickets, dwarfism, aschondroplasia, and acromegaly, among other defects, are obvious abnormalities which can be discovered by the investigating officers and checked against the skeletal remains.

For example, an almost totally skeletalized head and trunk were washed ashore in Wales, the only soft tissues extant were some adipocere and ligaments. The facial appearance was obviously acromegalic, and there was a penetrating fracture into a frontal sinus, with surrounding new bone indicating its *in vivo* origin. After some three months, the Missing Persons list turned up a candidate bearing the facial appearance of acromegaly, who had had a head injury in a traffic accident seven years previously. The hospital notes and films confirmed that both acromegaly and a forehead wound had been present, and the clinical skull radiographs compared with radiographs of the dead skull showed that the unique outline of the frontal sinuses were identical.

Less obvious abnormalities can sometimes be used in identity, but this usually depends upon the provisional identities having medical records available. Bone cysts, any small skeletal idiosyncrasy, and, of course, dental identity, come under this heading. One such case was a homicide in a northern English city, where the wife of a detective was strangled by her husband and dropped with attached weights into a river. Some six weeks later, the highly-decomposed body floated to the surface and a difficult identity problem was eventually resolved by virtue of the fact that the woman had had a road accident a year before and sustained injuries to her legs. Not only were the scars still barely evident, but radiography revealed an unusual sesamoid bone in the Achilles tendon at the ankle, which was matched with films retrieved from the hospital where she had been treated.

Foreign bodies. Bullets, other missiles, shrapnel and broken knife points are rarely found, but may of course assist in coming to a conclusion about the cause of death—a rare event in skeletal examination. Other metallic objects useful in determining identity are surgical or orthopaedic prostheses and devices such as femoral pins and plates or artificial joints, which may correspond with something known in the medical history of the potential matching person.

RADIOGRAPHY IN SKELETAL IDENTIFICATION

Several examples in which radiographs proved very useful in establishing identity have already been mentioned. They can be used in two ways, apart from assisting in the determination of general groupings described earlier in this article. First, they can be used to detect and delineate bony lesions known about from a history or description of the possible identitee—such as finding a well-healed old fracture of the midshaft of the left femur that was mentioned by a relative. More often, they are used for a point-by-point visual comparison with radiographs obtained during the life of the person and retrieved from hospital records or the archives of a physician. These may be used to compare pathological features, such as fractures, bone-related disease, congenital or acquired defects, and so on. The prerequisite for this was the discovery of antemortem films. For example, another bone that washed ashore in South Wales was so dense and heavy that it was thought to be fossilized, but radiography revealed a disease resembling the Albers-Schönberg "marble bone" condition. Unfortunately, since no potential candidate for a match was ever found, no antemortem film—the usual stumbling-block for this technique—was obtainable for comparison.

Apart from comparing signs of trauma or disease, radiography has become a very sophisticated way of comparing anatomical similarities when both antemorten and postmortem films are available. The details must be studied in either the original monographs or in my reviews of *Forensic Radiology* given in Krogman's book.

Basically, the methods of comparison that use radiography consist of two main methods:

1. Comparing anatomical structures that are unique in any individual. Foremost are the frontal sinuses, which are different in every person, even identical twins. The size and configuration of these sinuses are fixed from about the twentieth year, though they first appear at about the second year of life. About 5 percent of adults have no sinuses, and disease such as chronic sinusitis may distort and blur the radiographic outlines; otherwise, they are as distinctive as fingerprints. Some military personnel, such as air crew members, have their skull radiographs on record for identification purposes in case of an air crash, since the frontal sinuses are well protected against even severe burning of the body.

Other bones used for direct comparison are the first rib (which is sometimes used in clinical radiology departments to check on a possible mix-up of chest films), clavicles, and the bones of the wrist and hand. The details can be found in the reference books mentioned. The techniques depend upon recognizable and comparable patterns in outline, density, internal trabeculation and casual idiosyncrasies such as small cysts and marginal spicules and nodules.

2. A more systematic method depends upon the anatomical dimensions of the skull. Sassouni developed a sophisticated technique of taking many measurements on radiographs of the cranium and face and analyzing them for the most significant matching. Voluter devised his "V-test", which depends upon the profile of the pituitary fossa in lateral radiographs, and which takes into account the configuration of the sella and the angles adjacent on the base of the skull.

In summary, these methods mean that where a substantial part of the skeleton is recovered, especially the skull, the possession of antemortem radiographs of a short list of possible match subjects will, almost without exception, lead to a positive identification.

DATING OF SKELETAL REMAINS

The dating of skeletal remains is a vital yet extraordinarily difficult aspect of the examination of bones, and one that has exercised researchers for many years, and is very important in a forensic, historical and archeological context.

The major concern of this article—the medico-legal aspect of dating—is intimately related to identification, for if the approximate date of death remains undetermined, then the decision of whether the remains fall below the 50- to 70-year forensic threshold remains unresolved. Equally important, the date range within which to search among missing persons for a match cannot be established if the approximate date of death cannot be determined.

Dating is extremely difficult and frequently impossible; it is an unfortunate fact that the degree of confidence regarding date that is expressed by a examiner is often inversely proportional to the examiner's experience in the matter. The more bones that have been seen, the more ready a doctor is to admit that the range of error can be wide.

The main problem is that the morphological, microscopic and physicochemical appearance of bones is more a function of environmental exposure than it is of time. Different bones from the same skeleton may be in quite different stages of preservation if scattered within a small area that has different types of soil, exposure to air and, especially, to moisture. Even different parts of the same bone may be so affected: the author has seen a femur lodged vertically in a cave rock-fall, the upper end of which was in good condition, yet the lower condyles were crumbled and partly missing due to seepage of water through the lower level.

Therefore, attempts at dating from visual and many other criteria are quite unreliable. Paradoxically, the oldest bones may be datable with a much better percentage of accuracy than more recent remains, and the archeologist often has an advantage over the forensic scientist in this respect. This is because the radiocarbon test can be used, which, given certain technical safeguards, can date ancient bones independently of any reliance on the physical and chemical changes that are distorted by environment.

The radiocarbon method depends upon the steady decay of the carbon isotope 14_C to 12_C, the half-life being in the region of 5,600 years. The test is difficult and expensive, but these drawbacks are added to in forensic investigations by the fact that the radiocarbon test cannot be used on samples less than at least a century old, and usually much older. The reason is that the half-life is too long to give a significant decrease of 14_C in that period, the very time during which medico-legal dating is so important.

How, then, is dating to be attempted in bones brought by law enforcement authorities? There are some shortcuts, mainly enabling the doctor to exclude the specimens from the realm of potential criminal activities by virtue of their antiquity. For instance, a number of bones seen by the author have shown prominent green staining, indicative of copper salts impregnating areas of the bone. Unless artifacts such as corroding ornaments or buckles are present, this usually indicates (at least in a European context) that bronze coffin nails had been used in a burial certainly earlier than this century. When the wooden coffin collapses, the corroding nails stain the adjacent bones. The presence of a coffin, which can also sometimes be confirmed by the presence of rotten wood, naturally excludes the possibility of a clandestine criminal burial.

Also, in a western European situation, the finding of a jaw with marked occlusal attrition of the teeth removes the death in time from this century. In Britain, severe grinding of the chewing surfaces of the teeth was common until the first half of the nineteenth century, but was rare later, except in cases of pathological tooth grinding, which sometimes occurs in the mentally affected. The reason for the severe attrition was the use of soft stone mill-wheels, which allowed a considerable amount of stone dust to enter the flour and, hence, bread. This acted as an abrasive, wearing down the tooth crowns by middle adult life. It is still seen in eastern Europe and many other parts of the world, but not in Britain.

These shortcuts, however, are no real help in the majority of cases. The following can be of some assistance in dating skeletal remains, but probably the majority of specimens will never be corroborated by any circumstantial evidence; hence the doctor rarely gets any confirmation or rebuttal of his attempts at accurate dating.

The General Appearance of the Bone

A fairly recent bone will be heavy and still "soapy" to the touch. Naturally, any soft tissue remnants will confirm a recent origin; tendon and ligaments tags, scraps of periosteum and remnants of articular cartilage usually indicate that the bone is less than about five years old. Much depends on the climate, the local environment, and animal and insect predators. Some shrivelled fibrous tags may persist for decades if dry conditions prevail, leading to a mummification of the more persistent elements. Conversely, a bone may be picked absolutely clean within days in some tropical climates with heavy predator infestation.

Where no soft tissue is present, bones that have been kept in optimum conditions may remain dense with a smooth, shiny surface, for a very long time. Those in an anatomy department, for instance, appear to last in this state for scores of years, and there is whole spectrum of appearances from perfection down to the crumbling, dry bones of extreme weathering.

Bones exposed to the elements progressively lose this smooth, hard external texture. Leaching by soil water, often of acid pH, attacks the inorganic material and hydrolysis and other chemical attack degrades the protein stroma. Waterlogging, freezing, drying and splintering of the surface in hot conditions progressively erodes the outer layers. Water and soil particles penetrate the marrow cavity and the contents are destroyed, sometimes being replaced by sand or soil, even though no apparent route of entry can be seen. The hard compact bone eventually breads down, especially over the ends where it is least thick and the fragile cancellous bone is exposed.

The texture of the bone gradually changes from a hard material to a lighter, porous material which may be scratched with a fingernail. The density of the bone, when hefted in the hand, becomes appreciably lighter. Sometimes, the bones are buried below the water table, which in marshy land or a bog may be at or near the surface. Where peaty conditions exist, with a low pH from humic acid, as in many swampy areas, the mineral of the bone may be rapidly destroyed. The author has seen dated burials in a cemetery in such a region, where the whole skeleton has vanished within 20 years of death, due to the acidity of soil water.

By contrast, Roman bones almost 2,000 years old have been found in well-drained sand dunes in such excellent condition that they could have been used to demonstrate anatomy to students. Thus, an opinion as to date of death by visual examination alone is fraught with error. A knowledge of the environment at the places of discovery is imperative. Making allowances for this, an arbitrary opinion can be ventured, but only within very wide margins of time. A heavy, shiny, greasy bone must be relatively recent; depending upon where it was found, it may be thought to be less than 10 years old.

Conversely, a ragged, chalky, light bone, with an eroded surface and exposed trabeculae at the extremities, may well be thought to be a century or more old, unless it was found in a place of extremely deleterious environment. Every effort should be made to extract as much collateral information as possible; any artifacts with the remains are vital. Even vegetation over or entwined with the bones may give a lead. The advice of a botanist may be needed if roots are growing within the marrow cavity of a broken bone; the botanist might be able to give the minimum time for such growth. One set of bones was found under a tree stump; the number of growth rings indicated the minimum period.

Manmade artifacts may be useful; some bones found buried above a beach were accompanied by some crude buttons nearby. They were characteristic of those carved in previous centuries by sailors from their own food bones, indicating ancient origins. In the case of the murdered woman mentioned above, found after 40 years in a cave, remnants of clothing, shoes and jewelry were dated by a costume expert to a narrow time span around 1920.

Chemical Analysis

Many chemical parameters have been used to date bones, but all suffer from the same fault as the morphological appearance: The rate of decay is more a function of adverse environment than of time.

The deterioration of the organic stroma is of more use in dating than is the mineral component. It has been claimed that a progressive conversion of calcium phosphate/apatite to carbonate is a useful criterion, easily demonstrated by adding dilute acid to the bone, when effervescence reveals the presence of carbonate. However, this is a late change and sometimes never occurs. It has no discriminatory value in dating.

The organic stroma is composed mainly of protein, largely in the form of collagen. The total amount of protein is approximately indicated by the total nitrogen present. A recent bone has about 4.5 percent by weight of nitrogen when subjected to conventional analysis, either by Kjeldahl method or more modern automated techniques. However, this level persists for a long, if variable, time, and a significant reduction is not seen during the first century after death. Thus, the total nitrogen is fairly reliable in differentiating between bones of great age from those of forensic significance, though the cutoff point of about 3.5 percent is almost always attained much later than the conventional medico-legal threshold of about 70 years.

The total protein is composed of a wide range of amino acids. A small quantity is found free in the bone, usually due to spontaneous hydrolysis, but the amount and nature of these free acids are not related to date. Though it is reasonable to assume that hydrolysis is continually taking place in a buried bone subject to soil water (often acid in nature), this very process of percolation will leach out the soluble amino acids from the residual bone. Extensive analysis has revealed no useful pattern.

In acid hydrolysis of the bone sample (achieved by heating bone powder with 6 Normal hydrochloric acid in a sealed ampoule at 110° C for 24 hours), all protein is converted to its constituent amino acids. These can be identified, either by thin-layer or paper chromatography, or more accurately by the use of an amino acid autoanalyser. As many as about 20 different amino acids can be recovered from recent bones.

Originally, it was hoped that proline and hydroxyproline, particular markers for collagen, could be used for dating. Early work by the author suggested that these two amino acids tend to vanish after about 50 years in average conditions. However, more careful analysis fails to confirm any quantitative difference until about 150 years have passed.

The same holds true for all the many other amino acids. Marked random variations occur from sample to sample within the first century. After this time, and especially after about 150 years, there is a progressive decline in the number and amount of amino acids recoverable. Glycine and alanine are in largest quantity and persist longest, often for several thousands of years. Unfortunately, there is no reliable discriminatory pattern in the early period of forensic interest. The calcium/nitrogen ratio is also useless.

Claims have been made for the analysis of fat as a reliable marker of time since death, even in the earlier years. The reader is referred to the papers of Villaneuva for details. The same author has published on the use of differential thermal analysis as a measure of date, but the present writer has had no success with this technique as a dating method.

Fluoresence in ultraviolet light is a crude marker of date. If a compact bone sample, such as the shaft of a long bone, is sawn across to expose a fresh surface, recent bones will glow a silvery-blue color when viewed in UV light of 350 Å.

As the bone ages, the periosteal surface and the marrow cavity surface lose their fluoresence as the protein stroma decays. After many years—often a century or more—the inert zones become wider and the "sandwich filling" of fluoresent bone becomes thinner, eventually fragmenting and vanishing altogether. Appreciable loss of fluoresence may be seen within a century and progressively increases until, after several hundreds of years, the whole bone is nonreactive. However, this is a very crude test for differentiating ancient bone from that of recent date, and great variations occur related to the environmental rate of loss of the protein stroma.

Tests for residual blood pigment, using the clinical and forensic techniques such as Kastle-Meyer or phenolphthalein-peroxide tests, will usually reveal a positive result (both on the outer surface of the bone or on bone powder) for a few years after death. Previously, the more sensitive benzidene test was used, but is now proscribed because of the alleged carcinogenic activity of the reagent. The other tests do not seem so sensitive—none of them are specific—and although occasional "maverick" samples may give a rapid positive reaction after 50 or more years since death, most bones lose their blood pigment in the vascular channels within five years. As a general rule, a strong immediate positive reaction indicates that the bone is being tested less than five years since death.

Serological activity is another marker of a recent bone. When bone powder is eluted with a weakly-alkaline buffer and the resulting extract concentrated to minimum volume, any residual antigenic activity can be detected by running against a potent anti-human serum such as Coombs' reagent, either by passive gel-diffusion or by crossover electrophoresis. Though originally this method gave positive results up to five or ten years after death, further work has shown that antigenic activity as measured in this way rarely survives more than a few months after death. Certainly, a positive reaction indicates that the bone is very recent. As with the blood pigment test, there may be obvious corroborating evidence apparent, such as the general appearance of the bone and periosteal tags.

Histological examination of bones has been uniformly disappointing as an indicator of date. In very old samples, the preparation of decalcified sections may be impossible, due to the carbonate replacement of apatite, causing the block to disintegrate during processing. This in itself is evidence of antiquity. Where successful sections are obtained, there seems little or no variation in the histological picture during the first century or so. Very recent bones—within months of death—will show fat and soft tissue elements, albeit autolysed, in the haversian canals, but amorphous debris is seen there for a very long time after death, certainly many decades.

A whole variety of stains, including haematoxylin-eosin, Luxol Fast Blue, van Gieson, peroxidase, Mallory's PTAH, trichrome, and others, have all shown marked staining variation from sample to sample and usually from one part of the same section to another, but none is related to the passage of time. The architecture of the haversian system seems remarkably persistent and can be easily recognized in some ancient bones of thousands of years since death.

SUMMARY

In summary, unless the more sophisticated methods listed in the references are repeated and more success obtained with a series of bone samples of known date, no physico-chemical or morphological techniques have yet been devised that will determine date independently of environmental deterioration. The only exception is the radiocarbon estimation in bones of greater antiquity than those of medico-legal interest. The best mentor in the examination of skeletal remains is experience. Unfortunately, the majority of samples brought to the medical examiner remain of unknown provenance, and this prevents the doctor from checking his expertise against the true facts of identity and dating.

The main point to bear in mind is that the tendency toward overinterpretation and dogmatic opinion should be avoided where the available data do not merit such a degree of certainty. There is no advantage in offering unfounded opinions to the investigators, since this might merely mislead them and perhaps cause them to exclude a class of possible identitees because the doctor has unwisely told them to look only within a certain bracket of date and identifiable factors. As in any branch of forensic medicine, it is dangerous to speculate where the facts cannot firmly support the opinion.

REFERENCES

Berg, S. 1963. "The Determination of Bone Age." In *Methods in Forensic Science,* edited by Lundquist, pp. 231–252. New York: Interscience Publishers.

Brothwell, Donald R. 1972. *Digging Up Bones.* 2d ed. London: Pergamon Press.

Cameron, J.M., and B.G. Simms. 1973. *Forensic Dentistry.* Edinburgh and London: Churchill-Livingstone.

Evans, K.T., and B. Knight. 1981. *Forensic Radiology*. Oxford: Blackwell Ltd.

Gradwohl. 1968. "Identification by the Skeletal Structures." Chapter 11 in *Legal Medicine*. 2d ed. Bristol: John Wright.

Harvey, Warren. 1976. *Dental Identification and Forensic Odontology*. London: Henry Kimpton.

Knight, Bernard. 1969. "Methods of Dating Skeletal Remains." In *Human Biology*. Detroit: Wayne State University Press, 41, (3):322.

Krogman, W.M. 1962. *The Human Skeleton in Forensic Medicine*. Springfield, IL: Charles C Thomas.

Lauder, I., and B. Knight. 1967. "Practical Methods of Dating Skeletal Remains." In *Medicine, Science and the Law*. London: Kluwer Publishing Ltd. 7(4):205.

Villanueva, E., F. Girela, and M.J. Castellanos. In *Forensic Science* 21(4):822.

Psychosocial Characteristics of Homicide and Suicide Victims

Lori G. Russell, Ph.D.

Among certain subgroups in the American population, suicide and homicide are leading causes of death, exceeding the toll taken by such well funded and researched diseases as cancer and heart disease.[1] Within the general population, they rank eleventh and thirteenth, respectively, among all causes of death.[2] Despite the number of people killed each year due to homicide and suicide, research on these subjects is generally of a descriptive nature. This may indicate that, while the phenomena are interesting to study from an academic perspective, there is a general lack of awareness or orientation toward the severe social health problems they present.

The major limitations of studies that delineate demographic characteristics of victims lie in the methods by which these characteristics are determined. Data are usually case oriented or they are collected at the environmental level only, specifically from census tract information. The results of studies using each type of methodology appear to parallel each other closely; however, once the effects of environmental characteristics are examined with respect to the characteristics of individual victims, the results based on each methodology may not be as parallel as is often assumed. A general purpose of this study was to use individual and environmental data simultaneously to aid in identifying high risk individuals more precisely, both demographically and situationally, within the City of Richmond, Virginia.

Once the high risk segment is identified, attempts to prevent suicide and homicide should include appeals that are targeted for these potential victims. Attempts to change these unfavorable conditions or to alert high risk individuals to their potential dangers are more likely to be effective if they are specific to the City of Richmond and in their identification of the contributing factors in these violent deaths.

Since some cases of homicide and suicide exhibit the same physical causes of death (i.e., gunshot wounds or strangulation), a method that could be employed in distinguishing between the two groups of victims was developed. The large amount of descriptive information available made it possible to identify key variables which were used to determine to which of the two groups a victim was most likely to belong. This process, a stepwise discriminant analysis, was performed to determine if the two groups were distinct, and to derive an equation from which predictions could be made.

EPIDEMOLOGY AND IDENTIFICATION OF HIGH RISK FACTORS

Case studies of a total of 114 suicide victims and 136 homicide victims fatally injured in the City of Richmond, Virginia during the years 1973–1976 were used to develop the data base. These were cases for which autopsy reports from the office of the Chief Medical Examiner of Virginia and complete police investigation reports from the Richmond Bureau of Police were available. At the environmental level, the appropriate census data were consulted for the City of Richmond.

The Suicide Victims

Generally, the findings of this study tend to replicate earlier research and to support the idea of status integration as a partial explanation for suicide. An outgrowth of Durkheim's classic theory of anomie,[3] status integration theory is specifically concerned with the effects of social role conflicts and strains. The approach generally postulates that individuals who experience high conflict due to incompatibility among the social roles they fill are likely to be more susceptible to suicide.[4] As an illustration, males in white collar positions are expected to experience greater social mobility. This would lower the status integration of such individuals because the change in their social roles would result in conflicts within previously defined relationships and in a breakdown of traditional roles and norms.

The present study supported the above premise at the univariate level for race, sex, and age of the victim, as seen in Table 1. Of the victims, 67 percent were male and 75 percent were white. These groups were more likely to experience status conflict due to greater social and occupational mobility. The peak frequencies by age were found among older individuals, especially those making the transition from middle age to old age. People between 45 and 64 accounted for 41 percent of all the suicide victims. For these age, sex,

TABLE 1. Modal Characteristics of Suicide

Victim-related variables	Modal characteristic
Sex	Male (67%)*
Race	White (75%)*
Age in years	55–64 (24%)*
Mean Age	45.1 years
Marital Status	Married (44%)
Occupational Group	Blue Collar (24%)
Employment Status	Employed (60%)
Previous record of arrest	None (84%)
Previous record of conviction	None (88%)
Previous psychiatric history	None (59%)
Event-related variables	**Modal characteristic**
Month of Injury	February (13%)
Day of Week	Weekday (59%)
Hour of Injury	12 PM - 6 PM (39%)
Census Tract Area	"6" (29%)
Type of Fatal Wound	Gunshot (70%)
Location of Fatal Wound	Head (48%)
Alcohol in Blood	None (63%)
Drugs in Body	None (85%)
Current Legal Problems	No (83%)
Current Psychiatric Problems	Yes (63%)
Current Domestic Problems	No (66%)
Current Medical Problems	No (65%)

Notes: *Significantly overrepresented within the Richmond population. †This group was underrepresented within the Richmond population.

and racial characteristics, the modal group was found to be significantly overrepresented as compared to their proportions in the general population.

The occupational group of the victim was one variable for which the original expectations were not totally supported. While suicide victims tended to be significantly different from other individuals in the City of Richmond, the groups that were overrepresented were not the ones expected. Blue collar workers committed suicide with the greatest frequency (24 percent), but they were underrepresented because they made up over 30 percent of the population. Furthermore, instead of white collar and professional workers being more susceptible to taking their own lives, the overrepresented groups were those of retired and other workers. Although different from the prediction, these results are not inconsistent with status integration theory. In fact, they partially support it. Retired persons would be likely victims simply due to their increased age, but they also have entered the stage of life where they have changed positions with respect to the work force. Rather than being an integral part of the system, retired individuals are separated from the labor force, often with the assumption that they are no longer productive, contributing members of society. This assumption can easily lead to a perceived loss of status for the individual and to increased social conflict resulting from changes in the relationships between the individual and his family or peers.

The second occupational group that was overrepresented among suicide victims was classified as "other." This group consisted mainly of students, and therefore it is not surprising to find them a potential problem as suicides. Students, whether they be in high school or college, are on the opposite end of the spectrum compared to retired persons. They have not yet entered the adult world, although they are preparing for it. Additionally, they are still developing and maturing emotionally and socially. These factors indicate that such persons would experience decreased status integration because they are in a period of growth or transition resulting in personal or social instability.

One single variable test that failed to support status integration theory was that of marital status of the victim. Although most people were married at the time they took their lives, no significant differences were found between the four groups. It was predicted that widowed and divorced persons would be more likely to commit suicide than those who were married. These two groups contained individuals who had experienced a dramatic transition within their primary social relationship, probably accompanied by a great amount of stress and conflict. Thus, it was predicted that they would be a higher risk for suicide. The failure to support this prediction is puzzling in that it is not consistent with past research findings.[5]

A second finding involving the marital status variable was only partially supportive of the predictions based on this theory. When the interaction of age and marital status was examined, the results were significantly different from chance variations; however, in some cases, no differences were found in areas where they were expected. In others, unexpected differences that accounted for a large amount of variability were discovered. In support of status integration theory, older individuals who were widowed or who were single were more susceptible to suicide. However, the data also revealed that many more single young adults committed suicide than anticipated. This discrepancy may be artificially high due to the fact that there are proportionately more single young adults in the general population than there are married or widowed young adults. Since the actual population proportions were not used as a control for this test, the higher frequency of suicides in this subcategory may be the result of extraneous factors not related to suicide per se.

The failure to find strong differences between expected and observed frequencies in any of the age groups under the divorced and separated marital status category appears to be nonsupportive of the status integration theory. Since the theory is partially supported by the rest of the age/marital status breakdown, the influence of divorce as a variable in this type of analysis is called into question. Past research indicates that the suicide rate for divorced persons is higher than for those in other marital status groups. In the present study, the number of subjects which fell into that category was small (12). However, while only 9.3 percent of Richmond's population was divorced or separated, 13 percent of the suicide victims held that status. When the cases were broken down into age groups, the majority of these fell into the two older age groups. Additionally, the number of divorced or separated suicide victims was slightly higher in these two age groups than was expected for the analysis, while the frequencies in the two younger age groups were slightly lower. Thus, while the predicted differences were small, they still tended to support the status integration theory.

From a descriptive standpoint, psychiatric problems were common to many suicide victims. A previous history of such difficulties was experienced by 41 percent, and 63 percent were experiencing current psychiatric problems, usually described as depression, at the time of their deaths. Few had legal problems or records of arrest and conviction; however, almost a third of the victims were experiencing domestic and/or medical difficulties. When examined with respect to the age factor, older victims tended to have significantly more medical problems than younger victims. There was no interaction between age and the other "problem" variables.

Contrary to popular belief that suicides occur more frequently in holiday seasons or on certain days, they tended to be evenly distributed over months of the year and days of the week in the present study. Although 39 percent of the fatal injuries were incurred between noon and 6:00 p.m., the remainder were almost equally spaced across the other time groups.

Over a third of the suicide victims had alcohol in their blood at the time they were fatally injured. The level was 0.10 percent or above for 22 percent of the victims, indicating that (according to Virginia law) almost a fourth were legally intoxicated. Only 15 percent of the victims were found to have drugs in their bodies. For instances of drug usage, barbituates were commonly ingested and such poisoning was often the method of achieving self-destruction.

Poisoning was the second most frequent means of death, accounting for 16 percent of the subjects. In achieving self-destruction, however, an overwhelming 70 percent of the victims preferred the use of a gun. Wounds to the head killed 48 percent of the suicide victims and another 17 percent died of gunshot wounds to the chest.

The last series of analyses that tested status integration theory presented mixed results. A simple assumption was made that individuals who were different from those who lived around them would be more likely to commit suicide because their differences would result in poorer social acceptance and in conflict with these others. Three variables which were expected to be critical were those of race, marital status, and occupation. The marital status of the victim was the one variable that had a significant impact on suicide victims: They were more likely to belong to a different marital status category than their neighbors (those living in the same census tract area). This is strong evidence that the marital status of an individual is an important factor in suicide, but it also indicates that the variable's role is somewhat complex and needs to be considered in conjunction with other information about the subject. In other words, simply knowing the marital status of the individual will not be of much practical value in assessing his or her risk potential. Knowledge about age and the area in which the subject lives is also necessary. For example, 29 percent of the suicides occurred in a predominantly white census area in the southwest part of the city. Further research should attempt to specifically identify which marital status groups are more susceptible to suicide when members of the group differ from those around them.

Even though the race and occupation of suicide victims would probably have contributed to a lowered level of status integration for these people, they did not differ significantly from others in their census areas with respect to these two characteristics. This apparent failure to support status integration theory on a more local level indicates that the approach may be too broad and may require refinement. Individuals who are members of subcultural community groups may be well integrated into the roles and expectations at the local level but not in the larger societal system, or they may experience the opposite problem, either of which may produce conflict and tension. Furthermore, differences in racial and occupational backgrounds often reflect specific differences in subcultural lifestyles, behaviors, and values. Thus, particular groups in the entire population may be more susceptible to suicide due to the direct interaction of their subcultural background and their life experiences. Status integration theory appears to need further development to include some learned or subcultural influences which would account for response differences between certain groups of individuals when individuals in these groups are faced with similar situations or similar levels of status integration/disintegration.

The Homicide Victim

In addition to the gathering of descriptive data, the information pertaining to homicide victims was analyzed with respect to a theoretical approach known as the subculture of violence.[6] Derived from Wolfgang's idea of victim-precipitated homicide,[7] this theory maintains that there exists a group of individuals that is not integrated into the dominant nonviolent culture. This group or subculture has a system of norms and values that condones and, in some cases, requires the use of violence in many social relationships. Due to their cultural physical segregation within urban areas, minorities such as blacks and Mexican-Americans are often considered part of this subculture of violence. In Richmond, minorities are all classified under the category "nonwhite," but the group consists predominantly of black individuals.

Like the results from tests of status integration theory, the subculture of violence theory was supported at the univariate level by all variables except that of marital status (see Table 2). It appears that this variable, considered independent of other information, adds little to one's knowledge about the potential risk of homicide or suicide for a given subject. Also, as in the previous section, the variables of age, sex, race, and occupation tended generally to support the predictions that had been hypothesized.

The sex and race of the victims indicated that nonwhite persons (68 percent) and males (77 percent) were murdered more often than other types of individuals and, as expected, the victims were overrepresented as blue collar workers (56 percent). The picture of the homicide victim emerges as an

TABLE 2. Modal Characteristics of Homicide

Victim-related variables	Modal characteristic
Sex	Male (77%)*
Race	Nonwhite (68%)*
Age in years	25–34 (30%)*
Mean Age	37.9 years
Marital Status	Married (52%)
Occupational Group	Blue Collar (56%)*
Employment Status	Employed (70%)
Previous record of arrest	None (65%)
Previous record of conviction	None (70%)
Previous psychiatric history	None (98%)
Event-related variables	**Modal characteristic**
Month of Injury	April (13%)
Day of Week	Weekday (56%)
Hour of Injury	6 PM - 12 AM (46%)
Census Tract Area	"2" (33%)
Type of Fatal Wound	Gunshot (72%)
Location of Fatal Wound	Chest (53%)
Alcohol in Blood	Present (55%)
Drugs in Body	None (96%)
Current Legal Problems	No (95%)
Current Psychiatric Problems	No (99%)
Current Domestic Problems	No (57%)
Current Medical Problems	No (100%)

Note: *Significantly overrepresented within the Richmond population.

employed working class male who is a member of a minority, although in Richmond, the nonwhite minority is a large group (42 percent of the population).

Age was also an important variable in homicide. As predicted, the victims were young: A full 30 percent of the victims were between 25 and 34 years of age. Persons in this age group are likely to be actively involved in the adult social organization, and the accepted practice of violence can easily lead to serious consequences, especially if the simple but lethal handgun is present.

As with suicide, past research on homicide has emphasized one variable at a time, although conclusions based on the results have implied that these variables often interact (i.e., that young nonwhite males were overrepresented in homicide). This study directly tested that interaction between age, sex, and race using the actual population characteristics of the city as a control. While females were underrepresented across age groups with respect to their proportions in the general population, and nonwhite females were victims as often as would have been expected, white males were moderately overrepresented only in the 35–54 year range. Most dramatically, however, nonwhite men between the ages of 15 and 54 were homicide victims with a frequency almost five times greater than would have been expected from random selection. While 10 percent of the Richmond population held membership in this group, 46 percent of the homicide victims shared these race/sex/age characteristics. Clearly, the adult black male was a high risk individual. These findings indicate that the inability to control lethal violence persists past the testing stages of young adulthood and well into the middle adult years.

A full 35 percent of homicide victims had a record of arrest and 30 percent had previous convictions. There were no racial differences across these variables. Furthermore, there were no differences in white and nonwhite victims' usage of alcohol just prior to their fatal woundings. Of those murdered, 55 percent had been drinking and 43 percent had a blood alcohol content at 0.10 percent or greater, the legal limit for intoxication in Virginia. The lack of race differences in alcohol use is not surprising, considering the effects of the drug on inhibition and behavior patterns and the fact that it is the major drug of abuse in all levels of American society. The presence of other drugs was noted for only 4 percent of the victims.

When considering the temporal characteristics, homicide was often similar to suicide. Deaths were distributed fairly evenly over months of the year. April had the highest frequency of deaths (13 percent), followed by August, with 12 percent of the murders over the span of the study. Cases were also evenly distributed over weekdays and weekends. An examination of hour of injury, however, revealed that evening hours were particularly hazardous. Of the victims, 46 percent were fatally wounded between 6:00

p.m. and midnight, and another 27 percent were killed between midnight and 6:00 a.m. One third of all victims were injured in a census area in the southeastern section of the city.

Typical of the American pattern, the majority of homicidal deaths in this study were the result of gunshot wounds. Although 17 percent were stabbed to death, 72 percent of all victims died from gunshots. The chest and upper back were the most frequent locations of these fatal injuries (53 percent), followed by head injuries in 36 percent of the cases.

With respect to other characteristics of homicide victims, they were not generally having any sort of personal or situational difficulties. Despite a higher arrest and conviction rate compared to the suicide victims, only a handful were experiencing any type of legal problem at the time of their deaths. None were reported to have had medical problems and current psychiatric difficulties were noted in only one case. The exception to this pattern occurred in their domestic relationships. Almost half of the victims (43 percent) were having problems with spouses, children, or other family members, and these same relatives were usually involved in the homicide. This finding again supports a subcultural view of some forms of violent behavior.

The last series of analyses were based on the predictions that homicide victims were more likely to be similar to those living around them than they were likely to be different. Again, race, marital status, and occupational group of the victim were tested, and only occupational category proved to have significant results. As predicted, the homicide victim was more likely to belong to the same occupational group as the majority of his neighbors than would be expected purely from proportional breakdowns of occupations in each area. Thus, at the job level, the victim was likely to be well integrated into the community. The theoretical explanations relating to race were not supported, on the other hand, indicating that the victim was not more likely to be of the same race as the majority of the people in the census area. This finding seems contradictory to other results that have revealed the great overrepresentation of nonwhite persons as homicide victims; however, while previous findings were based on the entire population, these are locally specific. Again, the conclusion must be drawn that the subculture of violence theory is too simplistic and that it is not supported as the level of investigation is refined and begins to examine elements closer to the subculture itself. The theory needs to be further developed to specify which situations and environmental contexts will play important roles in evoking violent behaviors that are accepted or condoned by the subcultural group. Additionally, the factor of race needs to be examined in depth to determine how much it is related to the occupational levels of the victims and to study the differences in subcultural norms for different racial minorities. Hopefully, this will decrease some of the circular reasoning that is seen in the subculture of violence approach to homicide.

The above conclusions are similar to those based on the findings related to suicide and status integration theory, indicating that a more generalized process is involved in both phenomena. It appears that one set of learned subcultural values and norms can influence the occurrence of homicide under one set of circumstances while the norms and values of a different subcultural group may result in members of that group having a greater propensity for committing suicide under a different set of circumstances. Thus, the explanation of both phenomena is founded on the same principle. This resolves a basic problem in terms of accounting for the existence of high risk groups, but it does not improve the usefulness of the approach for prediction. In order to specify which groups and which situations are likely to be high risk for homicide or suicide, it will be necessary for an in-depth sociological review of the cultural heritages and traditions of the many subcultural groups that exist in this geographic area to be undertaken. Attitudes toward suicide and homicide differ greatly from group to group, and it is likely that the occurrence of each phenomenon within a group will reflect these differences.

THE DISCRIMINANT ANALYSIS

In many instances of violent death, there are no witnesses, and it falls to the investigating officer and the medical examiner to determine if the death was the result of homicide or suicide. Usually, such a determination is not difficult; however, some cases are ambiguous. The amount and nature of the information available in this study permitted the development of an empirical method of predicting whether a subject died as a result of homicide or suicide. A stepwise discriminant analysis was conducted using a computer to determine whether the two groups of victims were distinct and to derive an equation from which predictions could bc made.

Although 21 variables were used in thc analysis, thcy varied in their usefulness in discriminating between the two groups. Those that met specific statistical criteria were selected and weighted according to their discriminatory power or strength. The 12 variables presented in Table 3 were chosen as the most precise combination for distinguishing between homicide victims as a group and suicide victims as a group. The standardized coefficients for these variables are combined to determine a single score for each subject, and this score is used to determine to which group the subject is most likely to belong (independent of the subject's actual group membership). The standardized form of the coefficients, which is the result of standardizing the raw scores into *z*-scores with a mean of 0 and a standard deviation of 1, is presented with each variable. The 12 variables are presented in the order of their contribution (highest to lowest) to the discriminant function. This is based on the absolute value of the coefficient regardless of whether it has a

TABLE 3. Original Discriminant Function

Variable	Standardized coefficient
1. Victim had current psychiatric problems	−0.67213
2. Victim had fatal chest wound	0.47314
3. Victim had current medical problems	−0.32267
4. Cause of death was "other"	0.32131
5. Race of victim	0.31168
6. Victim had current legal problems	−0.25886
7. Victim had fatal abdominal wound	0.23848
8. Cause of death was stabbing	0.20362
9. Victim had current domestic problems	−0.18251
10. Victim had multiple fatal wounds	−0.17883
11. Victim was injured in census area 2	0.16546
12. Time of injury	0.16045

Notes: Variables selected by the discriminant function (F value = 2.0). Standardized coefficients are shown for each variable. Canonical correlation = 0.800.

positive or a negative value. The sign (+ or −) associated with each variable indicates whether that variable loads heavily on homicide or suicide. Negative coefficients indicate that the variable is more often related to suicide while positive coefficients indicate that the variable is more often related to homicide. Caution should be exercised in using any one variable as a discriminator or a predictor, since the discriminant function is valid as a predictor only when all the selected variables are considered as a combined whole. The canonical correlation presented at the bottom of Table 3 provides an estimate of the variability between the two groups that can be accounted for by these variables considered together. Thus, the canonical correlation of 0.80 indicates that approximately 64 percent of the variability can be attributed to these variables.

When discriminant scores are computed for each subject, they are used to predict the group (homicide or suicide) to which the subject is most likely to belong. The predicted group membership can then be compared to the actual group membership to determine the accuracy of the function for that set of subjects. Table 4 reveals that 90.67 percent of the subjects were correctly classified, an extremely high level of accuracy. Of the actual suicides, 13 percent were incorrectly classified, but only 6 percent of the homicide cases were inaccurately predicted.

In an effort to validate the discriminant function, data on an additional 57 subjects was obtained and their scores were determined based on the original function. When the accuracy of the scores for prediction was assessed, 93 percent of the cases were found to be correctly classified, as shown in Table 5. Again, the suicide group tended to have more misses (9.5 percent of suicide victims and 5.5 percent of homicide victims).

TABLE 4. **Prediction of Group Membership I (based on second discriminant function)**

Actual group	Number of cases	Predicted group membership: Suicide	Homicide
Suicide	93	81 (87%)	12 (13%)
Homicide	100	6 (6%)	94 (94%)

Note: Percent of subjects correctly classified = 90.67%.

Finally, Table 6 presents a second discriminant function that was computed using the 193 subjects in the original sample in combination with the 57 subjects in the second sample. Only 11 variables were used in this function and 10 of these variables were also selected in the original function. With the additional data, the variable of whether or not the victim was currently experiencing domestic problems ceased to improve the discriminant function, and whether or not a victim was married did contribute to its accuracy. As expected, the larger sample size ($n+250$) increased the accuracy of the procedure: 92 percent of the subjects were correctly classified, as shown in Table 7. The canonical correlation was also increased to 0.816, accounting for approximately 66.7 percent of the variability. These findings indicate that the majority of characteristics associated with discriminative prediction are quite stable and consistent, in addition to their strength and accuracy.

The discriminant function does not provide information that is of value for theoretical applications in this study. One would expect suicide and homicide victims to be different simply because two different phenomena are being considered. Instead, the equation is of great practical value. The first area of value is that it provides a place to start in determining a cause of death for an unclassified victim, as mentioned in previous paragraphs. Secondly, it provides an empirical test for unusual cases where some information is contradictory or where the medical examiner has a high index of suspicion that the history of the fatal injury is false. For instance, a witness

TABLE 5. **Prediction of Group Membership II (based on second discriminant function)**

Actual group	Number of cases	Predicted group membership: Suicide	Homicide
Suicide	21	19 (90.5%)	2 (9.5%)
Homicide	36	2 (5.5%)	34 (94.5%)

Note: Percent of subjects correctly classified = 93.0%.

TABLE 6. Second Discriminant Function

Variable	Standardized coefficient
1. Victim had current psychiatric problems	−0.72486
2. Victim had fatal chest wound	0.48919
3. Cause of death was "other"	0.36103
4. Race of victim	0.28228
5. Victim had current medical problems	−0.24732
6. Cause of death was stabbing	0.21618
7. Victim had fatal abdominal wound	0.20545
8. Victim had current legal problems	−0.19638
9. Victim was injured in census area 2	0.16050
10. Time of injury	0.13363
11. Victim was married	−0.12890

Notes: Variables selected by the discriminant function (F value = 2.0) using all 250 subjects. Standardized coefficients are shown for each variable. Canonical correlation = 0.816.

to a death may state that the victim committed suicide while other evidence indicates that a homicide occurred.

The discriminant function can be a useful tool to both the medical examiners and the police officers in the City of Richmond. A note of caution must be mentioned, though. The equation was developed based on data for that city only; therefore, it may not be valid as a predictor outside Richmond. Also, as time passes and populations and trends shift, the equation will require updating to assure predictive accuracy. Even the addition of another year's data revealed that changes had occurred which de-emphasized the importance of domestic problems in identifying homicide victims and emphasized the importance of the victim's marital status. Finally, since the equation does have a 10 percent error rate in classifying victims, it should not be used as the sole means of categorizing a death. The equation is intended as a support measure along these lines, so that it can supplement the investigator's findings with an unbiased evaluation of the background information available about a deceased individual.

TABLE 7. Prediction of Group Membership III

		Predicted group membership	
Actual group	Number of cases	Suicide	Homicide
Suicide	114	99 (86.8%)	15 (13.2%)
Homicide	136	5 (3.7%)	131 (96.3%)

Notes: Prediction of group membership for all subjects based on the discriminant function in Table 9. Percent of subjects correctly classified = 92.0%.

CONCLUSIONS

A single conclusion can be stated based on the results testing both status integration theory and subculture of violence theory: They need further refinement and specificity. The data focusing on suicide victims revealed that other factors besides status integration per se may play an important role in determining which individuals are high risk for this type of death. Certain groups of individuals may have a greater propensity for suicide based on learned subcultural values about acceptable behavior in very stressful or unhappy situations. This is quite similar to the premise of the subculture of violence theory, in which the killing of another is considered acceptable or is condoned under certain conditions by some subcultural norms. This theory of homicide, however, is not refined to the point where it specifies which conditions and/or situations are high risk for homicidal violence. This is the major limitation of both approaches.

Further empirical research is needed to determine more specifically what types of situational components and individual characteristics coincide with the occurrence of either homicide or suicide. The discriminant analysis that was conducted provides some information, especially with respect to the occurrence of suicide and the likelihood of the victim's having a current psychiatric or medical problem. However, even in these areas, the information available is neither detailed nor consistent enough to specify which types of medical or psychiatric problems are most likely to have an influence on the propensity for suicide. The data collected in this study, additionally, are not sufficiently thorough or complete to provide a good assessment of the situational variables that were salient to these cases. Such information, once collected and analyzed, could then be integrated into sociological information pertaining to specific subcultural groups' norms and modes of interaction so that a clearer picture (although an undoubtably complex one) of high risk persons and situations could be developed and tested.

REFERENCES

1. Braught, Loya, and Jamieson. 1980. "Victims of Violent Death: A Critical Review." *Psychological Bulletin* 87(2):309.
2. U. S. Public Health Service. *Mortality Trends for Leading Causes of Death: United States 1950–1959.* HRA 76-1853. Vital and Health Statistics, Monograph Series 20, No. 16.
3. Durkheim. 1951. *Suicide.* Translated by Spaulding and Simpson. Free Press.
4. Stack. 1978. "Suicide: A Comparative Analysis." *Social Forces* 57(2):644.
5. Dublin and Bunzel. 1933. *To Be or Not To Be.* Random House.
6. Lundsgaarde. 1977. *Murder in Space City.* Oxford University Press.
7. Wolfgang. 1958. *Patterns in Criminal Homicide.* Petterson Smith.

Blood Alcohol Concentrations: Factors Affecting Predictions

Charles L. Winek, Ph.D., and Francis M. Esposito, M.S.

The alcohol found in alcoholic beverages is known as ethyl alcohol or ethanol. Other common names include grain alcohol or neutral spirits. It is a clear, odorless liquid with a pleasant odor and burning taste. The odor associated with an alcoholic beverage is usually from the raw material used to make the drink, or the added flavoring.

Ethanol is produced synthetically and by fermentation. Synthetically produced alcohols are usually used for industrial purposes and are denatured with small amounts of substances to make them unfit for human consumption. Fermentation is the process by which drinking ethanol is made from sugars and starches of various sources, in the presence of yeast. Some raw starting materials include fruit juices, grain, rye, barley, corn and molasses. Maximum alcohol content of a fermented beverage is 14–15 percent by volume.

A further process known as distillation is required to attain the high alcohol concentrations found in such liquors as whiskey, rum, brandy, and gin. The process involves heating a mixture of alcohol and water at a temperature where only the alcohol boils, then catching and cooling the resultant steam. By repeating the process, nearly pure ethanol can be produced.

The quantity of alcohol in wines and distilled liquors is expressed as present by volume or proof. The proof of a beverage is twice the percentage of alcohol by volume. Thus, an 86 proof bottle of whiskey contains 43 percent alcohol by volume.

Most regulations involving alcohol exist to control its availability (e.g., age limitation, and its use with regard to motor vehicle operation). There are also regulations prohibiting the operation of airplanes, as well as motorboats or other water vessels, while intoxicated. Statutes in each of the states prohibit the operation of a motor vehicle while under the influence of alcohol. Penalties for driving while intoxicated include revocation or suspension of a driver's license and fines and/or incarceration.

Numerous investigators have studied the relationship between the level of alcohol in a subject's blood and impairment of abilities necessary to safely operate a motor vehicle. These studies have led to legislation governing the operation of a motor vehicle while "under the influence of an intoxicating liquor." Most states consider persons with .05 percent or less alcohol by weight in their blood or breath not under the influence of intoxicating liquor. Those tested who have in excess of .05 percent, but less than .10 percent, alcohol by weight in the bloodstream may or may not be under the influence, and should be considered with other competent evidence, such as sobriety tests. And, finally, those tested having a blood alcohol concentration (BAC) of .10 percent or more are presumed to be under the influence of alcohol.

Chemical tests for intoxication estimate the amount of alcohol absorbed into the brain by analyzing blood or breath. These tests are important in that they eliminate speculation about the sobriety of an individual. In addition to motor vehicle accidents, ethanol intoxication is frequently a contributing factor in violent crimes, industrial accidents, accidental falls and adult pedestrian accidents.

The forensic toxicologist is involved in antemortem and postmortem ethanol determinations and interpretation of ethanol levels in medico-legal investigations. The extent of alcohol intoxication of a person is very important in that it may affect insurance claims or it may be a factor in driver or pilot error in accidents. The forensic toxicologist is frequently requested to predict blood alcohol levels from certain pertinent data. To do this, all factors leading to a final blood alcohol prediction must be investigated; the important factors affecting blood alcohol concentration are discussed below.

ABSORPTION

Alcohol, typically, is swallowed and absorbed through the gastrointestinal tract. Alcohol may also gain entry into the body through inhalation in industrial settings, but the amount would be minimal and certainly not to a level of intoxication. About 5 percent or less of the alcohol absorbed into the bloodstream is through the stomach wall. The remainder is absorbed from the small intestine.

Absorption through the stomach wall is slow, whereas absorption from the small intestine is rapid. Therefore, anything that delays the emptying time of the stomach will slow the absorption of alcohol. The rate of flow from the stomach to the small intestine is controlled by the pylorus, situated at the base of the stomach, which opens and closes to control passage of solids, semisolids and liquids. Food in the stomach slows stomach emptying time, hence absorption of alcohol is delayed. This applies to eating while drinking and to eating shortly before drinking. Thus, a blood alcohol level will have a lower peak value and a slower rise to that level following a meal, compared with alcohol consumption on an empty stomach.

Absorption rate also depends on the concentration, composition, and amount of alcohol ingested; it is slow in dilute and strong beverages, and is fastest for an approximately 20 percent solution. The slow absorption is due to a delayed evacuation of the stomach and irritation of the gastrointestinal walls. Maximum absorption and, in turn, maximum blood concentrations, follows when alcohol is taken in moderate amounts. The presence of carbon dioxide in carbonated beverages, sparkling wines, and champagne promotes evacuation of the stomach, which enhances the absorption of alcohol.

The rate of absorption also varies from person to person. Generally, most alcohol is absorbed in 20–30 minutes in a fasting person after a single dose. Nearly 90 percent is absorbed within one hour. When drinks are consumed successively over time, the blood alcohol levels rise with each drink, reaching a maximum in about 20 minutes, then the levels decline from this maximum. When several drinks are consumed in a very short period of time, maximum blood alcohol levels may be delayed until 45 minutes or longer after ingestion of the last drink.

To summarize, factors that delay stomach emptying time, such as food in the stomach or large amounts of a strong or dilute drink, will lead to a lower blood alcohol concentration, as compared to blood levels attained from rapid absorption in the small intestine as a result of increased stomach motility.

DISTRIBUTION

Alcohol is absorbed into the blood through the stomach and small intestinal wall, travels through the portal vein to the liver, and then to the heart and lungs, and from there back to the heart. From the heart it is pumped to all parts of the body. Alcohol is distributed to the body organs and tissues in proportion to their water content and blood supply. When absorption and distribution are complete, equilibrium is achieved and the alcohol concentration in body tissues and organs is directly proportional to its water content.

Blood is the specimen routinely submitted for ethanol quantitation and interpretation of alcohol intoxication. However, in postmortem analyses, it is sometimes necessary to resort to other bodily substances when blood is unavailable or contaminated. Our laboratory has recently examined bone marrow as an alternative tissue in extrapolating blood ethanol levels. Bone marrow is highly vascular and well protected within the bones of the body. In forensic cases involving severe trauma, other tissues and fluids may become damaged and contaminated, whereas bone marrow should remain intact and free of contamination, allowing for accurate ethanol analysis. To date, our studies have shown that blood ethanol levels can be predicted accurately from rib bone marrow ethanol levels once the lipid (fat) content of marrow specimens is taken into consideration.

The literature also lists other specimens analyzed in situations when blood is unavailable, including brain, liver, bile, urine, vitreous humor, and spinal fluid. Brain and vitreous humor are the most common substitute specimens, but they may not always be used for an absolute prediction of a blood alcohol level. One of these specimens along with bone marrow can best be utilized to validate a blood level when blood is suspected of possible contamination, or they may be used in conjunction with one another to calculate a blood level when blood is unavailable.

The following is a demonstration in predicting a blood alcohol level from a bone marrow level. First the distribution ratio of alcohol between blood and bone marrow at equilibrium must be established. Our laboratory has determined this ratio to be 1.26. This ratio times the marrow alcohol level would thus give a predicted blood level by using the following formula:

$$\text{Calculated blood level} = \text{marrow level} \times \text{distribution ratio.}$$

The marrow alcohol level used in the above equation is determined, then corrected for lipid content, since alcohol is distributed solely in the aqueous portion of the original marrow sample. As an example: The original marrow sample taken for analysis is 1000 milligrams and the lipid content is determined to be 340 mg, then the aqueous portion would be 0.660 (1000 mg − 340 mg = 660 mg and 660 mg/1000 mg = 0.66).

If the determined (observed) bone marrow ethanol level is 150 mg%, the next step would be to correct this value by accounting for the lipid portion according to the following formula:

$$\text{Corrected bone marrow ethanol (mg\%)} = \frac{\text{observed marrow ethanol (mg\%)}}{\text{aqueous fraction}}$$

$$= \frac{150\ \text{mg\%}}{0.66}$$

$$= 227 \text{ mg\%}$$

The corrected marrow ethanol level is then incorporated in the first equation above to give a predicted blood level which, in this example, would be 286 mg% (227 mg%×1.26 = 286 mg%).

ELIMINATION

Once alcohol is absorbed into the bloodstream, the body immediately begins to eliminate the alcohol by direct excretion and metabolism. The amount eliminated by excretion is generally about 2 percent. This small amount is excreted directly through breath, urine, tears, and perspiration. Since the quantity of alcohol eliminated in this matter is minute, any attempt to increase its disappearance through excretion would be futile. This would include such procedures as strenuous physical exercise, increased diuresis by drugs or coffee, and hyperventilation.

About 90 to 98 percent of ethanol in the body is metabolized in the liver to carbon dioxide and water. Calories are generated by this process of oxidation, hence alcohol has been considered to be a food; however, it has no basic food value, since proteins and vitamins are absent.

It has been established that ethanol is eliminated from the body principally by metabolism and to a minor extent by excretion. The rate of metabolism varies from person to person; the normal range reported is 7.5 to 10 gm of ethanol per hour. Based on an average of 50 liters of body water, the above-mentioned rate of metabolism would cause a blood alcohol concentration to decrease by .015 to .02 percent per hour. The rate of elimination is essentially linear, so that for any given person alcohol elimination per hour will be constant.

Various disease states of the liver may decrease the elimination rates. Chronic alcoholics with cirrhosis of the liver show depressed alcohol metabolism. Other diseases producing liver necrosis also show impaired elimination.

BLOOD ALCOHOL CONCENTRATION CURVE

Many factors affect the height and shape of a blood alcohol concentration (BAC) curve, as illustrated in Figure 1. To reiterate, food in the stomach or a strong or dilute beverage will delay absorption and result in a lower BAC curve, with the plateau of the curve maintained for a longer period of time than would be obtained if the stomach were empty. A fasting

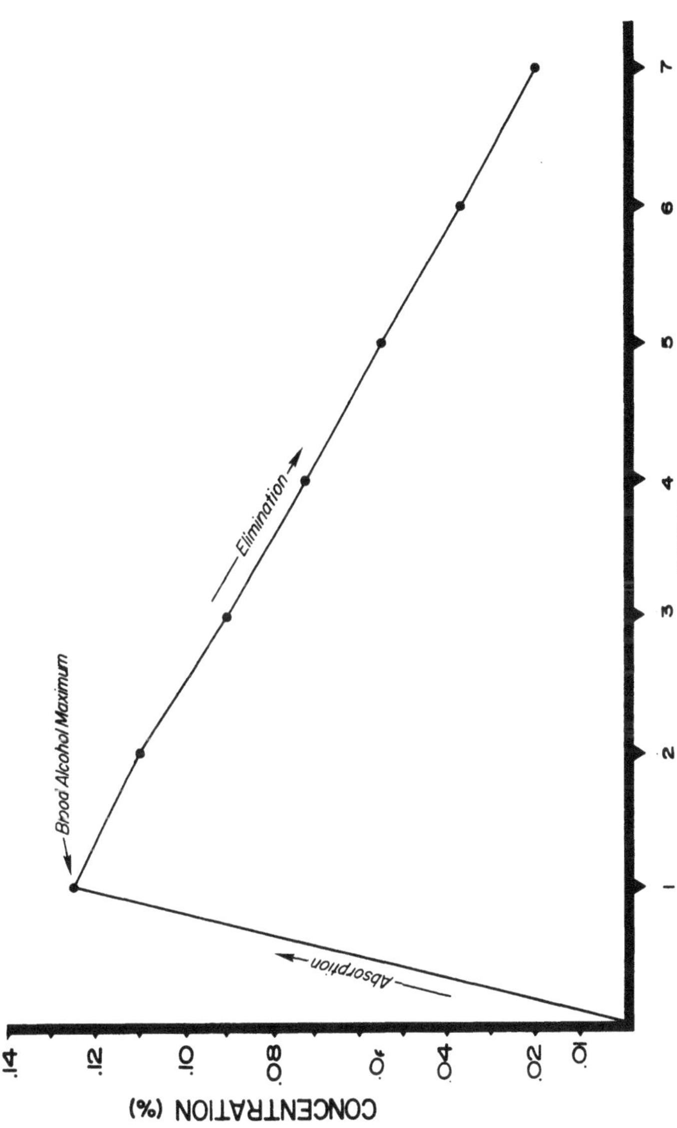

FIGURE 1. Hypothetical curve of the blood alcohol level of a 130-lb. person after consuming 5 oz. of 100 proof whiskey at a dissipation rate of .018% per hour.

subject drinking a 20 percent solution of a carbonated alcoholic beverage will have a higher and earlier BAC maximum. When several drinks are consumed in a very short period, peak BACs may not appear until about 45 minutes or longer, after the last drink. And finally, when alcohol is consumed successively over a period of time, the blood alcohol curve, as illustrated in Figure 2, will rise with each drink and then decline as the alcohol is eliminated.

To reach a particular BAC, a heavier person can consume more alcohol than a lighter one, since the heavier one has more body water for the distribution of ethanol. Table 1 shows estimated blood ethanol concentration by number of drinks in relation to body weight. As an example, if a 180-pound person had all the alcohol from 5 drinks in his body at one time, the blood ethanol level would be .104%. The time elapsed since the first drink must also be considered, since alcohol is continually being eliminated from the body. Although one's individual elimination rate is not known, the average value is .018% per hour. This figure times the number of hours since the first drink is the amount of alcohol eliminated. Subtracting this amount from the blood level found in the table will give an approximate BAC. Thus, a 180-pound person who consumed 5 drinks would have a BAC of .050% three hours after the first drink (.104% minus (.018%×3)=.050%).

TABLE 1. Estimated Blood Ethanol Concentrations (given in percentages)

	Number of drinks											
Body weight	**1**	**2**	**3**	**4**	**5**	**6**	**7**	**8**	**9**	**10**	**11**	**12**
100 lb.	.038	.075	.113	.150	.188	.225	.263	.300	.338	.375	.413	.450
110 lb.	.034	.066	.103	.137	.172	.207	.241	.275	.309	.344	.379	.412
120 lb.	.031	.063	.094	.125	.156	.188	.219	.250	.281	.313	.344	.375
130 lb.	.029	.058	.087	.116	.145	.174	.203	.232	.261	.290	.320	.348
140 lb.	.027	.054	.080	.107	.134	.161	.188	.214	.241	.268	.295	.321
150 lb.	.025	.050	.075	.100	.125	.151	.176	.201	.226	.251	.276	.301
160 lb.	.023	.047	.070	.094	.117	.141	.164	.188	.211	.234	.258	.281
170 lb.	.022	.045	.066	.088	.110	.132	.155	.178	.200	.221	.244	.265
180 lb.	.021	.042	.063	.083	.104	.125	.146	.167	.188	.208	.229	.250
190 lb.	.020	.040	.059	.079	.099	.119	.138	.158	.179	.198	.217	.237
200 lb.	.019	.038	.056	.075	.094	.113	.131	.150	.169	.188	.206	.225
210 lb.	.018	.036	.053	.071	.090	.107	.125	.143	.161	.179	.197	.215
220 lb.	.017	.034	.051	.068	.085	.102	.119	.136	.153	.170	.188	.205
230 lb.	.016	.032	.049	.065	.081	.098	.115	.130	.147	.163	.180	.196
240 lb.	.016	.031	.047	.063	.078	.094	.109	.125	.141	.156	.172	.188

Note: A drink equals one 12-ounce beer or one ounce of 100 proof liquor consumed within one hour.

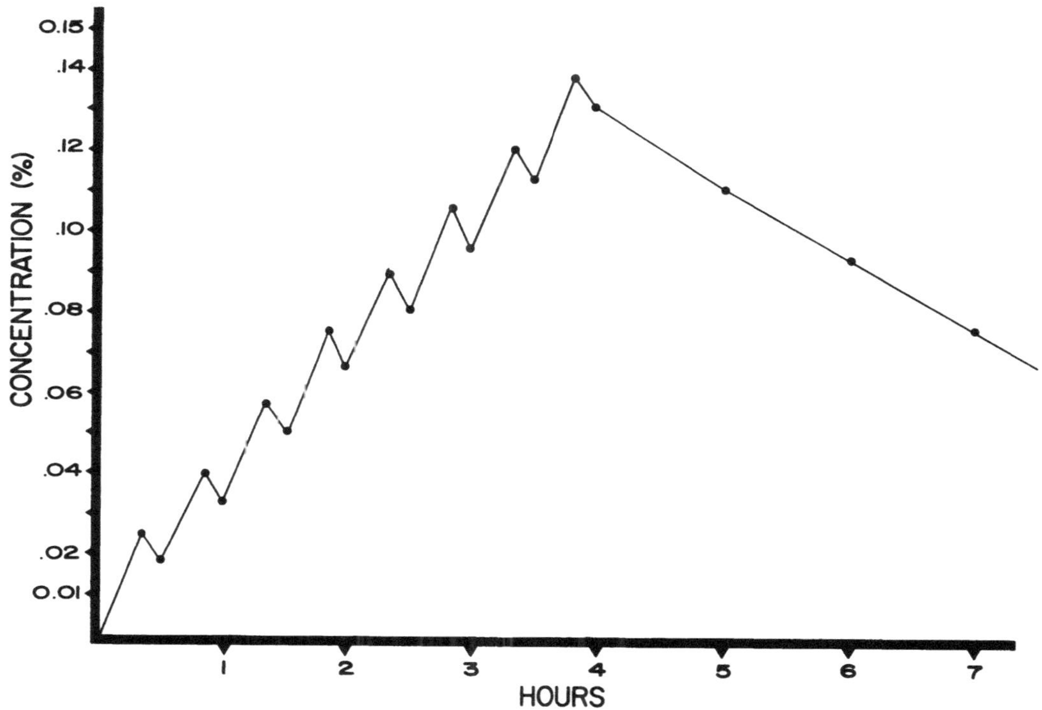

FIGURE 2. Hypothetical curve of the blood alcohol level of a 150-lb. person consuming 1 oz. of 100 proof whiskey every one-half hour for 4 hours at a dissipation rate of .018% per hour.

ALCOHOL EFFECTS ON THE CENTRAL NERVOUS SYSTEM

The principal pharmacodynamic actions of alcohol affect the central nervous system. Its early affects are a reduction of tension, release of inhibitions and a mild euphoria. These effects lead to the misconception that alcohol is a stimulant. Actually, alcohol produces a depressant effect on nerve cells which is directly proportional to the BAC. As the blood level increases, alcohol causes a progressive deterioration of body functions beginning with a disruption of the intellect, followed by impairment of motor coordination, loss of consciousness, respiratory depression, circulatory collapse and death. It affects the most recently developed part of the brain first (i.e., the cerebral cortex, which controls a person's judgment and morals). Its last effect is on the oldest portion of the brain which controls the automatic body functions. It must be emphasized that not all people are affected to the same degree at the same blood alcohol level; nor can one predict the social behavior of a person during alcohol consumption, since the personality and mental attitude of the drinker influences the behavior.

The depressant effects of alcohol on the central nervous system consist of impairment of sensory and motor functions. Visual impairment includes diminished acuity, peripheral vision and distance judgment. The pupils of the eye generally dilate so that reaction to light becomes sluggish and

TABLE 2. Blood Alcohol Levels and Corresponding Effects

Blood alcohol level	Description	Effects
0–.05%	Normal behavior	No apparent influence or mild euphoria
.05%–.10%	Slight intoxication	Euphoria; decreased inhibitions; diminished attention and judgement
.10%–.20%	Under the influence	Impaired sensory response and muscular coordination; flushed face; dilated pupils; increased reaction time; thick speech; loss of restraint and judgement
.20%–.30%	Grossly impaired	Slurred speech; incoordination; staggering gait; vomiting; apathy; sensory depression; mental confusion and disorientation
.30%–.40%	Stuporous	Sleep or stupor; marked incoordination and decreased response to stimuli
.40% and greater	Comatose or death	Anesthesia; unconsciousness, coma or death; reflexes absent; loss of sphincter control

resistance to glare decreases. Diplopia may occur due to the inability to completely fuse the vision from each eye into a single image. At elevated blood alcohol levels, hearing, taste, touch, and smell are all diminished to some extent.

Impairment of muscular coordination occurs at low blood alcohol levels due to increased reaction time. Thus, motor skills become progressively impaired with increasing levels of blood alcohol.

Table 2 shows the different signs and symptoms associated with blood ethanol levels. Not all people are affected the same at the same BAC. In addition, there are no precise blood alcohol levels for a particular sign or symptom. The common symptoms of alcoholic influence can be listed as follows: Odor of alcoholic beverages on the breath, staggering gait, poor muscular coordination, confusion, sleepiness, disorderly appearance, slurred speech, dizziness, nausea, visual disorder and flushed skin. The list is not all-inclusive, nor does any one symptom or combination of symptoms mean that the person is intoxicated, for numerous illnesses or injuries produce the same symptoms as alcoholic influence.

ETHANOL COMBINED WITH OTHER DRUGS

Ethanol is often combined with other drugs, frequently producing a more intoxicated state. The combination of alcohol and drugs can be suspected if the alcohol level found in the blood or breath is not consistent with the observed intoxicated condition of the subject.

The combined effects of alcohol and depressant drugs will be added together (additive) and, in some instances, the resultant effect will be greater than the expected combined effect of the two drugs (synergism). These central nervous system depressant drugs include narcotics, analgesics, antihistamines, tranquilizers, barbiturates, and sedative-hypnotics. Such depressants are used widely and indiscriminately by the public; their use with alcohol may be detrimental.

The central nervous system stimulants such as amphetamine, caffeine and ephedrine do not counteract the depressant effects of alcohol. They are only temporarily effective against the gross signs of intoxication. They have been effective for temporary arousal in severe intoxication, but arousal is short and a greater depression may occur.

TOLERANCE TO ALCOHOL

It is well known that some people are better able to "hold their liquor" than others. Individuals with the same weight, consuming the same amount of alcohol, may perform differently within limits. Furthermore, different individuals at the same BAC may react differently. Persons accustomed to alcohol use will learn to compensate for some of the effects of alcohol and in turn perform certain acts better than those unaccustomed to drinking. For example, they learn to minimize swaying by standing with their feet apart and they gradually learn to walk a straight line when mildly intoxicated. It is, however, the opinion of most investigators that tolerance is limited and occurs at blood alcohol levels in the lower levels of intoxication as opposed to higher levels.

The exact reasons for differences in tolerance to alcohol are unknown, but the following reasons have been proposed: Increased elimination, increased tissue tolerance, increased water content of the body, delayed absorption, decreased penetration of the central nervous system and enzyme induction. Of these, increased dissipation is the most likely explanation in the chronic alcoholic.

ESTIMATION OF A BLOOD ALCOHOL CONCENTRATION

The forensic toxicologist is frequently requested to determine whether or not the blood alcohol concentration (BAC) of a person corresponds to the reported quantity of alcohol ingested, or to estimate the quantity of alcohol consumed based on the measured BAC. Examples of both situations are illustrated below. These estimations of BACs must be based on sufficient information, without which the estimation cannot be made. Essential information includes body weight, percent and number of alcoholic beverages, and length of the drinking period. As mentioned previously, some of the factors that affect the rate of absorption will in turn influence the final BAC. For example, food in the stomach or a strong or dilute beverage will delay absorption, which will lessen the expected BAC. Also, an individual's dissipation rate is an important unknown factor that will determine one's BAC over an extended drinking period.

A standard example of calculating a blood alcohol concentration is as follows: A person weighing 150 pounds will attain a BAC of .025% upon complete absorption of one 12-ounce beer (4 percent ethanol) or one ounce of 100 proof (50 percent ethanol) alcohol beverage. The amount of alcohol is the same in both beverages, that is, they contain about 15 ml, or one-half ounce, of pure alcohol. Should the person weigh more or less than 150 pounds, or the alcohol beverage concentration be less or greater than 50 percent, the BAC will be lower or higher. The following formula is then utilized to calculate the BAC:

$$\frac{150}{A} \times \frac{B}{50} \times C \times .025\% = D, \qquad (1)$$

Where A = Body weight,
B = Percent of alcoholic beverage,
C = Number of one-ounce drinks (or number of ounces), and
D = Level attained upon complete absorption.

The forensic toxicologist might be asked to calculate, for example, the BAC of a man weighing 200 pounds upon complete absorption of five 12-ounce beers. Using Equation 1 we can determine, given body weight = 200 pounds, percent alcohol of beer = 4%, and number of ounces = 60, that D, blood alcohol concentration, is .090 percent:

$$D = \frac{150}{200} \times \frac{4}{50} \times 60 \times .025\% = .090\%.$$

The BAC for this man would be the same if five shots of 100 proof whiskey were consumed in place of the beers, where $B = 50\%$ (100 proof) and $C = 5$:

$$D = \frac{150}{200} \times \frac{50}{50} \times 5 \times .025\% = .094\%.$$

If the above person consumed both five 12-ounce beers and five one-ounce shots of 100 proof whiskey, his BAC would be the combined concentration from beer and whiskey (.090% + .094% = .184%).

Note above that the percentage of alcohol by volume is one-half of the proof of an alcoholic beverage. Thus, an 86 proof bottle of whiskey contains 43 percent alcohol by volume.

As soon as alcohol is absorbed into the bloodstream the body starts to eliminate it. The average rate of elimination is approximately .018 percent per hour, but the rates may vary between .015 percent to .020 percent per hour. If drinking is spread out over a period of time, the dissipation rate times the number of hours after the first drink must be subtracted from the BAC to give a BAC at the time in question. The equation is as follows:

$$\text{BAC} - (\text{Dissipation rate} \times \text{Number of hours after first drink}). \qquad (2)$$

Since the rate of alcohol elimination is variable and differs from person to person, three calculations involving the above equation can be made, one using the higher dissipation rate (.020 percent/hour), one using the lower rate (.015 percent/hour), and one using the average rate (.018 percent/hour).

The following example illustrates the use of Equations (1) and (2).

A woman weighing 120 pounds started drinking at 8:00 P.M. and continued to drink until 11:00 P.M. During the course of the evening she consumed six 12-ounce bottles of beer. What was her BAC at 12:00 A.M.?

Equation 1: $\frac{150}{A} \times \frac{B}{50} \times C \times .025\% = D$

A = Weight = 120 pounds
B = Percent alcohol of beer = 4%
C = Number of ounces = 72
D = Blood alcohol concentration

$$D = \frac{150}{120} \times \frac{4}{50} \times 72 \times .025\% = .180\%$$

Since drinking was spread out over a period of three hours, plus an additional hour to the time in question, the amount of alcohol eliminated in four hours must be subtracted from .180%, according to Equation (2), using the low, high and average dissipation rates:

a. BAC − (.015% × 4) = .180% − .060% = .120%
b. BAC − (.018% × 4) = .180% − .072% = .108%
c. BAC − (.020% × 4) = .180% − .080% = .100%

As mentioned previously, the elimination rate of alcohol has been determined to be constant (linear). This permits the calculation of an alcohol level at a previous time by back calculation. To be more accurate, the average dissipation rate with ranges should be used. The back calculation is only accurate in the elimination phase of the blood alcohol curve (Figure 1) and does not apply to the absorption phase. Extrapolation is frequently used in situations where there is a delay between the submission of a blood or breath sample and the actual occurrence. The equation for the extrapolation is as follows:

BAC + (Dissipation rate × Number of hours elapsed). (3)

The following example demonstrates a back calculation utilizing the average dissipation rate and ranges. Suppose a person was drinking from 8:00 P.M. to 10:00 P.M. and was involved in an accident at 11:30 P.M. A blood sample drawn at 1:30 A.M. revealed a BAC of .07 percent. What was the person's BAC at the time of the accident?

BAC + (Dissipation rate × No. of hours elapsed)

a. $.07\% + (.015\% \times 2) = .100\%$
b. $.07\% + (.018\% \times 2) = .106\%$
c. $.07\% + (.02\% \times 2) = .110\%$

Several examples employing Equations (1) through (3) are given below.

Example: A man weighing 220 pounds started drinking at 5:00 P.M. and continued to drink until 1:00 A.M. During this time he neglected to eat any food. During the course of the evening he consumed seven 16-ounce beers and ten one-ounce shots of whiskey (86 proof). At 3:00 A.M. he was involved in an automobile accident. At 4:00 A.M. a blood sample was drawn for alcohol content. What was his BAC at the time the blood was withdrawn?

Solution:

$$\frac{150}{A} \times \frac{B}{50} \times C \times .025\% = D \qquad (1)$$

A = Weight = 220 pounds
B = Percent of alcohol beverage = 4% for beer and 43% for whiskey
C = Number of ounces = 112 (beer) and 10 (whiskey)
D = Maximum level attained upon complete absorption

$$\text{BAC from beers} = \frac{150}{220} \times \frac{4}{50} \times 112 \times .025\% = .153\%$$

$$\text{BAC from whiskey} = \frac{150}{220} \times \frac{43}{50} \times 10 \times .025\% = .147\%$$

Total BAC from beer and whiskey = .300%

The elapsed time between the first drink (5:00 P.M.) and the blood sample withdrawal (4:00 A.M.) is 11 hours. The amount of alcohol dissipated during this time is estimated using Equation (2) and a range of dissipation rates.

BAC − (Dissipation rate × Number of hours after first drink) (2)

a. $.300\% - (.015\% \times 11) = .300\% - .165\% = .135\%$
b. $.300\% - (.018\% \times 11) = .300\% - .198\% = .102\%$
c. $.300\% - (.020\% \times 11) = .300\% - .22\% = .080\%$

Example: A woman drinks from 4:00 P.M. to 8:00 P.M. She has a reported BAC of .10 percent at midnight. What is her BAC at 9:00 P.M.?

Solution:

$$\text{BAC} + (\text{Dissipation rate} \times \text{Number of hours elapsed}) \tag{3}$$

a. $.10\% + (.015\% \times 3) = .145\%$
b. $.10\% + (.018\% \times 3) = .154\%$
c. $.10\% + (.02\% \times 3) \quad = .160\%$

The examples presented to this point have been predicting a BAC based on a certain number of drinks, their alcohol percentage and the weight of the individual. Reverse calculations are also possible; that is, an estimation of the amount of alcohol in a person's body can be obtained from a given BAC. The formula was developed by a pioneer in alcohol research, E.M.P. Widmark. It is based on the distribution of alcohol in the body as a whole, compared to blood. It should not be considered as a means of specifying actual amounts consumed. The formula is as follows:

$$A = \frac{WRCT}{0.8} \tag{4}$$

Where A = Ethanol in the body in milliliters (ml)
W = Body weight in grams (g)
R = Distribution ratio = 0.68 for men and 0.55 for women
CT = Chemical test (decimal equivalent of % BAC)
0.8 = Specific gravity of alcohol

An example using Widmark's formula is as follows: How many fluid ounces of 100 proof whiskey are in the body of a 150-pound man who has a BAC of .20%?

Solution:

$$A = \frac{WRCT}{0.8}$$

1 pound = 454 grams
30 ml = 1 fluid ounce (approximate)
100 proof = 50% alcohol = 0.50

A = ml of ethanol

W = Body weight in grams =
150 lbs × 454 g/lb. = 68,100 grams
R = 0.68 for men
CT = Decimal equivalents of a BAC of .20% =
0.0020

$$A = \frac{WRCT}{0.8} = \frac{68{,}100 \times 0.68 \times 0.0020}{0.8} = \frac{92.6}{0.8} = 115.8 \text{ ml}$$

A = 115.8 ml ÷ ml/ounce =
3.86 ounces of pure alcohol (200 proof or 100%)

$$\frac{3.86 \text{ oz.}}{.50} = 7.72 \text{ fluid oz. of 100 proof whiskey (50\%)}$$

Another example using Widmark's formula follows: The toxicology report of a deceased woman showed she had a BAC of .25%. Witnesses state that she was drinking "boilermakers" for about 3 hours. She weighed 130 pounds. Estimate in terms of beer and whiskey how many drinks she consumed if she died 3 hours after leaving the bar.

Solution:

$$A = \frac{WRCT}{0.8}$$

Where W = 130 lbs. × 454 g/lb. = 59020 g
R = 0.55 (women)
CT = .25% = 0.0025

$$A = \frac{59020 \times 0.55 \times 0.0025}{0.8} = \frac{81.2}{0.8} = 101.4 \text{ ml of 100\% alcohol}$$

The amount of alcohol dissipated during and after drinking (6 hours) must also be calculated and added to the above figure to attain an estimate of the total amount of alcohol ingested. Using Equation (2), the amount of alcohol dissipated, presuming a metabolic rate of .018%/hour, would be:

$$.018\% \times .108\% \qquad (2)$$

This figure is then converted to a quantity of alcohol as illustrated above using Widmark's formula (Equation 4):

$$A = \frac{WRCT}{0.8}$$

Where $W = 59020$
$R = 0.55$
$CT = .108\%$ or $.00108$

$$A = \frac{59020 \times 0.55 \times 0.00108}{0.8} = 43.8 \text{ ml of } 100\% \text{ alcohol}$$

The total estimated amount of alcohol ingested is thus:

$$101.4 \text{ ml} + 43.8 \text{ ml} = 145.2 \text{ ml of } 100\% \text{ alcohol}$$

This is equivalent to 4.84 oz. of 100% alcohol:

$$\frac{(145.2 \text{ ml}}{(30 \text{ ml/oz.}} = 4.84 \text{ oz.})$$

Converting this to ounces of 100 proof whiskey or 4 percent beer is:

a. Whiskey = 100 proof = 50% = 0.50

$$\frac{4.84 \text{ oz.}}{0.50} = 9.68 \text{ oz. of } 50\% \text{ alcohol} = 10 \text{ shots (approximate)}$$

b. Beer = 4% = 0.04

$$\frac{4.84 \text{ oz.}}{0.04} = 121 \text{ oz. of } 4\% \text{ beer} = 10 \text{ beers (approximate)}$$

The above calculations show that the woman consumed an equivalent of 10 beers or 10 shots of whiskey to give a BAC of .25% six hours after her initial drink. A "boilermaker" is considered to be a shot and a beer, thus she consumed approximately 5 "boilermakers."

The final example presented below typifies the calculation a toxicologist is frequently requested to perform in order to support or discredit the testimony of an accused subject. A hypothetical situation follows:

Example: A man was involved in an accident at 3:30 A.M. A breath test administered at 4:30 A.M. showed his alcohol level was .20%. The defendant denied being intoxicated, implying the Breathalyzer was not operating properly. However, the police report stated that he showed visible signs of gross intoxication. He testified that he drank 6 beers from 7:00 P.M. to 10:00 P.M. at Bar A, then he drank 4 beers from 12:00 midnight to 2:00 A.M. at Bar B. However, witnesses stated that he consumed 10 beers at Bar A and 7 beers at

Bar B. He had nothing to eat during this time. His weight is 170 pounds. Was the testimony of the accused man or the witnesses accurate? How many beers did he consume to give a BAC of .20%?

Solution:

The first step of this hypothetical problem would be to predict the man's BAC at different times of the evening according to the number of drinks he allegedly consumed. At Bar A the defendant stated he drank 6 beers from 7:00 P.M. to 10:00 P.M., whereas a witness stated the defendant drank 10 beers. Using both testimonies, his BAC upon complete absorption can be calculated using Equation (1):

$$\frac{150}{A} \times \frac{B}{50} \times C \times .025\% = D$$

Where A = Weight = 170
B = Percentage of alcohol beverage = 4%
C = Number of ounces = 72 (defendant's testimony)
120 (witness's testimony)
D = Level attained upon complete absorption

$$D = \frac{150}{170} \times \frac{4}{50} \times 72 \times .025\% = .127\%$$

$$D = \frac{150}{170} \times \frac{4}{50} \times 120 \times .025\% = .212\%$$

Since drinking is dispersed over a period of time, the dissipation rate times the number of hours after the first drink must be subtracted from the BAC to give a BAC at the time in question. Presuming his elimination rate is .018%/hour, his BAC at different times from 10:00 P.M. to 12:00 midnight can be determined using Equation (2):

$$\text{BAC} - (\text{Dissipation rate} \times \text{Number of hours after first drink}).$$

If the accused testimony is used, his BAC at about 10:00 P.M., presuming all alcohol consumed was absorbed, would be calculated using Equation (2):

$$.127\% - (.018\% \times 3) = .073\%$$

At 11:00 P.M. his BAC would be .055% and at 12:00 midnight, upon arriving at Bar B, .037%.

Using the testimony of the witness, his BAC at 10:00 P.M. would be:

$$.212\% - (.018\% \times 3) = .158\%$$

At 11:00 P.M. his BAC would be .140%, and at midnight, .122%.

The defendant then stated he drank four beers from midnight until 2:00 A.M., but a witness stated she served him at least seven beers. His BAC upon complete absorption is again calculated using Equation (1):

$$\frac{150}{A} \times \frac{B}{50} \times C \times .025\% = D$$

Where $A = 170$
$B = 4$
$C = 48$ (defendant's testimony)
84 (witness's testimony)
$D =$ Blood alcohol concentration

$$\frac{150}{170} \times \frac{4}{50} \times 48 \times .025\% = .085\%$$

$$\frac{150}{170} \times \frac{4}{50} \times 84 \times .015\% = .148\%$$

The blood alcohol concentrations accumulated at Bar A are added to these values and the amount of alcohol dissipated from 12:00 midnight to 2:00 A.M. is subtracted. So, using the defendant's testimony for calculations, at 2:00 A.M. his BAC would be .037% (from Bar A) + .085% (from Bar B) − (.018% × 2) = .086%. It follows that his BAC at 3:00 A.M. would be .068%, and .041% at 4:30 A.M. If the waitress's statement is used, his BAC at 2:00 A.M. would be .122% (from Bar A) + .148% (from Bar B) − (.018% × 2) = .234%. It also follows that his BAC at 3:00 A.M. would be .216%, and .189% at 4:30 A.M.

A graph showing hypothetical blood alcohol curves through the evening according to the testimony of the defendant and the witnesses are shown in Figure 3. It is apparent that the testimony of the defendant was not accurate, whereas statements from witnesses agreed with the Breathalyzer result of .20% at 4:30 A.M.

As illustrated earlier in this text, an estimation of the amount of alcohol in a person's body can be obtained from a given BAC (Equation 4). Applying this formula to this hypothetical case, the number of beers consumed by the defendant over the evening can be estimated from the Breathalyzer result and be compared to the testimonies given by the defendant and witnesses:

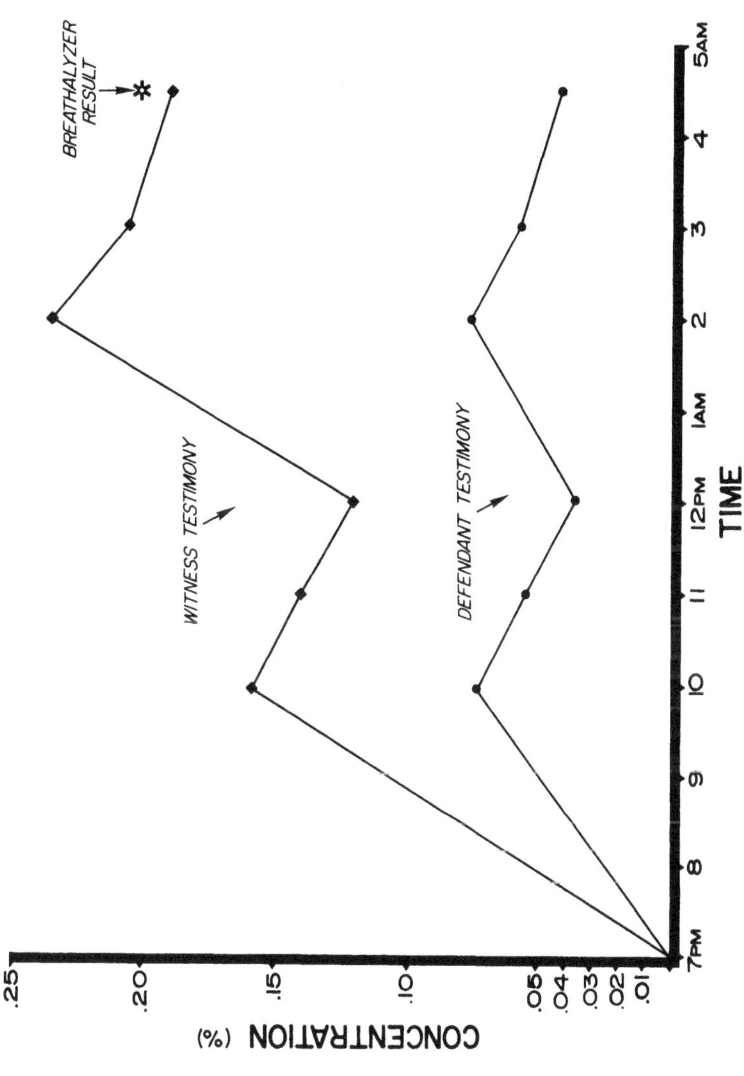

FIGURE 3. Blood alcohol concentration based upon testimony from defendant and witness.

$$A = \frac{WRCT}{0.8}$$

Where A = Ethanol in milliliters (ml)
W = Body weight in grams = 454 g/lb. × 170 lbs. = 77180 g
CT = Decimal equivalent of % BAC = .20% = 0.0020
R = Distribution ratio = 0.68 for men

$$A = \frac{77180 \times 0.68 \times 0.002}{0.8} = 131 \text{ ml of } 100\% \text{ alcohol}$$

$$\frac{131 \text{ ml}}{30 \text{ ml/oz.}} = 4.37 \text{ oz. of } 100\% \text{ alcohol}$$

$$\frac{4.37}{0.04} = 109 \text{ oz. of } 4\% \text{ beer} = 9 \text{ beers}$$

Again the amount of alcohol dissipated during the evening must be added to this figure. Using Equation (2), and presuming a metabolic rate of .018%/hour, the amount of alcohol dissipated during the course of the evening (7:00 P.M. to 4:30 A.M.) was .018%/hour × 9.5 hours = .171%. This concentration is then converted to a quantity of alcohol, again using Equation (4):

$$A = \frac{77180 \times 0.68 \times 0.0017}{0.8} = 111.5 \text{ ml of } 100\% \text{ alcohol}$$

$$\frac{111.5 \text{ ml}}{30 \text{ ml/oz.}} = 3.72 \text{ oz. of } 100\% \text{ alcohol}$$

$$\frac{3.72}{0.04} = 92.9 \text{ oz. of } 4\% \text{ beer} = 7.7 \text{ beers}$$

So, the total number of beers consumed during the evening would be approximately 17 beers. This figure agrees with the statement from witnesses who claimed the defendant drank about 17 beers. The defendant stated he drank 10 beers during the evening. From the calculations based on the presumed number of drinks consumed and based on the Breathalyzer reading of .20%, it is obvious that the testimony of the defendant was inaccurate.

These examples have illustrated both the use of predicting a BAC and estimating the quantity of alcohol consumed, based on a given BAC, using pertinent data. These predictions must be used with caution, for certain variables, such as an individual's metabolic rate, food in the stomach, and length of the drinking period, will have an effect on the outcome of the estimation.

CONTAMINATION OF ANTEMORTEM BLOOD SAMPLES

The collection of a blood specimen for ethanol analysis with subsequent legal use requires the specimen to be taken by a nurse or technician under the direction of a physician. Records should be made to identify the person withdrawing the blood, along with the date and time the sample was withdrawn. A chain of possession must also be documented. Finally, contamination of the sample must be eliminated. The question of contamination usually arises when an antiseptic swabbing compound containing ethanol is used. A study conducted in our laboratory evaluated the possibility of altering a BAC by swabbing with rubbing alcohol (70 percent ethanol) prior to blood collection using the Vacutainer apparatus. Technicians were instructed to swab an arm with ethanol and then use their usual clinical technique to draw the blood sample. Other technicians were told to be excessively sloppy when swabbing and drawing blood samples.

Technicians using the usual clinical technique showed an average increase of .0006 percent with a range of .0002 percent to .002 percent. Although ethanol was used for swabbing, a negligible increase occurred, hence the actual BAC would not be altered. For example, a person with an actual BAC of .17 percent would have a BAC of .172 percent maximum, should ethanol be used for swabbing, using standard withdrawal procedures.

Technicians told to be excessively sloppy when swabbing and withdrawing blood samples showed that significant contamination may occur. An average increase of .09 percent from the actual BAC was noted, with a range of .0 percent to 2.225 percent. Thus, should a sloppy technique be used, it is possible to elevate a BAC determination to a level of intoxication. For example, a BAC of .04 percent could be elevated to .13 percent, or more. To resolve the suggestion of contamination through swabbing with ethanol, it is recommended that nonethanol antiseptics, such as aqueous Zephiran chloride, be employed.

Another possible means of altering the BAC is via transfusion of donor blood that contains ethanol. Normally, blood banks will refuse donors that exhibit signs of alcohol intoxication. In order to establish the incidence and significance of donor blood containing ethanol, our laboratory analyzed 1,450 samples from several blood-banking organizations. We found that 2 percent of the samples contained ethanol. The average BAC was .03%, with a range of .007% to .15%. The rare occurrence of contaminated transfusion blood, together with the dilution of the blood by the recipient's body fluids, indicates that alteration of a BAC from this source would be negligible. For example, a unit of blood (450 ml) with an alcohol level of .15% contains 0.675 grams of ethanol (0.675 g/450 ml = 0.15 g/100 ml = .15%). Should this blood be transfused to a 160-pound person, it would be diluted with approximately 42,350 grams of body water (average total body water), assuming that the alcohol diffused equally throughout the total body water. This would give an insignificant increase in the BAC by .002% (0.675 g/42,350 ml = 0.0016 g/100 ml = .0016%). Thus, a person with a BAC of .14% receiving a unit of blood that has an alcohol content of .15% would elevate the actual BAC to .142%, an insignificant change. Similarly, should an accident victim receive therapy with an alcohol-containing drug prior to blood sample withdrawal for a BAC determination, the quantity of alcohol received would be insignificant due to the above described dilution. There are several injectable medications that contain ethanol, including Valium (10 percent ethanol), Nembutal (10 percent ethanol), and Crystodigin (49 percent ethanol). Again, a BAC will not be altered should a person be given one of these drugs. For example, if a person received 3 injections of Valium (2 ml each time, 10% of which is ethanol), they would be given approximately 0.6 grams of ethanol. The alcohol received would then be distributed in a person's body fluids (approximately 42,000 ml), resulting in a BAC of .0014% (0.6 g/42,000 ml = 0.0014 g/100 ml = .0014%). Thus, if the actual blood alcohol level were .15%, a contribution of .0014% would not change the BAC significantly.

Although not truly considered contamination of antemortem blood samples, the ingestion of prescription or over-the-counter products can add to or produce a significant blood alcohol level. Certain elixirs contain as much as 43 percent alcohol. A BAC in the legal range may be unintentionally elevated to an intoxicated level should an elixir or similar medication be taken simultaneously with social drinks. For example, if a person weighing 130 pounds has a BAC of .05% and then consumes three ounces of an elixir containing 43 percent alcohol, what would be the new BAC?

Solution:

$$\frac{150}{A} \times \frac{B}{50} \times C \times .025\% = D$$

$$\frac{150}{130} \times \frac{43}{50} \times 3 \times .025\% = .074\%$$

Where A = Weight in pounds = 130
B = Percent alcohol of product = 43
C = Ounces = 3
D = Blood alcohol level

Adding this amount to the existing BAC of .05% results in a significantly elevated BAC of .124%. This example also illustrates how a high alcohol level may be unintentionally attained even if there isn't a preexisting BAC. Caution must be exercised when consuming medications containing alcohol.

POSTMORTEM CHANGES OF ETHANOL LEVELS

There are many factors that may alter the concentration of alcohol present in autopsy samples. These factors include exposure of the samples to air, delay in obtaining and/or analyzing the samples, contamination due to severe trauma or the use of nonsterile technique. The greatest factor, however, seems to be the postmortem synthesis of alcohol either in the body or in the samples after removal and storage. This postmortem ethanol production requires the presence of microorganisms. These microorganisms can be inhibited by using a preservative and storing the samples under refrigeration.

Putrefaction is often accompanied with postmortem synthesis of ethanol, which may create a problem in medico-legal cases. It is recommended that several different specimens be collected and analyzed, such as urine, bile, vitreous humor, and bone marrow. Should the alcohol values for the various specimens agree within the range of distribution variation, then it can be assumed safely that the alcohol concentrations detected are due to ingestion.

ALCOHOL CONTENT IN EMBALMED AND EXHUMED BODIES

The toxicologist may be forced to analyze fluids for ethanol after the body has been embalmed, and/or embalmed and exhumed. This presents several problems in interpreting the blood alcohol results. Most embalming fluids contain one or more of the common alcohols: ethanol, methanol, or isopropanol. Since embalming fluid is forced into the circulatory system of the body, all fluids normally used in an alcohol analysis will be contaminated with the embalming fluid. Thus, a blood ethanol analysis is of no value if the embalming fluid contained ethanol. Furthermore, one cannot predict the presence or absence of ethanol prior to death, since all fluids of the body become contaminated, including urine, bile and vitreous humor. An embalming fluid containing an alcohol or a liquid other than ethanol will dilute the blood, which, in turn, lowers the true ethanol value. Hence, any attempt to predict a blood ethanol level prior to death after embalming is purely conjecture. This is also true for exhumed bodies, since dehydration in addition to contamination or dilution of the blood is often prevalent. All body tissues are contaminated in an embalmed-exhumed body. Further research is needed to see if bone marrow might be a specimen of choice shortly after vascular embalming.

STORAGE OF ANTEMORTEM BLOOD ALCOHOL SAMPLES

A current project being conducted in our laboratory is an *in vitro* study in which ethanol levels are monitored to establish what effects a delay in analysis and storage temperatures have on antemortem blood samples taken by sterile techniques. This project has practical application in cases where a police officer or laboratory procrastinates in delivering or analyzing a blood alcohol sample.

Blood samples were withdrawn from alcohol positive volunteers. The samples were stored without being opened for analysis until a specified day. Storage conditions included refrigeration and nonrefrigeration of blood samples in tubes, with and without preservatives. Table 3 summarizes the data. The ethanol levels of samples stored unopened were not significantly different from the levels obtained immediately after collection. Therefore, if a sample is collected using sterile tubes and technique, analysis may be delayed for up to 14 days with reasonable certainty that the ethanol level reflects that which was present upon collection. This holds true for refrigerated and nonrefrigerated samples, with and without preservatives.

UNITS

Blood alcohol concentration may be reported by various laboratories in different units. The most common manner of reporting a BAC is as a percent, for example, .19%. This concentration is equivalent to 190 mg percent, and since there are 1000 mg in each gram, the decimal point is moved three places to the left, giving a .190 gram percent. The unit gram is left out when reporting the concentration, since the unit is understood. So, a BAC of .19% means there is 0.19 gram percent or 0.19 grams of ethanol in every 100 ml of blood. Percent means parts per hundred. Note that the gram and milligram (mg) are units of weight and it is a weight of alcohol that is being reported, as opposed to volume. One would actually expect a liquid to be reported in terms of volume, as opposed to weight. Alcohol is a liquid, but is reported on a weight basis because of the language of the motor vehicle codes. A BAC may also be reported as 190 mg/dl. The dl represents deciliter, and is the same as percent. So a BAC of 190 mg/dl is the same as

TABLE 3. Effect of Storage on Blood Ethanol Levels in Antemortem Samples

		Refrigerated		Room temperature	
Day analyzed	Sodium fluoride	Average blood ethanol level (mg%)	Average percent difference	Average blood ethanol level (mg%)	Average percent difference
1	+	88	—	87	—
	−	87	—	86	—
2	+	87	+1.27 (±2.60)	86	−0.48 (±2.1)
	−	87	−0.44 (±2.81)	85	+0.44 (±1.51)
5	+	88	+2.01 (±2.5)	87	−1.05 (±2.07)
	−	88	+0.64 (±2.64)	85	−1.31 (±2.21)
7	+	88	+2.53 (±3.12)	87	−0.62 (±3.3)
	−	89	+1.57 (±2.38)	86	+0.08 (±2.22)
14	+	90	+0.98 (±3.33)	84	−2.12 (±1.61)
	−	87	+1.59 (±3.60)	86	!0.65 (±1.89)

Notes: All values are the average of six volunteers. The average percent difference refers to the respective value when compared to the day 1 value for blood ethanol level.

.19%. Another reporting unit is the liter. A BAC of 1900 mg/L is equal to 190 mg% or .19 percent.

SUMMARY

As a result of extensive alcohol research conducted on both humans and animals, it is possible to predict a BAC, given pertinent data. In addition, it is possible to estimate from a given BAC the quantity of alcohol consumed. Caution must be used in these predictions, for certain factors will affect the final estimation. Absorption of alcohol is influenced by gastrointestinal contents and motility, and also the composition and quantity of the alcoholic beverage. The vascularity of tissues influences the distribution of alcohol, and their water content will determine the amount of alcohol present after equilibrium. Elimination of alcohol begins immediately after absorption. The elimination rate varies for individuals but falls between .015 percent to .020 percent per hour, with an average of .018 percent per hour. In addition to these factors, a BAC will depend on the subject's weight, percentage of alcohol in the beverage, and the rate of drinking.

The principal effect of alcohol in the body is on the central nervous system. Its depressant effect consists of impairment to sensory, motor and learned functions. When combined with some other drugs, a more intoxicated state occurs. Although tolerance to alcohol at low blood concentrations is possible, the tolerance most noted is a learned tolerance among chronic drinkers.

Contamination of antemortem blood samples collected for alcohol analysis is minimal when swabbing with an ethanolic antiseptic is performed with routine clinical technique; sloppy swabbing has been shown to increase the BAC determination significantly. The alcoholic content of blood used for transfusion does not contribute significantly to the BAC of the recipient, since extensive dilution occurs; nor does the alcohol present in injectable medication contribute significantly.

Although many factors may alter the concentration of alcohol present in autopsy specimens, postmortem synthesis of alcohol receives the most attention. The microorganisms that cause postmortem ethanol production can be inhibited by adding a preservative to the samples and storing them under refrigeration. Should putrefaction be present, it is recommended that, in addition to blood, several different specimens be collected and analyzed for the presence of alcohol.

Antemortem blood samples containing ethanol, collected using sterile tubes and techniques, may be analyzed up to 14 days later with reasonable certainty that the ethanol level reflects that which was present at the time of collection.

REFERENCES

American Medical Association. 1970. *Alcohol and the Impaired Driver,* 15–34.

Aspects of Alcoholism. 1962. Vol. 1, pp. 16–19. Philadelphia: J.B. Lippincott.

Collum, W.D. 1974. "Postmortem Synthesis of Alcohol." In *The Toxicology Annual,* edited by C.L. Winek, pp. 169–274. New York: Marcel Dekker, 1975.

Larson, C.P. 1969. "Alcohol: Fact and Fallacy." In *Legal Medicine Annual, 1969,* edited by C.H. Wecht, pp. 241–268. Appleton-Century-Crofts.

National Institute on Drug Abuse. 1977. *Drugs and Driving,* edited by R. Willette.

Paul, L.J. 1982. "The Effect of Short Term Storage Conditions on Blood Alcohol Determinations in Living Human Subjects." Masters Thesis, Dusquesne University, Pittsburgh.

Stewart, C.P., and A. Stolman. 1961. *Toxicology: Mechanisms and Analytical Methods.* Vol. 11, pp. 145–162. New York: Academic Press.

Wallgren, H., and H. Barr III. 1970. *Actions of Alcohol.* Vol. 1, pp. 17–53. Elsevier Publishing.

Widmark, E.M.P. 1981. *Principles and Application of Medicolegal Alcohol Determination,* pp. 47–82. California: Biomedical Publications.

Winek, C.L., and T. Eastly. 1976. "Factors Affecting Contamination of Blood Samples for Ethanol Determinations." In *Legal Medicine Annual, 1976,* edited by C.H. Wecht, pp. 145–162. Appleton-Century-Crofts.

Winek, C.L., and F.M. Esposito. 1981. "Comparative Study of Ethanol Levels in Blood versus Bone Marrow, Vitreous Humor, Bile and Urine." *Forensic Science International* 17:27.

The Effective Use of a Questioned Document Examiner in Medical Malpractice Cases

David A. Crown

INTRODUCTION

To prove the issue of medical malpractice an attorney has to demonstrate that a physician was negligent based upon "a reasonable degree of medical probability." Conversely, Holder states "if a physician can prove that he followed due care in diagnosis and treatment of a patient's complaint, the patient obviously cannot prove, regardless of the gravity of the untoward result, that the physician was negligent."[1]

Holder further states "if a negligence suit is filed subsequent to alteration of a record and that alteration is apparent, it will undoubtedly be construed as a dishonest attempt to avoid liability."[2]

In considering the potential for a medial malpractice suit, there exists the possiblity of the following types of activity with medical records:

- alteration of records
- obliteration of records
- substitution of records
- newly created records
- additions to records

Additionally, at times there is concern regarding: (a) identifying the individual who wrote a portion of a medical record, or (b) determining whether there are superimposed writings or impressions that have evidential value.

USE OF A QUESTIONED DOCUMENT EXAMINER

The assistance of a questioned document examiner is indicated in any case where any of the above possibilities, circumstances or conditions are suspected, or where there is doubt about the identity of the individual who wrote something that is crucial in a record. In some cases, the absence of identity could be the issue, in that it may be essential to prove that a specific individual did not write a specific record entry, and where it is not of crucial significance to prove who actually did write the entry, if the claimed individual did not write it.

The significance of any evidencial matter is determined by a legal expert; however, it is obvious that changes to an existing record after initial completion may be indicative of the state of mind of the perpetrator.

The Medico-Legal Document Expert Team

In considering the significance of various aspects of medical records, theoretically the efforts of three different types of professionals may be required to effectively assess such records. The medical expert determines what is of significance in the records that would indicate an irregularity of medical practice, treatment, care, responsibility or supervision. The legal expert determines if the issue has legal significance within the terms of the allegations. The questioned document examiner determines what changes, substitutions, or other alterations have occurred in the records, or is asked to identify a specific writer, or typewriter, and so on.

Questioned document examiners are not equipped to answer questions of medical significance, nor are they trained or legally allowed to handle questions regarding the legal significance of any evidence. It is unwise to put questioned document examiners in the position of giving advice or counsel on matters outside their area of expertise. Particular care should be exercised in making sure that opinions or conclusions requested or expressed by questioned document examiners are in line with the scientific and/or legal potential of the evidence examined. Questioned document examiners who go beyond the true potential of the evidence examined could prove disastrous in a courtroom situation where the opposing side has a proper medico-legal document examiner team of experts.

Choosing a Questioned Document Examiner

The terms of questioned document examiner, document examiner, document expert, forensic document expert, and examiner of questioned documents will be used interchangeably in this chapter. The descriptor "Graphologist" is not used as a synonym for questioned document examiner.

What the attorney is seeking in a questioned document examiner is an individual who is technically competent, ethical in his relationships, and effective in court. Having a competent professional document examiner on an attorney's team can also be of value in the delicate area of negotiations as well as in court.

Currently in the United States the legal rules governing the claims of expertise and the testimony of expert witnesses are such that any individual claiming knowledge superior to the average layman in a field of technical skill or expertise may be allowed to testify at the discretion of the trial judge. Obviously, many different types of individuals can claim expertise in the field of questioned documents. It is possible for any individual claiming to be a questioned document examiner to advertise in the Yellow Pages and to have perviously testified as an expert witness.

Because of the lack of standards advocated, established, or enforced by the legal profession, the attorney is on his own in assessing the qualifications of prospective questioned document examiners. To say the least, there is a rather odd assortment of individuals offering to do questioned document work. There is a plethora of organizations that claim to offer mail order training and/or certification of dues paying members.

Only two of the many organizations for questioned document examiners have minimum standards for membership that specify academic background and specific on-the-job or internship requirements for training under a recognized questioned document examiner. These are the American Society of Questioned Document Examiners (ASQDE) and the Questioned Document Section of the American Academy of Forensic Sciences (AAFS). Membership in these organizations is restricted to individuals who are fulltime document examiners with demonstrated professional training in questioned document analyses and evaluation.

In the last decade, Department of Justice funds were used to set up the American Board of Forensic Document Examiners, a certifying board for professional questioned document examiners. At this time, over 250 individuals have been certified as Diplomates of the American Board of Forensic Document Examiners (ABFDE). Recertification, guaranteeing that a certified document examiner is "current" with the new developments in questioned documents, is now under way.

In the past, the adoption of the three-way test for attorneys or other individuals seeking competent questioned document examiners has been advocated.[3] If a questioned document examiner is a member of the ASQDE and AAFS, and is Board Certified by the ABFDE, there is every possibility that the individual is competent and ethical. Membership in these three groups is not a guarantee that an individual is right in any one specific case; it merely demonstrates that an individual has been granted peer acceptance by other professionals in the field.

Many attorneys ask their secretaries to call around for information on questioned document examiners. Often, the secretaries seem to fix on the topic of fee schedules rather than qualifications, in the mistaken belief that they can or should save money for their employer. Shopping for the lowest price may be the most expensive mistake an attorney can make. It is recommended that the attorney himself make the selection of a questioned document examiner on the basis of demonstrable qualifications rather than on the basis of anticipated savings.

Facilities of the Questioned Document Examiner

The facilities of the professional questioned document examiner fall into three areas. The first is that of equipment. One would expect a professional to have optical equipment such as magnifying glasses, stereoscopic and comparison microscopes, test plates for measuring typewriting, complete photographic facilities, radiation equipment such as ultraviolet lights, infrared converters, electrostatic detection equipment, and chromatographic, electrophoretic and/or spectrophotometric equipment for ink analysis.

The second area is that of reference files on topics such as typewriters, and research files of past and present technology culled from the professional journals over the last 50 years. An adequate library of all the current and past texts in the field is expected. A collection of books on graphology would not be a substitute for a professional library.

The last and most important part of the document laboratory is the proven experience and judgment of the professional document examiner. All the equipment and reference files in the hands of an incompetent will not help solve technical problems.

Technical Range of Questioned Document Examiner

Handwriting

The questioned document examiner should be able to identify handwriting, determine if a signature is a forgery, and determine the number of different writers involved in the preparation of a document. In a predictive sense, the examiner may be able to state in the broadest terms where a subject learned to write from the handwriting system used. All of the above is predicated upon having adequate materials for comparison, and the questioned writing having sufficient identification potential. It will not be possible in all cases for the document examiner to reach a definite conclusion regarding all aspects of a case. Less than definite conclusions must be expected when the evidence is less than conclusive for technical reasons.

It is axiomatic among professional questioned document examiners, as defined by the ABFDE, that they do not determine personality characteristics or behavioral patterns from handwriting. Whether graphology is a harmless parlour game or a tricky boardwalk scam is beyond the scope of this chapter. The merits, if any, of the wild and wonderful world of graphology should be debated at another time and place.

Typewriters

It is possible to determine the make and model of typewriter used to produce a document, subject to numerous qualifications. With the older typebar typewriters, this is a more specific activity. At the present time, with a few type wheel manufacturers producing typefonts for a multiplicity of typewriter manufacturers, it is much more difficult to make predictions. The habit of cloning successful type fonts produced by other manufacturers also complicates the problem. It is possible to differentiate two different classes of typewriters without being able to specifically delineate the make and/or model of either typewriter.

Typewriter identification is possible if there is sufficient individuality to identify one typewriter out of all the typewriters of the same class. The older typebar typewriters had a greater potential for identification than the more modern type wheel and type ball typewriters. Sometimes, it is possible to differentiate typewriting without being able to definitely identify either typewriter; for example, the presence or absence of a key individuality in the same time period would be evidence of two different typewriters.

It is possible to date typewriting by the dates of introduction of the type style used on a specific class of machine and by the periodic changes that manufacturers introduce in type fonts. Complete data on all type font introductions and type font changes is not available, but the professional questioned document examiner will have most of the known data available. Thus, it is possible to show that a document could not have been typed on the date claimed because the type font had not yet been introduced.

There are occasions when it is possible to determine whether or not a carbon copy has been made on a specific typewriter, if the typewriter has a specific fault. Sometimes, it is possible to determine the number of carbons made at one time on a typewriter.

Typewriter ribbon inks can be compared and differentiated. There is no known complete collection of typewriter ribbon inks, nor is it possible to make a definite identification of a specific typewriter ribbon ink. Comparisons of typewriting could show the presence of two different ribbons.

A frequent problem is that of determining if a typewritten entry on a document was added after the document was initially typed. Special ruled plates are used to determine vertical and horizontal alignment, since it is impossible to re-insert a document into a typewriter in precisely the same position it was previously.

Paper

Paper has class characteristics rather than individual characteristics; hence, paper cannot be identified on the basis of composition. On the other hand, torn paper can be individualized with regard to the connection of two elements by virtue of random tears. The potential exists in some cases to date paper by virtue of unusual fiber, filler or sizing constituents, or by the date of introduction of a watermark. In a few cases, the possible source of a paper can be determined by the presence of certain unusual constituents. Papers can be compared for class characteristics by a host of reactions to chemicals, radiation equipment or optical equipment. The substitution of a sheet of paper can be established by comparison with other sheets in evidence. It can be demonstrated in cases that a specific sheet of paper differs from all other sheets in a file and has characteristics in common with another source of paper.

Inks are class evidence and do not have individual characteristics except under specific conditions. Since inks of all types are made in large batches, many ink cartridges all made on the same day, and filled from the same mixing vats, will have the same precise constituency. Considering, also, that ink formulations are prepared from rather precise formulas, differences between batches are ordinarily nondetectable. An ink can become individual only if something happens to that specific pen that sets it apart from all other pens of the same class. Naturally, this very rarely occurs, considering the mode of pen production and current writing instrument usage. The point of the writing instrument may become individual on occasion. Ballpoint pen balls may develop sufficient individuality by way of striated grooves on the ball. One wear striation is not at all uncommon; hence, more than one regularly reproducible striation is needed.

Inks of all types can be compared and differentiated. Differences in constituency can be expressed by using chromatographic, dichroic, electrophoretic, spectrophotometric, and spectrophotofluorometric techniques, by differences in optical or photographic appearances, or by differences in chemical reactions. The technical literature of questioned documents is rich with descriptions of techniques designed to assist the document examiner in differentiating two inks. An agreement in test results does not mean that the examiner has been able to individualize the ink; it only means that two inks have similar class characteristics.

Libraries of ballpen inks exist; however, none of these is complete. Any claims of a complete collection of inks should be viewed with skepticism. The most complete collection, of all known collections, is that maintained by the Document Laboratory of the Bureau of Alcohol and Tobacco Tax of the Department of Justice. Samples of ballpen inks and other types of inks are maintained along with standard thin-layer chromatograms and data on the date the ink was first introduced. The limitations of this collection have been previously detailed.[4]

The dating of inks by comparing the ink formulation determined by thin-layer chromatography with chromatograms in a reference library is valid if certain conditions are met. The ink examiner must be able to demonstrate that the ink reference collection used is so complete that the possibility of a second brand of available ink having the same thin-layer chromatographic pattern can be excluded. One must always consider the possibility of a foreign-made pen's being used that is not represented in an ink reference collection.

Claims made regarding techniques for determining the age of ink lines must be viewed very circumspectly at this time. Research to date has not resulted in any technique that has the acceptance of the scientific community. Further work in this area is to be anticipated. There are several complicating factors in the determination of ink age. For instance, aging patterns for one ink cannot be used to predict the aging of a second ink. Also, aging may vary depending on the surface involved and the storage of documents.

Ink examinations can be destructive or nondestructive. Any destructive testing of an ink on a document must be done with the consent of all interested parties. While some destructive testing requires very minimal amounts of ink, it does change the document in some small way. In some cases, a court order may be necessary before any destructive testing can be carried out. Nondestructive testing, on the other hand, will leave no trace on the document. In many cases, nondestructive techniques, including infrared, infrared luminescence, ultraviolet, and dichroic filter examinations, along with microscopic comparisons, suffice to differentiate two different inks. Thin-layer chromatography is a destructive technique, even though minimal amounts of ink are removed for testing.

Pencils

Pencils, like ink pens, do not have a potential for individualization unless something unique happens to a specific pencil to set it apart from all other similar pencils. The clay-graphite mixtures can be compared and frequently, but not always, differentiated. Pencils also pose problems in that points wear down, become broader, or break, and then are resharpened. A recently sharpened pencil may present a different visual appearance when compared with writing done when the pencil point was worn.

Printing

Printed matter can be compared to determine if the same or a different class of printing ink was used to print two different documents. Printing typefaces can also be categorized by style and potentially by source, if the typeface design is unusual enough. Printing format and mode of printing also provide areas of investigation and comparison. Date of printing is always of concern, and there are occasions when evidence can be developed to show the time before which a printed document could not have been produced. In a recent case, the existence of a scratch on an engraved plate occurring after a certain date provided conclusive evidence that a document could not have been prepared on the date claimed.

In some cases, dates are printed onto forms indicating when the form first came into use. In other cases, there are printer's marks or union labels that can be researched to discover when the form was first introduced.

Rubber Stamps

This type of evidence bridges both categories of class evidence and evidence that can be individualized. Many rubber stamps can be produced from one master mold, but a specific rubber stamp can acquire individuality after sufficient wear that might result in individual scars or marks. Stamp pad inks can be compared and differentiated just as writing inks.

The forgery of rubber stamps requires the exact duplication of the original in text, line weight and spacing, with the duplication of all wear marks and scars—a rather complex task.

Computer Records

The use of the computer and computer printer is medical recordkeeping and bookkeeping requires the questioned document examiner to cover new areas. While computer operation and software interaction is a specialized area outside of the ken of the examiner, the printed record produced by a computer printer is squarely within the field of expertise of the questioned document examiner. There are many different types of printers used today, from daisy wheel machines to inkjet printers. Bases exist to differentiate the various types of printers, to categorize by design and spacing within types of printers, and in many cases to individualize printers if sufficient individuality exists. The interaction between software and hardware (i.e., the printer) requires a team effort.

Medical Records

The usual hospital record will have a series of forms regularly used in that specific institution. The forms and or records to be anticipated include:

- admission records
- physical examination records
- physicians' order sheets
- patients' history sheets
- medication records
- nurses' notes
- physicians' progress notes
- vital signs graph charts
- consultation reports
- laboratory pathology reports
- x-ray reports
- consent forms
- incident report forms
- operation records
- anesthesiologist records
- case summary and discharge sheets
- autopsy reports[5,6]

Medical office records may be less formal, depending on the whim and desire of the individual physician, but should include:

- patient history forms
- treatment notes and comments
- laboratory and pathology reports
- x-ray reports
- consultation reports
- insurance forms

In each type of record, a specific individual is normally expected to fill in each section (i.e., the physician fills in one portion of the record, the nurse fills in another portion, and the office secretary initiates the entry for a specific office visit). Personnel records can establish who was on duty at a specific time, should such be necessary. The writing of extraneous individuals in records that should have a regular fill-in pattern should be reviewed carefully. Likewise, consideration must always be given to the issue of correct sign-off signatures in records that require a specific titled individual, for example, Chief of OB/GYN, to sign off on an entry.

Alteration of Medical Records

One of the most frequently encountered document problems in the medical malpractice area is the medical record that has been altered. Alteration requires the physical or chemical erasure of part of the record and the addition of text, or whatever is more consistent with the desires of the perpetrator. Both mechanical erasure and chemical erasure normally leave traces of disturbed paper fibers or chemical residues that react with chemical reagents or radiation equipment. The person doing the erasure is faced with the problem of erasing too much, thus leaving obvious traces of erasure, or not erasing enough, thus leaving traces of the original text. While the presence of an erasure does establish that the record has been altered, it is always desirable, if at all possible, to decipher the original text to show what was removed and what has been substituted. Nondestructive testing is normally used to this end. Infrared, infrared luminescence, ultraviolet examinations, transmitted and oblique lighted microscopic examinations, and photographic techniques may all serve to decipher an erased text. Traces of erased pencil writing, for example, can be picked up with infrared photography or with an infrared converter.

On many occasions, the full text of the erased writing cannot be demonstrated because of the excesses in erasure. The presence of the erasure alone demonstrates that normal hospital procedures, usually the crossing out of the original text with a single line and initialing, were not followed.

There will be occasions where the sequence of strokes (i.e., the lines of the "new" text) will not be in the correct position in regard to existing ink, typewriting or rubber stamped impressions. It could well be that the physical format of the record requires that a rubber stamp impression be on top of the text of the ballpen nurses notes, for example.

Sequence of stroke examinations require a full range of laboratory facilities for the examiner, and even then the results may not be conclusive. Because dark lines appear to be uppermost, and lighter lines recede, false evaluations may be made. In many cases, the only correct conclusion may have to be that the examination has been inconclusive. Any positive conclusion regarding sequence of strokes should be demonstrable to judge and jury.

Obliterations on Medical Records

The covering up of text on medical records can be accomplished with an instrument of either the same class or a different class. If a different class of instrument was used, there is a range of photographic, optical, radiant energy and even chemical techniques that can be used to read through the offending upper layer. The most difficult cases are those involving the same class of instrument, because there are no constituency differences to exploit. Detailed examinations under the stereomicroscope may be fruitful in some instances. In all cases, successful decipherment should be demonstrable in court. Destructive techniques, such as the chemical removal of the upper layer, should not be used if nondestructive techniques can achieve the same results.

Additions to Medical Records

Some additions to medical records may be obvious by the visual differences in writing instruments used. This type of addition is quite different from the addition made with an instrument of the same class that also changes the total meaning of a record. Frequently, the addition of one phrase or sentence can be shown to be totally incongruous with the usual and normal record-keeping pattern and style of the author. Unless an individual consistently adds to a record after it was initially written or prepared, one must view with suspicion any addition that could be self-serving. Additions could be accomplished by writing above the existing line of writing or by overwriting an existing word.

Adding a sentence to change the meaning of an entry does occur. The added crucial entry may result in a narrower vertical spacing than is normally used by the writer, or by the person who always keeps the records. The key in such examinations is to compare the consistent habits of a specific writer or office with the questioned addition—what is typical and what is atypical? In a recent case, it was observed that for two crucial entries the medical doctor used two different pens on each occasion. While at first it might seem unusual to have four pens involved in two crucial entries, subsequent examination of other representative case files of the doctor revealed that he had a consistent pattern of switching pens or using more than one pen for an entry.

There will be occasions when it can be demonstrated that an addition to a record has been made by a writer other than the writer of the original entry. Typewritten additions potentially can be shown to be made either by a different typewriter, or to be out of alignment with the original typing.

Additions may also be shown to be in the wrong sequence in relationship to other writings on the record. The addition may be over some unit of the record, such as a rubber stamp impression that should be over the total entry. In this as in other addition problems, incongruity is the key to the examination.

Substitution of Medical Records

The substitution of one page for another page in a medical record or the addition of an extra page requires the perpetrator to manufacture another page with the same precise characteristics as the original page or pages (the same paper, typewriter, ink, handwriting, etc). One small difference in materials or writers will be enough to show what has occurred. Differences in watermarks, or unexplained changes in typing or typewriter ribbons, might all be used to show that a record page was not an original page.

The use of an Electrostatic Detection Apparatus (ESDA) may show the indented traces of the original true page on an underlying sheet of the record.

An examination of the staple holes in a record may reveal one sheet that does not match the other sheets in a record.

In a recent case, a record card was shown to be a substitute because of errors in dating—the date was chosen a year in advance and then corrected to the desired year. It is axiomatic that one does not write dates in the future, but one may very well forget the current year and write a prior year, especially in the first few months of the year.

In the case of bound records, it is impossible to duplicate the tear borders of one sheet with a substitute sheet. Again, indented traces of the original page may be found on the sheet below.

Creating Records

On occasion, totally new medical records will be created that were prepared at one time, or within a short time span, but are purported to be medical records prepared over a long period of time, with each entry accomplished on the day indicated. Examination in these cases must focus on whether the writing instruments and the substrate were in existence on the date claimed, on the format used, and on the choice of writing instruments over a long time period. The use of three or four pens in a repetitive cycle over a period of several years could be indicative of fraudulent preparation.

In some cases, a perpetrator preparing a record all at once gets bored with the project and tries to find shortcuts to get the job over with. This may result in incongruous elements in the records. Aging a record is not an easy task, and a perpetrator may not get everything right. In one instance, a loose-leaf record allegedly prepared daily over a span of four years had loose-leaf punch holes exhibiting no wear.

Circumstances of Preparation of Medical Records

Since medical records have a logical progression in preparation, because of standardized institutional procedures, records accomplished in the ordinary course of business should leave traces of the writing on the page below. As discussed above, ESDA examinations may disclose agreements or non-agreements in text which may be significant.

It is possible to develop fingerprints on documents many years after the documents have been touched. Various reagents such as iodine, silver nitrate, and Ninhydrin can be used to make latent fingerprints visible, depending on the time interval involved. Not every person leaves traces of fingerprints on documents. The development of fingerprints on a document may result in prints that are inappropriate to claims made, or prints may be found that are placed in such a location as to contradict positions taken.

FIGURE 1. Facsimile of record created at one time rather than day by day as claimed. The date "1-3-77" was originally written as "1-3-81" and then corrected to read "1-3-77." Note the pristine condition of the paper punch hole on a sheet of loose-leaf paper that had allegedly been in a notebook where data was entered daily.

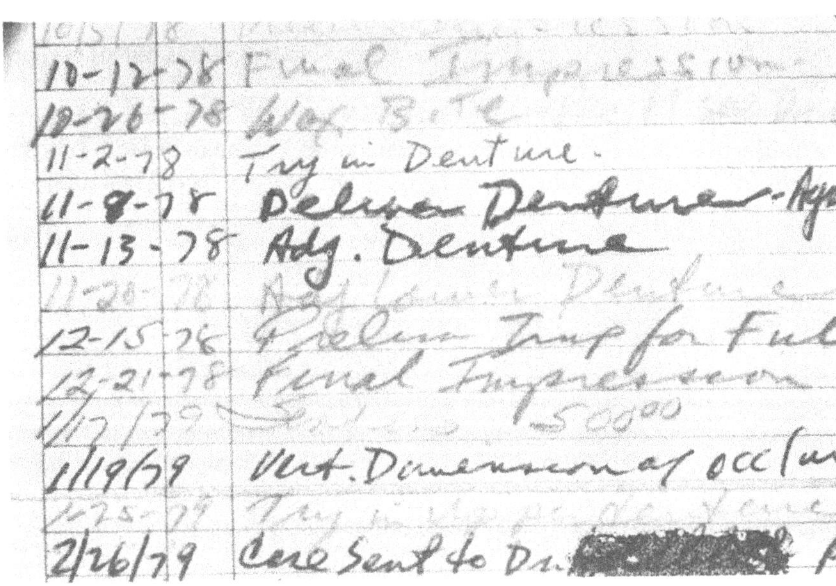

FIGURE 2. The original entry for 11-8-78 "Deliver Dentures" on this dental record was overwritten with a second ballpoint pen so that the total entry would appear to match the added entry beginning with the word "Agree" to the right of the original entry. Courtesy of Leslie Auerbach, Esq. Silver Spring, MD.

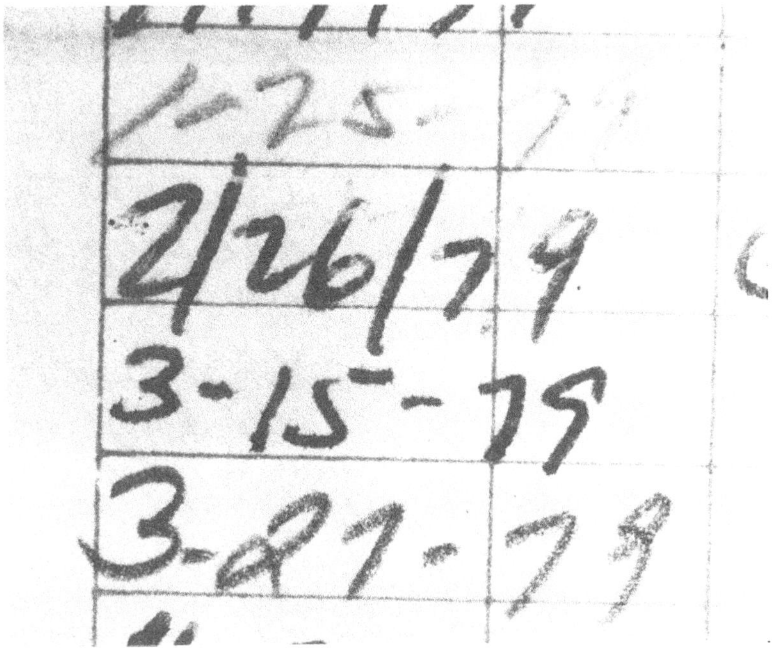

FIGURE 3. There are traces of erased writing under the date "2/26/79." The entry on the line was erased and the "new" entry substituted. Courtesy of Leslie Auerbach, Esq., Silver Spring, MD.

Age of Medical Records

While the legal profession would like to have techniques available that would positively establish the age of all writings and writing substrates, the reality of the situation is that no such techniques exist. Age can be approached from the positive or negative standpoint. Questions about positive age are normally phrased as, "Was this document written on August 23, 1976, or not"? Negative age concerns setting time barriers before which a document could not have been prepared, without proving when the writing instrument or substrate was actually used.

Negative dating is regularly used by questioned document examiners to prove that medical records could not be what they claim to be—the paper, typewriter, printing plate, ink or even photocopy machine wasn't manufactured before the date on the document. Proper reference materials and contacts with manufacturers are requisite to this type of dating. In a recent case, it was possible to show that a letter could not have been typed on the

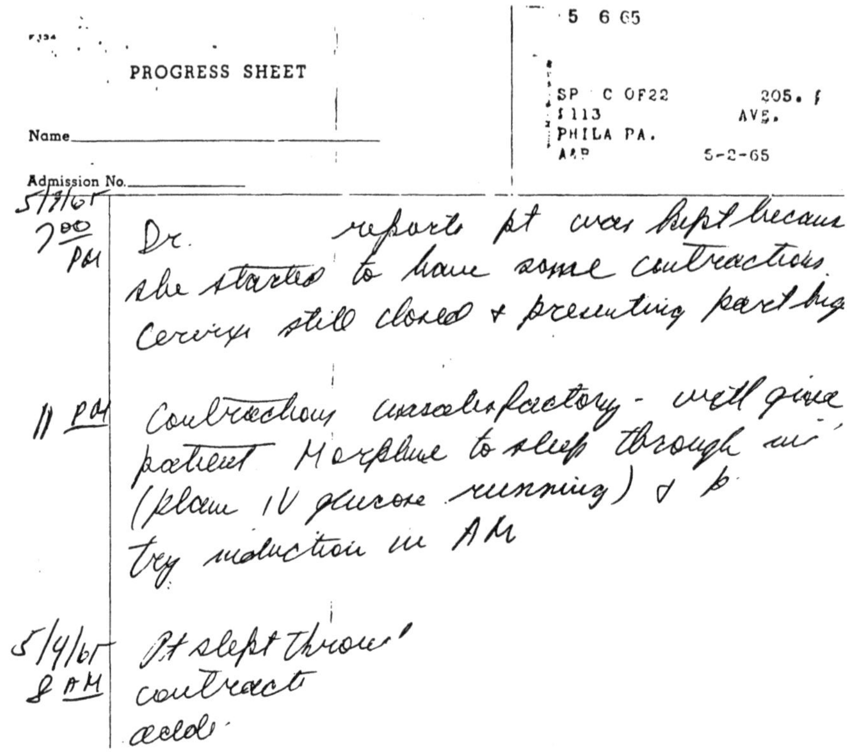

FIGURE 4. Substituted Progress Sheet in a medical record. The date on the stamp plate impression at the top of the sheet does not agree with the dates in the left margins.

date claimed because the typewriter used was not purchased until after the date in the document, because the letterhead involved was not in use on the date claimed, and because the letter was not copied on the photocopy machine available in that office during the time period under discussion.

At this time there are no proven techniques accepted by all document examiners that can be used to establish the positive age of paper, ballpen inks, or typewriting. However, there are a multiplicity of techniques available that can show that a medical record is not what it is purported to be.

Identification of Handwriting and Typewriting

Frequently, a question arises about whether a specific individual signed a report or wrote an entry on a medical record. Assuming that adequate comparison exemplars are available, this problem can be addressed by the questioned document examiner. Typewriter identification also requires adequate exemplars. In all cases, identification of a specific writer or typewriter requires sufficient individuality upon which to base an identification.

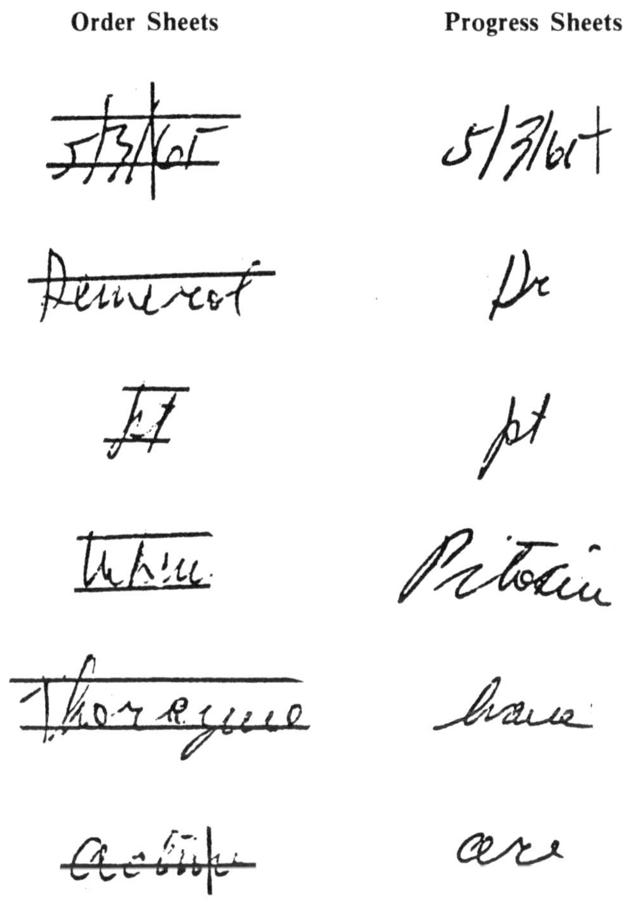

FIGURE 5. Handwriting chart prepared to illustrate basis for an expert opinion that a specific physician had written certain crucial entries in a medical record.

CONCLUSIONS REACHED BY DOCUMENT EXAMINERS

It is not possible, in all cases, for questioned document examiners to make definite identifications or eliminations of writers. Individuals claiming a very high rate of success in making identifications should be viewed with caution. When the evidence warrants it, definite identifications should be reached, but when the evidence is less than conclusive, a qualified conclusion must be expressed, with an explanation of why the opinion is less than conclusive.

The conclusion reached by an examiner is technically the opinion of the examiner, but it is better described as the "expert opinion" of the examiner. The phrase "just your opinion" is heard on occasion in court as a means of denigrating the conclusion reached by an examiner after hours of examination and deliberation. An expert opinion should be backed by the demonstrable reasons upon which it is based.

The vague generalization that a medical record is "suspicious" should not be used by a questioned document examiner since it lacks specificity. If there are reasons to doubt the authenticity of a record, they can be detailed without using pejoratives.

USING THE QUESTIONED DOCUMENT EXAMINER

Before engaging the services of a questioned document examiner, decide in advance exactly what you want the expert to examine. Decide what areas of the medical records seem to contain evidence of change, alteration, addition, substitution, or the like. The phrase "run it through the laboratory" may sound impressive on television, but it is essentially meaningless. Unfocused examinations without boundaries can run up high bills without usable results.

Just as evidence of alteration, obliteration, substitution, or addition, is of value to an attorney, it is equally important for him to know that a focused examination of the medical records has failed to disclose any demonstrable evidence of alteration. Likewise, it is important for an attorney to know what another competent examiner, hired by the opposition, will find if he makes an impartial examination of a certain medical record.

A questioned document examiner should always offer to provide a written laboratory report after giving a verbal report. There should be no difference in content between the two reports. There may be proper legal reasons for an attorney not to want a written report from an examiner, but the offer should always be made.

PRE-TRIAL CONSIDERATIONS

All implications of the written report of the examiner should be discussed prior to the trial. In the ordinary course of events, the examiner will supply the attorney with written qualifying questions, since the examiner best knows how to bring out his true qualifications. Ignoring these written questions may fail to bring out qualifications and thus endanger credibility with the judge and/or jury. In the pre-trial conference, the direct examination and potential areas of cross-examination should be covered. Both the examiner and the attorney should know what to expect in the direct examination. There should be no surprises for the side calling the expert.

The examiner will be informed of the date of the trial in advance and may ask if the attorney wishes the time to be blocked, giving the attorney exclusive call on that time unit. One must expect to pay for this service, since the examiner will refuse all other assignments during this time period. Cancellations given less than 48 or 72 hours in advance may incur financial penalties.

Arrangements to get the examiner in and out of court speedily will result in savings to the attorney and his client. If the examiner spends three days waiting in the corridors of a courthouse, he will have to charge for the total time involved, not just the time spent in court.

It is the responsibility of the hiring attorney to protect his witness from unusual harassment. The examiner can cope with the standard cross-examination questions but may have difficulties if the opposition becomes abusive. If the examiner declines to make any examination on the stand, the hiring attorney must support his position. It should be recalled that any examination requested of an examiner on the stand can only benefit the opposition. It is unscientific to examine evidence with limited time and equipment in the pressure cooker of the courtroom. Any conclusions reached from such examinations would be closer to guesses than carefully reasoned conclusions.

FEES OF QUESTIONED DOCUMENT EXAMINERS

The fees of questioned document examiners vary just as the fees of attorneys vary. In general, fees are set by the education, experience, and professional standing of the examiner, and by the willingness of attorneys to pay that fee. One must always discuss the fee structure beforehand. Some examiners charge by the hour, some by the day, and some by the case. One should get some type of estimate beforehand and, if necessary, set realistic upper limits. On occasion, one encounters an attorney who underdescribes his case to get a lower fee quote and then at a later time brings in many more documents to be examined. A competent questioned document examiner has to charge for his time; added documents will take more time and result in additional billing. Questioned document examiners are not permitted by the Canons of Ethics of the American Society of Questioned Document Examiners from taking cases on a contingency basis.

CROSS-EXAMINING THE INCOMPETENT DOCUMENT EXAMINER

It is common to find incompetent individuals attempting to testify as expert witnesses on the topic of questioned documents. A detailed examination of the individual on voir dire should bring out the educational and experience deficiencies of the individual. For example, one may find an individual trying to substitute a keen interest in graphology for on-the-job training in a recognized questioned document laboratory, or using law enforcement experience as a qualification for examining documents. The work of a check investigator or a fingerprint examiner does not encompass the technical area of expertise of the questioned document examiner.

An examiner may testify about conclusions reached concerning documents and may describe techniques used for the examination that are inappropriate to the results claimed. It may be possible to show that an examiner, while otherwise qualified, made an inadequate or superficial examination. The Frye Ruling[7] may be invoked when an expert describes technology that has not received general acceptance within the scientific community.

Finally, it may be possible to show that an opposing examiner has abandoned his objectivity in his examination and has become an advocate. Testifying for one side does not make one an advocate, but ignoring significant aspects of evidence to reach a predetermined conclusion does make one an advocate.

Harassing an examiner because he is "being paid to testify" is not a worthy topic to pursue. A competent examiner earns his income by examining documents and must charge for his time. He does not charge for testifying, per se, but for the time involved, whether it is in examining documents, travelling to court, or waiting or testifying.

DISAGREEMENTS AMONG DOCUMENT EXAMINERS

True disagreements between competent document examiners are rare, if both examiners examined the same exhibits with the same types of equipment and had the same amount of time to make the examination. Differences in degrees of conclusions can be anticipated when the evidence is less than clear-cut. One examiner might feel that an identification is "highly probable" while another might not feel any stronger than "a distinct possibility." Such differences are of more of a semantic nature than a true disagreement, and should be anticipated when more than one document examiner examines a case.

Some types of cases, such as those involving sequence of strokes, may produce variant opinions. The best answer in some of these cases could be an opinion that there is no determination possible given the conditions in the case.

If a competent examiner is opposed by an incompetent or dishonest individual, then different opinions may be expressed. Judges and juries can usually tell the difference between the competent and the incompetent expert witness. Ultimately, decisions are based on demonstrable reasons, not on conclusions without supporting reasons.

SUMMARY

The successful use of questioned document examiners in medical malpractice cases requires

1. Knowing what a document examiner can do in examining medical records
2. Defining in advance the areas of the records to be examined and the specific purposes thereof
3. Choosing a properly qualified questioned document examiner
4. Agreeing with the examiner on the cost and scope of his examination and prospective testimony
5. Evaluating the examiner's laboratory report in light of the claims made in the case
6. Conducting a proper pretrial conference with the examiner, covering not only the examiner's prospective testimony but possible opposing testimony.

REFERENCES

1. Holder. 1975. *Medical Malpractice Law,* p. 294. Wiley.
2. *Ibid.,* p. 297.
3. Crown. 1979. "Choosing a Questioned Document Examiner." *Security Management* 23(10):72.
4. Crown, Brunelle, and Cantu. 1976. "The Parameters of Ballpen Ink Examination." *Journal of Forensic Sciences* 21(4):917.
5. Calloway. 1984. "Understanding Hospital Records." *The Practical Lawyer* 30(1): 11.
6. Curran, and Shapiro. 1970. *Law, Medicine and Forensic Science,* p. 66. Little Brown.
7. Frye v. US, 54 App D.C. 46, 293 F. 1013, 1014.

The Use of Polygraph Testing in Civil Litigation

Terrance G. Furlow, M.D., J.D., and
Elizabeth A. Principi, J.D., LL.M.

Polygraphs have had a long and wary experience in the American court system. In the 1920s they were rejected as having no proven reliability.[1] Over the years they have proven to have a relative degree of accuracy and are routinely used out of court by law enforcement officials and employers who screen applicants for sensitive jobs. Nevertheless, the majority of jurisdictions hold that they are inadmissible at trial[2] and the remainder have rigid criteria for admissibility.[3]

Since there are known personality types who give unreliable results[4] and there is a significant percentage of unexplained erroneous results,[5] courts have found it difficult to conclude that the probative value of a "lie detector" outweighs its prejudicial risk. Because the answers to questions used during the polygraph examination are often the very conclusion that the judge or jury is asked to decide, there is a heightened mistrust that the polygraph will subvert our American judicial system.

We developed interest for this article from a recent medical malpractice suit in which polygraph results were used to resolve a major issue in contention. This case was unusual, since most judicial experience with polygraphs has been in the criminal courts. This litigation offers an excellent opportunity to review the theory, accuracy and shortcomings of polygraphs as well as the procedural safeguards courts should use when deciding whether or not to admit into evidence, or otherwise use, polygraph results.

FACTS OF THE CASE

Late one evening a two-and-one-half-year-old white female child was seen in a hospital emergency room. According to the mother, the child had a slight fever, a hard black stool, and her vomitus had black specks. By history several family members had had symptoms consistent with gastroenteritis the preceding week.

On physical examination by the emergency room physician, a general practitioner, the patient was described as very uncomfortable, with some grunting respirations. The temperature was 100.9° F. The head, eyes, ears, nose, throat and lungs were normal. The abdomen was distended. Bowel sounds were decreased. During examination the patient vomited green material with black particles. The emesis tested positive for blood; a rectal swab was negative. Blood tests and urinalysis were normal. The chest x ray was interpreted by the general practitioner as normal, and the upright and flat plate films of the abdomen were thought to show increased amounts of bowel gas.

The emergency room physician then called the pediatrician on call and recommended that the child be admitted to the pediatric ward. The pediatrician agreed with the plan of treatment, which included intravenous fluids, and stated he would see the child in the morning. At 6:00 A.M. the child appeared to be feeling better and was sitting in her mother's lap. Her mother stated that her eyes suddenly became dilated and she stopped breathing. Cardiopulmonary resuscitation was begun at 6:25 A.M. and continued for 50 minutes. She was pronounced dead at 7:15 A.M., nine hours after admission. The cause of death was certified as due to massive aspiration (the child vomited during resuscitation). At 8:30 A.M. one of the hospital radiologists read the x rays obtained on admission and discovered free air under the diaphragm. This finding becomes crucial in the malpractice action discussed below.

Both natural parents refused consent for a postmortem examination by the hospital pathologist. An autopsy was performed by a private civilian pathologist. He attributed death to generalized peritonitis due to rupture of the duodenum caused by hemorrhagic gastroenteritis.

THE MALPRACTICE ACTION

The natural parents of the child subsequently sued for the wrongful death of their daughter. They alleged that the emergency room physician was not qualified to read x rays and that he failed to diagnose a rupture of the duodenum. The failure to detect the ruptured bowel resulted in the otherwise preventable death of the child.

In the initial investigation of the claim, filed by the natural parents, defense attorneys began to suspect child abuse. They referred the case to the state district attorney for investigation, but no action was taken. Initially, defense attorneys were hesitant to raise child abuse as a defense, but as the investigation proceeded it became inevitable. The defense "Reply to Plaintiff's

Response" stated "I would have been seriously derelict in my duties and perhaps bereft of common sense, if with the available information, I had not advised this Court and made it a matter of record that the main issues in this lawsuit were not merely the disputed facts about the alleged medical malpractice, but also that the death was caused by what appeared to be intentionally inflicted injuries which became fatal due to ensuing complications."

Plaintiff's attorney flatly denied these counterallegations. The local press became preoccupied with each allegation and counterallegation between the opposing parties. The publicity became so intense that the defense attorneys made an offer to the plaintiffs that if they would take and pass a polygraph test, the defense would admit liability in the death of the child. However at this stage, the plaintiffs consistently refused to submit to a polygraph examination.

After months of pretrial conferences, depositions and readiness conferences passed, the judge became aware of the offer made by the defense. Because of the complicated pretrial battle between the parties the judge also decided that the parents should undergo polygraph testing. At an *in camera* meeting the day before the trial the judge convinced the plaintiffs to submit to a polygraph, which was administered by a local policeman.

Both plaintiffs, the noncustodial, natural father and the custodial, natural mother "passed" the test. The polygrapher concluded that the parents "had no knowledge of the injury sustained" by their daughter prior to her arrival at the hospital. The parents were also pointedly asked if they had ever mistreated the child.

After this the government conceded liability and trial was held on the issue of damages only. The parents were awarded $300,000.00 for the wrongful death of their daughter. No appeal was taken.

POLYGRAPH THEORY AND MECHANICS

The physiological basis of the polygraph testing technique is the measure of the response of the sympathetic nervous system to a perceived threat or stress. Assuming that the examinee perceives the question of the examiner as threatening the machine will measure this response.

The physiologic parameters measured by the polygrapher are inspiration-expiration, pulse rate, blood pressure and secretion by sweat glands measured as the galvanic skin response (GSR). The sympathetic and parasympathetic nervous systems are homeostatic. When stress is perceived by the subject the sympathetic nervous system becomes more active than the parasympathetic nervous system. Later, parasympathetics predominate over sympathetics when the stress has passed. The polygraph machine measures and records breathing patterns, pulse rate, changes in mean blood pressure and electrodermal responses. This is done in order to obtain physiological evidence that the sympathetic and the parasympathetic subdivisions of the autonomic nervous system have been activated during a polygraph examination, in response to pointed questions.

The machine is divided into three units. The first unit, which most experts consider the most essential, is a pneumatically operated recorder of changes in respiration, blood pressure, and pulse. One pneumograph tube, with the aid of a beaded chain, is fastened around the chest, and another one around the abdomen to measure the respiration patterns. A blood pressure cuff is secured around the examiner's upper right arm. A second unit records the galvanic skin reflex, or electrodermal response, which is based upon the change of electrical conductivity of the skin. Electrodes are attached to the examiner's left hand or fingertips. There is a third unit for recording muscular movements and pressures. This is accomplished by a sensor in the examination chair.

Precautions and Limitations

The reliability of the polygraph examination is subject to much discussion. In 1965 the Moss Committee Report found that the polygraph machine is not a "lie detector" nor does the operator who interprets the graph detect lies. Many physical and psychological factors make it possible for the examinee to give erroneous answers without detection by the machine or examiner. The report cites the following conditions which would invalidate a polygraph examination:

> Extreme nervousness... Physiological abnormalities... excessively high or low blood pressure, heart disease... respiratory disorders (even the common cold), toothaches, severe headaches, or practically any painful ailment. Mental abnormalities... pronounced neuroses, psychoses... abnormally low intelligence... state of self hypnosis or temporary amnesia... pathological liars... unresponsiveness. A lack of emotional response can seriously hamper accurate testing. Extreme fatigue or mental exhaustion ... a person under the influence of alcohol... drugs... bodily movement. Physical movement or muscular activity can lead to the misleading blood pressure readings....[6]

The report went on to chastise the field by stating "Federal investigators have given thousands upon thousands of polygraph tests, yet there has been no attempt to determine the validity of the procedure... no statistical proof has been compiled... no scientific proof has been produced."[7] The report did admit "There is some evidence that the polygraph technique works in the laboratory... [having] achieved as much as 80/90 percent accuracy in the laboratory studies. But the scientists admitted this does not mean the machine works in actual practice."[8] The committee recommended that the federal government "Prohibit the use of polygraphs in all but the most serious national security and criminal cases."[9] Reliability studies have now been done, but again primarily in the laboratory instead of the field or actual practice. The following table shows the results of uncontrolled studies in the field research reliability.[10]

INVESTIGATOR	PERCENT OF CONSISTENCY
Bittermant Marcuse 1947	84%
Rourke 1941	89%
Huntert Ash 1973	85%
Barland 1975	84%
Horvant 1974	77%
Average Agreement	84%

Laboratory studies have shown a mean reliability of 88 percent.[11] Research indicates, therefore, that the reliability can be high if the examinations are conducted by competent examiners. "The exact degree of accuracy will probably never be known because of the limitations inherent in both laboratory and field experimentation."[12]

Variables and Reliability of Testing

Several aspects of the testing situation must be controlled for an examination. These include the environment, the interview questions, the examiner and the examinee.

The room must be quiet, private and nearly sound-proof. There should be no individuals present other than the examiner and the examinee.

A proper and adequate pretest interview is required where the test questions are formulated. The examinee is instructed on the operation of the instrument, and a test rapport is developed between the examiner and the examinee.

Relevant, irrelevant and control questions must be developed by an experienced and knowledgeable examiner. The relevant question must have a true relationship to the actual incident under investigation. The nuances and theories of the case must be familiar to the examiner. For example, in the case under consideration, not only should the question "did you beat your daughter?" be asked, but also the accomplice-type questions "did you see your husband beat your daughter?," "did you believe he may have beaten her?," "did she tell you she had been hit?," and "had you suspected prior instances of abuse?" should be asked. It is necessary to structure questions to defeat rationalization by the examinee. The problem of gradation of truth and lying also affects the outcome of testing. For example, the degree of involvement or guilty knowledge associated in the trauma to this child would not be accurately adjuged by the "yes" or "no" answer required on a polygraph test.

The training and experience of the examiner has significant effect on the conduct and quality of a polygraph exam. Most authorities in the field find that the critical factor in any examination is the ability, experience, education and integrity of the examiner himself. A college education, a sensitive, amiable personality, and an unprejudiced, objective mind are all necessary. Six months' minimum training in an internship and several years of experience in conducting examinations are also basic requirements. This becomes a difficult variable of the exam.

Even the most adamant supporters of polygraph testing admit that there are certain subjects who will not generate meaningful polygraph data. Above all, the subject must overtly cooperate with the examination.[13] Without such cooperation no examination can take place.

Health problems of the examinee that affect reliability include cardiac irregularities, respiratory problems and fatigue. Covert attempts to "beat" the machine physically include voluntary muscular contraction of the arm and sphincters, or pressing down with the fingers or toes. Control of respiration and self-induced pain (e.g., a tack in the shoe) have been employed to mislead the examiner. One writer has found that such undetected behavior has reduced the reliability of testing from 75 percent to 10 percent.[14] Many authors, however, have found this behavior to be easily detectable.[15]

The retarded, psychotics and young children are generally regarded as inappropriate subjects for polygraph testing.[16] The usual explanation for the difficulty with these groups is that they are unable to appreciate the consequences of lying, and therefore will not experience the physiologic fear reaction which the polygraph is designed to detect.

Certain other subjects may also be able to deceive the examiner because their personality makeup flattens the fear response. The "pathologic liar" is the prototype in this category; however, neurotic personalities probably increase the rate of erroneous results.[17] "Circumscribed amnesia" has also been described, in which one's act is so reprehensible that one completely represses memory of the occurrence.[18]

Although we are unaware of studies that challenge the use of polygraphs in the detection of child-abusing parents, studies of personality and other psychological characteristics of battering parents should make one scrutinize polygraph reliability in this setting. One study of 89 mothers imprisoned on charges of killing or attempted murder of their children revealed 14 psychotics, 19 with reactive depression, 38 with personality disorders, 4 with markedly subnormal intelligence and 14 with no abnormal psychiatric diagnosis.[19] In another study of battering parents, 33 out of 89 battering fathers and 17 of 125 mothers were found to have psychopathic personalities as opposed to none of the controls.[20] In the same study 60 of the 125 (48 percent) mothers were found to be neurotic as opposed to 5 of the 51 (9.8 percent) control mothers.

In another study blood pressure, pulse and skin conductance were studied in admitted, abusing mothers and control mothers in reaction to infant smiles and cries.[21] All mothers experienced increases in pulse rate, blood pressure and skin conductance when viewing an audiovisual tape of crying infants. However, when viewing a smiling infant the abusing mothers had similar responses, as opposed to the control mothers who had no change or a decline in the tested parameters. Although one might speculate that battering parents may give indeterminate polygraph results, at this point in the development of polygraph science, this remains unknown.

Another concern in the reliability of lie detection in abusing parents is their tendency to deny their culpability and to blame others.[22] Lying is a natural response for anyone who wishes to avoid earned punishment. However, denial, coupled with projection of guilt onto others, is a deeply seeded aberration from a normal appreciation of honesty and falsehood.[23] This abnormal appreciation of truth is likely to have an adverse effect on the emotional response detected by polygraph testing.

Authorities conflict greatly concerning the effect of drugs on polygraph results. Polygraph advocates assert that drugs, especially tranquilizers, will blunt all physiologic responses of deceitful subjects, and thus polygraph results will be inconclusive, rather than erroneous.[24] Advocates also argue that subjects taking significant amounts of drugs will be clinically obvious.[25] Others have found that drugs cause significant false negative results and that the examiner is unable to detect which subjects are taking drugs.[26] To resolve doubts concerning drug use, polygraph advocates have suggested performing a drug screen on a urine sample taken at the time of testing.[27]

The most significant difficulty in resolving questions about polygraph reliability is the lack of generally acceptable research protocols to study the problem scientifically. Polygraph advocates maintain (and it is obvious from polygraph theory) that the accuracy of polygraph results depends on the subjects' belief that punishment or other severe adverse results will occur if the truth is divulged. Thus, the fear of lying is heightened. In the laboratory setting, however, subjects may view lying more as a game, and fear is consequently lessened. The use of matched control subjects and placebos may correct for deficiencies of the laboratory setting, but this still remains unsettled. The only well controlled study, of which we are aware, strongly challenges the accuracy of polygraph results in subjects taking tranquilizers.[28]

POLYGRAPH USE IN CIVIL SUITS

Resistance to admissibility of polygraph results as evidence in litigation exists because of limited reliability,[29] their prejudicial effect,[30] and their possible invasion into the province of the jury as the finder of fact. The general rule in jurisdictions that do admit polygraph results is that the results are admissible only upon stipulation by the parties. This applies to civil and criminal cases.[31]

The majority of jurisdictions, however, still prohibit their admission in criminal and civil cases.[32] Some jurisdictions have even prohibited the mention of the fact that the plaintiff in a civil case took a polygraph test.[33] In one jurisdiction the court found that it was prejudicial error that could not be corrected by remedial jury instructions.[34] In another jurisdiction a statute restricts judges in civil actions from requiring or suggesting that any party take a polygraph test.[35]

Civil courts have had increasing experience with polygraphs in recent years. In 1962 the Superior Court in Los Angeles, California, began a controlled experiment to admit stipulated results in civil cases determining child custody and paternity. The results have been favorable and well received by the bar and judiciary.[36] This trend has received approval *via dicta* in the United States Court of Appeals, which has jurisdiction over California.

Administrative hearings have taken a quite liberal view toward polygraph admissibility. Even in the jurisdictions where admissibility is strictly prohibited in civil and criminal cases the rule is relaxed for administrative hearings. The Illinois appeals court held recently that in an administrative hearing, if the proper foundation is laid out the polygraph examiners are subject to cross examination, the results are admissible over the objection of the opposing party.[37] Other courts have found that their admission in administrative hearings is purely discretionary and is proper even without a proper foundation being laid for admission.[38] Several jurisdictions, however, construe administrative hearings as civil actions and restrict admissibility on that basis.[39]

Oklahoma has done a turnabout on the issue. The Oklahoma Supreme Court held in *Castleberry v. State* that in criminal cases admissibility would lie upon stipulation by both parties.[40] However, in 1975 they retreated from this holding in *Fulton v. State* when they proclaimed that no such evidence is to be introduced at trial for any purposes due to "the potential unreliability of polygraph examinations at this time."[41]

The Tenth Circuit, which is the Federal Appeals Court for Oklahoma, has consistently denied the admission of polygraph results.[42]

CONCLUSIONS

Polygraph testing remains both an art and a science. It significantly improves detection of deceit over other methods. However, even its advocates concede that polygraph examiners are fallible just as other expert witnesses are.[43] The major concern with polygraph results is that their prejudicial effect may outweigh their probative value. This was the heart of the problem in the use of polygraphs in our principle case. Not only were the results used as conclusive evidence that the subjects had not battered their child, but also the procedural safeguards of our judicial process were given secondary priority.

We suggest the following guidelines for the admissibility and use of polygraph results in civil litigation. We think that polygraph testing should have restricted utility in litigation until its scientific validity is better defined. Similar guidelines have been developed in criminal litigation.[44]

1. Polygraph results may only be used in civil litigation if admitted into evidence and made part of the record. Off the record use of such evidence lends itself to coercion of parties and makes meaningful appellate review impossible.
2. There must be a prior agreement between all parties on both sides of the controversy stipulating their use.
3. The suggestion to use polygraph results must originate from a party to the controversy and the stipulation agreement must be reached only through free bargaining between the parties. Such a suggestion by a judge leaves a reluctant party in a compromised position.
4. On petition by all parties under the guidelines of a written stipulation agreement, the judge must decide whether the polygraph results are admissible under the rules of evidence.
5. The party offering polygraph results with the evidence must lay a proper foundation, demonstrating that the examiner is qualified, appropriate protocol was followed, and the results of the test are the opinion of the examiner based on certain physiologic responses to questioning.
6. Any part of the test in which responses were inconclusive must be disclosed.
7. Notwithstanding any provision of the stipulation agreement to the contrary, any party must be able to cross examine the polygraph examiner concerning his qualifications, the conditions of the test, the protocol, the limitations of and possibility of errors in the polygraph technique.
8. The judge should freely admit into evidence scientific treatises which support or discredit polygraph testing.
9. The judge must instruct the jury that polygraph results are merely nonconclusive opinion evidence of the polygraph examiner.
10. When the judge is the finder of fact, his memorandum opinion must explicitly state what weight of evidence was given to the polygraph results and how they influenced his final decision.

REFERENCES

1. Frye v. United States, 54 U.S.App.D.C. 46, 293 Fed. 1013 (1923).
2. State v. French, 403 A.2d 424 (1979), 53 A.L.R.3d 1005, 1973, 3 F. Wharton Criminal Evidence § 630.
3. State v. Valdez, 91 Ariz. 274, 371 P.2d 894 (1962).
4. Abrams, S. 1973. "Polygraph Validity and Reliability: A Review." *Journal of Forensic Science,* 18(113):313–326.
5. *Ibid.,* 316–322.
6. *Use of Polygraphs as "Lie Detectors" by the Federal Government.* H. R. REP. NO. 198, 89th Cong., 1st Sess. 1965, H. R. REP. NO. 2081, 89th Cong., 2nd Sess. 1966.
7. *Ibid.*
8. *Ibid.*
9. *Ibid.*
10. Abrams, S. 1977. *A Polygraph Handbook for Attorneys.* Lexington, Mass.: D.C. Heath & Company. 106.
11. *Ibid.*
12. *Ibid.,* 115.
13. *Ibid.,* 140.
14. *Ibid.,* 54.
15. *Ibid.,* 148.
16. Camps. F. E., ed. 1976. *Gradwohl's Legal Medicine 3rd Ed.* John Wright & Sons. 527.
17. Heckell, R. V., et al. "Polygraphic Variations in Reactivity Between Delusional, Non-Delusional and Control Groups." *Journal of Criminal Law and Criminology* 53(167):380–383.
18. Abrams, *Polygraph Handbook,* 47.
19. d.'Orban, P.T. 1979. "Women Who Kill Their Children." *British Journal of Psychiatry* 134:560–71.
20. Smith, S.M., R. Hanson and S. Noble. 1973. "Parents of Battered Babies; A Controlled Study." *British Medical Journal* 4:388–391.
21. Frodi, A.M. and Lamb, M.E. 1980. "Child Abusers: Responses to Infant Smiles & Cries." *Childhood Development* 51:238–241.
22. Blumberg, M.L. 1974. "Psychopathology of the Abusing Parent." *American Journal of Psychotherapy* 28:21, 23–25.
23. *Ibid.*
24. Abrams, *Polygraph Handbook,* 3.
25. Camps, *Gradwohl's Legal Medicine,* 527.
26. Waid, W.M., et al. 1981. "Meprobamate Reduces Accuracy of Physiological Detection of Deception. *Science* 212:71–72.
27. *See* n. 26; *also see* Matte, J.A. 1980. *The Art & Science of the Polygraph Technique,* 194. Springfield, IL: Charles C Thomas.
28. Waid, et al., "Meprobamate Reduces Accuracy."
29. Matte, *Polygraph Technique,* 213.
30. Abrams, *Polygraph Handbook.*

31. Justice v. City of Case Grande, 567 P.2d 1195 Ariz. Appl. 1977.
32. Pierson v. McClanahan, 531 S.W.2d 672 Civ. App. 1975, *but see:* Cravens v. Cravens, 533 S.W.2d 372 Tex. Civ. App. 75 (stipulated agreement to offer polygraph results would be enforceable in a divorce action), People v. Liddell, 234 N.W.2d 669 Mich. App. 1975.
33. Powers v. Carvalho, 281 A. 2d 298, 531 S.W.2d 672 R.I. 1971.
34. *Ibid.*
35. Alm v. General Telephone Co. of Illinois, 327 N.E.2d 523, Ill. Appl. 1975 (*see* Ill.Rev.Stat. Ch. 10, § 54.1).
36. Abrams, *Polygraph Handbook,* 11.
37. Bart v. State Dept. of Law Enforcement, Div. of State Police, 53 Ill. Dec. 332 (Ill. App. 1981).
38. Manaleu Dept. of Police, 376 So.2d 607 (La. App. 1979).
39. 234 N.W.2d 669.
40. 522 P.2d 257 (Okla. Cr. 1974).
41. 541 P.2d 871 (Okla. Cr. 1975).
42. United States v. Rodgers, 419 F.2d 1315 (10th Cir. 1969); Marks v. United States, 260 F.2d 377 (10th Cir. 1950).
43. Abrams, *Polygraph Validity and Reliability,* 313–326.
44. 371 P.2d 894.

Stress and Ulceration: Medico-Legal Aspects

Nathaniel Shafer, M.D., Robert Shafer, M.D.,
and Charles Wolf

Medical science has long been aware of the relationship between stress and peptic ulceration. Hippocrates, in a detailed description of a patient with gastric hemorrhage, observed the relationship between emotional tension and gastric symptoms.[1] Swan[2] made one of the earliest references to acute stress ulcers in 1823. Curling[3] and Cushing[4] wrote two early classic papers in 1842 and 1932, respectively. Their papers delineated the relationship between acute stress ulcerations, burns, and intracranial lesions (particularly those of the hypothalamus).

The presence of psychogenetic components is accepted by most specialists even in those patients whose ulcers are not caused purely by stress.[5] Today, stress ulceration is additionally important, since it can occur after trauma or surgery even though the victim has overcome his initial problem. According to Butterfield,[6] "Patients with trauma, hemorrhage, burns, neurologic injury, and sepsis, survive their initial injurics only to succumb to the bleeding complications of their ulcers." Butterfield[6] goes on to statc that "it is reported that in some large metropolitan hospitals, stress ulcers are the most common cause of upper GI bleeding."

Stress ulcer has been defined as an acute ulcer of the upper gastrointestinal tract which develops after a patient has been exposed to stress. Stress ulcers can develop in response to stress due to physical and emotional trauma in any patient, irrespective of their previous gastrointestinal and/or ulcer history.[7] Brooks[7] noted the gravity of the relationship between stress and physical well-being: "life-threatening ulcers may develop in patients under stressful circumstances." For the purposes of this discussion, the term *stress ulcer* will be used to describe only *acute* peptic ulcers, although a preexisting, dormant ulcer that is reactivated by an emotionally or physically traumatic event will be considered a stress ulcer.

Peptic ulceration is a process of sharply circumscribed loss of tissue which results from the digestive action of acid gastric juices.[8] The wall of the stomach or duodenum (the first portion of the small intestine which leads from the stomach) begins to erode, and eventually several layers of the wall have been penetrated and the ulcer resembles a crater or jagged hole.

The pathology of peptic ulceration is intimately tied to the workings of the digestive process. Digestion truly begins in the perception of food. The expectation, sight, and smell of comestibles, the perception of ingestion and of chewing, stimulate the vagal nerve centers of the brain, thus preparing the stomach to receive food. This early stage of digestion is known as the cephalic (i.e., thinking or brain-centered) phase. As masticated food moves from the esophagus (food pipe) to the stomach in the form of a bolus (ball), it triggers a vagovagal distention reflex which in turn evokes acid secretion—the gastric phase of digestion. Neuroreceptors in the pyloric area of the stomach release a hormone, gastrin, from specialized cells in the mucosal cavity (stomach lining). Gastrin, in turn, stimulates the stomach's parietal cells, causing them to secrete acidic juices. Peptic ulcers result from the digestion of the mucosa by gastric juices containing hydrochloric acid and pepsin.

Acid production is a normal function of the stomach, but ulceration results when the stomach is stimulated to produce an excess of digestive juices. Dr. J. Barton found that patients with duodenal ulcer secrete almost twice as much acid as normal patients.[9] Bralow[10] found that "both parietal cell mass, which is intimately involved in the secretion of gastric acid, and the maximal acid output are, on the average, twice as great in duodenal ulcer patients as in control subjects."

INCIDENCE

Postmortem examinations have provided the best data on the relationship between trauma and stress ulcer. Hummel, et al., found 17 acute ulcers among 80 patients who died of burns.[11] At the Mayo Clinic, Spencer, et al.,[12] found acute erosions or ulcers in 30 percent of 274 postmortems where death had been caused by intracranial tumors, though only 13 percent of a control group showed signs of ulceration. McDonnell and McCloskey,[13] at Jefferson Medical College Hospital, reported five acute ulcers among 179 examinations where death had been caused by intracranial disease, and eight among 243 patients who had died within two months of some operation other than an intracranial or central nervous system surgical procedure. Hebert[14] found five examples of acute peptic ulcer in 1,750 consecutive autopsies of patients who died following operations on areas other than the upper gastrointestinal tract. Mears[15] found eight examples of acute ulcer in 375 postmortems where there was also a fracture of one of the long bones. Watson and Netsky[16] described six cases of acute ulceration in autopsies of patients who had died from a variety of neurological diseases. Moncrief, Switzer, and Teplitz[17] found that the incidence of acute ulceration among burn cases increased over time, rising from 6.5 percent in 1954 to 21.3 percent in 1962. Drye, Schoen, and Ross reported that of 42 patients with duodenal ulcer who had other than gastric surgery, three had a definite reactivation of their ulcers.

Garvey[18] described 20 patients who developed acute gastro-duodenal ulceration as a result of a major fracture, burn, or laceration-contusion; none of these patients had experienced injury to the stomach or duodenum. He also described 30 cases where surgery preceded the development of peptic ulceration, though only in one case did a patient have gastric or duodenal surgery (for lye stricture of the esophagus by colon interposition). Crawford[19] reported 3.6 percent of postmortem examinations revealed acute ulceration. He found that 55 percent of these acute ulcerations had been diagnosed prior to death, indicating that this disorder may be much more common than those following any other type of trauma. A study of a series of autopsies showed that 65 percent of patients with acute ulcers had undergone surgery of some description. A study of clinically diagnosed ulcers showed that 52 percent (of the clinical patients) had undergone surgery, compared to 21 percent of the autopsy study and 19 percent of the clinical series, whose ulcers followed on disorders of the nervous system. Crawford concluded that ulcers are quite common after surgery, trauma, burns, and other stressful experiences. In his review of experimental stress ulcers, Butterfield[6] cites both experimentally-induced stress and burns as causal in ulceration of experimental animals. Law, et al.,[20] reviewed autopsies of trauma patients over a ten year period. He found that 46.9 percent of 81 burn cases had erosive lesions, and 23.5 percent had frank ulcers. Gastric lesions were present in 27.7 percent of these cases, and duodenal lesions were found in 11.1 percent. Of the frank ulcerations, 11.1 percent were in the stomach, and 8.6 percent in the duodenum. Spencer[12] concluded that acute duodenal erosions and ulcers occur four times as often in cases where there are associated intracranial neoplasms than in those where there exists no significant intracranial pathologic state.

Ulceration, then, often follows trauma. Because of the complexity of surgical procedures, the modern developments in intestine resuscitation, and the ever-increasing number of multiple life-threatening injuries resulting from the carnage on our highways, the incidence of acute stress ulcerations can do nothing but increase.[21]

EMOTIONAL INFLUENCE ON ULCERATION

"It is well established that emotional factors can alter gastric function."[22] The influence of the nervous system on peptic ulceration was first observed over 100 years ago. Peptic ulcers have been found in association with almost every type of brain disease. Cushing[4] blamed the autonomic nervous system when he observed instances of perforation by ulcer after operations for brain tumor.

Trauma or stress leads to ulceration when the vagus nerve which innervates the stomach wall is stimulated (as a result of such trauma), causing hypersecretion of stomach acids. A local spasm of the muscular wall is produced by the changes in the motility and tonicity of the stomach itself. In this way, any physical emotional stress may lead to the development of an ulcer, or aggravate a quiescent one. Cecil and Loeb have observed that "direct epigastric trauma is occasionally followed by the prompt appearance of the symptoms of ulcer and indeed by its subsequent roentgenological demonstration." McCombs,[23] professor of Graduate Medicine, concurred. "Stress," he argued, "both physical and emotional, is recognized as an important factor in the production of a peptic ulcer and in the reactivation of healed ulcers,"[24] and that "psychic disturbances such as increased emotional tension and psychological conflicts play an exceedingly important role in the mechanism of ulcer formation."[25] Emerson and Taylor[26] reported that peptic ulcers "seem to develop in persons who are emotionally tense."

A good deal of tension can be said to exist in wartime, particularly under battlefield conditions. Hincks[27] reported that a quarter of all Canadian troops brought home from England during the early days of World War II were evacuated because of ulcers. Between 1942 and 1945, 53,450 men were separated from the U.S. Army and, in a three-year period for the U.S. Navy during World War II, 77,000 cases of duodenal ulcer were identified.[28] Many of these ulcers were preexisting but had been dormant and were reactivated during military service.

Cole and Elman[29] showed that the autonomic nervous system, which controls both secretory and muscular activities, is involved in the pathogenesis of ulceration. "Worry, fatigue, and tension greatly aggravate the clinical severity of peptic ulcer, undoubtedly because of their influence on gastroduodenal secretion and motility via the autonomic nerves, notably the vagus." Cecil and Loeb[8] have emphasized the important role of emotional factors in ulceration, citing studies that demonstrate the response of the stomach to various psychological states. Though they recognized that "the central nervous system through the vagus may produce hypermotility and quantitative hypersecretion," they admitted as well that "it is premature to conclude that peptic ulcer is purely psychosomatic disorder." Harrison, et al.,[30] noted that "the occurrence of peptic ulcer in individuals who are high-strung, tense, and possessed of more than the average of ambition, drive and responsibility, as well as in persons who are subjected to emotional conflicts and upheavals, strongly suggests that psychogenic influences play an important role in the pathogenesis (of peptic ulceration). A great deal of evidence has accumulated to indicate that such emotional disturbances give rise to gastric hypertension, hypermotility, and hypertonus. The association of acute peptic ulcer in the stomach or duodenum with lesions in the central nervous system, as well as the results of the vagotomy operation for the treatment of peptic ulcer, indicate that the impulses responsible for the abnormal gastric physiology arise in the central nervous system and are mediated through the parasympathetic division of the autonomic nervous system."

Reference to the stomach in everyday conversation such as "I can't stomach it," or "he has no guts," reflect the extent to which the stomach is seen as the sounding board of the emotions. In the relationship between emotional trauma, mental anguish, and ulceration, then, we see a concrete physiologic justification for belief in this naive assumption.

Ulcer patients have been found to have an unusually high incidence of "Type A" behavior.[31] They have been described as tense people who are always in a hurry, who possess an unusual drive, who are self-sufficient to the extreme, independent, overly conscientious and who, although given to great worry, do not give way to emotion easily. Ulcer patients have also been found to be more depressed and anxious than non-ulcer individuals.[32] They also appeared to have had greater incidence of financial and domestic strife than the control population.[33]

Within such a personality typology, the incidence of ulceration can be assumed to be much greater than the 10 to 20 percent incidence of ulceration among the general population. Other influences on ulcer formation aside from physical trauma include changes in blood concentration, steroids, the hormonal response to trauma, age, central nervous system changes, and sepsis (a general reaction to the result of bacterial action and effects). Hereditary, constitutional, racial, allergic, infectious and occupational factors, as well as the presence of associated disease processes, can also be said to play a part in ulcer development. No matter what the case, though, it is generally accepted that ulcers are "common morphological changes that follow exposure to stress."[34]

TRAUMA AND ULCERATION

Roberts[35] emphasizes that there is a strong tie between accident and/or operation trauma and peptic ulceration. He showed that peptic ulceration may follow or be reactivated by injury and operation; that it may be present as bleeding, penetration, or perforation; and that it may cause death, or be an incidental finding after death. It was his conclusion, based on this evidence, that peptic ulceration after trauma is the abnormal reaction of an ulcer-prone patient to a physiological stimulus.

Ulcers exist with no external manifestation whatsoever, so the connection between external trauma and ulceration may be difficult to conceptualize. When ulceration exists, there need be no marks on the abdomen or any tenderness to reveal its presence. But there exists a wealth of evidence supporting the fact that physical insult often leads to peptic ulceration. David, McIlrath, and Higgins,[36] at the Mayo Clinic, studied 197 ulcer patients, most of whom were between 50 and 70 years of age. Ulceration was often accompanied by some other illness, and many ulcers were associated with multiple complications.

Other studies link peptic ulcerations to burns, neurologic, abdominal, thoracic and cardiovascular operations, diffuse diseases of the central nervous system, myocardial infarction, and acute respiratory insufficiency. The incidence of ulceration seems to depend on the type of operation or trauma patients were subjected to, in addition to their particular predisposition to ulceration. Relatively safe operations, for example, produce less ulceration than those operations known to be of greater risk; thus, emotional stress, or preoperative anxiety, is clearly a factor in the precipitation of ulceration. Crawford,[19] in a study of ulcer following stress, underlines the notion that even when predisposing factors are different, the commonality of stress in preoperative patients permits all operative, trauma-related ulceration to be considered as having some common and basic cause—the stress itself.

Severity of Trauma

As there is clearly a difference between a rear end "fender bender" automotive collision and one in which a car is completely demolished, so there are differences in the severity of emotional stress due to physical and other traumas. We can assume that there is a positive, though not necessarily linear, relationship between the degree of severity of the stress and the progress of ulceration. There is at the present, however, no clear, concise, unambiguous methodology for measuring degrees of stress. David, McIlrath and Higgins,[36] in their careful study at the Mayo Clinic, found that "it is difficult to establish the degree of 'stress' present in these cases." However, they also recognized that the "incidence (of ulceration) increases in direct proportion to the severity of the stressful circumstances." And, as stress is to some degree a function of a subjective psychological disposition as well, the trauma leading to the stress need not be great in magnitude in order to produce peptic ulceration.

Latency after Trauma

Peptic ulcer symptoms rarely appear directly after a traumatic experience. A period of latency is a common phenomenon and a common feature of infectious diseases in general. Symptoms of mumps do not appear until one month after the invasion of a virus. Infectious hepatitis does not manifest itself until three months after exposure. Certain diseases, such as syphilis and dissecting aortic aneurysm, develop for years before they manifest themselves clinically. Ulceration is a gradual process and not an infectious syndrome; its latency period is much more variable. David, McIlrath and Higgins[36] reported that the lapse between initial insult and the first clinical evidence of acute ulceration ranged from 1 to 28 days. The length of the latency period for a particular ulcer, however, is a crucial factor in the analysis of its pathology. In the aforementioned study of 39 patients who developed ulceration 14 days or more after an initial insult, only six (15 percent) survived, as compared to 17 (43 percent) of the patients in the entire sample who survived.

MECHANISM OF ULCERATION

Three factors—increased acid secretion, the breakdown of normal protective membranes (the mucosa), and reduced blood supply due to open arteriovenous shunts—work in combination to produce ulcer.[7] Each of these three factors can itself be said to be caused or influenced by an interaction of the autonomic nervous system and the endocrine glands, particularly the adrenals.

The hypothalamus, a pivotal gland in the endocrine system, secretes a hormone called corticotropin in response to stress or traumatic situations. Corticotropin activates the pituitary gland which stimulates the adrenal gland to increase corticoid production. The corticoids, in turn, stimulate the gastric glands, causing increased acid and pepsin production, which result in ulcer.

A trauma, such as an automobile accident, evokes an immediate physiological reaction from the affected individual, a physiological "fear response." This response is quite normal—it prepares the body for impending shock. The individual becomes pale as blood travels from skin to muscles and internal organs as a state of general readiness is attained. This blood flow stimulates all of the glandular mechanisms of the body, especially those glands related to peptic ulceration. Leonard, et al.,[37] showed that the hypothalamus is related to hydrochloric acid secretion as well as gastric blood flow in animals, and that proper low frequency stimulation of the anterior hypothalamus results in increased gastric secretion.

Selye[38] believed that any systemic stress, such as that accompanying acute gastrointestinal ulceration, will evoke an alarm reaction in the organism. He considered the alarm reaction to be constituted of two distinct phases: the shock phase, characterized by hypothermia (lower than normal body temperature), hypotension (lower than normal blood pressure), depression of the nervous system, decreasing muscular tone, hemoconcentration (an increase in the concentration of blood cells resulting from loss of plasma or water from the bloodstream), deranged capillary and cell-membrane permeability, generalized tissue breakdown, hypochloremia (reduction in the blood potassium), acidosis (a reduction of the alkali reserve), a transitory rise in blood sugar, leukopenia (a subnormal amount of leukocytes in the peripheral blood), eosinophilia (an increase above the normal amount of eosinophilia in circulating blood or tissues), and acute gastrointestinal erosion which heals rapidly; and the countershock phase, characterized by a reversal of all the manifestations of shock as well as by enlargement of the adrenal cortex and acute involution of the thymicolymphatic (that which affects the thymus and lymphatic structures such as the spleen, lymph nodes and lymphoid aggregates) apparatus. Selye[38] believed that the gastrointestinal erosions produced by shock are the result either of an intense autonomic discharge occurring in the splanchnic area (an internal area) or of the release of a histamine-like substance with toxic effects on the gastrointestinal tract.

Curling[3] suggested that patients with severe burns are extremely prone to peptic ulcers. Chu-Jeng Chiu[39] studied a group of rats that had been scalded and then fasted for twenty-four hours. He found that the general cellular metabolic depression caused by burns is at least reflected in the alteration of the gastric mucous. Due to the action of various pathological conditions and agents acting directly or through neural, vascular, and humoral mediators, the intestinal mucosal epithelium (covering) is lifted away bit by bit, allowing digestive enzymes and acids to eat away at the stomach wall.

Dragstedt, et al.,[40] and Beck, et al.,[41] have argued that acidity plays little part in ulcer formation. Instead, they contend, ulceration occurs when the mucosal coat becomes more susceptible to the action of acid as a result of trauma. Both Menguy and Master[42] and Desbaillents and Menguy[43] have recently shown that cortisone or ACTH reduced the secretion of gastric mucous and altered its biomedical composition. Menguy and Masters[42] found that the administration of exogenous ACTH and cortisone alters both the volume and mucopolysaccharide constituents of the gastric mucous, leading to a reduction of the resistance to peptic or tryptic proteolysis. They also showed that these compounds prolong gastric cell regeneration time, perhaps leading to a greater susceptibility to injury. Much of Selye's work[38] with the stress and general adaptations syndrome has been based on increased

ACTH and cortisone output through the hypothalamus-pituitary-adrenal complex.

Thus, the relationship between increased levels of acid secretion and stress ulceration is still controversial. O'Neil[44] and Dragstedt[40] found that hydrochloric acid secretion remained normal in their stress ulcer patients, and it was the breakdown of the protective mucosal structures that made the stomach wall vulnerable to even normal acid secretion. Menguy[45] has gathered more recent evidence to support the view that focal mucosal necrosis results from an energy deficit that is particularly severe in the corpus of the stomach because its energy metabolism is primarily aerobic. The foci of ischemic necrosis then undergo acid peptic digestion with bleeding before healing by all migration from the crypts can occur.

The mechanism of ulceration is the same in either case. An imbalance between aggressive acid-pepsin factors and the gastrointestinal protective mechanism of mucous and the mucosal barrier results in ulceration of the mucosal wall.

SYMPTOMATOLOGY

The principal manifestation of acute, or chronic, peptic ulcer is abdominal pain, usually burning in character, and located in the upper abdomen, at midline or slightly to the right, although pain may also occasionally be present on the left side, and may radiate to other areas of the abdomen or the back, especially the latter when a penetrating or deep ulcer condition exists. Radiation of pain in the chest may mimic heart disease.

The severity of the pain varies from a sense of discomfort or indigestion to a severe burning sensation. Ulcer pain is periodic and has a relationship to the intake of food. In the case of chronic ulcers, distress can last for six or seven years,[8] with attacks predominately in the spring and fall. Attacks occur in greatest frequency between October and March, and also during the month of June.[8] Periods of remission, of similar duration to the attacks, follow, but as the disease progresses these periods of remission become shorter, and attacks come to dominate the clinical picture.

Ulcer pain is related to the digestive cycle in the same way for both gastric and duodenal ulcer, though specific location does have an effect on the time between meals and the onset of pain. Pain is almost always absent in the morning before breakfast, appears one to four hours after breakfast, and lasts thirty minutes or more, perhaps until relief is obtained at the noon meal.[7] Pain at night is frequently reported. There may be long periods with no pain, or pain may be constant.

Ulcer pain as alternatively described is a gnawing or aching sensation, a burning, hurting, annoying or cramplike feeling. It is often compared to hunger pains, though usually referred to as much greater in intensity. Peptic ulcer patients seem to be always hungry, and will eat soon after a regular meal or nibble constantly between meals. Because ulcer pains are relieved by food, especially milk or an alkaline substance which neutralizes stomach acid, patients learn that eating helps make them more comfortable even before diagnosis is confirmed. Many obese individuals who eat uncontrollably and many addicts of drugstore remedies are actually suffering from peptic ulcer.

Nausea, water brash (a combination of excessive saliva and acid regurgitation), constipation, and diarrhea are other less common manifestations of peptic ulcer. Frequent eating in order to relieve ulcer pain may result in a weight gain.[8] Weight loss is uncommon unless chronic duodenal obstruction has been present.

DIAGNOSIS

With the advent of fiberoptics, gastroscopy has become the best method for the diagnosis of actively bleeding ulcers. A *British Medical Journal* editorial[46] emphasized that "pride of place is now accorded to fibroscopy in the investigation of massive upper gastrointestinal hemorrhage." In experienced hands, a firm endoscopic diagnosis can be made in at least 90 percent of patients examined.[47]

When the problem is less acute and there is no bleeding, a radiological study of the upper gastrointestinal tract often reveals the presence of ulceration. But, if the duodenal bulb has been scarred by chronic disease, or if there is an ulcer in the pyloric channel, radiology alone cannot detect ulceration in these areas. Therefore, a combined approach, using both endoscopy and radiology, is necessary in the diagnosis of ulcer disease.

COMPLICATIONS

Peptic ulcers and the symptoms that accompany them often recur, even with medical treatment. Failure to adhere to dietary regimen, continued use of nicotine and alcohol, ingestion of irritating substances such as aspirin, and continued emotional stress all work to cause recurrence. Reactivation of ulcer has been called the "peptic ulcer diathesis" and is often brought on when the factors that originally caused the condition continue to be operative.

Microscopic amounts of blood are found in the stools of many ulcer patients, and stool analysis is a convenient way of detecting reactivation prior to the onset of new pain. This is especially important for individuals who bleed but do not manifest any of the other "warning" symptoms—a fairly frequent occurrence, particularly in acute ulcers. In the Mayo Clinic study,[36] massive upper gastrointestinal hemorrhage was found to be the most common manifestation of ulceration. In gastric ulcer, hematemesis is usually present, as well as melena. In duodenal ulcer, it occurs in about one-fourth of the cases. Gross hemorrhage with bloody stools or vomitus occurs in about 25 percent of ulcer patients.[8] Other symptoms of hemorrhage include shock or prostration, weakness, and fainting. Occasionally, the hemorrhage remains undetected, or presents itself as anemia of unknown cause.

Perforation is "the most dangerous complication of peptic ulcer and accounts for 65 to 85 percent of the deaths."[8] It occurred in 13 percent of 197 ulcer patients studied at the Mayo Clinic.[36] Perforation manifests itself in a sudden onset of excruciating pain starting in the epigastrium and migrating to the lower right quadrant. Nausea is often present and the face becomes pallid and haggard, with beads of cold sweat covering it.

Obstructive symptoms resulting from swelling or scarring adjacent to the ulcer may be present as the first clinical manifestation of ulceration. Initial vomiting is often preceded by pain, which is then relieved, and vomitus usually contains undigested food ingested within twenty-four hours of a given attack. Obstruction often resembles retention, which may be present in the absence of gastric disease, but obstruction is always due to a spasm of the pylorus, to edema and inflammatory swelling about a pyloric or duodenal ulcer, to cicatricial stenosis or to a combination of these factors. If obstruction is not relieved, the patient will become weak, lose a dramatic amount of weight, and may finally starve.

Generalized peritonitis usually ensues in untreated patients. The ulcer becomes so deep that it penetrates the outside wall of the stomach, emptying the contents of the stomach into the abdominal and thoracic (chest) cavities. Pain becomes sharp and quite severe. The abdomen loses its boardlike character, but not its rigidity or tenderness. It becomes distended and the pulse becomes gradually rapid, weak, and feeble. Respiration becomes more rapid and shallow. Hippocratic facies appears, and the patient dies a typical peritonitic death within two to five days. The condition is imminently fatal unless promptly treated.

PREVENTION AND TREATMENT

The basis of treatment revolves around maintaining the pH of the stomach and duodenum at 5 or 6 by the administration of antacids. Patients who are conscious and can tolerate liquids are given antacids orally. However, many patients are so ill after serious trauma or surgery that they may not be able to tolerate oral liquids, and thus cannot be given antacids. It is with these patients that Khan[48] and his associates found that the giving of antacids via a nasogastric tube each hour on the hour, while maintaining suction, was almost 100 percent effective in preventing stress ulcers. Similar results were found by Hastings, et al.,[49] and McAlhany, et al.,[50] where stress-induced bleeding was nearly eliminated from the upper GI.

In an editorial discussion of the Hastings, et al.,[49] and McAlhany, et al.,[50] studies, the *British Medical Journal* notes that side effects may occur due to the amount of antacid required for treatment.[51] It notes, however, that these side effects are not usually severe, and certainly less severe than continued bleeding. Cimetidine, an H_2-receptor antagonist, also appears to be able to control stress-induced bleeding.[52] According to Hetzel,[52] cimetidine has fewer side effects than antacids, and may be given intravenously, thus precluding the necessity of a functioning gut. However, it is not clear whether cimetidine controls stress-induced bleeding due to its action on gastric acid, or due to antifibrinolytic properties.[51] Tentatively, it would seem that a combination of antacid and cimetidine would be most effective.[52]

Strong emphasis should be placed on prevention, which is the keynote of treatment, since stress ulcers, once developed, complicate an already compromised patient. In the words of Dr. Rene Menguy, "surgical mortality rates exceeding 50 percent underscore the need for studies of prophylaxis."[53]

Once the ulcer develops, treatment is aimed at maintaining adequate circulatory volume with whole blood transfusions. Preferably, the transfusions should be accomplished with fresh blood, because banked blood is often lacking in crucial clotting factors. The patient is given an ice water lavage and placed on nasogastric suction, or perhaps, cimetidine as well. If the patient's condition becomes stable, one can start a regimen of antacids. Continued bleeding is indicative of the need for surgical intervention.

SUMMARY

This paper outlines the possibility of acute, and perhaps, fatal, if not diagnosed, stress ulcers precipitated by trauma, surgery, or other potentiating events. It should once again be emphasized that prevention is the best treatment for the stress-induced ulcer, and that this prevention may occur at both a secondary level (defusion of emotive or physical precipitators) and a primary level (reduction of gastric acid and/or bleeding).

REFERENCES

1. Smith, L.A., and A.B. Rivers. 1953. *Peptic Ulcer, Pain, Patterns, Diagnosis, and Medical Treatment.* New York: Appleton-Century-Crofts.
2. Swan, J. 1823. "Case of Severe Burn." *Edinburgh Med. J.* 19:344.

3. Curling, T.B. 1842. "On Acute Ulceration of the Duodenum in Cases of Burn," translated by Roy Med-Chir. *London* 25:260–281.
4. Cushing, H. 1932. "Peptic Ulcers and the Interbrain." *Surg Gynec Obstet* 55:1034.
5. Day, Stacey B. 1982. *Life Stress,* p. 323. New York: Van Nostrand Reinhold.
6 .Butterfield, W.C. 1975. "Experimental Stress Ulcers, A Review." *Surg Annu* 7:261–78.
7. Brooks, F.P. 1966. "Stress Ulcer: Etiology, Diagnosis, and Treatment." *Med Clin N Amer* 50:1447–1455.
8. Cecil and Loeb. 1959. *A Textbook of Medicine.* Philadelphia: W.B. Saunders.
9. Baron, J.H. 1971. "Physiological Control of Gastric Acid Secretion." *Proc R. Soc Med* 64(July):739–41.
10. Bralow, P.S. 1971. *Practice of Medicine.* Vol. 7. New York: Harper and Row.
11. Hummel, R.P., G.F. Lanchantin, and C.P. Artiz. 1957. "Clinical Experiences and Studies in Curling's Ulcer." *JAMA* 164:141.
12. Spencer, J.A., C.G. Morlock, and G.P. Sayre. 1959. "Lesions in Upper Portion of the Gastrointestinal Tract Associated with Intracranial Neoplasms." *Gastroenterology* 37:20–27.
13. McDonnell, W.V., and J.F. McCloskey. 1953. "Acute Peptic Ulcers as a Complication of Surgery." *Ann Surg* 67.
14. Herbut, P.A. 1945. "Acute Peptic Ulcers Following Distant Operations." *Surg Gynec & Obst* 80:410.
15. Mears, F.B. 1943. "Autopsy Survey of Peptic Ulcer Associated with Other Diseases." *Surgery* 34:640.
16. Watson, J.M., and M.G. Netsky. 1964. "Ulceration and Malacia of the Upper Alimentary Tract in Neurologic Disorders." *Arch Neurol & Psychiat* 72:426.
17. Moncrief, J.A., W.E. Switzer, and C. Teplitz. 1964. "Curling's Ulcer." *J. Trauma* 4:481.
18. Garvey, J.M., and Fogelman. 1966. "Septic Peptic Ulceration." *J Trauma* 6:644–665.
19. Crawford, F.A., et al. 1971. "The Stress Ulcer Syndrome: A Clinical and Pathologic Review." *Amer J Surg* 121(June):644–9.
20. Law, E.J., et al. 1971. "Autopsy Findings in the Upper Gastrointestinal Tract of 81 Burn Patients: A Review." *Arch Surg* 102(April):412–15.
21. Girvan, D.P., et al. 1971. "Acute Stress Ulceration with Bleeding or Perforation." *Arch Surg* 103(August):116–21.
22. Grossman, Morton I. 1975. "Peptic Ulcer: Pathogenesis and Physiology." In *Textbook of Medicine,* edited by Paul, Beeson, Walsh, and McDermott. 14th ed. Philadelphia: W.B. Saunders.
23. McCombs, R.P. 1960. *Internal Medicine.* Chicago: The Year Book Publishers.
24. Gray, S.J. 1957. "Relationship of the Adrenal Gland to Peptic Ulcer." *Med Clin N Amer* 41:147.
25. Lyght, C., et al. 1961. "Pepsin Ulcer." In *The Merck Manual.* 10th ed. Rahway, N.J.: Merck, Sharp & Dohme Research Laboratories.
26. Emerson and Taylor. 1950. *Essentials of Medicine.* Philadelphia: Lippincott.
27. Hincks, C.M. 1941. "Mental Hygiene in the Emergency Work in Canada." *Ment Hyg* 25:10.
28. Hamilton, E.L., B.H. Sullivan, Jr., and E.D. Palmer. 1952. "Duodenal Ulcer in

Military Personnel: Studies on the Military Effectiveness of the Ulcer Patient." *U.S. Armed Forces Med J.* 3:831.
29. Cole and Elman. 1952. *Textbook of General Surgery.* 6th ed. New York: Appleton-Century-Crofts.
30. Harrison, T.R. 1950. *Principles of Internal Medicine.* New York: The Blakiston Co.
31. Paulley, J.W. 1979. "Ulcers, Heart Disease, and Type-A Behavior." *Lancet,* 2(8154, December 8):1238.
32. Feldman, Edward J., and Karen A. Sabovich. 1980. "Stress and Peptic Ulcer Disease." *Gastroenterology* 78(May):1087–1089.
33. Alp, M.H., J.H. Court, and A.K. Grant. 1970. "Personality Pattern and Emotional Stress in the Genesis of Gastric Ulcer." *Gut* II:773–777.
34. Tache, Jean, et al. 1979. *Cancer, Stress and Death,* p. 4. New York: Plenum Medical Book.
35. Roberts, P.A.L. 1954. "A Danger of Peptic Ulceration: A Survey of Eight Cases Complicating Surgery and Trauma." *Brit. Med J* 1:1295–98.
36. David, E., D.C McIlrath, and J.A. Higgins. 1971. "Clinical Experience with Acute Peptic Gastrointestinal Ulcers." *Mayo Clinic Proceedings,* 46:15–24.
37. Leonard, A.S., D.M. Long, L.A. French, E.T. Peter, and O.H. Wagenstein. 1964. "Pendular Pattern in Gastric Secretion and Blood Flow Following Hypothalamic Stimulation: Origin of Stress Ulcer." *Surgery* 56:109.
38. Selye, Hans. 1950. *Stress.* Montreal: Acta.
39. Chiu, C.J., et al. 1971. "Gastric Mucosal Changes Following Burns in Rats: A Morphological and Metabolic Approach to the Stress Ulcer Problem." *Arch Surg* 103(August):147–152.
40. Dragstedt, L.R., H. Ragins, L.R. Dragstedt II, et al. 1956. "Stress and Duodenal Ulcer." *Ann Surg* 144:450–463.
41. Beck, I.T., H.W. Fletcher, R.D. McKenna, et al. 1960. "Effect of Small and Massive Doses of Prednisone on Gastric Secretory Activity." *Gastroenterology* 38:740–749.
42. Menguy and Masters. 1963. "Effects of Cortisone on Mucoprotein Secretion by Gastric Antrum of Dogs: Pathogenesis of Steroid Ulcer." *Surgery* 54:19–28.
43. Desbaillets, L., and R. Menguy. 1967. "Inhibition of Gastric Mucous Secretion by ACTH: An Experimental Study." *Amer J Dig Dis* 12:282–588.
44. O'Neil, J.A. Jr., B.A. Pruitt, J.A. Moncrief, et al. 1967. "Studies Related to the Pathogenesis of Curling's Ulcer." *J. Trauma* 7:275–287.
45. Menguy, Rene, and V.F. Masters. 1974. "Gastric Mucosal Energy Metabolism and Stress Ulceration." *Ann Surg.* 180:538–548.
46. Editorial. 1974. "Massive Upper Gastrointestinal Bleeding." *Brit Med J.,* March 9.
47. Lightdale, C.J., R.C. Kurtz, C.C. Boyle, P. Sherlock, and S.J. Winawer. 1973. "Cancer and Upper Gastrointestinal Tract Hemorrhage: Benign Causes of Bleeding Demonstrated by Endoscopy." *JAMA* 226:139.
48. Kahn, F. 1977. "New Regimen Avoids Stress Ulcer Deaths." *Medical Tribune* 18(3, Jan. 19):1, 34.
49. Hastings, P.R., J.J. Skillman, L.S. Bushnell, and W. Silen. 1978. "Antacid Titration in the Prevention of Acute Gastro-Intestinal Bleeding: A Controlled, Randomized Trial in 100 Critically Ill Patients." *N. Eng. J. Med.* 298:1041–45.

50. McAlhany, J.C., A.J. Czaja, and B.A. Pruitt. 1976. "Antacid Control of Complications from Acute Gastrointestinal Disease After Burns." *J. Trauma* 16:645–47.
51. Editorial. 1980. "Prevention or Cure for Stress-Induced Gastrointestinal Bleeding?" *Brit Med J.* 181(Sept. 6).
52. Hetzel, D. 1980. "Response to Editorial: Prevention or Cure...." *Brit Med J.* 281(Nov. 15).
53. Menguy, R. 1980. "The Prophylaxis of Stress Ulceration." *N Eng J. Med.* 302(8, Feb. 21):461–462.

A Skeleton Only Clad with Skin: The Medico-Legal Aspects of Anorexia Nervosa

Elizabeth A. Principi, J.D., LL.M.

> Mr. Duke's Daughter in St. Mary Axe, in the year 1684 and the eighteenth year of her Age, in the Month of July, fell into a total suppression of her Monthly Courses from a multitude of Cares and Passions of her Mind, but without any symptom of the Green-Sickness following upon it. From which time her Appetite began to abate, and her Digestion to be bad; her flesh also began to be flaccid and loose, and her looks pale....
>
> I do not remember that I did ever in all my Practice see one, that was conversant with the Living, so much wasted with the greatest degree of a Consumption (like a Skeleton only clad with skin); yet there was no Fever, but on the contrary a coldness of the whole body; no Cough, or difficulty of Breathing nor an appearance of any other distemper of the Lungs, or of any other Entrail; no looseness or any other sign of a Colliquation or Preternatural expence of the Nutritious Juices. Only her Appetite was diminished and her Digestion uneasie, with Fainting Fits, which did frequently return upon her.... She was after three months taken with a Fainting Fit and Dyed.[1]

This graphic and interesting case study is the first known description of a disease that is as baffling today as it was three centuries ago when the English physician Morton treated Mr. Duke's daughter. The symptomatology remains the same. Morton noted the essential features of the illness: amenorrhea, loss of appetite, constipation, loss of weight, and the lack of any fever or cause for the illness.

Morton named the disease "phthisis nervosa." The disease was rediscovered and renamed in 1868 by Gull who called it "anorexia nervosa," the term generally used in English speaking countries.[2] The Germans aptly call it "Pubertatsmagersucht" or puberal emaciation.[3]

BASIC DIAGNOSTIC CRITERIA

Though the etiology of the syndrome of anorexia nervosa is unclear, there is now widespread acceptance of basic diagnostic criteria originally proposed by Feighner and associates.[4] They outline five primary criteria that must be fulfilled for a diagnosis of anorexia. These criteria must present together for an accurate diagnosis:

1. *The patient must be under twenty-five at the onset of the illness.* The typical patient is a girl just past puberty. Although boys also develop anorexia nervosa, only one in fifteen cases is male,[5] with onset frequently prepubertal.[6]
2. Anorexia with accompanying weight loss of at least twenty-five percent of original body weight, or in adolescents twenty-five percent below accepted standards for age and height.
3. The patient holds a "distorted, implacable attitude towards eating, food, or weight that overrides hunger, admonitions, reassurance and threats." Patients seem to have a virtual "weight phobia"[7] that expresses itself through a relentless pursuit of thinness. They manifest this attitude in a variety of ways which may include denying their illness even when they are emaciated; manipulating or deceiving medical personnel and family; obtaining overt pleasure from refusal and weight loss; expressing distorted judgments of nutritional needs and intake; and developing unusual patterns of food handling (e.g., hoarding, or the excessive cooking for others, frequently reported by family members).
4. *The patient has no medical illness that could account for the disease.*
5. *The absence of any other psychiatric disorder.* Psychometric testing is generally normal. Despite a basically normal personality, anorexics are perfectionists, overachievers, or highly eager to please. Body image is often distorted,[8] but primary affective disorders, schizophrenia and obsessive-compulsive or phobic neuroses are not present.

In addition to these five criteria, at least two of the following signs or symptoms must be present for a diagnosis of anorexia nervosa: amenorrhea, lanugo, bradycardia, periodic overactivity, episodic bulimia, and vomiting (which may be self-induced).

In addition to the primary criteria, there are numerous supporting signs and symptoms of anorexia nervosa. These include constipation, hypothermia, cold intolerance, hypotension, pitting edema, dry or scaly skin, acrocyanosis, petechiae, disturbed sleep, leukopenia, absence of anemia, normal breast tissue, maintenance of axillary and pubic hair, and normal intelligence.[9,10] In addition, there are complex metabolic and endocrine changes, none of which are pathognomonic that may be reflected in abnormal laboratory findings.[11,12]

Thus, the symptomatology of anorexia can be divided into three categories: (a) psychopathological characteristics, (b) functional disturbances that are not direct consequences of malnutrition, and (c) the psychological effects of the mentally determined fasting. These closely resemble the effects of enforced starvation. It is of note, however, that the anorexia nervosa patient rarely shows starvation, edema, or avitaminosis. Even in advanced stages of marasmus, they are usually active and full of energy.

THEORIES OF ETIOLOGY

It is clear that the medical diagnosis of anorexia nervosa is becoming less difficult. However, anorexia nervosa continues to be etiologically a mystery. Theories are rampant as to its cause, and they remain multifaceted. The proposed theories of its etiology can be grouped into six general categories: Psychodynamics; Family Interaction; Behavioral; Medical; Perceptual Distortion; and Cultural.

Psychodynamic Theory

Bruch is the leading proponent of this theory. She describes the anorexic as a regressive individual who is fixated in the oral-anal stage of sexual development, attempting to avoid normal adolescent sexuality. Characteristically, the anorexic is of a stubborn and obsessive trait who becomes totally preoccupied with eating and bowel-bladder functions, all symptomatic of anal-oral fixation. The regression at its worst leads the patient into childlike mannerisms with a loss of secondary sexual characteristics. The ultimate outcome can be a total infantile dependence, where the anorexic must be fed and cared for.[13]

Family Interaction Theory

Family psychopathology has been implicated in two different stages of the disease. Crisp observed in the early 1960s that the family plays no active role until the anorexic is improved and returned to the home.[14] On the other hand, Minuchin proposes an earlier input from the family "organizing" around the patient's refusal to eat, and focusing so much on this alone that the family avoids handling other interpersonal conflicts. The anorexic attempts to control her environment and family in the only way she can—not eating. The anorexic's symptoms serve to stabilize a precarious or dysfunctional family.[15] Some observers consider the family the prime mover in the syndrome to the extent that among the myriads of treatments suggested only one has received almost unanimous agreement: patients must be removed from their home environments.[16]

Behavioral Therapy

This theory holds that the behavior of the anorexic in rejecting food is reinforced by the attention it receives. The anorexic becomes the center of attention and becomes extremely manipulative of her environment. Behavior toward food is disordered in a variety of ways. Absolute food intake may be decreased. There may be, however, an increase in the amount ingested through episodic outbreaks of gorging followed by attempts to prevent weight gain by vomiting, purgatives, or physical activity. The patient subsists on high bulk, low calorie food primarily, though she may desire rich food. Food selection may be bizzare and idiosyncratic, often limited to one food. Vomiting may be induced. These women keep themselves busily immersed in food-related activities. Some find refusal of food pleasant. Food becomes the center of her life and as she becomes thinner she receives more attention. Behavioral modification by a system of rewards and punishments used in a hospital setting has become a useful tool in treatment.[17]

Medical Theory

The medical or organic theory of causation has been stimulated by the physical manifestations of the disease. Particularly, the high incidence of amenorrhea, sometimes before other symptoms have appeared, has led endocrinologists to investigate and find a number of hypothalamic-pituitary abnormalities. Abnormal function was consistently found in thermoregulation, water conservation, delayed release of trophic hormones, LH, FSH, and TSH, and carbohydrate metabolism.[18]

Distorted Body Perception

Another theory of anorexia nervosa's etiology is distorted body perception. Anorexics persistently believe that they look fat and cannot be dissuaded from this view. Slade and Russell have documented a perceptual distortion of body size in anorectics by measuring their overestimation of body size.[19] In most cases, however, their perception of others remains intact.

Cultural Factors

The theory of culturally induced anorexia nervosa may be lent credence by the recent increase in the prevalence of this disease. We have become a body oriented society carefully supervised and encouraged by the Madison Avenue ethic. Peer pressure's being so invasive at the normal age of anorexia nervosa onset cannot be underestimated. Hilde Bruch considered the "relentless pursuit of thinness" to be the central theme of these patients.[20] The prevalence in our Western society may now be as high as one in 100 or one in 200 among sixteen- to eighteen-year-old school girls in upper socioeconomic groups.[21]

The treatment of this disease is widely variable. However, in the crisis stage where the weight loss approaches sixty pounds, the treatment mandated is hospitalization,[22] where the support of basic physiological functions can be achieved. This therapy may include tube feeding, hyperalimentation, and respiratory support.

INTERVENTION

Aside from crisis, intervention general management must have a dual orientation. One set of objectives is aimed at restoring nutritional balance and generating weight gain, sufficient to allow independent functioning.

For a number of reasons the patient should be hospitalized for nutrition therapy. The patient will be in a controlled environment where food intake and output, medications, and activity can be monitored, and she will be separated from the probable cause of her disease—her family. The nutritional approach may include a firm encouragement of food intake, force feeding, feeding of high calorie formulas, drug therapy, and hormones.

Once nutrition has been improved, the other set of objectives on the psychological plane can be instituted. This may include again drug therapy, electroconvulsive therapy, hypnosis, psychotherapy, family therapy, behavior modification, and leukotomy.[23] Successful outcomes have been reported for all these therapeutic regimens. Newly on the treatment horizon are self-help groups, similar to Alcoholics Anonymous, which have earned considerable respect and referral from the medical community.

The prognosis for anorexia nervosa, like every other aspect of this disease, is generally uncertain. An estimated 40 to 60 percent of patients recover completely. The remaining numbers suffer severe and recurrent episodes or continue to manifest some sort of eating disorder or psychopathology.[24] Prognostic signs correlated with favorable longterm recovery include younger age at onset; absence of premorbid obesity, vomiting or laxative abuse; absence of multiple psychosomatic, depressive, or obsessive-compulsive symptoms; membership in upper socioeconomic groups; being female rather than male; and lack of preoccupation with body size or nutrition within the family.[25]

MEDICO-LEGAL ISSUES

The medico-legal issues of anorexia nervosa predominate in the diagnostic stage. The fourth criteria listed in the primary criteria of the diagnosis needs to be carefully examined: *The patient has no medical illness that could account for the disease.*

The majority of the court cases reported were medical malpractice cases wherein the issue was a failure to diagnose an underlying metabolic or organic disease.

One case involved the failure by a hospital laboratory to report glycosuria in a young teenage girl hospitalized for anorexia nervosa. The complaint also alleged that the internist should have intervened more vigorously in the patient's therapy and that he unduly relied on the psychiatric diagnosis of anorexia nervosa to the detriment of the decedent.[26]

A California case involved a ten-year-old girl who was initially suspected of having an intracranial neoplasm by a school pediatrician. He immediately referred her for admission to a local children's hospital. Her subsequent discharge diagnosis was anorexia nervosa. An intriguing story then began to unfold. It included monkey bites, mysterious evening visits by the patient to a locked outpatient clinic, numerous hospitalizations at several hospitals, and a deteriorating relationship between the girl's mother and the girl's physicians. Two years later a psychiatric consultant suggested the diagnosis of craniopharyngioma and recommended a series of tests. Because the girl's attending physician felt the consultant was "winging it," the tests were never completed. During the following year the girl became progressively worse and her mother became increasingly concerned that the daughter had leukemia. The leukemia was subsequently ruled out and the mother became the object of some ridicule by the succession of physicians treating her daughter. The child's diagnosis continued to be anorexia nervosa. Finally, three-and-one-half years after the diagnosis of intracranial tumor was initially suspected, the diagnosis of craniopharyngioma was confirmed.[27]

A more recent Michigan case involved a nineteen-year-old woman who arrested and died from unknown causes while hospitalized for treatment of anorexia nervosa. Plaintiffs attempted to show that the diagnosis of anorexia nervosa was incorrect, that she was instead suffering from a severe depression, that she was prescribed contraindicated drugs, and that her treatment modality contributed to her death from starvation or malnutrition. Defendants contended that she was properly diagnosed as an anorexic, that she was treated appropriately, and that despite adequate medical intervention, she succumbed. The defendants' theory that a physician is not a guarantor of results was successful and a "no cause of action" verdict was returned and subsequently upheld on appeal.[28]

A search of reported cases found several other areas where anorexia nervosa was involved. Of special note is a child custody case, in which a father who had had actual (de facto) and continual physical custody of his two-year-old daughter was awarded legal custody on appeal.[29] Following a custody hearing, pursuant to the mother's petition for legal separation, the mother was awarded physical and legal custody. The father appealed. The appeals court found that the 65-pound mother was "ravaged" by the disease of anorexia nervosa, that the disease was life-threatening, and that her ritual of overeating, vomiting, and starving left her with no energy to care for her healthy 31-pound two year old. The court reviewed the uncontroverted testimony regarding the mother's unstable emotional condition and its life-threatening physical symptoms, in contrast to the father's demonstrated desire and ability to provide a stable wholesome home for the child. This review convinced the appeals court that the trial judge's decision to award custody to the mother was erroneous and that he was unduly influenced by the obsolete "maternal preference" rule. Taking into account the modern rule, "in the best interest of the child," the appeals court, in quite strong language, found that the father was not only the better equipped parent, but the *only* parent equipped to care for the child. The court went on to find that, "even if the mother was capable of physically caring for the child, which is questionable, her distorted self-image, mental instability, and bizarre habits would certainly have an adverse impact on the psychological development of this (female) child." Based on the above analysis, the appeals court found the mother physically unfit and emotionally unstable, while finding it in the child's best interest to remain in the continuous care and affection provided by the father's stable mental and physical health.

In a Social Security disability appeal, among other issues addressed, the United States Court of Appeals for the Fifth Circuit opined that anorexia nervosa may be considered a disabling condition.[30] Tangential involvement of anorexia, primarily dictum, was found in a criminal dissent opinion,[31] a damages for emotional distress case,[32] and a health insurance litigation case.[33]

The recent interest in anorexia nervosa by the lay press indicates a growing awareness of the disease by the general public. The medico-legal implications underscore the need to thoroughly search for and rule out any underlying metabolic or organic disease before relying solely on the psychiatric diagnosis. This caveat equally applies to the recent theories that weight gain experienced by the recovering anorexic may cause additional complications.[34] Any diagnosis of anorexia nervosa must involve a comprehensive medical workup before the diagnosis is accepted and must include collateral medical consultation and support through convalescence and recovery.

Anorexia nervosa is and remains an elusive disease medically and legally. Mr. Duke's daughter continues to intrigue.

REFERENCES

1. Morton, R.R. 1689. *Phtisiologia—or a Treatise of Consumption.* London: Smith.
2. Gull, W.W. 1868. "Address in Medicine Delivered before Annual Meeting of the British Medical Association at Oxford." *Lancet* 2:171.
3. Bruch, Hilde. 1970. *Changing Approaches to Anorexia Nervosa.* Boston: Little, Brown.
4. Feighner, J.P., et al. 1972. "Diagnostic Criteria for Use in Psychiatric Research." *Arch. Gen. Psychiatry* 26(1):57.
5. Crisp, A.H., and D.A. Toms. 1972. "Primary Anorexia Nervosa or Weight Phobia in the Male: Report on 13 Cases." *British Med. J.* 1:334.
6. Bruch, Hilde. 1973. *Eating Disorders: Obesity, Anorexia Nervosa and the Person Within.* New York: Basic Books.
7. Crisp, A.H. 1970. "Anorexia Nervosa: 'Feeding Disorder,' 'Nervous Malnutrition,' or 'Weight Phobia'?" *World Rev. Nutr. Diet* 12:452.
8. Garner, D.M. 1977. "Measurement of Body Image in Anorexia Nervosa." In *Anorexia Nervosa,* edited by R.A. Vigersky. New York: Raven Press.
9. Crisp, 452.
10. Morgon, H.G. 1975. "Value of Family Background and Clinical Features as Predictors of Long Term Outcome in Anorexia Nervosa: Four Year Follow-up Study of 41 Patients." *Psychol. Med.* 5:355.
11. Warren, M.P. 1973. "Clinical and Metabolic Features of Anorexia Nervosa." *Am. J. Obstet. Gynecol.* 117:435.
12. *Ibid.*
13. Rampling, D. 1978. "Anorexia Nervosa: Reflections on Theory and Practice. *Psych.* 41:296–301.
14. Crisp. A.H. 1965. "Clinical and Therapeutic Aspects of Anorexia Nervosa—A Study of 30 Cases." *J. Psychosom. Res.* 9:67–78.
15. Minuchin, S., et al. 1978. *Psychosomatic Families: Anorexia Nervosa in Context.* Cambridge, Mass.: Harvard University Press.
16. Thoma, H. 1967. *Anorexia Nervosa.* New York: International Universities Press, Inc.
17. Agras, S. 1977. "Behavior Modification in Anorexia Nervosa: Research Foundations." In *Anorexia Nervosa,* edited by R.A. Vigersky. New York: Raven Press.
18. Vigersky, R.A. 1976. "Anorexia Nervosa: Behavioral and Hypothalmic Aspects." *Clinics in Endocrin. and Metab.* 5:2.
19. Slade, P.D., and G.F.M. Russell. 1973. "Awareness of Body Dimensions in Anorexia Nervosa: Cross Sectional and Longitudinal Studies." *Psych. Med.* 3:188–199.
20. Bruch, *Eating Disorders.*
21. Crisp, A.H. 1976. "How Common Is Anorexia Nervosa? A Prevalence Study." *Br. J. Psychiatry* 128:549.
22. Bliss, E.L. 1960. *Anorexia Nervosa: Its History, Psychology, and Biology.* New York: Paul B. Hoeber.
23. *Ibid.*
24. Crisp, A.H., et al. 1977. "The Long Term Prognosis in Anorexia Nervosa: Some

Factors Predictive of Outcome." In *Anorexia Nervosa,* edited by R.A. Vigersky. New York: Raven Press.
25. Halmi, K. 1973. "Prognosis in Anorexia Nervosa." *Ann. Intern. Med.* 78:907.
26. Kern v. Kogan, 93 N.J. Super. 459 (1967).
27. Whitfield v. Ross, 10 C. 3d 874 (1974).
28. Warfield v. City of Wyandotte, 117 Mich. App. 83 (1982).
29. Spohrer v. Spohrer, 428 So.2d 1350 (La. 1983).
30. Strickland v. Harris, 615 F.2d 1103 (1980).
31. Missouri v. Mitchell, 563 S.W.2d 18 (Mo. 1978).
32. Battalia v. State of New York, 10 NY 2d 237 (1961).
33. Bridals v. Mutual Benefit, 62 Ill. App. 3d 542 (1978).
34. Rockwell, W.J. 1982. "Anorexia Nervosa: Review of Current Treatment Practice." *South Med. J.* 75:1101.

Legal Aspects of Neuroleptic-Induced Movement Disorders

Robert M. Wettstein, M.D.

INTRODUCTION

A variety of involuntary movement disorders are known to occur commonly following the use of neuroleptic medication (Ayd 1961). Neuroleptic medication denotes those neuropharmacologic agents that have antipsychotic activity and produce symptoms resembling disorders of the nervous system. The various syndromes differ according to phenomenology and clinical presentation, clinical course, time of onset after medication ingestion, timing and frequency of reversibility or persistence, response to pharmacological intervention or discontinuation of antipsychotic medication, demographic characteristics, association with other types of movement disorders, and complications or disability and disfigurement.

This chapter is organized into several sections. First, in order to orient the reader, a thorough review of the neuroleptic-induced movement disorders,, including acute dystonic reactions, pseudoparkinsonism, akathisia, tardive dyskinesia, and tardive dystonia will be presented. Several relevant, spontaneous movement disorders will also be discussed. Second, the malpractice aspects of neuroleptic-induced movement disorders will be reviewed, particularly focusing on negligence, breach of contract, fraud, and negligent misrepresentation. Third, a discussion of informed consent as it pertains to iatrogenic movement disorders will be presented. The fourth and final section addresses several recent areas of potential concern and liability for the practicing physician. This chapter will be primarily concerned with the antipsychotic medications and will not explicitly contend with the medicolegal implications of the numerous other medications that induce movement disorders. These include lithium carbonate, antihistamines, tricyclic antidepressants, amphetamines, methylphenidate, phenytoin and levodopa.

Acute Dystonic Reaction

Acute dystonic reactions are a heterogeneous group of movement and posture disorders which typically and abruptly develop within hours or days of the initial ingestion of antipsychotic medication (Ayd 1961; Swett 1975; Keepers et al. 1983). They consist of involuntary, sustained muscle contractions or an abnormality in muscle tone resulting in a disorder of posture of the face, neck, trunk, or limbs. Acute dystonic reactions usually manifest themselves as sustained retroflexion (opisthotonos) or twisting (torticollis) of the neck, upward deviation of the eyes (oculogyric crisis), facial grimacing, or involve the tongue, but may also affect pharyngeal or laryngeal muscles and be associated with respiratory distress (Bernstein 1983), dysphasia and dysarthria. Unusual or atypical reactions include carpopedal spasm, writhing limb movements, dystonic gait and scoliosis (Sovner & DiMascio 1978) which can occur in conjunction with other dystonic manifestations. Their onset may be sudden and alarming to the unprepared patient, and, though generally self-limited and benign, they may be temporarily disabling or painful (Cavenar et al. 1979). The disorders responds rapidly to an intramuscular or intravenous dose of anticholinergic medication as well as diphenhydramine or diazepam (Gagrat et al. 1978). Anticholinergic medication is sometimes prescribed as prophylaxis when antipsychotic medication is initially started (Keepers 1983). There is generally no need to decrease the dose of antipsychotic medication once the dystonia appears, but maintenance with an anticholinergic medication early in treatment generally forestalls a subsequent dystonia (Keepers 1983).

Prevalence data of the acute dystonias is imprecise and available data indicates that drug-induced dystonias occur frequently, in up to 64 percent of all patients in some reports (Chiles 1978). The reactions are more prevalent in men than women and decline in frequency with age; the peak incidence of dystonia is said to be in adolescence (Ayd 1961; Chiles 1978; Keepers et al. 1983). Prescription of the high potency neuroleptics, for example, butyrophones, thioxanthenes and the piperazine class of phenothiazines, is an additional risk factor (Swett 1975). The diagnosis of acute dystonic reactions is usually not difficult but they are sometimes misdiagnosed as conversion reactions (Bumpass & Knoll 1982; Lesser & Fahn 1978), seizure disorder, tetanus, stroke, dislocation, encephalo-meningitis, drug intoxication or calcium deficiency (Lee 1977). The etiology or pathophysiology of acute dystonias remains ill defined (Sovner & DiMascio 1978; Marsden & Jenner 1980; Tarsy 1983a).

Pseudoparkinsonism

Antipsychotic medication also induces pseudoparkinsonism which occurs at varying intervals, sometimes weeks to months, of continuous treatment (Ayd 1961; Rifkin et al. 1975). Ayd (1961) reported that 90 percent of cases of parkinsonism developed within the first 72 days of therapy. Like the acute dystonias, its presentation can be patient-related or dose-related (Freedman 1973). The most common drug-induced parkinsonian symptom is akinesia (Wells & Duncan 1980) with its attendant slowness in movements or hesitancy in initiating movements (bradykinesia), flattening of facial expression (hypomimia, amimia), micrographia and microphonia which can mimic and be confused with a depressive syndrome or the negative symptoms of a schizophrenic disorder (Rifkin et al 1975; Van Putten & May 1978). Such symptoms may be subjectively distressful to a patient and contribute to medication noncompliance (Jellinek et al. 1981; Van Putten 1974). Rarely, a drug-induced catatonic syndrome appears with waxy-flexibility, negativism, mutism, incontinence, withdrawal and posturing (Gelenberg & Mandel 1977). Use of a research rating scale (Simpson & Angus 1970) is sometimes helpful in distinguishing symptoms and establishing standardized, reliable and quantifiable symptom ratings over time. Other more typical parkinsonian features such as resting tremor, rigidity, anteroretropulsion, festinating gait, loss of postural reflexes, drooling, and sialorrhea also occur with treatment using antipsychotic medications (DeVeaugh-Geiss 1982). Pseudoparkinsonian symptoms generally disappear within a short time following the discontinuation of antipsychotic medication, though in some cases this may take many months (Klawans et al. 1973), and in 1 percent of cases, symptoms persist indefinitely (Marsden & Jenner 1980). As with the acute dystonias, pseudoparkinsonism has been reported to be more prevalent in men, and in those with decreasing age (Keepers et al. 1983; Moleman et al. 1982), though conflicting data exists (Ayd 1961) and precise prevalence data are unavailable. An incidence range of 2 to 56 percent has been reported, depending in part upon the definition of the syndrome (Donlon & Stenson 1976; Rifkin et al. 1978). High potency antipsychotic medications are more likely to induce such symptoms. Reduction in antipsychotic dosage or treatment with an antiparkinsonian medication is sometimes required for symptom relief for time-limited periods, though drug-induced parkinsonian symptoms may gradually and spontaneously disappear during the course of treatment. There is considerable controversy over the need for long-term prophylactic or maintenance treatment with antiparkinsonian medications (Klett & Caffey 1972; Johnson 1978; Jellinek et al. 1981; Rifkin et al. 1978). Prophylactic antiparkinsonian medication is effective to various degrees depending upon the patient's age and sex and antipsychotic type and dosage (Keepers et al. 1983; Moleman et al. 1982); maintenance antiparkinsonian medication may result in adverse anticholinergic symptoms, aggravate other disorders such as tardive dyskinesia, or interfere with the metabolism or activity of antipsychotic medication (Gautier et al. 1977), and be superfluous as tolerance to pseudoparkinsonism or antiparkinsonian medications develop. Though definitive answers to these questions remain unavailable, several recommended clinical management strategies have been made (McEvoy 1983):

1. Physicians should repeatedly question and assess patients for pseudoparkinsonian symptoms during neuroleptic treatment, and especially attend to its subtle, subjective or akinetic manifestations.
2. The dosage of antipsychotic medication should be directed to maximize therapeutic benefit and minimize side effects.
3. Anticholinergic agents should be used when the patient requires a dosage of antipsychotic medication that results in parkinsonian symptoms (i.e., when the parkinsonian symptoms cannot be controlled by antipsychotic dosage reduction and are intolerable to the patient).
4. Physicians should be aware of the side effects of anticholinergic agents and treatment for these side effects (Donlon & Stenson 1976).
5. Dosage of antipsychotic and anticholinergic medications should be maintained at the lowest possible levels.

Pseudoparkinsonism may be indistinguishable from idiopathic Parkinson's disease in an older patient (Wells & Duncan 1980). Clinical features of pseudoparkinsonism that may help to differentiate it from the idiopathic disease include its transient and nonprogressive course, onset early in the course of treatment, disappearance upon continuation of medication, bilaterality of signs, and response to anticholinergic medication (Hausner 1983). Both disorders, however, appear to be due to a functional deficiency of dopamine in nigro-striatal pathways (Tarsy, 1983). In making a diagnosis of pseudoparkinsonism, the diagnostician must exclude a variety of other neurologic, toxic, infectious, endocrine, and iatrogenic disorders (Klawans & Barr 1983).

The "rabbit syndrome" is a late onset antipsychotic drug-induced syndrome characterized by 5–5.5 per second rhythmic, involuntary perioral movements that mimic the masticatory movements of a rabbit. This syndrome is thought to be a form of drug-induced parkinsonism as it responds to antiparkinsonian agents, or withdrawal of neuroleptic medication, and may coexist with typical parkinsonian features (Villeneuve 1972; Jus et al. 1972; Sovner & DiMascio 1977). It has only been reported in middle-aged or older patients who have received antipsychotic medication for several years. It thus must be distinguished from the buccal-lingual-facial movements of tardive dyskinesia (*infra*), though the two syndromes may also coexist (Sovern & DiMascio 1977). Masticatory movements in the rabbit syndrome are more rapid and regular than those in tardive dyskinesia, and the tongue is not involved (Todd et al. 1983). Lastly, as noted above, the syndrome responds to antiparkinsonian medication, while tardive dyskinesia is often exacerbated by this intervention (Todd et al. 1983; Jus et al. 1974; Sovner & DiMascio 1977).

Akathisia

Akathisia, also commonly associated with antipsychotic medication, is a syndrome of motor restlessness composed of both subjective and objective elements, which has enjoyed a wide variety of clinical descriptions in the literature. In its mildest form, akatnisia presents subjectively with few observable signs (Braude et al. 1983). Patients report a nearly indescribable compulsion to move constantly, experience feelings of unease, and an inability to remain still whether sitting, lying or standing, which may be associated with or mistaken for generalized anxiety and fear. More severe akathisia presents with detectable signs such as agitation, frequent changes of posture and truncal or limb position, inability to remain standing, sitting or lying, shifting body weight from foot to foot, walking-on-the-spot, and semipurposeful leg and foot movements. The patient's activity is not stereotyped but appears to afford some relief to the inner restlessness and agitation. Its subjective distress has been reported to have precipitated suicide (Shear et al. 1983), or self-destructive behavior (Van Putten 1975), violence (Keckich 1978), exacerbation of psychosis (Simpson et al. 1976; Van Putten 1975; Van Putten et al. 1974), loss of concentration and job loss, and noncompliance with antipsychotic medication (Van Putten 1974).

Lack of precise diagnostic criteria or pathognomonic movements complicate the assessment of akathisia. It can readily be misidentified as psychotic agitation (Freedman 1973) which, if managed by increasing antipsychotic dosage, aggravates the syndrome. Its objective features may be difficult to distinguish from other disorders such as tardive dyskinesia (Munetz & Cornes 1982 refer to this as "pseudoakathisia"), though akathisia may coexist with tardive dyskinesia (Munetz & Cornes 1982, 1983; Braude & Barnes 1983; Barnes et al. 1983b), and parkinsonism (Braude et al. 1983; Van Putten 1975).

Akathisia, like acute dystonias and pseudoparkinsonism, is a prevalent side effect of antipsychotic drug therapy. Studies report frequencies of 21 percent (Ayd 1961, period prevalence), 25 percent (Braude et al. 1983, period prevalence), 26 percent (Keepers et al. 1983), period prevalence without anticholinergic prophylaxis), and 45 percent (Van Putten 1975, period prevalence) depending in part upon antipsychotic potency (Kane et al. 1978) and dosage (Braude et al. 1983). Frequency rates are higher for women than for men (Ayd 1961) and decline with age; those patients 20–40 years of age have the highest rates (Ayd 1961; Keepers et al. 1983; Braude et al. 1983). Onset of akathisia usually occurs within several weeks of neuroleptic treatment (Ayd 1961; Wells & Duncan 1980; Braude et al. 1983) but in some cases it becomes apparent after several months or years of treatment; this disorder has been referred to as "tardive akathisia" (Weiner & Luby 1983; Braude & Barnes 1983; Munetz & Cornes 1983). Its symptoms may spontaneously appear or disappear over time. Anticholinergic medication is only variably effective in prophylaxis and treatment (Keepers et al. 1983; Braude et al. 1983), though benzodiazepines have also been helpful. Decrease in neuroleptic dose or changing to a different class of antipsycotic medications is an often recommended treatment strategy. Rarely, akathisia persists for months after withdrawal of antipsychotic medication (Kruse 1960; Weiner & Luby 1983). The pathophysiology of akathisia is unknown and several hypotheses relating to pre- or postsynaptic dopamine receptor antagonism have been invoked to account for it (Marsden & Jenner 1980). Its sensory component may indicate that different neural systems are involved from those associated with the other neuroleptic side effects (Sovner & DiMascio 1978).

Tardive Dyskinesia

The discussion so far has focused on the transient acute dyskinesias (acute dystonias) which appear early upon the initiation or increase of treatment and disappear rapidly, and the subacute dyskinesias (pseudoparkinsonism and akathisia) which appear insidiously or later in treatment and disappear within weeks of its withdrawal. Mention was also made of reports of the late onset of akathisia (tardive akatnisia) or the chronic or persistent presentation of akathisia or pseudoparkinsonism even after discontinuation of treatment (Tarsy 1983b). Tardive dyskinesia shares some features of these chronic dyskinesias, since it is late (tardive) in onset during antipsychotic drug treatment and frequently persists after neuroleptic withdrawal.

The initial reports of tardive dyskinesia appeared in the German literature. Schonecker (1957) described three elderly women who developed lip-smacking movements following two to eight weeks' treatment with chlorpromazine. The dyskinesias persisted for at least four to eleven weeks in two of the patients following discontinuation of the phenothiazine. All three patients were described as having cerebral arteriosclerosis. Subsequent reports and investigations of the prevalence of tardive dyskinesia throughout the world have attracted increasing attention from a variety of disciplines including epidemiologists, endocrinologists, pharmacologists, neurologists, psychiatrists, and their affiliated disciplines. The American Psychiatric Association has recently published a Task Force Report on tardive dyskinesia (Baldessarini et al. 1980), offering a compendium of available clinical and research data on the subject while recommending several therapeutic and prophylactic intervention strategies.

The syndrome of tardive dyskinesia encompasses a variety of abnormal involuntary movements, excluding tremor, that appear late in the course of prolonged treatment with antipsychotic medication and that are not attributable to an alternative factor (Tarsy 1983b). The pharmacotherapy is thought to be a necessary but insufficient variable in the development of tardive dyskinesia, since not all patients receiving antipsychotic medication develop this syndrome. Dyskinesias affecting the mouth, lips, tongue and face are typically noted and include involuntary chewing, mouthing, sucking, puckering, smacking, and licking movements. Dyskinesias of the fingers, hands, arms, feet, trunk and diaphragm can also develop, the latter of which present with tachypnea, dyspnea (Jeste & Wyatt 1982a; Weiner et al. 1978) and dysarthria (Faheem et al. 1982). The movements of tardive dyskinesia are generally described as choreo-athetoid, though tics, grimacing, and dystonic forms also occur (*infra*) (Mueller & Aminoff 1982). Tardive dyskinesia is exacerbated by changes in arousal, anxiety, and stress, and improves with sedation and is abolished during sleep; it spontaneously fluctuates in severity and distribution (Gardos & Cole 1980). Its frequency and amplitude are attenuated or abolished by voluntary activity of the muscles in the affected areas, but are increased by movements in distant parts (Crane & Naranjo 1971). Researchers have used videotaped rating techniques (Barnes & Traver 1982), instrumentation (e.g., electromyography), and several quantitative rating scales to more accurately assess tardive dyskinesia (Gardos et al. 1977). In marked contrast to the subjective distress of a patient with akathisia, patients are often unaware of or untroubled by their tardive dyskinesia movements (Ananth 1980; Alexopoulos 1979; Deveaugh-Geiss 1979) until they become severe (Rosen et al. 1982).

Diagnostic criteria for tardive dyskinesia, as they are for other involuntary movement disorders, are currently in evolution (Classification of Extrapyramidal Disorders, 1981). While most authorities assert that antipsychotic drug use for many months or even years precedes the onset of tardive dyskinesia, tardive dyskinesia has developed following one month of drug exposure (Chouinard & Jones 1979; Schonecker 1957). Various subtypes of tardive dyskinesia have been described; it may initially and insidiously appear during antipsychotic drug therapy or following a reduction or withdrawal of drug therapy. The latter, designated "withdrawal-emergent dyskinesias," is sometimes not considered to represent tardive dyskinesia. In this case, antipsychotic agents, possibly through their hypokinetic or parkinsonian effects, are considered to have masked tardive dyskinesia. Either subtype may remit or persist following the withdrawal of antipsychotic medication, though transient or withdrawal dyskinesias may represent reversible phases in the evolution of persistent tardive dyskinesia (Tarsy 1983a; Gardos et al. 1978). Schooler & Kane (1982) have recently proposed uniform research diagnostic criteria for tardive dyskinesia.

Not all dyskinetic movements of patients taking antipsychotic drugs represent tardive dyskinesia, and an extensive list of dental, medical, neurologic, toxic and infectious conditions must be excluded (Granacher 1981; Tarsy 1983a). Use or intoxication with levodopa, tricyclic antidepressants (Fann et al. 1976), lithium carbonate (Beitman 1978; Apte & Langston 1983), amphetamines, antihistamines (Thach et al. 1975), phenytoin (Chadwick et al. 1976), benzodiazepines (Kaplan & Murkofsky 1978), and antimalarials (Osifo 1979) have also been reported to induce dyskinesias resembling tardive dyskinesia. Some differentiating features may be present, for example, tardive dyskinesia has been reported to primarily affect orofacial areas, while levodopa-induced dyskinesias more often involve trunk and limbs (Karson et al. 1983). The appropriate diagnostic evaluation of a patient with dyskinetic movements must be individualized, but might include neurological consultation, serum chemistry profile, liver and thyroid function tests, urinary copper levels, serum ceruloplasmin and electroencephalography (Baldessarini et al. 1980).

Cross-sectional epidemiological studies report a considerable range of tardive dyskinesia incidence and prevalence depending on diagnostic criteria for the syndrome, the patient sample, and the locus of treatment. A recent review of 56 studies of patient populations exposed to antipsychotic medication calculated an average prevalence of tardive dyskinesia of 15 percent (Kane & Smith 1982), after correcting for the rates of spontaneous dyskinesias (*infra*). Tardive dyskinesia is prevalent in outpatient psychiatric populations as well as inpatient samples (Mukherjee et al. 1982). Some studies indicate that the prevalence of tardive dyskinesia has increased significantly over the past 20 years (Kane & Smith 1982). Rates are strongly related to increase in age between 40 and 70 years and possibly to female sex (Kane & Smith 1982; Jeste & Wyatt 1981). Increasing age has also been correlated with increasing symptom severity (Smith & Baldessarini 1980). Children rarely develop tardive dyskinesia during antipsychotic drug treatment, but may develop withdrawal emergent dyskinetic symptoms when antipsychotic medication is discontinued (Polizos & Engelhardt 1978). In part because of methodological considerations, the literature does not as yet support a firm relationship between the incidence or prevalence of tardive dyskinesia and several hypothetical risk factors: drug type, maximum drug dose, cumulative drug exposure, length of drug exposure, psychiatric diagnosis, presence of associated neurological conditions, or previous extrapyramidal side effects (Baldessarini et al. 1980; Jeste & Wyatt 1982a). It has been suggested that patients with major affective disorders have a higher risk of developing tardive dyskinesia (Rush et al. 1982; Yassa et al. 1983); state dependent dyskinesias have been reported in the depressed phase of manic-depressive patients which remit in the manic phase (Cutler & Post 1982). Both psychotic and nonpsychotic individuals develop tardive dyskinesia when exposed to antipsychotic medication (Klawans et al. 1974). Concomitant use of anticholinergic drugs has also been thought to be a risk factor in the development or course of tardive dyskinesia, but there is conflicting data about this (Gardos & Cole 1983a).

Information on the natural history of tardive dyskinesia, whether antipsychotic medications are maintained or not, is of critical clinical and legal significance. Some earlier reports of its clinical course suggested that tardive dyskinesia was an irreversible or "permanent," if not a progressively disabling, disorder (Crane 1971), though increasing data dispute this. Remission of dyskinetic symptoms following drug termination has varied from 0 to 92 percent depending on the particular study, patient population, duration of drug exposure, and follow-up interval (Baldessarini et al. 1980). Jeste and Wyatt (1982a) concluded that reversal of dyskinetic symptoms after neuroleptic withdrawal occurs in 37 percent of dyskinetic patients, and suggest that the reversal rate is highest within the first three months of drug withdrawal. Because of the masking effects of antipsychotic medication, however, many studies report a short-term exacerbation of dyskinetic symptoms when medication is withdrawn (Branchey et al. 1981). Further, some reports indicate reversal only after several drug-free years (Klawans & Tanner 1983; Yagi et al. 1976; Itoh & Yagi 1979), so the longer the withdrawal, the greater the chance of symptom remission (Jeste & Wyatt 1982a; Gardos & Cole 1983b). Advancing age (over 30 years) has been consistently correlated with irreversibility, though this observation is contaminated in that the fewer years remaining in a patient's lifetime, the less opportunity there is for a late-occurring reversibility of the syndrome. Other prognostic factors have yet to be identified (Smith & Baldessarini 1980; Gardos & Cole 1983b). Drug holidays, periods of drug discontinuation, have been recommended to decrease the longitudinal risk of tardive dyskinesia, but their value remains undetermined (Shenoy et al. 1981; Pyke & Seeman 1981; Seeman 1981). One study reported that an increased number of drug-free intervals of at least two months each was associated with persistent, not reversible, tardive dyskinesia (Jeste et al. 1979). Because antipsychotic medication reduction or withdrawal so frequently exacerbates psychotic symptoms, reversibility of dyskinetic symptoms is more properly viewed in the context of continued antipsychotic therapy. Few prospective studies of this issue are, however, available. In one recent representative report, Barnes et al. (1983a), in a three-year prospective longitudinal study of the course of tardive dyskinesia in 99 patients regularly receiving maintenance antipsychotic medication, found that the point prevalence increased from 39 percent to 47 percnt. Of the patients, 63 percent did not change their tardive dyskinesia status; 38 percent remained free of dyskinesia throughout the three-year period, while the condition persisted in 25 percent. Tardive dyskinesia developed anew in 37 percent of those who did not initially have dyskinesia, while remission of symptoms occurred in 36 percent of patients who initially had tardive dyskinesia. The investigators speculated that the apparent symptom remission while on increased maintenance medication represented covert or masked dyskinesia rather than a genuine remission. They reported that orofacial movements, but not limb or trunk movements, increased over the course of drug treatment. Other recent studies indicate that dyskinetic symptoms will not typically worsen with continued antipsychotic medication, and may be stable or improve over time, particularly if the dosage of medication is reduced (Kane et al. 1983; Gardos 1983; Wegnar & Kane 1982; Kane et al. 1982; Iton & Yagi 1979). Indeed, there is reason to question the notion that persistent tardive dyskinesia is an irreversible state (Itoh & Yagi 1979). Further research is clearly indicated to determine the outcome of patients with tardive dyskinesia, whether or not they continue to receive medication, as well as to explore the risk factors for persistent tardive dyskinesia. It is important to note that tardive dyskinesia can progressively worsen or result in a number of physical and emotional complications: embarrassment and ostracism (DeVeaugh-Geiss 1982), dental problems, oral ulcerations, dysarthria, and swallowing disorders, as well as respiratory, gastrointestinal and gait disturbances which can become life-threatening (Casey & Rabins 1978; Jeste & Wyatt 1982). Dyskinesias have also been reported to interfere with manual dexterity (Breuning 1982). One report of increased mortality in patients with tardive dyskinesia has not been reiterated (Mehta et al. 1978).

The etiology and pathophysiology of tardive dyskinesia remain the subject of intense investigation, and excellent reviews of this subject are available (Baldessarini et al. 1980; Jeste & Wyatt 1982). It has been predominantly hypothesized that tardive dyskinesia is associated with postsynaptic dopamine receptor hypersensitivity consequent to prolonged neuroleptic dopamine receptor blockade (Baldessarini et al. 1980). Numerous therapeutic strategies for tardive dyskinesia have been proffered with generally unsuccessful results (Jeste & Wyatt 1982b). Withdrawal of antipsychotic drugs may transiently aggravate tardive dyskinesia, but later frequently reverses it. Increase in antipsychotic dosage may acutely suppress the dyskinetic movements but may worsen them in the long run. Intervention is directed to primary or secondary prevention, with temporizing tardive dyskinesia, until nonneuroleptic antipsychotic medication becomes available (Baldessarini et al. 1980).

Tardive Dystonia

Though choreiform movements have predominately characterized presentations of tardive dyskinesia since its earliest reports, there have been occasional reports of chronic persistent or late onset dystonia as a movement disorder related to antipsychotic medication. Cases of persistent opisthotonus

(Shields & Bray 1976), scoliosis, retrocollis (Druckman et al. 1962), torticollis (Angle & McIntire 1968), orofacial-mandibular (Weiner et al. 1981) and limb dystonia (Dabbous & Bergman 1966) have been described. Barnes et al. (1983b) reported that 9.3 percent of 182 psychiatric patients receiving antipsychotic medication for at least one year experienced dystonic movements or postures. Systematic epidemiological and clinical data has, however, been unavailable in this area. Burke and colleagues (1982a, 1982b) reported recently their cumulative experience with 42 patients who developed persistent dystonia during or within two months after treatment with antipsychotic drugs. The investigators designated the condition as tardive dystonia if chronic dystonia were present, antipsychotic drug therapy preceded or occurred with the onset of dystonia, causes of secondary dystonia (Parkinson's disease, Huntington's disease, Wilson's disease, mass lesions, cerebral lipidosis) were excluded by appropriate clinical and laboratory evaluation, and the patient's family history were negative for dystonia. These authors remarked, however, that tardive dystonia is a particular type of tardive dyskinesia rather than a distinct or separate entity from choreic tardive dyskinesia. Indeed, some of their patients had oral or peripheral chorea, tremor, or myoclonus as well. The age of onset of tardive dystonia varied from 13–60 years, with a mean of 34 years, and was related to bodily distribution of dystonia.

The mean age of onset for men was 29.0 years, less than that of 41.5 years for women, but dystonia severity did not vary between the sexes. Though tardive dystonia usually developed after several years of antipsychotic drug therapy (mean 3.7 years), it presented within three days in one patient, and within one month in another. The type or duration of antipsychotic drug therapy did not correlate with the severity of dystonia. The patients were followed for as long as eleven years after symptom onset; generally, "dystonia was insidious in onset, progressive for months or years and then persistent but stable for years" (Burke et al. 1982b, 1339). Almost all patients had the onset of dystonia during treatment with antipsychotic medication, but tardive dystonia typically persisted following discontinuation of therapy, sometimes for years. As with tardive dyskinesia, increase in the dose of antipsychotic medications sometimes suppressed the dystonia, but dopamine depletion with tetrabenazine, not available in the United States, was frequently beneficial. In contradistinction to tardive dyskinesia, anticholinergic medication was beneficial in 39 percent of cases of chronic dystonia.

In these reports, tardive dystonia was phenomenologically indistinguishable from idiopathic torsion dystonia or secondary dystonia *(infra).* In contrast to idiopathic dystonia, the tardive dystonia patients had limb or trunk involvement with dystonia of face and neck, and tardive dystonia did not progress to a severely disabling condition as would be expected with idiopathic dystonia. The authors acknowledged the possibility of a coincidental appearance of idiopathic chronic dystonia during the course of antipsychotic drug therapy, but considered this unlikely.

While the Burke et al. (1982a, 1982b) reports should be considered accumulated case reports rather than systematic epidemiological or controlled data, they represent a significant contribution to the literature on tardive dystonia. Accumulated experience with tardive dystonia, the dystonic form of tardive dyskinesia, remains meager, and firm conclusions about prevalence, complications, treatment, pathophysiology, and its relationship to other forms of dystonia or tardive dyskinesia, remain unavailable.

Spontaneous Movement Disorders

Of great clinical and legal significance are reports of spontaneous movements in individuals never exposed to antipsychotic drugs which have been reported for decades in chronically hospitalized patients (Bleuler 1950). Such movements have been noted in chronic schizophrenic or psychiatric populations, in neurologic patients (Appenzeller & Biehl 1968), in geriatric or nursing home populations, and in dental clinics. Mannerisms, unusual ways of carrying out purposeful activity, and stereotypies (repetitive, perhaps ritualistic, isolated purposeless movements) have been observed and can be difficult to distinguish from each other or from the choreo-athetotic movements of neurologic or iatrogenic disorders (Marsden et al. 1975). In view of the critical importance of the spontaneous disorders, a brief discussion and review of the recent research is in order.

Bourgeois et al. (1980) surveyed 211 elderly residents of a retirement home in France who had not been exposed to antipsychotic medication. Eighteen percent of this group was noted to have oral-facial-lingual or extremities movements. Women had twice the incidence of dyskinesias (27 percent) as did the men (12 percent). Comparison of this nondrug exposed sample with 59 other residents who had been treated with antipsychotic medication in the past revealed that 42 percent of the latter had a movement disorder. Thus, antipsychotic medication increased the risk of developing dyskinesias by a factor of 2.35. Greenblatt et al. (1968) determined that 2 percent of nursing home patients not exposed to antipsychotic drugs presented with dyskinesias at any bodily site, while 39 percent of the patients receiving antipsychotic drugs were so affected. Varga et al. (1982) surveyed nursing homes and senior citizen centers and rated 365 subjects for the presence of oral dyskinesias. Though the investigators were unable to calculate the exact incidence of dyskinesia, they reported that a minimum of 10.3 percent of patients had oral dyskinesia. Blowers et al. (1982) investigated dyskinetic movements in geriatric nursing home patients. Dyskinesias were detected in 11 percent of women and 21.6 percent of men unexposed to neuroleptics. Dyskinesias were much more prevalent among women who had received neuroleptics (21.6 percent) than among those who had not, though this was not true of the men. Kane et al. (1982) reported that 4 percent of 127 senior citizens in the community without a psychiatric or neurologic history had abnormal involuntary movements when evaluated with the Simpson Dyskinesia Scale (Baldessarini et al. 1980).

Barnes et al. (1983b), using a single-blind standardized videotape rating technique, evaluated 85 nonpsychiatric controls with a median age of 38 as part of a larger study of involuntary movement disorders. Of this group, 52.4 percent manifested "semi-purposeful or purposeless normal movements," 9.8 percent manifested "oral-facial dyskinesias," and 2.4 percent showed "choreiform movements" of a pathological nature. Oral-facial dyskinesia was significantly more likely to be present in those people over age 50; there were significantly more subjects below age 50 with no significant movements. Klawans and Barr (1982) surveyed a nonpsychiatric population between the ages of 50 and 79 who had no history of neuroleptic use, "overt brain disease" or dentures who had been referred to neurologic consultation. Of their 661 patients, 4.7 percent had lingual-facial-buccal dyskinesias. The incidence increased with age by decade: 0.8 percent of patients between the ages of 50 and 59, 6.0 percent between the ages of 60 and 69, and 7.8 percent between the ages of 70 and 79. Of those between 60 and 79 years of age, the incidence was greater in women (8.4 percent) than men (4.6 percent), with a combined incidence of 6.8 percent. In a study of 240 patients between 60 and 99 years of age, not exposed to antipsychotic medication, Delwaide and Desseilles (1977) reported that 36.7 percent presented with involuntary repetitive buccolinguofacial movements and 4.2 percent with stereotypic movements of the limbs. The incidence of the dyskinesia did not increase with age, but 44 percent of the women, compared with 15 percent of the men, manifested dyskinesias. Brandon et al. (1971) examined psychiatric inpatients for facial dyskinesia and determined that 19.7 percent of 285 patients never exposed to antipsychotic medication were so afflicted. By sex, 29.3 percent of women and 12.3 percent of men had facial dyskinesia; the authors excluded "simple habits" and stereotypies such as "bizarre grimacing movements" from the results.

In a unique investigation, Owens et al. (1982) were able to identify 47 hospitalized chronic schizophrenic patients with a mean age of 66.7 years who had never been exposed to antipsychotic medication. Using standardized rating instruments for abnormal involuntary movements, they determined that more than half of the sample had abnormal movements to at least a mild degree, and 36.2 percent showed abnormal movements to a moderate degree in any body area. The bodily distribution and severity of abnormal movements in this sample were very similar to those in a hospitalized neuroleptic-treated schizophrenic group.

Lieberman et al. (1983) surveyed 400 medically healthy individuals over 65 years of age in the community using standardized dyskinesia rating scales. Only 1.2 percent of the sample showed a spontaneous movement disorder. This was in contrast to 4.8 percent of a sample of elderly patients hospitalized for medical conditions, and 16.5 percent of a group of institutionalized, elderly antipsychotic medication-treated patients. Serious medical conditions and antipsychotic treatment each increased the dyskinesia incidence by a factor of four.

Orodyskinesias have also been reported in nonpsychiatric, medically healthy persons who are edentulous, or wear dentures with grossly incorrect occlusions. Koller (1982) reported that 16 percent of edentulous patients, with a mean age of 62 years, had orofacial dyskinesias involving the jaw, lips or tongue which spared the upper face and limbs. Tooth extraction averaged 12 years before the onset of the movements. This investigator referred to this syndrome as "edentulous orodyskinesia." Sutcher and colleagues (1971) reversed their edentulous patients' dyskinesias with a dental prosthesis or proper construction of complete dentures. Lastly, Brandon et al. (1971) noted that edentulous institutionalized psychiatric patients over 50 years of age were a high risk group for tardive or spontaneous facial dyskinesia. Forty-six percent of such patients had facial dyskinetic movements, compared to 21 percent of patients who had more than four teeth or wore dentures.

In conclusion, as with tardive dyskinesia, a wide incidence or prevalence range for spontaneous involuntary movements has been reported. Studies variously include tics, habits, grimacing, mannerisms, or stereotypic movements along with dyskinetic movements. One report concludes that a prevalence of 5–10 percent of spontaneous dyskinetic movements in institutional populations is accurate (Kane & Smith 1982). Despite some conflicting data (Blowers et al. 1982; Owens et al. 1982) suggesting that a syndrome of abnormal involuntary movements may be a manifestation of a disease process such as schizophrenia rather than of its treatment (Crow et al. 1982), almost all studies conclude that prolonged use of antipsychotic medication significantly increases the risk of developing the dyskinetic movements.

It also should be mentioned that persistent dystonias occur spontaneously, unrelated to the use of antipsychotic medication. Specific focal disorders such as blepharospasm (Jankovic et al. 1982), torticollis (Matthews et al. 1978), or heterogeneous idiopathic syndromes such as torsion dystonia appear spontaneously in adults and may be more familiar to neurologists than psychiatrists (Marsden 1976a; Marsden & Harrison 1974). As noted above with regard to the acute dystonias, there is some controversy over the etiology and prevalence of some chronic dystonias, implicating both organic and functional factors (Cavenar et al. 1978; Volow et al. 1980). Spontaneous oral-facial-cervical dystonias have attracted increasing attention in recent years, though such a syndrome was first reported by Meige in 1910 (Tolosa & Klawans 1979). Currently denoted by a variety of terms, Meige's disease, Meige's syndrome, idiopathic orofacial dystonia (Tolosa 1981), blepharospasm-oromandibular dystonia, and Brueghel's syndrome (Marsden 1976b), the syndrome may include persistent blepharospasm and prolonged focal or generalized dystonic spasms of the face, lips, tongue, jaws, larynx, neck, trunk or extremities (Jankovic & Ford 1983). The disorder may be confused with a variety of functional conditions including Gilles de la Tourette's Syndrome (Tolosa 1981), though may coexist with other neurologic conditions such as essential tremor, parkinsonism, akathisia and multiple sclerosis. Its differential diagnosis from tardive dyskinesia or tardive dystonia may not be easy (Glazer et al. 1983; Jankovic 1981). Lastly, the disorder can progress in intensity or distribution to a severely disabling or incapacited state; no consistently effective pharmacological intervention has yet been identified.

While each of the spontaneous and antipsychotic drug-induced movement disorders have been presented individually, it is well known that these disorders coexist in various combinations. Drug-induced parkinsonism, for example, can be associated with tardive dyskinesia (Wolf et al. 1983; Richardson & Craig 1982), akathisia, dystonia (Moleman et al. 1982), rabbit syndrome, Meige's Syndrome (Jankovic & Ford 1983), and tardive dystonia (Burke et al. 1982b). Tardive dyskinesia can be seen with parkinsonism, akathisia (Brandon 1971), rabbit syndrome (Sovner & DiMascio 1977) and tardive dystonia (Burke et al. 1982b). Lastly, akathisia can be found with pseudoparkinsonism (Moleman et al. 1982), Meige's Syndrome (Jankovic & Ford 1983), and tardive dyskinesia (Munetz & Cornes 1982). Such combinations of spontaneous and neuroleptic effects complicate clinical management of the patient, as the use of anticholinergic drugs, for example, may suppress the patient's parkinsonian features but exacerbate the dyskinetic movements. Continual monitoring of the patient's neurologic and psychological status while minimizing polypharmacy as much as possible remains the prudent standard of care. As with the presentation of any medication side effect, it is important to evaluate the benefits of antipsychotic drug therapy in light of its risks. This is particularly a problem with the neuroleptic medications, since decrease or withdrawal of the medication when one or more side effects develop so frequently exacerbates the presenting psychotic disorder.

With a review of the clinical aspects of neuroleptic-induced movement disorders in mind, we can now begin a discussion of their legal aspects.

NEGLIGENCE

Many physicians have become accustomed to real increases in malpractice insurance premiums over the last decade allegedly consequent to escalating numbers and costs of medical malpractice claims. Recurrent medical malpractice "crises," whether referring to the prevalence of medical misconduct or the escalation in litigation and premiums, have often been alleged. The frequency and severity of medical malpractice claims against physicians increased dramatically in the early 1970s and many private insurance carriers withdrew from the market when premiums lagged behind claim costs (Danzon 1983). According to a recent Rand Corporation study using data available through 1980, physician malpractice claim frequency sharply tapered off between 1975 and 1980 but claim severity (awards) increased throughout the decade and outpaced the general rate of inflation (Danzon 1982). Between 1971 and 1978, the mean incurred cost per claim against physicians increased at 12.4 percent per year, compared to 18.9 percent for claims against hospitals. Increases in medical malpractice claim frequency exceeded increases in other tort litigation (e.g., product liability bodily injury claims, manufacturers' and contractors' bodily injury claims) but severity of the latter claims exceeded that for malpractice. Danzon (1982) reported that the increased density of physicians (number per capita) correlated positively with the frequency of claims against physicians, but not with their severity. Thus, the 40 percent increase in practicing physicians between 1960 and 1978 accounted for 24 percent increase in claims over this interim. The increase in lawyer density was positively related to claim severity but not frequency. Even after controlling for higher physician and attorney density in urban states, it was found that urbanization was the single most powerful predictor of claim frequency and severity in the 1970s, as higher awards were adjudicated by urban courts. The Rand study also determined that several pro-plaintiff changes in common law doctrines contributed significantly to the escalation in claims against physicians in the early 1970s. States that abolished the locality rule and governmental or charitable immunity, and adopted doctrines of informed consent and *respondeat superior* by 1970 had claim costs per capita in 1976 over twice as high as states that had not incorporated any of these changes. The last two mentioned doctrines, particularly informed consent, appeared to have had the greatest impact in increasing claim costs (Danzon 1982). In response to the physicians' malpractice crisis in the mid 1970s, many states enacted tort reforms to reduce litigation and awards. States that mandated the offset of compensation from collateral sources and those that limited awards significantly reduced claim severity within two years. The impact of other tort reforms, such as reducing the statute of limitations, limiting contingency fees, restricting the informed consent and *res ipsa loquitur,* eliminating *ad damnum* clauses, introducing structured settlements or binding arbitration and malpractice screening panels, could not be ascertained given the short outcome period in the study. Such reforms, however, did not appear to account for the post-1976 reduction in claim frequency against physicians. Despite these reported frequency reductions, however, claim frequency and severity recently appears to be escalating and large premium increases have again been requested of physicians (Malpractice Awards 1982; Curran 1983). In 1978, for example, plaintiffs won 13 verdicts of $1 million or more; there were 45 such verdicts in 1981 (Lavin 1983). Physicians' malpractice crises are regularly reported in the medical news (Litigation 1983; Lavin 1983) and major reforms in the tort system, such as no-fault compensation for medical injuries, continue to be advocated (Tancredi 1982a). Such calls for reform become particularly significant when it is realized that at most one in ten incidents of malpractice result in a claim, and less than half of these, or one in twenty-five of total injuries, receive payment (Danzon 1983). Further, for every dollar that reaches a plaintiff as compensation, one dollar is spent on litigation and another on insurance overhead (Danzon 1983).

Such frequency surveys of malpractice claims have, however, been predominantly concentrated upon claims against physicians. Data regarding claims against hospitals is less available because of hospital self-insurance. Information about malpractice claims against drug manufacturers or nonphysician healthcare providers such as nurses, pharmacists and psychologists is also less available.

Malpractice actions against psychiatrists, who prescribe the vast majority of antipsychotic medication, are said to be relatively scarce compared to those against other medical practitioners or specialists. It has been estimated that one out of four nonpsychiatric physicians will file a malpractice claim with an insurer each year, while one out of twenty-five psychiatrists is expected to file a claim (APA Malpractice 1983). Fishalow (1975) has ascribed the relative scarcity of professional malpractice claims against psychiatrists to several factors:

1. The imprecise nature and diagnosis of mental disorders.
2. The patient's consequent difficulty in formulating clear expectations for the results of treatment and evaluating treatment.
3. Difficulty establishing the cause of emotional injuries, given the limited knowledge about psychiatric etiology.
4. Difficulty in establishing acceptable clinical standards because of the diversity of therapeutic schools and techniques.
5. Reluctance of patients to publicize their psychiatric histories and conditions.
6. Reluctance of patients to sue their psychiatrists, with whom they may have developed a close relationship over a long period of time.
7. The alleged ability of the psychiatrist to dispel the patients' negative therapeutic reaction.

Taub (1983) suggests that increased expectations of the efficacy of psychiatric treatment, an emphasis on patients' rights in recent mental health litigation, and the publication of sizable verdicts in psychiatric malpractice cases have contributed to an increase in psychiatric malpractice claims. Indeed, the American Psychiatric Association malpractice insurance program reports that claim frequency and severity have doubled over the last five years (APA Malpractice 1983). The cost of an average claim in the American Psychiatric Association's insurance program, whether or not it proceeds to trial, is currently $35,000. The types of claims, and their proportion to the total number of cases have not, however, changed over the years of the program. Improper treatment, constituting one-quarter of the claims against psychiatrists, is the most common complaint, while suicides and drug treatment failures or reactions each account for one-fifth of the recent complaints. Less than 15 percent of claims arise from failure to diagnose/improper diagnosis, or failure to restrain a patient. Hogan (1979) and Slawson et al. (1978) have provided a compendium of psychiatric malpractice cases for the interested reader.

Psychiatrists and physicians in general have been found liable for their patients' neuroleptic-induced movement disorders under several causes of action including negligence and informed consent. Physicians are potentially liable as well for injuries due to breach of contract, fraud, and negligent misrepresentation. Hospitals have been held liable for the negligent acts and omissions of their physician employees or medical staff which have resulted in antipsychotic drug-induced movement disorders. Lastly, pharmaceutical manufacturers have been found liable for inadequately warning of the risks of their antipsychotic drugs when their use has resulted in movement disorders.

It is well established in tort law that the plaintiff-patient has the burden of proving by a preponderance of the evidence that the physician-defendant's conduct deviated from the applicable standard of medical care, that the patient suffered damages because of the negligent conduct, and that the physician's conduct was the proximate cause of the patient's injuries (Slovenko 1981). Negligence is not presumed from an adverse result but is defined as that "conduct which falls below the standard established by law for the protection of others against unreasonable risk of harm."[1] Analogously, the physician is not liable for any adverse consequence of treatment, but is only obligated to exercise that degree of care and skill ordinarily employed under similar circumstances by experts in his field. Neurologists, psychiatrists or other specialists voluntarily assume and are held to a higher standard of care than generalists because of their additional training and experience.

As suggested above, despite the fact that antipsychotic drug-induced movement disorders are iatrogenic complications of medical treatment, their presence is not presumptive evidence of negligence. It must be demonstrated that the disorder proximately resulted from negligent care by the physician. Such malpractice cases against physicians are representative of those for any drug use or reactions in general. The physician risks liability for injuries sustained from negligence in the areas of history taking, physical examination and laboratory evaluation prior to treatment (Beresford 1972; Tozer & Kasik 1967), prescription of a drug without customary medical indication, prescription of a Federal Drug Administration approved drug for a non-Federal Drug Administration approved usage, prescription of an excessive dosage,[2] prescription of an inadequate dosage,[3] prescription of medication for inappropriately short or long time periods, failure to recognize, monitor or treat side effects or toxicity,[4] failure to abate the possibility of drug reactions or interactions (Junewicz 1979), failure to consult the necessary experts (Twardy 1978; Gutheil & Appelbaum 1982) or refer the patient to the necessary consultant.

With regard to iatrogenic movement disorders, the physician is potentially liable for negligent prescription of antipsychotic medications in excessive dosages, for improper indications, or for an excessive period of time. It might be alleged that the physician did not attempt to reduce or withdraw medication during the course of treatment. Should acute or persistent dystonia, pseudoparkinsonism, akathisia or tardive dyskinesia develop, there is conceivable liability for a failure to detect, diagnose and monitor its presence. Tardive dyskinesia, in particular, may be overlooked in part because patients may be unaware of, unconcerned with, or deny the presence of, their involuntary movements (Ananth 1980; Alexopoulos 1979; DeVeaugh-Geiss 1979; Rosen et al. 1982). Or, as indicated earlier, concomitant parkinsonism, akinesia or bradykinesia can mask or attenuate tardive dyskinesia (Richardson & Craig 1982). Negligence in diagnosis of the iatrogenic movement disorders can occur in a variety of ways. Clinicians can misattribute the signs and symptoms of the neuroleptic related disorders to other disorders, for example, spontaneous movements, conversion disorder, Huntington's chorea, or Meige's syndrome. They can also overdiagnose an iatrogenic disorder, thus failing to diagnose another condition, for example, neoplasm, dental problem, or manganese intoxication. Lastly, physicians might negligently fail to diagnose all coexisting neuroleptic related disorders, if more than one exists, or confuse one such disorder with another, for example, mistaking akathisia for tardive dyskinesia (Munetz & Cornes 1983). Clinicians are similarly liable for negligent failure to appropriately treat these disorders if they fail to at least consider reducing or withdrawing neuroleptics once tardive dyskinesia, tardive dystonia, or disabling akathisia appear, fail to adequately treat acute dystonias or pseudoparkinsonism with anticholinergic or other medication, or if they fail to obtain appropriate neuropsychiatric consultation.

The fragmentary state of our knowledge about these disorders, particularly tardive dyskinesia and tardive dystonia, creates several problems in pursuing or defending a negligence cause of action. One cannot speak of a single or consensual standard of care when clinical and research opinion is heavily divided about the acceptability or efficacy of:

1. Primary or secondary prophylaxis of acute dystonias, pseudoparkinsonism, or akathisia with anticholinergic medication.
2. Maintenance of anticholinergic medication while a patient is on antipsychotic medication.
3. Drug holidays for patients maintained on antipsychotic medication.
4. Periodic attempts to decrease or withdraw antipsychotic medication in high-risk patients who readily decompensate, whether or not the patients have tardive dyskinesia or tardive dystonia.
5. Routine expensive diagnostic tests such as electroencephalogram, computerized axial tomography of the head, slit-lamp examination, urinary copper determination or neurological referral.
6. A variety of treatment approaches to tardive dyskinesia and tardive dystonia, most of which have met with inconsistent or unsatisfactory results.

In the absence of a uniform method of assessment, particularly for tardive dyskinesia, symptom ratings become idiosyncratic according to the individual examiner. In the absence of specific biological markers for these disorders, their diagnosis and classification are descriptive, not objective or etiological, in nature.

In contrast to the earlier so-called conspiracy of silence among physicians which rendered expert testimony under the locality rule nonexistent, a plaintiff's attorney should have little difficulty obtaining an expert willing to testify to virtually any purported medical standard derived in retrospect, despite any possible deviation from majority or representative opinion (Falk & Conn 1983). Beyond the fact that medical standards in developing medical disciplines may be precariously egocentric, any such standards evolve over time with the state of the art (Sanbar & Thompson 1983). Thus, for example, while drug holidays were uniformly recommended several years ago to decrease the longitudinal exposure to antipsychotic drugs, and thus the risk of developing tardive dyskinesia or tardive dystonia, such advice is no longer so widely dispensed. Similarly, as more longitudinal information about the reversibility of tardive dyskinesia and tardive dystonia or the consequences of neuroleptic withdrawal becomes available, then it might become less (or more) advisable to decrease or withdraw neuroleptic medication when movement disorders first present.

Standards of care for medical malpractice litigation do not, of course, always redound to professional opinion testimony, whether representative or otherwise. If available, guidelines or standards from medical or health associations, specialty boards, licensing authorities, accrediting organizations, governmental rules, regulations, guidelines, or statutes may define the appropriate standard by which to judge a defendant's conduct. Thus, the violation of a state or hospital rule requiring neurological evaluation for all patients receiving antipsychotic medication for longer than one year might be argued as evidence of negligence. Rarely, courts have rejected medically defined standards of care and articulated their own,[5] though they more typically defer to expert opinion.[6] Organizational or authoritative treatises as well as the *Physicians' Desk Reference* are also used to cite medical standards. The *Physicians' Desk Reference,* however, contains prescribing information for only those pharmaceuticals for which documentation establishes certain indications. According to the Food and Drug Administration, "once a drug has been approved for marketing, a physician may prescribe it for uses or in treatment regimens of patient populations that are not included in the approved labeling. Such unapproved or, more precisely, unlabeled uses may be appropriate and rational in certain circumstances and may, in fact, reflect approaches to drug therapy that have been extensively reported in medical literature" (FDA Drug Bulletin 1982). Neither the *Physicians' Desk Reference* nor the manufacturer's package inserts are intended to be a pharmacology textbook; Food and Drug Administration control over the contents of the package insert is not intended to legislate the practice of medicine. With few exceptions, therefore,[7] deviation from the package insert's recommendations for use will not represent negligence per se (Shapiro 1978). Further, the *Physicians' Desk Reference* does not necessarily address all aspects of drug prescription; for example, it does not specify the maximum permissible dose of most antipsychotic medications when used in an adult psychiatric setting.

The establishment of causation in a negligence cause of action for the persistent neuroleptic-induced movement disorders can also be problematic, as in many medical malpractice cases: there may be difficulty in proving the absence of a preexisting or coexisting noniatrogenic movement disorder such as spontaneous dyskinesias or Parkinson's disease; the patient may have been prescribed other nonantipsychotic medications known to cause dyskinesias; coexisting medical problems such as chronic obstructive pulmonary disease, perhaps aggravated by the patient's use of tobacco, may exacerbate involuntary movements (Campbell et al. 1983); the natural course of akathisia, tardive dyskinesia and tardive dystonia with probable spontaneous fluctuations in symptom severity, distribution and reversibility is unknown; the etiology of tardive dyskinesia and tardive dystonia is sufficiently unclear that at present, use of neuroleptices is just one risk factor among many for the onset of movement disorders; and lastly, the typically long interval between initiation of drug therapy and the onset of the tardive dyskinesia and tardive dystonia permits a question of intervening cause, such as the underlying disorder itself or other disorders such as cerebral ischemia.

Nevertheless, successful professional negligence cases for neuroleptic-induced involuntary movement disorders have occurred, though they are difficult to locate. Individual insurance carriers, drug manufacturers or other defendants rarely publish their data, and its acquisition is largely anecdotal. Psychotropic drug treatment failures or adverse reactions in general accounted for one-fifth of the American Psychiatric Association's malpractice insurance program's recent claim experience (APA Malpractice 1983), though the proportion of this group of claims related to neuroleptic-induced movement disorders is unavailable. Related cases of negligent diagnosis of movement disorders in neurology have also been reported (Malpractice 1977). The following cases of iatrogenic movement disorders have been cited in the literature.

In Lesser v. Farb and Smith Kline and French Laboratories,[8] a 30-year-old woman brought suit against her prescribing physician and the drug manufacturer. The patient had been prescribed Stelazine for depression, and developed grimacing, blinking, and parkinsonian tremor. The plaintiff charged the physician with negligence in continuing to prescribe Stelazine after the patient developed side effects. She also alleged that the manufacturer's warnings in the *Physicians' Desk Reference* and the manufacturer's package inserts that such side effects were rare and readily reversible were misleading, given the medical literature reports of irreversible extrapyramidal disorders. The suit was settled for $180,000 after two days of trial.[9]

In Collins v. Cushner,[10] a 56-year-old housewife consulted a family practitioner for treatment of anxiety. The physician diagnosed "spactic colon" and prescribed low doses of Stelazine for six years between 1969 and 1975. For a 29-month period, the patient was not seen by the defendant physician but received renewals of her prescription by telephone. The patient developed jerking movements in her arms and hands and the defendant discontinued the Stelazine for two months but then reinstituted Stelazine within a month and doubled the dose. Six months later, the physician prescribed Cogentin to treat her involuntary facial movements. In the lawsuit, the plaintiff charged that the defendant continued to prescribe Stelazine despite product information warnings regarding its use in the treatment of anxiety as well as warnings of long-term use by females in the patient's age bracket of developing tardive dyskinesia. She further alleged that treatment with Cogentin had aggravated rather than relieved her condition. The litigation was settled for $125,000.[11]

In Torres v. Bronx Lebanon Hospital,[12] a jury awarded $400,000 to a young woman who suffered persistent extrapyramidal symptoms and a seizure disorder as a result of an excessive dose of Compazine (prochlorperazine). A 17-year-old girl, without a past history of neurologic or psychiatric illness, presented to a hospital emergency room complaining of nausea and vomiting. She was given a 25 mg intramuscular injection of Compazine and discharged from the emergency room with a prescription for additional Compazine, of which she took little or none. Over the next 36 hours she developed extrapyramidal symptoms including oculogyric crisis and spasms of the tongue, and returned to the hospital into which she was then admitted. She was subsequently discharged to the clinic with a diagnosis of pseudoparkinsonism secondary to Compazine and was prescribed Artane. The plaintiff developed recurrent grand mal seizures with an abnormal electroencephalogram over one month following her initial dose of Compazine. Extrapyramidal symptoms persisted despite continued treatment with Artane. At the time of trial, the extrapyramidal symptoms were in remission but her seizure disorder required maintenance anticonvulsant medication. The jury awarded $400,000 for negligent prescription of an excessive intramuscular dose of Compazine, two to five times the regular dose according to the *Physicians' Desk Reference,* and $2000 for failure to inform the patient's mother, her legal guardian, of the risk of extrapyramidal symptoms, a known side effect of phenothiazines.[13]

In Rector v. Gilbert,[14] a 26-year-old female teacher consulted a general practitioner for treatment of flu symptoms. The defendant physician did not perform a physical examination but diagnosed depression due to a chemical imbalance after administering a "scratch test" as well as the Zung Depression Rating Scale. The patient was admitted to the hospital nine days later and was diagnosed as having a flu syndrome as well as a central nervous system dysfunction with multiorgan complaints. The physician initially prescribed Elavil, Stelazine and Librium in the hospital where the patient remained for nine days. Elavil 300 mg each day, Stelazine 20 mg a day, and Valium 20 mg a day were prescribed for the plaintiff as an outpatient in addition to her weekly visits with the physician. The patient developed blurred vision, drowsiness and tremors which impaired her orientation, concentration, attention, memory, muscle coordination, mood and affect. The patient complained to her physician about her side effects but was told that if she did not continue to take her medication she would die from her inherited chemical imbalance. Her school performance and social life deteriorated and she resigned from her teaching position. The medication was continued for two and one-half years, in the last six months of which the patient did not see her physician, until she spontaneously terminated treatment. Subsequent psychological and psychiatric evaluation revealed mild organic brain damage affecting memory, learning, and concentration in the absence of movement disorder, which was assumed to be permanent in nature. The suit against the physician alleged negligent diagnosis, improper treatment with inappropriate medication in excessive doses for unnecessary duration, and failure to recognize and treat medication side effects. A jury returned a $238,000 verdict, following a 30 percent reduction for the plaintiff's comparative negligence in remaining in the care of the physician. Damages included permanent organic brain damage and psychological sequela.[15]

In Faigenbaum v. Oakland Medical Center et al.,[16] a 50-year-old Michigan woman began to experience symptoms of tardive dyskinesia involving her face and limbs in 1976, after an undetermined number of years of antipsychotic drug treatment, starting in 1964, particularly with Thorazine. She had in the past been treated as an inpatient and outpatient for a recurrent depressive disorder but had also been diagnosed as suffering from a schizophrenic disorder. She voluntarily admitted herself in 1976 to Clinton Valley Center, a state psychiatric hospital, for evaluation and treatment of her movement disorder, and remained there for over one year. During this time, when her movement disorder progressed to involve her face, neck, mouth, speech, throat, extremities and gait, she was simultaneously referred for neurological evaluation at the adjacent Oakland Medical Center, a state operated medical-surgical facility. There, a neurologist employed by the Medical Center diagnosed Huntington's chorea although the patient's family history was negative for the disease, and recommended that the patient be treated with Haldol. Haldol, up to ten milligrams daily, sometimes in conjunction with Mellaril or Triavil, was prescribed by several treating psychiatrists at Clinton Valley Center during her hospitalization in 1976 and 1977, as the physicians apparently relied on the neurologist's diagnosis and ignored a diagnosis of tardive dyskinesia made by two other consulting physicians. Her antipsychotic medication was discontinued in November, 1977 at the family's request and the patient was discharged from Clinton Valley Center in January, 1978 with a diagnosis of Huntington's chorea and hysterical neurosis, conversion type. A diagnosis of major affective illness or schizophrenia was not made at that time though secondary psychiatric problems consequent to the prolonged involuntary movement disorder were alleged. After the patient was discharged from the hospital, her family obtained medical consultation elsewhere and a diagnosis of tardive dyskinesia was made. Suit was brought against the consulting neurologist, eight psychiatrists, two internists, Clinton Valley Center, Oakland Medical Center, Sinai Hospital, William Beaumont Hospital, and the manufacturers of Haldol, Mellaril and Thorazine. Causes of action against the physicians included negligent failure to consider tardive dyskinesia within a differential diagnosis, failure to obtain a drug or neurological history, and improper prescription of antipsychotic medication. The psychiatrists in particular were alleged to have improperly relied exclusively upon the consultant's diagnosis and report. *Res ipsa loquitur,* absence of informed consent to the patient and her family, assault and battery, and fraudulent misrepresentation were also alleged by the plaintiff. Defendant hospitals were charged with the vicarious liability for the negligent and intentional tortious acts of the physician-defendants who were employed by or worked in those facilities. Defendant pharmaceutical manufacturers were alleged, in product liability action, to have failed to adequately warn physicians of the side effects of their antipsychotic drugs, and to have failed to adequately warn after a time in which the defendant knew or should have known of the side effects of the drug. The *Physicians' Desk Reference* through 1982 stated that persistent tardive dyskinesia was "rarely reported with Haldol," allegedly contrary to clinical experience. The plaintiff settled for $378,000 against several defendants, including the neurolgist, three psychiatrists and two hospitals (Sinai and William Beaumont) which had treated her prior to her state hospitalization. The court determined that governmental immunity for state psychiatric institutions and their employees shielded Clinton Valley Center and three other psychiatrists from liability even though the patient was treated primarily for a physical disorder at that facility. Oakland Medical Center, the state medical-surgical facility, was not immune from suit and a 1 million dollar jury verdict was obtained, plus $350,000 for costs and interest. Subsequent settlements totalling $100,000 with drug manufacturers for inadequate warnings to physicians of the risks of tardive dyskinesia were also obtained. The court made its determination on grounds of negligence, but ruled against theories of implied contract, *res ipsa loquitur,* and intentional torts, the last of which would not have been immune from suit. Damages were assessed for medical expenses, compensation for injuries, and pain and suffering but not for lost wages or future earnings.[17]

In Clites v. State of Iowa,[18] a mentally retarded patient at a state hospital-school brought action against the hospital for medical malpractice. Admitted to a state residential facility for the mentally retarded at age 11, the patient was prescribed a "myriad of different tranquilizers, administered in various combinations, under the auspices of several different physicians" for "aggressive behavior" beginning at age 18.[19] Medication continued for five years before tardive dyskinesia of the face and extremities was diagnosed. After expert testimony about the standard of care for such a patient, the court determined that (1) medication was inappropriately used for the convenience of the staff, not for the treatment of the patient. Evidence of the severe aggression or self abuse required to justify such use of major tranquilizers was lacking; (2) the patient was improperly monitored as he "was not regularly visited by a physician and physical exams had not been conducted for a three-year period"; (3) the staff, "without justification, ignored the known risks of uninterrupted use of major tranquilizers";[20] (4) the medical staff negligently failed to react to the patient's symptoms of tardive dyskinesia and alter the drug treatment program; (5) the attending physician, being unfamiliar with tardive dyskinesia, negligently failed to obtain consultation; (6) polypharmacy, the concurrent use of multiple drugs, was not warranted by the patient's status and the particular drugs involved; and (7) that the patient's "parents were never informed of the potential side effects of the use, and prolonged use, of major tranquilizers, nor was consent to their use obtained" violated the "standard that requires some form of informed consent prior to the administration of major tranquilizers."[21] The absence of such consent to medication, the court said, contrasted with the hospital's requirement for written consent to use the patient's photograph at a presentation. The trial court also rejected the defendant's argument that the patient's parents implicitly consented to the treatment, since they were "not informed of the risks attendant to the treatment program".[22] The Iowa Court ruled for the plaintiff and awarded $385,165 for future medical expenses, and $375,000 for past and future pain and suffering. The District Court's ruling was subsequently upheld in the Iowa Court of Appeals.[23]

A wide variety of general and specialty practitioners prescribe antipsychotic medications and are confronted with the panoply of involuntary movement disorders as adverse reactions. Both nonpsychiatric and psychiatric patients, many of whom may not be psychotic or severely disturbed, receive such medication. While it is unclear whether the practitioner not specializing in neurology or psychiatry will be held to the same standard of care in the diagnosis and treatment of these disorders, it appears that all physicians will at least be required to become aware of the existence of such disorders, take notice of such disorders when they clinically present, make the appropriate differential diagnosis, modify their treatment regimen, or refer the patient for neuropsychiatric consultation. The physician is additionally expected to document his observations, conclusions and treatment plan in the patient's medical record.

Because of their potential persistence, severity, and disability, tardive dyskinesia and tardive dystonia represent the greatest potential legal liability to the physician compared to acute dystonias, parkinsonism, or akathesia, though multiple movement disorders may be alleged to be present. Thus, it is important to question the prolonged prescription of such medication in nonpsychotic, especially nonpsychiatric patients or those over age 50 years, particularly if it is borne out that psychiatric patients with affective disorders are at higher risk of developing tardive dyskinesia. Even the short-term use of antipsychotic medications, however, can result in significant or persistent involuntary movement disorders, particularly in children, so such use must be judicious and informed. The primary care physician, whether psychiatrist or general practitioner, must not relinquish responsibility to his consultant for the diagnosis and treatment of these disorders. The primary care physician risks liability for either disregarding or overrelying upon the consultant's diagnosis and recommendations. He must independently evaluate the patient's condition, utilizing his own skills and knowledge, while appropriately documenting his reliance or rejection of the consultation report.

The considerable prevalence of tardive dyskinesia and tardive dystonia among inpatients as well as hospital-based outpatients constitutes high risk liability for hospitals as well as for the prescribing and consulting physicians. Hospitals are vicariously, though not directly, liable for the negligent acts of their employees within the scope of their employment, whether physicians, nurses, or other medical staff, under the doctrine of *respondeat superior.* Hospitals may also be liable for the negligent acts of independent contracting physicians when the latter are apparent or ostensible agents of the hospitals under an expansion of *respondeat superior* (Southwick 1983). The doctrines of "captain of the ship" and "borrowed servant" have also been restricted by the courts in recent years, resulting in further expansion of vicarious hospital liability. Yet, hospitals are also directly liable under the doctrine of corporate negligence when the hospital owes a defined legal duty directly to the patient which is not delegable to its personnel. Beyond the corporate duties to select and maintain hospital equipment, buildings and grounds, hospitals must exercise reasonable care in selecting and retaining employees and its medical staff (Miller 1983). While case law regarding a hospital's duty to monitor the quality of hospital-based medical care is in various stages of development in different jurisdictions (Hollowell 1982), the hospital administration or governing board must be certain that an organized medical staff is periodically reviewing clinical care by staff physicians (Southwick 1983). Many public hospitals (and their employees), where the majority of chronically medicated psychiatric patients reside, are shielded from liability for unintentional torts by governmental immunity. But, in some jurisdictions, as in the Michigan case reported above, immunity is highly selective and depends upon the type of medical care rendered in the facility.[24] With regard to the neuroleptic-induced movement disorders, then, hospitals will be vicariously liable for the negligent omissions and acts of their employed physicians, consultants and nursing staff when the employees fail to meet the standard of care in the use of antipsychotic medication and in the diagnosis and treatment of movement disorders. In addition, hospitals should have guidelines or policies concerning the indications and dosage of antipsychotic medications when used singly or multiply, resources and provisions for periodic neurological assessment of patients maintained on antipsychotic drugs, and an adequate capacity to transfer or refer patients with serious complications referable to these drugs. An appropriate medical record keeping system for both inpatients and hospital clinic outpatients is critical to adequately assessing the persistent movement disorders over time and over change in locus of treatment. Hospitals have the right, if not the duty, to suspend, terminate or otherwise modify the hospital privileges of those independent or contracting staff physicians, whether generalists or specialists, who do not conform to contemporary usage of antipsychotic medication, or those who show inappropriate disregard for the development or presence of persistent tardive dyskinesia and tardive dystonia.

BREACH OF CONTRACT

Epstein (1976, 93) states that "the typical malpractice case raises issues of both tort and contract." The "relationship between physician and patient is contractual insofar as the former provides services and the latter pays for them" (Ficarra 1980, 194). The physician is not, however, held to be a guarantor of results. While the defendant's negligence is usually the issue in malpractice litigation, suits against physicians for breach of contract or warranty occasionally occur. This happens when the doctor promises or is understood to have promised a particular result, often a cure, which does not eventuate (Wilkinson 1981).[25] Courts have held that it is for the finder of fact to determine whether the physician's statements were reassurances or promises, and whether he failed to fulfill that warranty.[26] In a breach of contract action, it is not necessary for the plaintiff to establish the defendant's negligence (Ficarra 1980), but such causes of action are difficult to prove. With regard to neuroleptic-induced movement disorders, a physician would be susceptible to such an action should he promise, or appear to promise, the absence of side effects to antipsychotic drugs, or success in the treatment of the disorder, even though his treatment met the standard of care.

FRAUD

Fraud in the physician-patient relationship has received only brief consideration in the medico-legal literature (Stevens 1983). Litigation against physicians for fraudulent diagnosis and treatment is uncommon, as suit is usually brought under other causes of action including negligence, assault and battery, or breach of contract. Fraud is an intentional tort whose elements include material misrepresentation by the defendant; knowledge of its falsity; intent to defraud (i.e., to induce reliance); justifiable reliance; and resulting injury.[27] The scienter, or knowledge, element of fraud has been subject to various interpretations, owning to different problems in its proof. Section 526 of the Restatement (Second) of Torts defines a misrepresentation as fraudulent if the maker "(a) knows or believes that the matter is not as he represents it to be, (b) does not have the confidence in the accuracy of his representation that he states or implies, or (c) knows that he does not have the basis for his representation that he states or implies". Physicians who falsely and deliberately assure a patient that a proposed procedure is without risk, who knowingly misrepresent the nature, outcome or prognosis of a completed procedure, or who by false reassurance willfully conceal negligence or disease from the patient are actionable for fraud (Holder 1978). Mere silence or nondisclosure by the physician is not actionable as fraud (James & Gray 1977). In such cases, the statute of limitations for a negligence cause of action will be tolled,[28] and the defendant is additionally liable for punitive damages for fraud, and if other physicians are involved, for conspiracy as well.[29] Further, the statute of limitations for a cause of action sounding in fraud may significantly exceed that in negligence, and many medical malpractice policies do not cover a physician for intentional torts. In Nelson v. Gaunt, the defendant physician was held to have knowingly and intentionally misrepresented the risks of the proposed treatment (silicone injections for breast augmentation) as having "absolutely no side effects",[30] and knowingly and intentionally represented that he could safely administer the silicone that in fact could be administered only under the restriction and controls of state and federal authority of which he did not inform the patient. The patient was awarded 1.5 million dollars in punitive damages plus $450,000 in special and general damages when injury necessitating six surgical procedures ensued.

The related tort of negligent misrepresentation, previously recognized in pecuniary transactions, has also recently been applied to physician-patient relationships.[31] Many courts, however, subsume actions for fraud and negligent misrepresentation under negligence or informed consent doctrines.[32] The Restatement (Second) of Torts, Section 311, notes the elements of a claim for negligent misrepresentation involving a risk of physician harm:

- One who negligently gives false information to another is subject to liability for physical harm caused by action taken by the other in reasonable reliance upon such information, where such harm results (a) to the other, or (b) to such third parties as the actor should expect to be put in peril by the action taken.
- Such negligence may consist of failure to exercise reasonable care (a) in ascertaining the accuracy of the information, or (b) in the matter in which it is communicated.

In Bloskas v. Murray, the court held that evidence that the defendant falsely reassured the patient of the non-risk of a complication which eventuated, and evidence that the defendant falsely but negligently represented his prior surgical experience to the patient should both be presented to the jury under the tort of negligent misrepresentation, independently of informed consent liability.

Liability for negligent or intentional (fraudulent) misrepresentation about a patient's proposed or completed treatment has been distinguished from that about a patient's condition. While courts have generally not required disclosure of a physician's own malpractice to the unawares patient,[33] some commentators have advocated such a duty by the negligent physician or any other medical personnel cognizant of such negligence (Vogel & Delgado 1980; LeBlang 1981). Such a duty would arise as a corollary to the physician's obligation to obtain informed consent from the patient, a goal of which is to promote the patient's autonomy and self-determination *(infra)*. It is argued that the patient's need for information is not confined to the pretreatment period, but that information about the posttreatment condition of the patient is also essential to the patient's physical and psychological well-being, particularly insofar as the patient may need to seek further treatment. It remains unclear, however, whether the negligent physician under such a duty would be obligated to inform the patient of the medical condition and its iatrogenesis or indicate further that such an iatrogenic injury constituted malpractice (i.e., a requirement which would represent a legal assessment or judgment).

There is currently no available case law pertinent to fraud or negligent misrepresentation with regard to neuroleptic-induced movement disorders (Hogan 1979). It seems clear that the physician, whether a general practitioner or specialist, should not misrepresent his credentials, experience or skills in the diagnosis and treatment of these disorders. When confronted with a patient with an iatrogenic movement disorder, the physician should so indicate this to the patient, though the latter may deny this, especially when mild tardive dyskinesia is involved. The physician should not misrepresent or deny, if the patient asks, and arguably should volunteer if the patient does not ask, that the involuntary movement disorder is a result of negligence, if the clinician believes this to be the case. The physician is not, however, generally under any affirmative obligation to volunteer this belief. Such an allegation might, in some circumstances, be difficult to sustain on behalf of any particular physician, especially where multiple treating and consulting physicians are involved in the patient's care, as in many public institutions and clinics. Lastly, a patient with a persistent iatrogenic movement disorder, particularly tardive dyskinesia and tardive dystonia, should not be informed even with benevolent intent that his movements are transient or insignificant, especially when they appear to be otherwise.

INFORMED CONSENT

The modern doctrine of informed consent to medical treatment and research has been the focus of considerable attention in law and medicine in its brief history. Its antecedents extend back in time for hundreds of years in English common law. Since the beginning of the century in the United States, nonconsented medical treatment was actionable under theories of trespass or assault and battery, notwithstanding the exercise of reasonable care in its performance; "any unlawful or unauthorized touching of the person of another, except it be in the spirit of pleasantry, constitutes an assault and battery."[34] When a physician exceeded the expressly consented diagnostic procedure and excised a fibroid tumor, Justice Cardozo wrote in 1914,

Every human being of adult years and sound mind has a right to determine what shall be done with his own body; and a surgeon who performs an operation without his patient's consent commits an assault for which he is liable in damages.[35]

The traditional law of consent, as opposed to informed consent, required only that the physician explain the nature of the proposed procedure to the patient and obtain express or implied consent, absent an emergency.[36] A successful action for battery did not require the patient to be physically injured by the medical intervention and did not require proof that the plaintiff would not have submitted to the procedure had the physician fulfilled the duty of advising the patient of its nature (Katz 1977). Further, nominal and punitive damages for dignitary injuries may be awarded. Nearly a half-century later, a California court ruled that the scope of a physician's disclosure to the patient must exceed that of the nature of the proposed procedure:

A physician violates his duty to his patient and subjects himself to liability if he withholds any facts which are necessary to form the basis of an intelligent consent by the patient to the proposed treatment. Likewise, the physician may not minimize the known dangers of a procedure or operation in order to induce his patient's consent.[37]

This court coined the term "informed consent" in its enlarging of the scope of the physician's disclosure, but ambiguously qualified the duty by according it with doctor's discretion:

In discussing the element of risk a certain amount of discretion must be employed consistent with the full disclosure of facts necessary to an informed consent.[38]

Three years later, the Kansas Supreme Court perpetuated this expansion of the law of battery in holding a radiologist liable for not disclosing the risks of cobalt radiation treatment to a postoperative mastectomy patient.[39] Emphasizing the principle of "self-determination" for a patient, the court specified the physician's obligation

to disclose and explain to the patient in language as simple as necessary the nature of the ailment, the nature of the proposed treatment, the probability of success or of alternatives, and perhaps the risks of unfortunate results and unforeseen conditions within the body.[40]

The court, treating the case as a negligence action, noted that the physician's duty of disclosure is limited to those disclosures that a reasonable medical practitioner would make under the same or similar circumstances. Lastly, and also in accord with the law of negligent malpractice, it required that the physician's failure to adequately disclose constitute a proximate cause of the patient's injury:

If, of course, the appellant would have taken the cobalt irradiation treatments even though Dr. Kline had warned her that the treatments he undertook to administer involved great risk of bodily injury or death, it could not be said that the failure of Dr. Kline to so inform the appellant was the proximate cause of her injury.[41]

Twelve years later, two courts continued the expansion of the judicial doctrine of informed consent and rejected a disclosure of medical information standard determined by the medical community as inconsistent with the premises of the doctrine, namely, the patient's right to self-determination and autonomy.[42] The Cobbs court ruled that giving physicians discretion as to their disclosures to patients is "irreconcilable with the basic right of the patient to make the ultimate informed decision regarding the course of treatment to which he knowledgeably consents to be subjected".[43] *Canterbury* articulated the scope of the medical disclosure according to its "materiality," defined as,

When a reasonable person, in what the physician knows or should know to be the patient's position, would be likely to attach significance to the risk or cluster of risks in deciding whether or not to forego the proposed therapy.[44]

Most, but not all, informed consent to treatment cases have sounded in negligence theory rather than battery,[45] where nondisclosure vitiates consent:

The battery theory should be reserved for those circumstances when a doctor performs an operation to which the patient has not consented. When the patient gives permission to perform one type of treatment and the doctor performs another, the requisite element of deliberate intent to deviate from the consent given is present. However, when the patient consents to certain treatment and the doctor performs that treatment but an undisclosed inherent complication with a low probability occurs, no intentional deviation from the consent given appears; rather, the doctor in obtaining consent may have failed to meet his due care duty to disclose pertinent information. In that situation the action should be pleaded in negligence.[46]

Battery theory differs from negligence actions in statute of limitations, need for expert testimony, proof of causation, and available damages (Ludlam 1978; Katz 1977). Battery theory is properly invoked where the physician fails to disclose the nature of, or obtain consent to, a procedure, obtains consent to perform a procedure but exceeds the scope of that consent, performs a substantially different procedure, or misrepresents its severity[47] (Ludlam 1978).

The legal doctrine of informed consent presupposes three indispensable elements: provision of information to the patient or the patient's representative by the physician, patient voluntariness, and patient competency (Meisel et al. 1977; Dickens 1981). Both case law and subsequent statutory developments have almost exclusively been concerned with the information disclosed by the physician to the patient and have ignored the more problematic issue of whether patients comprehend or utilize the provided data.

Informed consent to treatment case and statutory law almost invariably indicate that the patient is entitled to medical information from the physician without having to ask for it. Oregon's informed consent statute[48] uniquely modifies this by requiring the physician to explain in general terms the procedure or treatment to be undertaken as well as the existence of treatment alternatives or treatment risks, without actually disclosing those alternatives or risks. It then requires the physician to ask if the patient wants additional explanation and disclose as a reasonable medical practitioner would. In theory, the legal doctrine requires the disclosure of several elements: the nature and purpose of the proposed procedure or treatment, the risks or hazards of the proposed intervention, and its anticipated benefits as well as any available alternatives. In practice, however, jurisdictions have only variably specified the requisite disclosure elements in case law or statute and are frequently silent on particular requirements (Meisel & Kabnick 1980). Supplementary disclosures which have sometimes been recommended include: the nature and diagnosis of the patient's condition, the probability of success and failure of the proposed intervention, the risks and benefits of alternative (Rosoff 1981; Taub 1982; Kraft 1980), or no treatment,[49] the right of the patient to receive or waive the disclosure, the right of the patient to decide or waive the decision about the intervention itself (Meisel 1979), and the patient's right to withdraw consent for the intervention at any time. Most of the litigation against physicians regarding informed consent, however, pertains to the nondisclosure of the risks of treatment rather than the nondisclosure of the other required or supplementary elements.

As noted above, the scope of the disclosure duty is determined by the professional or patient oriented standard.[50] The professional standard requires disclosures that correspond to those made by a reasonable medical practitioner or by prevailing medical practice. This standard is established by the medical profession and is the duty of disclosure in the vast majority of jurisdictions (Miller 1980). Some jurisdictions have retained or adopted a locality rule with the customary medical standard, thus requiring the physician to make disclosure "in accordance with the accepted standard of medical practice among members of the profession with similar training and experience in the same or similar medical community".[51] In contrast, several appellate courts,[52] but just two state statutes,[53] have adopted a lay or material risk standard of disclosure. Here the physician is required to disclose information that a person "would be likely to attach significance to the risks or cluster of risks in deciding whether or not to forego the proposed therapy."[54] Such materiality may be viewed in the subjective case of the particular patient or in the objective or hypothetical case, the former of which has been criticized as burdening the physician with having to guess the informational needs of his patient.[55]

Despite judicial proclamations of what constitutes materiality, particularly with regard to medical risks, it does not seem possible to articulate this with any degree of reliability, clarity, or uniformity. While the relevant parameters of materiality with regard to disclosure of risks include likelihood (foreseeability) of the risk and severity of the injury, disproportionate weight may be given to the severity of injury in cases of very severe, though rare, side effects (Halligan 1980). Ozzi (1982) notes that courts have

found physicians liable for failure to disclose a 3 percent chance of death, a 1 percent chance of loss of hearing, a one eight-millionth chance of anemia, a 1.5 percent chance of loss of an eye (and) a one five-hundreth chance of perforation of the esophagus (Ozzi 1982, 123).

Conversely, a risk that occurs frequently, regardless of severity, may be considered material. Some jurisdictions specify that "common," "known," "remote," or "minor" risks need not be disclosed (Meisel & Kabnick 1980). The disclosure of risk burden may also be a function of the benefits or alternatives of treatment, as burden may be greater when the benefit-risk ratio is low or where comparable treatment alternatives exist, as well as inversely (Mills 1974; Miller 1980). One court has also introduced a temporal parameter, ruling that a physician had a duty to warn his patient of risks when he learned of them subsequent to his initial intervention.[56] This lack of clarity in articulating disclosed rules prompted Hawaii and Texas to create administrative agencies empowered to standardize what information, particularly risks of treatment, must be disclosed prior to specific medical or surgical diagnostic and treatment procedures.[57] Risk disclosure in Texas depends upon a predetermined list of certain medical procedures and their risks, disclosure of which on the approved written consent form creates a rebuttable presumption that informed consent was obtained. The physician need not volunteer the risks of procedures on another established list, but would be compelled to do so should the patient so request (Richards & Rathbun 1982). Such a standardized disclosure-nondisclosure system has been criticized as dehumanizing, unethical and unconstitutional (Meisel & Kabnick 1980; Curran 1979b).

The breach of a duty of care in a negligence cause of action does not establish liability. Similarly, a physician is not held liable for failing to disclose a medical risk without the patient's having been physically harmed, though a dignitary injury may have ensued (Goldstein 1975). Indeed, that undisclosed risk must materialize in damages which must occur as a proximate cause of the breach of care. This requirement has been referred to as "injury causation" (Meisel & Kabnick 1980). Further, the plaintiff must prove that he would have refused the proposed procedure or treatment had he been properly informed about it. This "decision causation" (Meisel & Kabnick 1980) may be viewed from the perspective of the particular plaintiff (subjective test) or the hypothetical reasonable person in the patient's situation (objective test). The objective test has been the more prevalently used test, given the issue of credibility of a plaintiff's retrospective judgment aided by hindsight and self-interest in the subjective test (Epstein 1976; Samuels 1982). The objective causation test, too, has received criticism in that it presupposes a single reasonable response to a medical situation (Katz 1977).

A final consideration from a legal prospective relates to the exceptions to the physician's duty to inform the patient and obtain consent (Meisel 1979; McClellan 1982). The exceptions, sometimes referred to as defenses, include emergency, therapeutic privilege, incompetency, and waiver. These are enunciated to various degrees in case law and statute but are typically recognized in dictum (Meisel & Kabnick 1980). Though easy to recite, they are neither simple to define nor apply. Definitions of an emergency, for example, the most commonly recognized exception to the requirements for informed consent, vary widely and the urgency of medical care is not so simply divisible into binary categories of emergency and nonemergency care. It is generally believed, though, that the physician can treat the patient in an emergency without disclosure or without consent when there is insufficient time to disclose and secure consent and "harm from the failure to treat is imminent and outweighs any harm threatened by the proposed treatment."[58] It is then unclear whether the physician should secure a surrogate's informed consent[59] or not. Therapeutic privilege, the second most commonly recognized exception (Meisel & Kabnick 1980) permits the physician to avoid disclosing any information, usually the risks of the procedure or the uncertainty of its success, which would be detrimental to the patient. The privilege might be invoked where divulgence would "foreclose a rational decision, complicate or hinder the patient, or perhaps even pose psychological damage to the patient"[60] but not where the patient would refuse the treatment if aware of the nondisclosed information. Such information may[61] or may not[62] then be disclosed to the patient's representative. Incompetence of the patient to consent to treatment, whether de jure or de facto (Meisel 1979) will also suspend either or both of the physician's duties to the patient. The absence of a uniform definition or threshold of acceptable decisional capacity renders this exception particularly troublesome to implement (Roth et al. 1977; Appelbaum & Roth 1982). Further, the determination of the identity of the proxy decisionmaker and the scope of the proxy's authority are often unspecified (Meisel & Kabnick 1980). Lastly, a patient may waive the physician's disclosure or treatment itself and prefer to have the physician decide; the physician should not disclose information against the patient's wishes.[63]

While the foregoing discussion of informed consent has focused on its legal aspects, its clinical, sociocultural and philosophical implications should not be neglected. Indeed, the theoretical and empirical literature on patient decision making and informed consent has grown tremendously over the last 25 years (Kaufmann 1983). Perhaps the piecemeal origins of the legal doctrine reflect a fundamental ambivalence of society's notion of the proper locus of medical decision making authority (Katz 1977). Admonished by Hippocratic tradition to conceal medical information from patients (Katz 1981), physicians in the past have indicated little interest or willingness to share information, much less decision making authority, with patients (McMahon 1975). Despite a relatively recent demand to restructure the traditional physician paternalism with patients, patients on their part, and the judiciary and legislature on their behalf, continue to defer to medical authority.[64] Even the patient-autonomy model of medical practice upon which the informed consent doctrine rests has been rejected as fundamentally inconsistent with the realities of medical illness with its incumbent physchological dependency and regression (Thomasma 1983). The recent report on informed consent by the President's Commission for the Study of Ethical Problems in Medicine and Biomedical and Behavioral Research (President's Commission 1982) concluded that informed consent is "essentially an ethical imperative" defined as "a process of shared decision making based upon mutual respect and participation, not a ritual to be equated with reciting the contents of a form that details the risks of particular treatments" (President's Commission 1982, 1:2). Observational research conducted for the Commission revealed that such collaborative decision making is in fact quite rare; rather

> (1) disclosure does not typically occur...
> (2) "decisions" are not made by patients. "Recommendations" are made by doctors to patients.
> (3) "Consent" does not exist. Instead what we find is "acquiescence," the absence of "objection," or occasionally a "veto" (President's Commission 1982, 2:401).

Reviews of other empirical research of the informed consent process have also suggested that the informed consent doctrine as originally envisioned has yet to be achieved (Meisel & Roth 1981; Meisel & Roth 1983), though does not confirm allegations that informed consent is a "charade" (Katz 1977), a "fairy tale" (Feldman 1978; Chayet 1976; Laforet 1976) or is "hazardous" to health (Denney et al. 1975; Lankton et al. 1977; Loftus & Fries 1979; Kaplan et al. 1977). Limitations in its implementation are a function of cultural (President's Commission 1982, 3:37–62), institutional (Lynn 1983), economic (Lynn 1983), psychological (President's Commission 1982, 3:83–116; Tancredi 1982; Eraker & Politser 1982; Tversky & Kahneman 1974; McNeil et al. 1982; Dyer 1978; Katz 1981), physiological (Stanley 1983), demographic (Roth et al. 1982b; Cassileth et al. 1980b; President's Commission 1982, 2:317–410), and illness variables (President's Commission 1982, 2:317–410, 411–477). As well, many patients simply prefer not to be informed about the nature and risks of their treatment (Alfidi 1975; Denney et al. 1975; Lankton et al. 1977; Rosoff 1981) and decline the legally available decisional authority (Brody 1980; Cross & Churchill 1982; Tancredi 1982b; Szasz & Hollender 1956; Vertinsky et al. 1974).

In response to these impediments to genuinely shared decision making, commentators have suggested that the physician's responsibilities for ensuring a truly informed consent exceed those of disclosing information and securing the patient's consent. The ethical physician thus might be said to have a duty to ascertain the patient's knowledge and familiarity with the condition, clarify the patient's distortions and misconceptions about the illness and the available treatments that affect decision making, elucidate the patient's values that affect decision making, and attend to patient vulnerability by minimizing coercion and manipulation (Ingelfinger 1972; Lynn 1983; Meisel & Kabnick 1980; Miller & Willner 1974; Richards & Rothburn 1982; President's Commission 1982). Finally, the President's Commission suggested that the quality of the consent process could be improved by divulging distressing information, reassessing patient competency and obtaining consent over a period of time rather than in an instant, encouraging patients to consult with other patients, the medical literature and their family, and utilizing supplementary written or audiovisual materials (President's Commission 1982, 1:113–128).

Informed Consent and Neuroleptic-Induced Movement Disorders

Informed consent issues arise in malpractice litigation principally in conjunction with claims of negligence in the medical care itself; most informed consent claims are appended to those alleging negligence and rarely occur as the sole issue of litigation (Rosoff 1981). Curran (1979a) reported that a primary claim of lack of informed consent to treatment constituted 2.5 percent of the claims of one malpractice insurance company between 1973 and 1978 (Connors 1979). Another report indicated that this was an issue in 1.7 percent of the malpractice claims of an insurance company between 1973 and 1982.[65] This low prevalence of informed consent allegations is equally true in psychiatry according to the American Psychiatric Association's malpractice insurance program over the last ten years (APA Malpractice 1983; Hogan 1979). Even less prevalent is litigation against physicians regarding informed consent to treatment with medication,[66] though drug manufacturers[67] and hospitals [68] are also subject to suit by patients on these grounds (Drugs and Litigation 1982).

Several cases have clearly indicated that informed consent disclosures by physicians prior to treatment with medication are as essential to informed medical decision making, as those prior to diagnostic or surgical intervention. Medical intervention is generally thought to be of significantly higher risk.[69] In neurology and psychiatry, for example, considerably more legal attention has been devoted to the nature and quality of patient decision making about psychiatric procedures such as insulin or electric shock therapy and psychosurgery than to decision making concerning the use of psychotropic or antipsychotic medications (Mills & Avery 1978; Tenebaum 1983).[70] Yet, there is case law, statute, regulations and guidelines pertinent to informed consent requirements where antipsychotic medications are prescribed.[71]

In Clites v. Iowa,[72] that the parents of a mentally retarded minor resident of a state hospital-school "were never informed of the potential side effects of the use, and prolonged use, of major tranquilizers" violated the "standard that requires some form of informed consent prior to the administration of major tranquilizers."[73] Judgment was rendered on behalf of the plaintiffs when tardive dyskinesia materialized after five years of treatment with antipsychotic medication.

Judge Brotman, in a right to refuse psychotropic medication case,[74] ordered that voluntary and involuntary hospitalized psychiatric patients be required to sign written informed consent prior to prescription of psychotropic drugs in nonemergencies. Such forms

> shall also state all known short-term and long-term side effects of the drug to be consented to, and may be supplemented by informal discussion by hospital staff with the patient concerning the risks and benefits of the drugs... Information on the rights of patients and the side effects of all psychotropic drugs used in a hospital shall be posted or made available on each ward.[75]

This order was subsequently reversed on appeal[76] in favor of a state Administrative Bulletin requiring that

> if a patient refuses to take the psychotropic medication that has been prescribed for him, the attending physician shall speak to the patient and attempt to explain: his assessment of the patient's condition; his reasons for prescribing the medication; the benefits and risks of taking the medication; and the advantages and disadvantages of alternative courses of action.[77]

In an analogous right to refuse medication case, the court indicated that "the scope of a psychiatrist's duty to inform mental health patients is not clearly defined,"[78] and rejected the notion that the "presumed incompetence" of committed psychiatric patients justified a "failure to provide a patient with sufficient information to make an informed treatment decision."[79] This court, too, referred to a state Department of Mental Health regulation which provided that involuntary patients have a right to

> be told in detail what is wrong with you, what alternative treaments are available, and to choose from these alternatives; (have the right to) be informed of the risks and possible side effects of treatment.[80]

As a result of litigation in California, hospitalized, competent patients who are prescribed antipsychotic medications, lithium carbonate and tricyclic antidepressants since June, 1980, must be informed of:

(a) The nature of the patient's mental condition
(b) The reasons for taking such medication, including the likelihood of improving or not improving without such medication, and that consent, once given, may be withdrawn at any time by stating such intention to any member of the treating staff
(c) The reasonable alternative treatments available, if any
(d) The type, range of frequency and amount (including use of PRN orders), method (oral or injection), and duration of taking the medications
(e) The probable side effects of these drugs known to commonly occur, and any particular side effects likely to occur with the particular patient
(f) The possible additional side effects which may occur to patients taking such medication beyond three months. The patient shall be advised that such side effects may include persistent involuntary movement of the face or mouth and might at times include similar movement of the hands and feet, and that these symptoms of tardive dyskinesia are potentially irreversible and may appear after medications have been discontinued.[81]

This regulation also requires a written consent form signed by the patient which indicates that items (a) through (f) have been discussed with the patient by the prescribing physician. Withholding of the requisite disclosures, based upon a therapeutic privilege, is not explicitly permitted. Such disclosures, documented by written consent form, are also required for involuntary psychiatric patients in California prior to administration of antipsychotic drugs, according to a recent consent decree.[82]

In another consent decree arising from litigation regarding standards for psychoactive drug use in Maine, the court ordered that prior to administration of psychotropic medication, a physician or nurse explain

> in lay terms to the resident and to the resident's correspondent the reasons for the treatment and possible benefits and consequences of the medication ... During a course of administration of psychotropic medication, the physician shall ensure that the resident's progress or response to the treatment, including adverse effects, are carefully monitored and recorded.[83]

An occasional statute may also specifically relate to informed consent disclosures prior to antipsychotic medication. The Mental Health System Act[84] encouraged each state to "review and revise, if necessary, its laws to ensure that mental health patients receive the protection and services they require,"[85] including

> the right to be provided with a reasonable explanation, in terms and language appropriate to such person's condition and ability to understand, of
>
> (i) such person's general mental condition ...
> (ii) the objectives of treatment
> (iii) the nature and significant possible adverse effects of recommended treatments
> (iv) the reasons why a particular treatment is considered appropriate.[86]

Lyon et al. (1982) report that state statutes in four states substantially comply with this subsection of the Mental Health Systems Act, while 15 others comply in part. An additional 13 states comply at least in part with another subsection of the Act which provides for a "right to ongoing participation... in the planning of mental health services to be provided such person."[87]

Lastly, several professional organizations have promulgated standards pertinent to the use of psychoactive substances. The standards on patients' rights of the Joint Commission on Accreditation of Hospitals states that

> As appropriate, the patient, the patient's family, or the patient's legal guardian shall be fully informed about... the risks, side effects, and benefits of all medications and treatment procedures used, especially those that are unusual or experimental.[88]

The American Hospital Association's Patient's Bill of Rights states that

> The patient has the right to obtain from his physician complete current information concerning his diagnosis, treatment and prognosis... such information should include... the specific procedure and/or treatment, the medically significant risks involved and the probable duration of incapacitation...[89]

Lastly, standards for the use of psychotropic medication proposed by the Accreditation Council for Services for Mentally Retarded and Other Developmentally Disabled Persons, adopted in 1977, provide that

> the individual's record contains written authorization for the use of behavior modifying drugs... (which) conveys in a simple, non-technical and comprehensible manner the drugs to be used, their expected benefits, and their possible hazards (Sprague 1982).

Despite the fragmentary legal or regulatory standards regarding the need for disclosures prior to the administration of antipsychotic medications, numerous psychiatric commentators have articulated their own standards though almost exclusively with regard to disclosing the long-term risks of tardive dyskinesia. These authors have indicated that the significant period prevalence of tardive dyskinesia in patients maintained on drugs in conjunction with its potential irreversibility despite neuroleptic withdrawal argues for its disclosure prior to long-term treatment, at least in a material risk jurisdiction (Ananth 1980; Ayd 1977; Baldessarini et al. 1980; Chayet 1978; Davis et al. 1983; DeVeaugh-Geiss 1979; Drug Toxicity 1980; Furrow 1980; Gutheil & Appelbaum 1982; Halleck 1980; Jeste & Wyatt 1981; Sovner et al. 1978; Stone 1981; Wettstein 1983). Disclosure of the risk of tardive dyskinesia with long-term treatment in a professional standard jurisdiction is less certain, given the absence of empirical data about physicians' actual disclosures to patients. Should the physician decide to inform the patient of the risk of developing tardive dyskinesia, he should also discuss its likely severity and reversibility, given the patient's age, sex, diagnosis, and history of medication ingestion. Authors have also commented that disclosure of the risks of developing tardive dyskinesia is unnecessary when only brief (under six months) treatment is contemplated, especially when the patient is severely psychotic, since tardive dyskinesia rarely occurs in this time period (Ayd 1977; Gutheil & Appelbaum 1982). Such a recommendation would require modification when the patient has received antipsychotic medications extensively in the past.

Disclosure of the risks of developing the other neuroleptic-induced movement disorders has provoked little professional comment. Though the risk of developing tardive dystonia after long-term treatment is presently incalculable and its materiality to either patients or physicians is uncertain, incorporating a discussion of this disorder with that of tardive dyskinesia would not be cumbersome. Discussing the risks of the acute neuroleptic movement disorders with a patient prior to treatment is, however, occasioned by the considerable prevalence of the acute dystonias and their resulting distress, despite the disorganization of an acutely ill patient and the usual treatability and spontaneous reversibility of these disorders, in contrast to tardive dyskinesia and tardive dystonia. Again, the need for such discussion will be tempered by the risk of the movement disorder (patient's age, sex, diagnosis, drug dose, and drug type) as well as the locus of treatment, as a hospital environment will provide continual monitoring, support, and treatment of any movement disorders. Psychiatrists have also been known to prescribe an as-needed dose of anticholinergic medication for ambulatory patients given antipsychotic medication, should they develop a dystonic reaction. As noted earlier, disclosure varies with the nature of the medical problem as well as its treatment. Some have argued, too, that use of antipsychotic medication for FDA unlabelled purposes requires disclosure of this fact and discussion with the patient. Lastly, when treating a legally incompetent patient, the proper informed consent dialogue should obtain with the appointed guardian.

Many disorders for which antipsychotic medication is prescribed are chronic rather than acute conditions. Recent research has revealed that the decision making process for patients receiving treatment for chronic conditions closely approximates the decision making envisioned by the informed consent doctrine (President's Commission 1982, 2:317–410). Such patients are better educated about their condition and the available interventions and enjoy greater decisional authority. While there is some evidence that psychiatric patients with chronic disorders are not so well informed about their conditions and treatments (Appelbaum et al. 1981; Appelbaum & Roth 1982; Roth et al. 1982a; Grossman & Summer 1980; Geller 1982; Linden & Chaskel 1981; Soskis 1978; Soskis & Jaffee 1979; Olin & Olin 1975; Palmer & Wohl 1972; Jaffe 1982), the long-term nature of the psychiatric intervention can greatly facilitate an ongoing process of informed consent (Dyer

1978). Indeed, the management of pseudoparkinsonism, akathisia, tardive dyskinesia, and tardive dystonia requires patient compliance with both antipsychotic medication and drug treatment for the iatrogenic complication, and can best be implemented by an informed and educated patient. In a long-term treatment relationship, there is ample opportunity to assess the patient's understanding of the primary and secondary disorders and their respective interventions, provide corrective information, monitor the patient's functional capacity to consent (Macklin 1982; Stone 1979; DeVeaugh-Geiss 1979; Munetz et al. 1982), reaffirm the patient's consent to treatment, and incorporate contemporary information about the patient's illness and treatment (Dickens 1981). Such a relationship is particularly important when a trial of unapproved drug therapy for tardive dyskinesia or tardive dystonia is implemented.

Documentation of the informed consent process through written consent forms for medical procedures and treatment has attracted considerable controversy. Though there is no case law or statutory requirement that written consent for treatment be obtained, the practice has developed because physicians and attorneys believe that the written form has evidentiary value in testimonial conflicts between the patient and the doctor (Meisel & Kabnick 1980). Though recent statutes create a variety of presumptions that a valid informed consent has been obtained through a written form,[90] the value of the statutory presumption is uncertain given that the burden of proof in negligence actions is on the plaintiff (Meisel & Kabnick 1980). Under some statutes, this presumption of validity may be rejected by demonstrating duress, misrepresentation, mistake or fraud.[91] Further, those written forms that only acknowledge in a conclusory manner that disclosure was made without reporting the content of the disclosure are even less valuable as a defense for the physician. Many physicians and attorneys mistake the process of informed consent with its documentation through the written form. Yet, written consent forms fail to promote information disclosure or patient understanding (Lidz & Roth 1983) and too frequently substitute for the consent dialogue itself (Moore 1978; Vaccarino 1978; President's Commission 1982, 2:317–410). Despite considerable publicity that consent forms are written at college or postgraduate level (Grundner 1980; Morrow 1980) or are excessively long (Epstein & Lasagna 1969), recent revisions remain problematic (Baker & Taub 1983; Kaufer et al. 1983). Physicians and other health care personnel obtain the patient's signature in a ritualistic manner (Zerubavel 1980) and patients view consent forms as legal formalities (Ashley et al. 1980; Fritz 1981), which protect the physicians (Cassileth et al. 1980a).

With regard to neuroleptic-induced movement disorders, some commentators, as well as the state of California, have favored a written consent form documenting disclosure of the risks of tardive dyskinesia (Chayet 1978; DeVeaugh-Geiss 1979; Halleck 1980; Sovner et al. 1978). Others have recommended a detailed note in the patient's record (Ayd 1977; Baldessarini et al. 1980; Gutheil & Appelbaum 1982; Wettstein 1983). Stone (1981) urged psychiatrists to audiotape informed consent sessions while others have recommended audiovisual aids (Barbour & Blumenkranz 1978). The President's Commission recommended that written information or brochures such as patient package inserts be dispensed to patients and the American Medical Association has implemented a voluntary patient medication instruction program for commonly used medications.[92] Though discussion of the acute risks of even the short-terms use of antipsychotic medications appears indicated for all but the most psychiatrically disturbed patient, obtaining a written consent to such use appears unreasonable. Again, the risk-benefit ratio in such situations is distinctly high, and the harm readily reversible. The cognitive disruption of many such patients renders any written communication of dubious validity, though not invariably so.

Compulsory Treatment

The preceding discussion of informed consent pertained to patients who consent to antipsychotic medications. A great deal of recent attention has been devoted to the legal justification of involuntary antipsychotic medication in psychiatric patients, particularly those who are involuntary hospitalized.[93] Considerable litigation has attempted to articulate a right to refuse medication for involuntary patients in a nonemergency, and such a right, though qualified, is prevalent in many jurisdictions (Callahan & Longmire, 1983). Viewed inversely, however, such a qualified right represents an authority to administer antipsychotic medication despite a patient's refusal. Such authority in civilly committed patients typically presupposes the patient's functional incompetence to assess the nature of his mental disorder, and the purposes, risks, benefits and alternatives of the proposed intervention (Roth et al. 1977). In such cases, the patient's refusal is said to be a product of his mental illness.[94] In other cases, however, compulsory medication may be administered to a functionally competent patient if he has been committed to the hospital under dangerousness criteria rather than *parens patriae* criteria.[95] Regardless of its foundation, such involuntary medication can be administered to a refusing patient for significant periods of their commitment.[96] An Ohio proposal, for example, permits this for 180 days (Hickman et al. 1982). A substantial period of involuntary medication can thus result when a patient is repeatedly civilly committed.

A second recent legal development authorizes compulsory antipsychotic medication for criminally committed patients. Michigan's statute for the disposition of criminal defendants adjudicated incompetent to stand trial has been interpreted to permit unconsented medication throughout the duration of the period of incompetency.[97] In Idaho, imprisonment in a state prison, "suspends all the civil rights of the person so sentenced including the right to refuse treatment authorized by the sentencing court."[98] Illinois defendants acquitted by reason of insanity of a criminal charge can be committed to outpatient, court-supervised psychiatric treatment by the criminal court for five years on conditional release status. If the defendant-patient fails to fulfill the conditions of release which may include maintenance antipsychotic medication, then the court may remand the defendant back to an inpatient facility.[99] Similar statutes in Maryland[100] and Oregon[101] also permit involuntary neuroleptic medication to insanity acquittees treated as outpatients for periods of years. In contrast to the forced medication of the civilly committed patients, the criminally committed patients are not alleged or adjudicated as incompetent to consent or refuse medication; instead, medication is permitted on the basis of the patient's proven past dangerousness to others and likelihood of recidivism in the absence of treatment.

Such prolonged involuntary medication in criminally committed patients, whether inpatients or outpatients, permits the development of both short- and long-term neuroleptic-induced movement disorders. The apparent acceptability of such medication and its side effects contrasts with the acute concern of some courts about the development of tardive dyskinesia with forced medication in civilly committed patients.[102] In either situation, physicians are in the precarious position of prescribing prolonged court imposed medication to a refusing patient, contrary to the informed consent doctrine. It is thus particularly incumbent upon the physician in such situations to use medication judiciously and conservatively. Again, the sometimes long-term nature of the treatment process permits a dialogue about the patient's experience of the medication, its side effects and their secondary management, despite an involuntary status. Thus, though two of the precursors of ethically valid decision making, voluntariness and competency, are sometimes suspended under court of administrative order, disclosure of information can still continue.

CONCLUSION

This chapter has reviewed several medico-legal aspects of the neuroleptic drug-induced movement disorders. The discussion has been principally focused on the perspective of the physician, though it has also been concerned with several matters pertinent to hospitals and drug manufacturers. These issues are, however, certainly of relevance to pharmacists, nurses and other health care providers (Dixon 1982).

It is worth emphasizing that the prevalence of these disorders dictates conservative use of the neuroleptic agents. Physicians should avoid their use in alleviating problems in living, mild anxiety or nonpsychotic depression.

When indicated, one should use the lowest effective dose for the shortest period of time (DeVeaugh-Geiss 1982). Periodic reassessment of antipsychotic drug dosage and regular examinations for involuntary movements are essential to responsible medical care. If a movement disorder develops, a proper differential diagnosis should be considered and consultation obtained if necessary. Intervention may be complex and require the active participation of the patient. A therapeutic alliance with the patient mandates that the drug related issues be discussed with the patient in an ongoing manner. Documentation of the drug prescription, ingestion, side effects, and dialogue is also required. Such will be the case until, and perhaps long after, a new generation of nonneuroleptic antipsychotic agents has been developed.

NOTES

1. Restatement (Second) Torts, Section 282, 1965.
2. Carter v. Metropolitan Dade County, 253 So. 2d 920; Chasse v. Banas, 399 A. 2d 608; Watkins v. United States, 589 F. 2d 214.
3. Jansen v. University Hospital, 26 ATLA L. Rep., April, 1983.
4. Brown v. State, 44 N.Y. 2d 1006 (1977); Brown v. City of New York, 63 App. Div. 2d 635 (1978); Annotation, 45 A.L.R. 3d 928.
5. Helling v. Carey, 519 P. 2d 981 (1974); Tarasoff v. Regents of the University of California, 551 P. 2d 334; Canterbury v. Spence, 464 F. 2d 772 (1972).
6. Youngberg v. Romeo, 457 U.S. 307.
7. Mulder v. Parke Davis, 181 N.W. 2d 882; Ohligschlager v. Proctor Community Hospital, 303 N.E. 2d 392 (1973).
8. New Jersey Superior Court, Law Division, Essex County, Docket Number L-44353-67, May, 1971.
9. 14 ATLA Newsletter 424, November, 1971.
10. Montgomery County, Maryland, Circuit Court, Number 48751, October 20, 1980.
11. 24 ATLA L. Rep. 185, 1981.
12. New York, Bronx County Supreme Court, index number 14232/72, February 4, 1982.
13. 25 ATLA L. Rep. 279, August, 1972; personal communication with plaintiff's attorney, Mr. Harold M. Fishman, November 8, 1983.
14. Kewaunee County Circuit Court, Wisconsin, Number 81-CV-104, May 28, 1982.
15. 26 ATLA L. Rep. 87, March, 1983; Plaintiff's brief; Personal communication with plaintiff's attorney David A. Saichek, October 4, 1983.
16. Wayne County Circuit Court, Number 79-904-736 NM, July 27, 1982.
17. 25 ATLA L. Rep. 473, December, 1982; Medical brief, trial brief; Personal communication with plaintiff's attorneys Geoffrey Fieger, September 20, 1983, and William Lamping, November 18, 1983.
18. Law No. 46274, Iowa District Court, Pottawattamie County, August 7, 1980.

19. Clites v. Iowa, 322 N.W. 2d 917, 918 (1982).
20. 322 N.W. 2d 920 (1982).
21. 322 N.W. 2d 922 (1982).
22. 322 N.W. 2d 923 (1982).
23. 322 N.W. 2d 917 (1982).
24. cf. Perry v. Kalamazoo State Hospital, 273 N.W. 2d 421 (1978) and Parker v. Highland Park Hospital, 273 N.W. 2d 413 (1978).
25. Johnson v. Rodis, 251 F. 2d 917 (1958).
26. Guilmet v. Campbell, 188 N.W. 2d 601 (1971); Marchlewicz v. Stanton, 50 Mich. App. 344 (1973).
27. Nelson v. Gaunt, 178 Cal. Rptr. 167, 173 (1981).
28. Lopez v. Swyer, 279 A. 2d 116; Weinstock v. Ott, 444 N.E. 2d 1227 (1983); Weinstock v. Eissler, 36 Cal. Rptr. 537 (1964).
29. Simcuski v. Saeli, 406 N.Y.S. 2d 259 (1978).
30. 178 Cal. Rptr. 173.
31. Bloskas v. Murray, 646 P. 2d 907 (1982).
32. cf. Woods v. Brumlop, 377 P. 2d 520 (1962).
33. Millett v. Dumais, 365 A. 2d 1038.
34. Mohr v. Williams, 104 N.W. 2d 12 (1905).
35. Schloendorff v. Society of New York Hospital, 105 N.E. 93 (1914).
36. Wall v. Brim, 138 F. 2d 478 (1943); Franklyn v. Peabody, 249 Mich. 363 (1930).
37. Salgo v. Leland Stanford Jr. University, 317 P. 2d 181 (1957).
38. 317 P. 2d 181 (1957).
39. Natanson v. Kline, 350 P. 2d 1093 (1960).
40. 350 P. 2d 1106 (1960).
41. 354 P. 2d 673 (1960).
42. Canterbury v. Spence, 464 F. 2d 772 (1972); Cobbs v. Grant, 8 Cal. 3d 229 (1972).
43. 8 Cal. 3d 243 (1972).
44. 464 F. 2d 787 (1972).
45. Dow v. Kaiser Foundation, 90 Cal. Rptr. 747 (1970); Hales v. Puttman, 576 P. 2d 493; Mink v. University of Chicago, 460 F. Supp. 713 (1978).
46. Cobbs v. Grant, 8 Cal. 3d 229 (1972).
47. Weinstock v. Eissler, 36 Cal. Rptr. 537 (1964).
48. Oregon Revised Statutes, Chapter 677.097 (1977).
49. Truman v. Thomas, 611 P. 2d 902 (1980).
50. Annotation, 88 ALR 3d 1008.
51. Florida Statutes Annotated 768.132 (1975).
52. Canterbury v. Spence, 464 F. 2d 772 (1972); Cobbs v. Grant, 8 Cal. 3d 229 (1972); Cowman v. Harnaday, 329 N.W. 2d 422 (Iowa, 1983); Harnish v. Children's Hospital Medical Center, 439 N.E. 2d 240 (Massachusetts, 1982).
53. Pennsylvania Statutes Annotated Title 40, Section 1301.103; Washington Revised Code Annotated, Section 7.70.050 (1) (a).
54. Canterbury v. Spence, 464 F. 2d 787 (1972).
55. Canterbury v. Spence, 464 F. 2d 787 (1972).
56. Tresemer v. Barke, 150 Cal. Rptr. 384 (1978).
57. Hawaii Revised Statutes, Section 671-3 (1976); Texas Revised Civil Statutes

Annotated, 4590 (i) (1977).

58. Canterbury v. Spence, 464 F. 2d 778 (1972).

59. Canterbury v. Spence, 464 F. 2d 789 (1972).

60. Canterbury v. Spence, 464 F. 2d 789 (1972).

61. Lester v. Aetna Casualty and Surety Company, 240 F. 2d 676 (1957).

62. Nishi v. Hartwell, 473 P. 2d 116 (1970).

63. Ferrara v. Galluchio, 152 N.E. 2d 249 (1958).

64. Youngberg v. Romeo, 457 U.S. 307; Reliance upon professional standards is evidenced in informed consent doctrine by the predominance of a medical standard of disclosure, by a therapeutic privilege regardless of the disclosure standard, by the need for compulsory expert testimony to establish the materiality of risk or the justification for therapeutic privilege, and by the objective standard of causality.

65. Medical World News, March 14, 1983, p. 173.

66. This contrasts with the extensive tort and constitutional litigation on consent to treatment in the context of right to refuse medication, discussed *infra.*

67. A comprehensive discussion of the liability of pharmaceutical manufacturers is beyond the scope of this chapter (Dixon 1982; McClellan 1978). Pertinent to informed consent, a manufacturer has a duty to warn prescribing physicians of all dangers of its medication which it knew or should have known (Woodill v. Parke Davis and Company, 402 N.E. 2d 194; Oksenhold v. Lederle Laboratories, 656 P. 2d 293 (1982)), but does not have a duty to directly warn the patient of such hazards (McKee v. Moore, 648 P. 2d 21 (1982); Carmichael v. Reitz, 95 Cal. Rptr. 381 (1971)), with limited exceptions such as oral contraceptives (Lukaszewicz v. Ortho Pharmaceuticals Inc., 510 F. Supp. 961 (1981)). A few courts, however, have held manufacturers to strict liability rather than negligence standards (Singer v. Sterling Drug, Inc., 461 F. 2d 1972); Davis v. Wyeth Laboratories, 399 F. 2d 121 (1968) (Polio vaccine); Cunningham v. MacNeal Memorial Hospital, 266 N.E. 2d 897 (1970) (blood products); Hasler v. U.S., 517 F. Supp. 1262 (1981)). Pharmaceutical manufacturers regularly modify their product warnings to physicians to conform to new clinical or research data (Ananth & Costin 1977) through changes in the *Physician's Desk Reference* and package inserts.

68. The potential liability against hospitals for failure to obtain informed consent to treatment is even more restricted and Ludlam (1978) reports that no such successful cases existed as of that date. A hospital would be liable for the failure of an employed physician but not an independent physician to obtain informed consent for treatment (Miller 1983) (Roberson v. Menorah Medical Center, 588 S.W. 2d 134 (1979); Cross v. Trapp, 294 S.E. 2d 446 (1982)). It would also be liable if it failed to intervene when it knew or should have known that an intervention was being performed without the proper disclosure and consent, it knew that the patient was incompetent to consent (Miller 1982), or it knew that the operation was per se an act of malpractice or not indicated (Fiorentino v. Wenger, 227 N.E. 2d 296 (1967); Magana v. Elie, 439 N.E. 2d 1319 (1982)).

69. Sharpe v. Pugh, 155 S.E. 2d 108 (1967) (fatal aplastic anemia from chloromycetin); Marsh v. Arnold, 446 S.W. 2d 949 (1969) (ototoxicity from kanamycin); Hamilton v. Hardy, 549 P. 2d 1099 (1976) (cerebrovascular accident from an oral contraceptive); but see Malloy v. Shanahan, 421 A. 2d 803 (1980) for the contrary view that the informed consent doctrine does not apply to suits involving prescription drugs and their known potentially dangerous side effects.

70. Kaimowitz v. Department of Mental Health, Civil Number 73-19434-AW (Wayne County, Michigan Circuit Court 1973) (voluntariness and competency to consent to psychosurgery); Woods v. Brumlop, 377 P. 2d 520 (1962) (informed consent to ECT); California Welfare and Institutions Code Section 5326 (ECT); The Illinois Mental Health and Developmental Disabilities Code states that: "no recipient of services shall be subjected to electro-convulsive therapy, or to any unusual, hazardous, or experimental services or psychosurgery without his written and informed consent," while it does not impose any requirements for informed consent for other mental health services (Chapter II, Article I, Section 2-110).

71. Regulations or guidelines for the use of antipsychotic medications or psychotropic medications are even more widely promulgated, as are surveys of the quality of drug prescription practices in psychiatry (Prien et al. 1978; Dorsey et al. 1979; James 1983). Indeed, it may be the case that standards for what physicians do are better defined than for what they say.

72. 322 N.W. 2d 917 (1982).

73. 322 N.W. 2d 922 (1982).

74. Rennie v. Klein, 476 F. Supp. 1294 (1979).

75. 476 F. Supp. 1313 (1979).

76. Rennie v. Klein, 653 F. 2d 836 (3d. Circuit 1981).

77. New Jersey Division of Mental Health and Hospitals, Administrative Bulletin 78-3, March 1, 1978, II B, cited in Rennie v. Klein, 462 F. Supp. 1131, 1150 (1978). The regulation does not mandate such disclosures when the patient does not protest the medication prescription.

78. Rogers v. Okin, 478 F. Supp. 1342, 1387 (1979).

79. 478 F. Supp. 1387 (1979).

80. Massachusetts Department of Mental Health Regulation 16-7, cited in Rogers v. Okin, 478 F. Supp. 1359 (1979). This statement of patient rights is required to be posted on hospital wards and is presented to patients on admission to the hospital.

81. Title 9, California Administrative Code, Subchapter 4, Article 5.5.

82. This consent decree in Jamison v. Farabee, initially applies to involuntary patients at Napa State Hospital but will be implemented at all state hospitals after one year. Mental Disability Law Reporter, Vol. 7, No. 5, September/October, 1983, pp. 436–439.

83. Wuori v. Zitnay, 1978, cited in Sprague, 1982.

84. 42 USC 9501, passed by Congress, October 7, 1980.

85. Section 501.

86. Section 501 (1) (C).

87. Section 501 (1) (C).

88. Consolidated Standards Manual for Child, Adolescent, and Adult Psychiatric Alcohol and Drug Abuse Facilities, 1981, Edition, JCAH, Chicago, Section 14.4(e).

89. American Health Association, 1972, cited in the Rights of the Mentally Disabled, 1982.

90. Florida: "A consent which is evidenced in writing and meets the requirements of [disclosure] shall, if validly signed by the patient or another authorized person, be conclusively presumed to be a valid consent," Florida Statutes Annotated Section 768.46(4)(a); Iowa: "Consent in writing... shall create a presumption that informed consent was given," Iowa Code Annotated Section 147.137.

91. Idaho: "...when the giving of such consent is recited in writing and expressly authorizes the care...to be furnished...such written consent, in the absence of convincing proof that it was secured maliciously or by fraud, is presumed to be valid..." Idaho Code Section 39-4304.

92. Among the psychotropic medications, patient medication instructions for Haldol, lithium carbonate and benzodiazepines are currently available at nominal cost.

93. Rennie v. Klein, 653 F. 2d 836 (1981); Rogers v. Okin, 634 F. 2d 650 (1980).

94. Jamison v. Farabee, Mental Disability Law Reporter, Volume 7, September/October, 1983, pp. 436–439.

95. *Ibid.*

96. Most mechanisms for involuntarily medicating committee patients require two separate procedures: one for the civil commitment and a second for the refusal for medication. The Utah commitment statute combines the two proceedings and denies committed patients the right to refuse medication: A.E. and R.R. v. Mitchell, 79-466 (1980).

97. The "court shall order him to undergo treatment to render him competent to stand trial," Michigan Compiled Laws 330.2032.

98. Senate Bill 1396, 1982; Idaho Code, Sections 18-310, 18-311.

99. Illinois Chapter 38, Section 1005-2-4.

100. Maryland Annotated Code Article 59, Section 28 (1979).

101. Oregon Revised Statutes, Section 161.319–161-351 (1979).

102. "If the plaintiff is likely to contract tardive dyskinesia through renewed administration of psychotropic drugs, the cure would be worse than the illness, and involuntary medication would not be permitted." Rennie v. Klein, 462 F. Supp. 1146 (1978). Others have proposed that criminally committed patients should not be less protected from side effects of treatment than those civilly committed (Hickman et al. 1982).

REFERENCES

Alexopoulos, G.S. 1979. "Lack of Complaints in Schizophrenics with Tardive Dyskinesia." *Journal of Nervous and Mental Disease* 167:125–127.

Alfidi, R.J. 1975. "Controversy, Alternatives, and Decisions in Complying with the Legal Doctrine of Informed Consent." *Radiology* 114:231–234.

Ananth, J. 1980. "Tardive Dyskinesia: Myths and Realities." *Psychosomatics* 21: 389–396.

Ananth, J., and A. Costin. 1977. "Dyskinesia with Thiothixene." *American Journal of Psychiatry* 134:689.

Angle, C.R., and M.S. McIntire. 1968. "Persistent Dystonia in a Brain-Damaged Child after Ingestion of Phenothiazine." *Journal of Pediatrics* 73(1):124–126.

Annas, G.J. 1978. "Informed Consent." *Annual Review of Medicine* 29:9–14.

Appelbaum, P.S., S.A. Mirkin, and A.L. Bateman. 1981. "Empirical Assessment of Competency to Consent to Psychiatric Hospitalization." *American Journal of Psychiatry* 138:1170–1176.

Appelbaum, P.S., and L.H. Roth. 1982. "Competency to Consent to Research." *Archives of General Psychiatry* 39:951–958.

Appenzeller, O., and J.P. Biehl. 1968. "Mouthing in the Elderly: A Cerebellar Sign." *Journal of the Neurological Sciences* 6:249–260.

"APA Malpractice Claim Types Constant, But Frequency, Costs Have Doubled." *Psychiatry News* 18(21, November 4, 1983):3.

Apte, S.N., and J.W. Langston. 1983. "Permanent Neurological Deficits Due to Lithium Toxicity." *Annals of Neurology* 13:453–455.

Ashley, M., R.M. Sestak, and L.H. Roth. 1980. "Legislating Human Rights: Informed Consent and the Pennsylvania Mental Health Procedures Act." *Bulletin of the American Academy of Psychiatry and the Law* 8:133–151.

Ayd, F.J. 1977. "Ethical and Legal Dilemmas Posed by Tardive Dyskinesia. *International Drug Therapy Newsletter* 12:29–36.

Ayd, F.J. 1961. "A Survey of Drug-Induced Extrapyramidal Reactions." *Journal of the American Medical Association* 175(12):102–108.

Baker, M.T., and H.A. Taub. 1983. "Readability of Informed Consent Forms for Research in a Veterans Administration Medical Center." *Journal of the American Medical Association* 250:2646–2648.

Baldessarini, R.J., J.O. Cole, J.M. Davis, et al. 1980. *A Task Force Report of the American Psychiatric Association.* Washington, D.C.: American Psychiatric Association.

Barbour, G.L., and M.J. Blumenkrantz. 1978. "Video Tape Aids Informed Consent Decision." *Journal of the American Medical Association* 240:2741–2742.

Barnes, T.R.E., T. Kidger, and S.M. Gore. 1983a. "Tardive Dyskinesia: A Three-Year Follow-up Study." *Psychological Medicine* 13:71–81.

Barnes, T.R.E., M. Rossor, and T. Trauer. 1983b. "A Comparison of Purposeless Movements in Psychiatric Patients Treated with Antipsychotic Drugs, and Normal Individuals." *Journal of Neurology, Neurosurgery and Psychiatry* 46: 540–546.

Barnes, T.R.E., and T. Trauer. 1982. "Reliability and Validity of a Tardive Dyskinesia Videotape Rating Technique." *British Journal of Psychiatry* 140:508–515.

Beitman, B.D. 1978. "Tardive Dyskinesia Reinduced by Lithium Carbonate." *American Journal of Psychiatry* 135:1229–1230.

Beresford, H.R. 1972. "Professional Liability of Psychiatrists." *Defense Law Journal* 21:123–167.

Bernstein, J.G. (ed.) 1983. *Handbook of Drug Therapy in Psychiatry.* Boston: John Wright.

Bleuler, E. 1950. *Dementia Praecox or the Group of Schizophrenias,* translated by J. Zinkin. New York: International Universities Press.

Blowers, A.J., M. Levin, B.I. Diamond, et al. 1982. "Neuropharmacologic Epidemiology of Dyskinesias in Geriatric Patients." *Neurology (NY)* 32(2):A187.

Bourgeois, M., P. Bouilh, J. Tignol, et al. 1980. "Spontaneous Dyskinesias vs. Neuroleptic-Induced Dyskinesias in 270 Elderly Subjects." *Journal of Nervous and Mental Disease* 168(3):177–178.

Branchey, M.H., L.B. Branchey, and M.A. Richardson. 1981. "Effects of Neuroleptic Adjustment on Clinical Condition and Tardive Dyskinesia in Schizophrenia Patients." *American Journal of Psychiatry* 138:608–612.

Brandon, S., H.A. McClelland, and C. Protheroe. 1971. "A Study of Facial Dyskinesia in a Mental Hospital Population." *British Journal of Psychiatry* 118: 171–184.

Braude, W.M., and T.R.E. Barnes. 1983. "Late-Onset Akathisia—An Indicant of

Covert Dyskinesia: Two Case Reports." *American Journal of Psychiatry* 140: 611–612.

Braude, W.M., T.R.E. Barnes, and S.M. Gore. 1983. "Clinical Characteristics of Akathisia: A Systematic Investigation of Acute Psychiatric Inpatient Admissions." *British Journal of Psychiatry* 143:139–150.

Breuning, S.E., V.J. Davis, J.L. Matson, et al. 1982. "Effects of Thioridazine and Withdrawal Dyskinesias on Workshop Performance of Mentally Retarded Young Adults." *American Journal of Psychiatry* 139:1447–1454.

Brody, D.S. 1980. "The Patients Role in Clinical Decision Making." *Annals of Internal Medicine* 93:718–722.

Bumpass, E.R., and J.L. Knoll. 1982. "Single Case Study: Emotional Factors in Oculogyric Crisis." *Journal of Nervous and Mental Disease* 170(6):366–370.

Burke, R.E., S. Fahn, J. Jankovic, et al. 1982b. "Tardive Dystonia: Late-Onset and Persistent Dystonia Caused by Antipsychotic Drugs." *Neurology (NY)* 32: 1335–1346.

Burke, R.E., J. Jankovic, C.D. Marsden, et al. 1982a. "Tardive Dystonia and Inappropriate Use of Neuroleptic Drugs." *Lancet* 1:1299.

Callahan, L.A., and D.R. Longmire. 1983. "Psychiatric Patients' Right to Refuse Psychotropic Medication: A National Survey." *Mental Disability Law Reporter.* 7:494–502.

Campbell, R.J., W.E. Fann, and J.I. Thornby. 1983. "Abnormal Involuntary Movements and Chronic Obstructive Pulmonary Disease." *Journal of Clinical Psychopharmacology* 3(3):179–182.

Casey, D.E., and P. Rabins. 1978. "Tardive Dyskinesia as a Life-Threatening Illness." *American Journal of Psychiatry* 135:486–488.

Cassileth, B.R., R.V. Zupkis, K. Sutton-Smith, et al. 1980a. "Informed Consent—Why Are Its Goals Imperfectly Realized?" *New England Journal of Medicine* 302:896–900.

Cassileth, B.R., R.V. Zupkis, K. Sutton-Smith, et al. 1980b. "Information and Participation Preferences Among Cancer Patients." *Annals of Internal Medicine* 92:832–836.

Cavenar, J.O., I.J. Brantley, and E. Braasch. 1978. "Blepharospasm: Organic or Functional?" *Psychosomatics* 19(10):623–628.

Cavenar, J.O., E.B. Hammett, and A. Maltbie. 1979. "Misdiagnosis of Severe Dystonia." *Psychosomatics* 20(3):209–210.

Chadwick, D., E.H. Reynolds, and C.D. Marsden. 1976. "Anticonvulsant-Induced Dyskinesias: A Comparison with Dyskinesias Induced by Neuroleptics. *Journal of Neurology, Neurosurgery and Psychiatry* 39:1210–1218.

Chayet, N.L. 1976. "Informed Consent of the Mentally Disabled: A Failing Fiction." *Psychiatric Annals* 6:82–96.

Chayet, N.L. 1978. "Patient Surrogates: A Possibility of Improving the Present System." In *Controversy in Psychiatry*, edited by J.P. Brady and H.K.H. Brodie. Philadelphia: Saunders.

Chiles, J.A. 1978. "Extrapyramidal Reactions in Adolescents Treated with High-Potency Antipsychotics." *American Journal of Psychiatry* 135(2):239–240.

Chouinard, G., and B.D. Jones. 1979. "Early Onset of Tardive Dyskinesia: Case Report." *American Journal of Psychiatry* 136:1323–1324.

"Classification of Extrapyramidal Disorders." *Journal of the Neurological Sciences* 51(1981):311-327.
Connors, P.J. 1979. "Malpractice and Informed Consent." *New England Journal of Medicine* 300:928-929.
Crane, G.E. 1971. "Persistence of Neurological Symptoms Due to Neuroleptic Drugs." *American Journal of Psychiatry* 127:1407-1410.
Crane, G.E., and E.R. Naranjo. 1971. "Motor Disorders Induced by Neuroleptics." *Archives of General Psychiatry* 24:179-184.
Crow, T.J., A.J. Cross, E.C. Johnstone, et al. 1982. "Abnormal Involuntary Movements in Schizophrenia: Are They Related to the Disease Process or Its Treatment? Are They Associated with Changes in Dopamine Receptors?" *Journal of Clinical Psychopharmacology* 2(5):336-340.
Curran W.J. 1983. "Medical Malpractice Claims Since the Crisis of 1975: Some Good News and Some Bad." *New England Journal of Medicine* 309(18):1107-1108.
Curran, W.J. 1979a. "Malpractice Claims: New Data and New Trends." *New England Journal of Medicine* 300:26-27.
Curran, W.J. 1979b. "Informed Consent, Texas Style: Disclosure and Non-Disclosure by Regulation." *New England Journal of Medicine* 300:482-483.
Cutler, N.R., and R.M. Post. 1982. "State-Related Cyclical Dyskinesias in Manic-Depressive Illness." *Journal of Clinical Psychopharmacology* 2(5):350-354.
Dabbous, I.A., and A.B. Bergman. 1966. "Neurologic Damage Associated with Phenothiazine." *Am J Dis Child* 3:291-296.
Danzon, P.M. 1982. *The Frequency and Severity of Medical Malpractice Claims.* Santa Monica, CA: Rand Corporation.
Danzon, P.M. 1983. "An Economic Analysis of the Medical Malpractice System." *Behavioral Sciences and the Law* 1(1):39-54.
Davis, J.M., P.M. Schyve, and I. Pavkovic. 1983. "Clinical and Legal Issues in Neuroleptic Use." *Clinical Neuropharmacology* 6(2):117-128.
Delwaide, P.J., and M. Desseilles. 1977. "Spontaneous Buccolinguofacial Dyskinesia in the Elderly." *Acta Neurologica Scandinavica* 56:256-262.
Denney, N.K., D. Williamson, and R. Penn. 1975. "Informed Consent." *Postgraduate Medicine* 60:205-209.
DeVeaugh-Geiss, J. 1979. "Informed Consent for Neuroleptic Therapy." *American Journal of Psychiatry* 136:959-962.
DeVeaugh-Geiss, J. (ed.) *Tardive Dyskinesia and Related Involuntary Movement Disorders.* Boston: John Wright.
Dickens, B.M. 1981. "Ethical Issues in Psychiatric Research." *International Journal of Law and Psychiatry* 4:271-292.
Dixon, M.G. 1982. *Drug Product Liability.* New York: Mathew Bender.
Donlon, P.T., and R.L. Stenson. 1976. "Neuroleptic Induced Extrapyramidal Symptoms." *Diseases of the Nervous System* 629-635.
Dorsey, R., F.J. Ayd, J. Cole, et al. 1979. "Psychopharmacological Screening Criteria Development Project." *Journal of the American Medical Association* 241(10):1021-1031.
Druckman, R., D. Seelinger, and B. Thulin. 1962. "Chronic Involuntary Movements Induced by Phenothiazines." *Journal of Nervous and Mental Disease* 135:69-76.

"Drug Toxicity and Physician's Liability." Massachusetts General Hospital Newsletter. *Biological Therapies in Psychiatry* (June 1980):21–22.

"Drugs in Litigation: Damage Awards Involving Prescription and Non-Prescription Drugs." By the editorial staff of the publishers of *Lawyer's Medical Cyclopedia.* Indianapolis: Allen Smith, 1982.

Dyer, A.R. 1978. "Reflections on the Doctor-Patient Relationship." In *Controversy in Psychiatry,* edited by J.P. Brady and H.K.H. Brodie. Philadelphia: Saunders.

Einhorn, H.J., and R.M. Hogarth. 1981. "Behavioral Decision Theory: Processes of Judgment and Choice." *Annual Review of Psychology* 32:53–88.

Epstein, L.C., and L. Lasagne. 1969. "Obtaining Informed Consent." *Archives of Internal Medicine* 123:682–688.

Epstein, R.A. 1976. "Medical Malpractice: The Case for Contract." *American Bar Foundation Research Journal* 87–149.

Eraker, S.A., and P. Polister. 1982. "How Decisions Are Reached: Physician and Patient." *Annals of Internal Medicine* 97:262–268.

Faheem, A.D., D.R. Brightwell, G.C. Burton, et al. 1982. "Respiratory Dyskinesia and Dysarthria from Prolonged Neuroleptic Use: Tardive Dyskinesia?" *American Journal of Psychiatry* 139(4):517–518.

Falk, A., and A. Cohn. 1983. "Refining the Standard of Care—A Medicolegal Imperative." *Medical Trial Technique Quarterly* 214–228.

Fann, W.E., J.L. Sullivan, and B.W. Richman. 1976. "Dyskinesias Associated with Tricyclic Antidepressants." *British Journal of Psychiatry* 128:490–493.

Feldman, W.S. 1978. "Is Informed Consent Possible in Psychiatry?" *Legal Aspects of Medical Practice* 29–31.

Ficarra, B.J. 1980. "Medical Negligence Based on Bad Faith, Breach of Contract, or Mental Anguish." In *Legal Medicine Annual,* edited by C. Wecht.

Fishalow, S.E. 1975. "The Tort Liability of the Psychiatrist." *Bulletin of the American Academy of Psychiatry and the Law* 3:191–230.

Freedman, D.X. 1973. "Neurological Syndromes Associated with Antipsychotic Drug Use." *Archives of General Psychiatry* 28:463–467.

Fritz, W.B. 1981. "Inpatients' Views of Staff-Patient Discussions about Major Treatment Decisions." *Hospital and Community Psychiatry* 32:791–795.

Furrow, B.F. 1980. *Malpractice in Psychotherapy.* Lexington: D.C. Heath & Co.

Gagrat, D., J. Hamilton, and R.H. Belmaker. 1978. "Intravenous Diazepam in the Treatment of Neuroleptic-Induced Acute Dystonia and Akathisia." *American Journal of Psychiatry* 135(10):1232–1233.

Gardos, G., and J.O. Cole. 1980. "Problems in the Assessment of Tardive Dyskinesia." In *Tardive Dyskinesia Research & Treatment,* edited by W.E. Fann, R.C. Smith, J.M. Davis, and E.F. Domino. New York: Spectrum.

Gardos, G., and J.O. Cole. 1983a. "Tardive Dyskinesia and Anticholinergic Drugs." *American Journal of Psychiatry* 140:200–202.

Gardos, G., and J.O. Cole. 1983b. "The Prognosis of Tardive Dyskinesia." *Journal of Clinical Psychiatry* 44:177–179.

Gardos, G., J.O. Cole, and R. La Brie. 1977. "The Assessment of Tardive Dyskinesia." *Archives of General Psychiatry* 34:1206–1212.

Gardos, G., J.O. Cole, and D. Tarsy. 1978. "Withdrawal Syndromes Associated with Antipsychotic Drugs." *American Journal of Psychiatry* 135:1321–1324.

Gardos, G., A. Perenyi, J.O. Cole, et al. 1983. "Tardive Dyskinesia: Changes after Three Years." *Journal of Clinical Psychopharmacology* 3(5):315–318.

Gautier, J., A. Jus, A. Villeneuve, et al. 1977. "Influence of the Antiparkinsonian Drugs on the Plasma Level of Neuroleptics." *Biological Psychiatry* 12(3):389–397.

Gelenberg, A., and M.R. Mandel. 1977. "Catatonic Reactions to High-Potency Neuroleptic Drugs." *Archives of General Psychiatry* 34:947–950.

Geller, J.L. 1982. "State Hospital Patients and Their Medication—Do They Know What They Take?" *American Journal of Psychiatry* 139:611–615.

Glazer, W.M., D.C. Moore, T.C. Hansen, et al. 1983. "Meige Syndrome and Tardive Dyskinesia." *American Journal of Psychiatry* 140:798–799.

Goldstein, J. 1975. "For Harold Lasswell: Some Reflections on Human Dignity, Entrapment, Informed Consent, and the Plea Bargain." *The Yale Law Journal* 84:683–703.

Granacher, R.P. 1981. "Differential Diagnosis of Tardive Dyskinesia: An Overview." *American Journal of Psychiatry* 138:1288–1297.

Greenblatt, D.L., J.R. Dominick, B.A. Stotsky, et al. 1968. "Phenothiazine-Induced Dyskinesia in Nursing-Home Patients." *Journal of the American Geriatrics Society* 16(1):27–34.

Grossman, L., and F. Summers. 1980. "A Study of the Capacity of Schizophrenic Patients to Give Informed Consent." *Hospital and Community Psychiatry* 31:205–206.

Grundner, T.M. 1980. "On the Readability of Surgical Consent Forms." *New England Journal of Medicine* 302:900–902.

Gutheil, T.G., and P.S. Appelbaum. 1982. *Clinical Handbook of Psychiatry and the Law*. New York: McGraw-Hill.

Halleck, S.L. 1980. *Law and the Practice of Psychiatry*. New York: Plenum.

Halligan, P.D. 1980. "The Standard of Disclosure by Physicians to Patients: Competing Models of Informed Consent." *Louisiana Law Review* 41:9–67.

Halperin, D.A. 1980. "Misinformed Consent." *Bulletin of the American Academy of Psychiatry and the Law* 8:175–178.

Hausner, R.S. 1983. "Neuroleptic-Induced Parkinsonism and Parkinson's Disease: Differential Diagnosis and Treatment." *Journal of Clinical Psychiatry* 44:13–16.

Hickman, F.J., P.J. Resnick, and K.B. Olson. 1982. "Right to Refuse Psychotropic Medication: An Interdisciplinary Proposal." *Mental Disability Law Reporter* 6(2):122–130.

Hogan, D.B. 1979. *The Regulations of Psychotherapists*. Vol. 3. Cambridge: Ballinger.

Holder, A.R. 1978. *Medical Malpractice Law*, 2d ed. New York: Wiley.

Hollowell, E.E. 1982. "Does Hospital Corporate Liability Extend to Medical Staff Supervision?" *Law, Medicine and Health Care* 225–236.

Horan, D.J., and M.E. Guerrini. 1981. "Developing Legal Trends in Psychiatric Malpractice." *Journal of Psychiatry and the Law* 9:65–89.

Ingelfinger, F.J. 1972. "Informed but Uneducated Consent." *New England Journal of Medicine* 287:465–466.

Itoh, H., and G. Yagi. 1979. "Reversibility of Tardive Dyskinesia." *Folia Psychiatrica et Neurologica Japonica* 33(1):43–54.

Jaffe, R. 1981. "Informed Consent: Recall about Tardive Dyskinesia." *Comprehensive Psychiatry* 22:434–437.

James, D.H. 1983. "Monitoring Drugs in Hospitals for the Mentally Handicapped." *British Journal of Psychiatry* 142:163–165.

James, F., and O.S. Gray. 1977. "Misrepresentation—Part I." *Maryland Law Review* 37:286–322.

James, F., and O.S. Gray. 1978. "Misrepresentation—Part II." *Maryland Law Review* 37:488–543.

Jankovic, J. 1981. "Drug-Induced and Other Orofacial-Cervical Dyskinesias." *Annals of Internal Medicine* 94:788–793.

Jankovic, J., and J. Ford. 1983. "Blepharospasm and Orofacial-Cervical Dystonia: Clinical and Pharmacological Findings in 100 Patients." *Annals of Neurology* 13:402–411.

Jankovic, J., W.E. Havins, and R.B. Wilkins. 1982. "Blinking and Blepharospasm: Mechanism, Diagnosis, and Management." *Journal of the American Medical Association* 248:3160–3164.

Jellinek, T., G. Gardos, and J.O. Cole. 1981. "Adverse Effects of Antiparkinson Drug Withdrawal." *American Journal of Psychiatry* 138(12):1567–1571.

Jeste, D.V., S.G. Potkin, S. Sinha, et al. 1979. "Tardive Dyskinesia—Reversible and Persistent." *Archives of General Psychiatry* 36:585–590.

Jeste, D.V., and R.J. Wyatt. 1981. "Changing Epidemiology of Tardive Dyskinesia: An Overview." *American Journal of Psychiatry* 138:297–309.

Jeste, D.V., and R.J. Wyatt. 1982a. *Understanding and Treating Tardive Dyskinesia.* New York: Guilford Press.

Jeste, D.V., and R.J. Wyatt. 1982b. "Therapeutic Strategies Against Dyskinesia." *Archives of General Psychiatry* 39:803–816.

Johnson, D.A.W. 1978. "Prevalence and Treatment of Drug-Induced Extrapyramidal Symptoms." *British Journal of Psychiatry* 132:27–30.

Junewicz, J.J. 1979. "Physicians' Liability for Failure to Anticipate and Control Reactions and Interactions Precipitated by Prescribed or Administered Drugs." *Medical Trial Technique Quarterly* 26:8–41.

Jus, K., A. Jus, J. Gautier, et al. 1974. "Studies on the Action of Certain Pharmacological Agents on Tardive Dyskinesia and on the Rabbit Syndrome. *International Journal of Clinical Pharmacology* 9(2):138–145.

Jus, K., A. Villeneuve, and A. Jus. 1972. "Tardive Dyskinesia and the Rabbit Syndrome During Wakefulness and Sleep." *American Journal of Psychiatry* 129(6):765.

Kane, J.M., A. Rifkin, M. Woerner, et al. 1983. "Low-Dose Neuroleptic Treatment of Outpatient Schizophrenics." *Archives of General Psychiatry* 40:893–896.

Kane, J.M., and J.M. Smith. 1982. "Tardive Dyskinesia." *Archives of General Psychiatry* 39:473–481.

Kane, J., F. Quitkin, A. Rifkin, et al. 1978. "Comparison of the Incidence and Severity of Extrapyramidal Side Effects with Fluphenazine Enanthate and Fluphenazine Decanoate." *American Journal of Psychiatry* 135(12):1539–1542.

Kane, J.M., P. Weinhold, B. Kinon, et al. 1982. "Prevalence of Abnormal Involuntary Movements (Spontaneous Dyskinesias) in the Normal Elderly." *Psychopharmacology* 77:105–108.

Kane, J.M., M. Woerner, P. Weinhold, et al. 1982. "A Prospective Study of Tardive

Dyskinesia Development: Preliminary Results." *Journal of Clinical Psychomacology* 2(5):345–349.

Kaplan, S.R., R.A. Greenwald, and A.I. Rogers. 1977. "Neglected Aspects of Informed Consent." *New England Journal of Medicine* 296:11–17.

Kaplan, S.R., and C. Murkofsky. 1978. "Oral-Buccal Dyskinesia Symptoms Associated with Low-Dose Benzodiazepine Treatment." *American Journal of Psychiatry* 135:1558–1559.

Karson, C.N., D.V. Jeste, P.A. LeWitt, et al. 1983. "A Comparison of Two Iatrogenic Dyskinesias." *American Journal of Psychiatry* 140:1504–1506.

Katz, J. 1977. "Informed Consent—A Fairy Tale? Law's Vision." *University of Pittsburgh Law Review* 39(2):137–174.

Katz, J. 1981. "Disclosure and Consent in Psychiatric Practice: Mission Impossible?" In *Law and Ethics in the Practice of Psychiatry*, edited by C.K. Hofline.

Kaufer, D.S., E.R. Steinberg, and S.D. Toney. 1983. "Revising Medical Consent Forms: An Empirical Model and Test." *Law, Medicine and Health Care* 11(4): 155–184.

Kaufmann, C.L. 1983. "Informed Consent and Patient Decision Making: Two Decades of Research." *Social Science and Medicine* 17(21):1657–1664.

Keckich, W.A. 1978. "Neuroleptics: Violence as a Manifestation of Akathisia." *Journal of the American Medical Association* 240(20):2185.

Keepers, G.A., V.J. Clappison, and D.E. Casey. 1983. "Initial Anticholinergic Prophylaxis for Neuroleptic-Induced Extrapyramidal Syndromes." *Archives of General Psychiatry* 40:1113–1117.

Klawans, H.L., and A. Barr. 1982. "Prevalence of Spontaneous Lingual-Facial-Buccal Dyskinesias in the Elderly." *Neurology (NY)* 32:558–559.

Klawans, H.L., and A. Barr. 1983. "The Extrapyramidal System: A Review of Function." *Clinical Neuropharmacology* 6(Suppl. 1):S3–S8.

Klawans, H.L., D. Bergen, and G.W. Bruyn. 1973. "Prolonged Drug-Induced Parkinsonism." *Confinia Neurologica* 35:368–377.

Klawans, H.L., D. Bergen, G.W. Bruyn, et al. 1974. "Neuroleptic-Induced Tardive Dyskinesias in Nonpsychotic Patients." *Archives of Neurology* 30:338–339.

Klawans, H.L., and C.M. Tanner. 1983. "The Reversibility of 'Permanent' Tardive Dyskinesia." *Neurology* 33(Suppl 2):163.

Klett, C.J., and E. Caffey. 1972. "Evaluating the Long-Term Need for Antiparkinson Drugs by Chronic Schizophrenics." *Archives of General Psychiatry* 26:374–379.

Koller, W.C. 1983. "Edentulous Orodyskinesia." *Annals of Neurology* 13:97–99.

Kruse, W. 1960. "Persistent Muscular Restlessness after Phenothiazine Treatment: Report of 3 Cases." *American Journal of Psychiatry* 117:152–153.

Laforet, E.G. 1976. "The Fiction of Informed Consent." *Journal of the American Medical Association* 235:1579–1585.

Lankton, J.W., B.M. Batchelder, and A.J. Ominsky. 1977. "The Emotional Responses to Detailed Risk Disclosure for Anesthesia, A Prospective, Randomized Study." *Anesthesiology* 46:294–296.

Lavin, J.H. 1983. "Malpractice—A New Storm Is Looming." *Medical Economics*, October 3.

LeBlang, T.R. 1981. "Disclosure of Injury and Illness: Responsibilities in the Physician-Patient Relationship." *Law, Medicine and Health Care* 4–7.

Lee, A. 1977. "Drug-Induced Dystonic Reactions." *Journal of the American College of Emergency Physicians* 6:351–354.
Lesser, R.P., and S. Fahn. 1978. "A Disorder Often Misdiagnosed as a Conversion Reaction." *American Journal of Psychiatry* 135(3):349–352.
Levinson, P., R. Malen, G. Hogben, et al. 1978. "Psychological Factors in Susceptibility to Drug-Induced Extrapyramidal Symptoms." *American Journal of Psychiatry* 135(11):1375–1376.
Lidz, C.W., and L.H. Roth. 1983. "The Signed Form—Informed Consent?" In *Solutions to Ethical and Legal Problems in Social Research,* edited by R.F. Boruch and J.S. Cecil. New York: Academic Press.
Lieberman, J. 1983. "Dyskinesia Incidence Held Very Low in Healthy Aged Population." *Clinical Psychiatry News* 11(9).
Linden, M., and R. Chaskel. 1976. "Information and Consent in Schizophrenic Patients in Long-Term Treatment." *Schizophrenia Bulletin* 7:372–378.
"Litigation Seen Forcing Ob-Gyns to Limit Practices, Increase Fees." *American Medical Association News* (Sept. 23, 1983):1.
Loftus, E.F., and J.F. Fries. 1979. "Informed Consent May be Hazardous to Health." *Science* 204(April 6).
Ludlam, J.E. 1978. *Informed Consent.* Chicago: American Hospital Association.
Lynn, J. 1983. "Informed Consent: An Overview." *Behavioral Sciences and the Law* 1(4):29–45.
Lyon, M.A., M.L. Levine, and J. Zusman. 1982. "Patients' Bill of Rights: The Survey of State Statutes." *Mental Disability Law Reporter* 6:178–201.
Macklin, R. 1982. "Some Problems in Gaining Informed Consent from Psychiatric Patients." *Emory Law Journal* 31:345–374.
"Malpractice Against Psychologist, Pediatrician and Neurologist—Dystonia Musculorum Deformans—Direct and Cross-Examination of Plaintiff's Expert (a Neurosurgeon)—Part I." *Medical Trial Technique Quarterly* 24(1977):83–120.
"Malpractice Awards Rise in Recent Years." *Chicago Medicine* (April 21, 1982): 453–454.
Marsden, D.C. 1976a. "The Problem of Adult-Onset Idiopathic Torsion Dystonia and Other Isolated Dyskinesias in Adult Life (Including Blepharospasm, Oromandibular Dystonia, Dystonic Writer's Cramp and Torticollis, or Axial Dystonia.)" *Advances in Neurology* 14:259–276.
Marsden, C.D. 1976b. "Blepharospasm-Oromandibular Dystonia Syndrome (Brueghel's Syndrome): A Variant of Adult-Onset Torsion Dystonia?" *Journal of Neurology, Neurosurgery and Psychiatry* 39:1204–1209.
Marsden, C.D., and M.J.G. Harrison. 1974. "Idiopathic Torsion Dystonia (Dystonia Musculorum Deformans): A Review of Forty-Two Patients." *Brain* 97:793–810.
Marsden, C.D., and P. Jenner. 1980. "The pathophysiology of Extrapyramidal Side-Effects of Neuroleptic Drugs." *Psychological Medicine* 10:55–72.
Marsden, C.D., D. Tarsy, and R.J. Baldessarini. 1975. "Spontaneous and Drug-Induced Movement Disorders in Psychotic Patients." In *Psychiatric Aspects of Neurologic Disease,* edited by D.F. Benson and D. Blumer, pp. 219–265. New York: Grune and Stratton.
Matthews, W.B., P. Beasley, W. Parry-Jones, et al. 1978. "Spasmodic Torticollis: A

Combined Clinical Study." *Journal of Neurology, Neurosurgery and Psychiatry* 41:485–492.
McClellan, F.M. 1978. "Strict Liability for Drug Induced Injuries: An Excursion Through the Maze of Products Liability, Negligence, and Absolute Liability." *Wayne Law Review* 25:1–36.
McClellan, F.A.M. 1982. "Informed Consent to Medical Therapy and Experimentation." *Journal of Legal Medicine* 3:81–115.
McEvoy, J.P. 1983. "The Clinical Use of Anticholinergic Drugs as Treatment for Extrapyramidal Side Effects of Neuroleptic Drugs." *Journal of Clinical Psychopharmacology* 3(5):288–302.
McMahon, F.G. 1975. "The Patient Package Insert." *Journal of the American Medical Association* 233:1089.
McNeil, B.J., S.G. Pauker, H.C. Sox, et al. 1982. "On the Elicitation of Preferences for Alternative Therapies." *New England Journal of Medicine* 306:1259–1262.
Mehta, D., A. Mallya, and J. Volavka. 1978. "Mortality of Patients with Tardive Dyskinesia." *American Journal of Psychiatry* 135:371–372.
Meisel, A. 1979. "The Exceptions to the Informed Consent Doctrine: Striking a Balance Between Competing Values in Medical Decisionmaking." *Wisconsin Law Review* 1979:413–488.
Meisel, A., and L.D. Kabnick. 1980. "Informed Consent to Medical Treatment: An Analysis of Recent Legislation." *University of Pittsburgh Law Review* 41(3): 407–564.
Meisel, A., and L.H. Roth. 1981. "What We Do and Do Not Know About Informed Consent." *Journal of the American Medical Association* 246:2473–2477.
Meisel, A., and L.H. Roth. 1983. "Toward an Informed Discussion of Informed Consent: A Review and Critique of the Empirical Studies." *Arizona Law Review* 25(2):265–346.
Meisel, A., L.H. Roth, and C.W. Lidz. 1977. "Toward a Model of the Legal Doctrine of Informed Consent." *American Journal of Psychiatry* 134:285–289.
Miller, L.J. 1980. "Informed Consent: 1." *Journal of the American Medical Association* 244:2100–2103.
Miller, R., and H.S. Willner. 1974. "The Two-Part Consent Form." *New England Journal of Medicine* 290:964–966.
Miller, R.D. 1983. *Problems in Hospital Law,* 4th ed. Rockville, MD: Aspen.
Mills, D.H. 1974. "Whither Informed Consent?" *Journal of the American Medical Association* 229:305–310.
Mills, M.J., and D. Avery. 1978. "The Legal Regulation of Electroconvulsive Therapy." In *Mood Disorders: The World's Major Public Health Problem,* edited by F.J. Ayd, pp. 154–183. Baltimore: Frank Ayd Communications.
Moleman, P., P.J.M. Schmitz, and G.A. Ladee. 1982. "Extrapyramidal Side Effects and Oral Haloperidol: An Analysis of Explanatory Patient and Treatment Characteristics." *Journal of Clinical Psychiatry* 43:492–496.
Moore, R.M. 1978. "Consent Forms—How, or Whether, They Should Be Used." *Mayo Clinic Proceedings* 53:393–396.
Morris, L.A., M. Mazis, and E. Gordon. 1977. "A Survey of the Effects of Oral Contraceptive Patient Information." *Journal of the American Medical Association* 238:2504–2508.

Morrow, G.R. 1980. "How Readable Are Subject Consent Forms?" *Journal of the American Medical Association* 244:56–58.

Morrow, G., J. Gootnick, and A. Schmale. 1978. "The Simple Technique for Increasing Cancer Patients' Knowledge of Informed Consent to Treatment." *Cancer* 42:793–799.

Mueller, J., and M.J. Aminoff. 1982. "Tourette-Like Syndrome After Long-Term Neuroleptic Drug Treatment." *British Journal of Psychiatry* 141:191–193.

Mukherjee, S., A.M. Rosen, C. Cardenas, et al. 1982. "Tardive Dyskinesia in Psychiatric Outpatients." *Archives of General Psychiatry* 39:466–469.

Munetz, M.R., and C.L. Cornes. 1983. "Distinguishing Akathesia and Tardive Dyskinesia: A Review of the Literature." *Journal of Clinical Psychopharmacology* 3(6):343–350.

Munetz, M.R., and C.L. Cornes. 1982. "Akathisia, Pseudoakathisia and Tardive Dyskinesia: Clinical Examples." *Comprehensive Psychiatry* 23(4):345–352.

Munetz, M.R., L.H. Roth, and C.L. Cornes. 1982. "Tardive Dyskinesia and Informed Consent: Myths and Realities." *Bulletin of the American Academy of Psychiatry and the Law* 10:77–88.

Olin, G.B., and H.S. Olin. 1975. "Informed Consent in Voluntary Mental Hospital Admissions." *American Journal of Psychiatry* 132:938–941.

Osifo, N.G. 1979. "Commentary: Drug-Related Transient Dyskinesias." *Clinical Pharmacology Therapeutics* 25:767–771.

Owens, D.G.C., and E.C. Johnstone. 1982. "Spontaneous Involuntary Disorders of Movement." *Archives of General Psychiatry* 39:452–461.

Ozzi, W.M. 1982. "Survey of the Law of Informed Consent in Physician-Patient Relationships." In *Legal Medicine 1982,* edited by C.H. Wecht. Philadelphia: W.B. Saunders.

Palmer, A.B., and J. Wohl. 1972. "Voluntary Admission Forms: Does the Patient Know What He Is Signing?" *Hospital and Community Psychiatry* 23:250–252.

Polizos, P., and D.M. Engelhardt. 1978. "Dyskinetic Phenomena in Children Treated with Psychotropic Medications." *Psychopharmacology Bulletin* 14:65–68.

President's Commission for the Study of Ethical Problems in Medicine and Biomedical and Behavioral Research. 1982. *Making Health Care Decisions,* Vols. 1, 2, 3. U.S. Govt. Printing Office.

Prien, R.F., M.B. Balter, and E.M. Caffey. 1978. "Hospital Surveys of Prescribing Practices with Psychotherapeutic Drugs." *Archives of General Psychiatry* 35: 1271–1275.

Pyke, J., and M.V. Seeman. 1981. "Neuroleptic-Free Intervals in the Treatment of Schizophrenia." *American Journal of Psychiatry* 138:1620–1621.

Richards, E.P., and K.C. Rathbun. 1982. "A Procrustean Approach to Informed Consent: The Texas Medical Disclosure Panel." *Law, Medicine and Health Care* 158–164.

Richardson, M.A., and T.J. Craig. 1982. "The Coexistence of Parkinsonian-Like Symptoms and Tardive Dyskinesia." *American Journal of Psychiatry* 139: 341–343.

Rifkin, A., F. Quitkin, J. Kane, et al. "Are Prophylactic Antiparkinson Drugs Necessary?" *Archives of General Psychiatry* 35:483–489.

Rifkin, A., F. Quitkin, and D.F. Klein. 1975. "Akinesia: A Poorly Recognized Drug-

Induced Extrapyramidal Behavioral Disorder." *Archives of General Psychiatry* 32:672–674.

Rights of the Mentally Disabled. Washington, D.C.: Hospital and Community Psychiatry Service of the American Psychiatric Association, 1982.

Roth, L.H., P.S. Appelbaum, R. Sallee, et al. 1982a. "The Dilemma of Denial in the Assessment of Competency to Refuse Treatment." *American Journal of Psychiatry* 139:910–913.

Roth, L.H., C.W. Lidz, A. Meisel, et al. 1982b. "Competency to Decide About Treatment or Research." *International Journal of Law and Psychiatry* 5:29–50.

Roth, L.H., A. Meisel, and C.W. Lidz. 1977. "Tests of Competency to Consent to Treatment." *American Journal of Psychiatry* 134:279–284.

Rosen, A.M., S. Mukherjee, S. Olarte, et al. 1982. "Perception of Tardive Dyskinesia in Outpatients Receiving Maintenance Neuroleptics." *American Journal of Psychiatry* 139:372–373.

Rush, M., F. Diamond, and M. Alpert. 1982. "Depression as a Risk Factor in Tardive Dyskinesia." *Biological Psychiatry* 17:387–392.

Samuels, A. 1982. "What the Doctor Must Tell the Patient." *Medicine, Science and Law* 22:41–46.

Sanbar, S.S., and C.S. Thompson. 1983. "Developing Standards of Care for the Diagnosis and Treatment of Coronary Artery Disease." *Journal of Legal Medicine* 4(1):87–108.

Schonecker, V.M. 1957. "Ein Eigentumliches Syndrom im Oralen Bereich bei Megaphenapplikation." *Nervenarzt* 28:35.

Schooler, N.R., and J.M. Kane. 1982. "Research Diagnoses for Tardive Dyskinesia." *Archives of General Psychiatry* 39:486–487.

Seeman, M.V. 1981. "Tardive Dyskinesia: Two-Year Recovery." *Comprehensive Psychiatry* 22:189–192.

Shapiro, S.A. 1979. "Limiting Physician Freedom to Prescribe a Drug for any Purpose: The Need for DFA Regulation." *Northwestern University Law Review* 73:801–872.

Shear, M.K., A. Frances, and P. Weiden. 1983. "Suicide Associated with Akathisia and Depot Fluphenazine Treatment." *Journal of Clinical Psychopharmacology* 3(4):235–236.

Shenoy, R.S., A.G. Sadler, C. Goldberg, et al. 1981. "Effects of a Six-Week Drug Holiday on Symptom Status, Relapse, and Tardive Dyskinesia in Chronic Schizophrenics." *Journal of Clinical Psychopharmacology* 1(3):141–145.

Shields, W.D., and P.F. Bray. 1976. "A Danger of Haloperidol Therapy in Children." *Journal of Pediatrics* 88(2):301–303.

Simpson, G.M., and J.W.S. Angus. 1970. "A Rating Scale for Extrapyramidal Side Effects." *Acta Psychiatrica Scandinavica* 212(Suppl):11–21.

Simpson, G.M., E. Varga, and E.J. Haher. 1976. "Psychotic Exacerbations Produced by Neuroleptics." *Diseases of the Nervous System* 37(7):367–369.

Slawson, P., W. King, B. Lee, et al. 1978. *Professional Liability Insurance and Psychiatric Malpractice: A Task Force Report of the American Psychiatric Association.* Washington, D.C.: American Psychiatric Association.

Slovenko, R. 1979. "On the Legal Aspects of Tardive Dyskinesia." *Journal of Psychiatry and Law* 295–331.

Slovenko, R. 1981. "Malpractice in Psychiatry and Related Fields." *Journal of Psychiatry and Law* 9:5–63.

Smith, J.M., and R.J. Baldessarini. 1980. "Changes in Prevalence, Severity and Recovery in Tardive Dyskinesia with Age." *Archives of General Psychiatry* 37:1368–1373.

Soskis, D.A. 1978. "Schizophrenia and Medical Inpatients as Informed Drug Consumers." *Archives of General Psychiatry* 35:645–647.

Soskis, D.A., and R.L. Jaffe. 1979. "Communicating with Patients about Antipsychotic Drugs." *Comprehensive Psychiatry* 20:126–131.

Southwick, A.F. 1983. "Hospital Liability—Two Theories Have Been Merged. *Journal of Legal Medicine* 4(1):1–50.

Sovner, R., and A. DiMascio. 1977. "The Effect of Benztropine Mesylate in the Rabbit Syndrome and Tardive Dyskinesia." *American Journal of Psychiatry* 134:1301–1302.

Sovner, R., and A. DiMascio. 1978. "Extrapyramidal Syndromes and Other Neurological Side Effects of Psychotropic Drugs." In *Psychopharmacology: A Generation of Progress,* edited by M.A. Lipton, A. DiMascio, and K.F. Killam, pp. 1021–1032. New York: Raven Press.

Sovner, R., A. DiMascio, D. Berkowitz, et al. 1978. "Tardive Dyskinesia and Informed Consent." *Psychosomatics* 19:172–177.

Sprague, R.L. 1982. "Litigation, Legislation, and Regulations." In *Drugs and Mental Retardation,* edited by S.E. Breuning and A.D. Poling. Springfield, IL: Charles C Thomas.

Stanley, B. 1983. "Senile Dementia and Informed Consent." *Behavioral Sciences and the Law* 1(4):57–71.

Stevens, G.E. 1983. "Fraud and Medical Malpractice." *Medical Trial Technique Quarterly* 29(3):291–301.

Stone, A.A. 1979. "Informed Consent: Special Problems for Psychiatry." *Hospital and Community Psychiatry* 30:321–327.

Stone, A.A. 1981. "Doctor Stone Replies." *Clinical Psychiatry News* (Dec.):7–8.

Sutcher, H.D., R.B. Underwood, R.A. Beatty, et al. 1971. "Orofacial Dyskinesia: A Dental Dimension." *Journal of the American Medical Association* 216(9):1459–1463.

Swett, C. 1975. "Drug-Induced Dystonia." *American Journal of Psychiatry* 132(5): 532–534.

Szasz, R.S., and M. Hollender. 1956. "A Contribution to the Philosophy of Medicine." *Arch Internal Medicine* 97:585–592.

Tancredi, L.R. 1982a. "Designated Compensable Events: A No-Fault Approach to Medical Malpractice." *Law, Medicine and Health Care* (October).

Tancredi, L.R. 1982b. "Competency for Informed Consent." *International Journal of Law and Psychiatry* 5:51–63.

Tarsy, D. 1983a. "Neuroleptic-Induced Extrapyramidal Reactions: Classification, Description, and Diagnosis." *Clinical Neuropharmacology* 6(Suppl. 1):S9–S26.

Tarsy, D. 1983b. "History and Definition of Tardive Dyskinesia." *Clinical Neuropharmacology* 6(2):91–99.

Taub, S. 1983. "Psychiatric Malpractice in the 1980s: A Look at Some Areas of Concern." *Law, Medicine and Health Care* (June).

Taub, S. 1982. "Cancer and the Law of Informed Consent." *Law, Medicine and Health Care* 61–66.

Tenenbaum, J. 1983. "ECT Regulation Reconsidered." *Mental Disability Law Reporter* 7(2):148–211.

Thach, B.T., T.N. Chase, and J.F. Bosma. 1975. "Oralfacial Dyskinesia Associated with Prolonged Use of Antihistaminic Decongestants." *New England Journal of Medicine* 293:486–487.

Thomasma, D.C. 1983. "Beyond Medical Paternalism and Patient Autonomy: A Model of Physician Conscience for the Physician-Patient Relationship." *Annals of Internal Medicine* 98:243–248.

Todd, R., S. Lippmann, M. Manshadi, et al. 1983. "Recognition and Treatment of Rabbit Syndrome, an Uncommon Complication of Neuroleptic Therapies." *American Journal of Psychiatry* 140:1519–1520.

Tolosa, E.S. 1981. "Clinical Features of Meige's Disease (Idiopathic Orofacial Dystonia): A Report of 17 Cases." *Archives of Neurology* 38:147–151.

Tolosa, E.S., and H.L. Klawans. 1979. "Meige's Disease: A Clinical Form of Facial Convulsion, Bilateral and Medial." *Archives of Neurology* 36:635–637.

Tozer, F.L., and J.E. Kasik. 1967. "The Medical-Legal Aspects of Adverse Drug Reactions." *Clinical Pharmacology and Therapeutics* 8:637–646.

Tversky, A., and D. Kahneman. 1974. "Judgement under Uncertainty: Heuristics and Biases." *Science* 185:1124–1131.

Twardy, S. 1978. "The Issue of Malpractice in Psychiatry." *Medical Trial Technique Quarterly* 25:161–176.

"Use of Unapproved Drugs for Unlabelled Indications." *Food and Drug Administration Drug Bulletin* 12:4–5.

Vaccarino, J.M. 1978. "Consent, Informed Consent and the Consent Form." *New England Journal of Medicine* 298:455.

Van Putten, T. 1975. "The Many Faces of Akathisia." *Comprehensive Psychiatry* 16(1):43–47.

Van Putten, T. 1974. "Why Do Schizophrenic Patients Refuse to Take Their Drugs?" *Archives of General Psychiatry* 31:67–72.

Van Putten, T., and P.R.A. May. 1978. "Akinetic Depression in Schizophrenia." *Archives of General Psychiatry* 35:1101–1107.

Van Putten, T., L.R. Mutalipassi, and M.D. Malkin. 1974. "Phenothiazine-Induced Decompensation." *Archives of General Psychiatry* 30:102–105.

Varga, E., A.A. Sugerman, V. Varga, et al. 1982. "Prevalence of Spontaneous Oral Dyskinesia in the Elderly." *American Journal of Psychiatry* 139:329–331.

Vertinsky, I.B., W.A. Thompson, and D. Uyeno. 1974. "Measuring Consumer Desire for Participation in Clinical Decisionmaking." *Health Services Research* 9: 121–134.

Villeneuve, A. 1972. "The Rabbit Syndrome: A Peculiar Extrapyramidal Reaction." *Canadian Psychiatric Association Journal* 17(SS-II):69–72.

Vogel, J., and R. Delgado. 1980. "To Tell the Truth: Physicians' Duty to Disclose Medical Mistakes." *UCLA Law Review* 28:52–94.

Volow, M.R., J.O. Cavenar, W.N. Grosch, et al. 1980. "The Diagnostic Dilemma of Blepharospasm." *American Journal of Psychiatry* 137:620–621.

Wegner, J.T., and J.M. Kane. 1982. "Follow-up Study on the Reversibility of Tardive Dyskinesia." *American Journal of Psychiatry* 139:368–369.

Weiner, W.J., C.G. Goetz, P.A. Nausieda, et al. 1978. "Respiratory Dyskinesias: Extrapyramidal Dysfunction and Dyspnea." *Annals of Internal Medicine* 88: 327–331.

Weiner, W.J., and E.D. Luby. 1983. "Persistent Akathisia Following Neuroleptic Withdrawal." *Annals of Neurology* 13:466–467.

Weiner, W.J., and E.D. Luby. 1983. "Tardive Akathisia." *Journal of Clinical Psychiatry* 44:417–419.

Weiner, W.J., P.A. Nausieda, and R.H. Glantz. 1981. "Meige Syndrome (Blepharospasm-Oromandibular Dystonia) after Long-Term Neuroleptic Therapy." *Neurology (NY)* 31:1555–1556.

Wells, C., and G. Duncan. 1980. *Neurology for Psychiatrists,* edited by F.A. Davis Co., Philadelphia.

Wettstein, R.M. 1983. "Tardive Dyskinesia and Malpractice." *Behavioral Sciences and the Law* 1(1):85–107.

Wilkinson, A.P. 1981. "Psychiatric Malpractice." *American Journal of Forensic Psychiatry* 2:3–9.

Williams, R.L., G.M. Trenholme, K.H. Rieckmann, et al. 1977. "The Use of a Test to Determine That Consent Is Informed." *Military Medicine* 142:542–545.

Wolf, M.E., J. Chevesich, E. Lehrer, et al. 1983. "The Clinical Association of Tardive Dyskinesia and Drug-Induced Parkinsonism." *Biol Psychiatry* 13(10):1181–1188.

Yagi, G., K. Ogita, N. Ohtsuka, et al. 1976. "Persistent Dyskinesia after Long-Term Treatment with Neuroleptics in Japan." *Keio Journal of Medicine* 25:27–35.

Yassa, R., A.M. Ghadirian, and G. Schwartz. 1983. "Prevalence of Tardive Dystinesia in Affective Disorder Patients." *Journal of Clinical Psychiatry* 44(11):410–412.

Zerubavel, E. 1980. "The Bureaucratization of Responsibility: The Case of Informed Consent." *Bulletin of the American Academy of Psychiatry and the Law* 8: 161–167.

The Current Status of Actions for Wrongful Life and Wrongful Birth

Sheila Taub, J.D.

INTRODUCTION

The planned birth of a normal, healthy child is usually an occasion for great rejoicing, but the birth of an unplanned child may be viewed as a lesser blessing, and the birth of a child with a serious mental or physical handicap is almost universally perceived as a great tragedy. Until fairly recently, such events were considered "acts of God," and parents dealt with them as best they could with whatever financial and emotional resources they happened to possess. Legal, medical, and social changes of the past few decades have greatly altered the picture, however, and parents who might formerly have railed at the Almighty for their misfortunes now seek financial compensation from more earthly beings.

The usual sources looked to for compensation are physicians who may have been negligent in performing unsuccessful sterilization or abortion procedures, in failing to counsel parents that they were at risk for producing a defective child, or in failing to diagnose a genetic defect in a fetus, thus depriving the parents of the opportunity to abort the child. (The term "defective child," although objectionable to some, will be used as a shorthand description for a child with a congenital mental or physical handicap.)

Among the societal changes which have contributed to the ever-increasing resort to the courts in these situations are the decriminalization of abortion by the United States Supreme Court decision in Roe v. Wade,[1] the great expansion in the ability to diagnose genetic defects in parents, children, and fetuses (via amniocentesis, and, quite recently, chorionic villus biopsy), the trend toward smaller families, with the consequent desire to provide each child with the optimum genetic, social, and economic endowment, the increasing litigiousness in society, especially toward the medical profession, and the increasing willingness of courts to recognize novel forms of action whenever a demonstrable injury has occurred. Consequently the picture has changed radically since 1967 when the New Jersey Supreme Court decided, in Gleitman v. Cosgrove,[2] that an obstetrician who failed to advise a pregnant woman who had had German measles in the first trimester of her pregnancy that she was at risk for producing a defective child could not be sued successfully either by the parents or by the child, who was subsequently born with numerous severe defects.

This article will not attempt a comprehensive review of the subject, since there already exist numerous articles and books which trace the history, theoretical basis, and outcome of wrongful life and wrongful birth claims.[3] It will instead discuss in detail a few recent cases which either break new ground in this area of the law or which summarize in a particularly lucid way the paths the various courts seem to be taking with these cases.

Terminology

"Wrongful birth" actions are those brought by parents seeking damages for the birth of a child who was either (1) healthy but unwanted, or (2) planned but defective. (It is, of course, possible for a child to be both unplanned and defective, which has occurred in several cases.) Cases in the first category generally result from unsuccessful sterilizations or abortions. It has been suggested that these cases be denoted "wrongful pregnancy" or "wrongful conception" cases, and that the term "wrongful birth" be reserved for cases where the child has been born defective. The latter usually result from failure to diagnose a genetic defect in the parents or in the fetus, or, sometimes, in an older sibling of the defective child. Parents typically allege that had they been made aware of the defect they either would not have conceived the child or would have aborted it. Recent decisions appear to be following the suggested distinction between actions for wrongful pregnancy or conception and actions for wrongful birth.

"Wrongful life" cases, on the other hand, are actions brought by the child himself, alleging that because of his defect, which may be physical, mental, or social, he would have been better off never having been born. In every wrongful life claim, the particular defect suffered by the child is one which could not have been prevented, under the current state of medical technology, except by preventing the birth of the child. Were it otherwise, and a child were found, for example, to have a defect which was curable in utero, but the physician negligently failed to cure it, the child would have an ordinary negligence action against the physician for a prenatal tort.

The term "dissatisfied life" has been suggested for claims brought by children who are illegitimate, but physically healthy and normal, to distinguish these claims from claims brought by children born with mental or physical handicaps. This term also seems to be gaining currency in some recent cases.

One author has suggested that the term "wrongful life" be replaced by the term "diminished life," in order to avoid misleading analogies to actions for wrongful death, as well as for other reasons,[4] but the term does not seem to have gained many adherents.

Although it might be desirable to limit the number of terms to two, "wrongful life" and "wrongful birth," since these are clearly distinguishable on the basis of (1) the plaintiff who brings the action, and (2) the nature of the harm for which damages are being sought, there is also some merit to adding the terms "wrongful pregnancy" or "wrongful conception" and "dissatisfied life," since courts tend to treat wrongful pregnancy/conception claims somewhat differently from other wrongful birth claims, and to treat dissatisfied life claims differently from other wrongful life claims. Wrongful pregnancy and wrongful birth claims will overlap when an unwanted child born of a faulty sterilization procedure turns out to be defective.

Wrongful Pregnancy

A claim for wrongful pregnancy[5] may arise out of negligence in filling a prescription for a contraceptive, in diagnosing pregnancy in time for an abortion to be obtained, or in performing an abortion or sterilization procedure. Whatever the means, the end result is a child that is usually, but not always, healthy, but unplanned and unwanted. Conceding that there was negligence on the part of the defendant, courts have nevertheless had great difficulty in awarding damages for the birth of a normal healthy child. Yet the Supreme Court has recognized, in a long line of cases,[6] the rights of individuals to decide when to procreate, and even to abort an unwanted child, so the negligent failure to perform medical procedures designed to effectuate these rights would seem to justify an action in tort. This conflict between the judicial desires to exalt the sanctity of life, on the one hand, and vindicate the rights of parents to make their own procreative decisions, on the other, has led courts in different jurisdictions to different solutions to the wrongful pregnancy dilemma. The general trend seems to be to recognize the existence of the cause of action, but to limit the damages to something less than all that would be available under recognized tort principles.

Basis of the action

Negligence. Most wrongful pregnancy claims are based on negligence. Under the traditional tort analysis, to prevail on a negligence claim plaintiff must establish all four elements of duty, breach of duty, proximate causation, and damages. In the usual wrongful pregnancy claim based on a failure of sterilization, there is no difficulty in establishing the first three elements. A few cases have questioned the existence of proximate causation, either on the grounds that the pregnancy resulted from the plaintiff's having sexual relations and not from the sterilization procedure, or on the grounds that plaintiff could have obtained an abortion after she discovered that she was pregnant.[7] The first argument has not carried much weight, for obvious reasons, and most courts have held that a plaintiff should not be required to undergo an abortion to mitigate damages. A plaintiff's testimony that she would have undergone an abortion had a timely diagnosis of pregnancy been made has been held sufficient to support a verdict.[8]

Informed consent. If the failure of a sterilization procedure is not due to negligence, but rather to an inherent risk of the procedure itself, then liability may be predicated on failure to obtain informed consent. The plaintiff may have difficulty recovering under an informed consent theory because of the need to prove, in jurisdictions where informed consent claims are grounded in negligence, that she would not have undergone the procedure had she been apprised of the risks.[9] In some cases, plaintiff might be able to demonstrate that she would have undergone a more drastic procedure, such as a hysterectomy, rather than undergo the risk of an unsuccessful sterilization.

Breach of contract. Where the physician is rash enough to guarantee that sterility will result from the procedure, the action may be based on breach of contract.[10] Disadvantages to the plaintiff of basing a wrongful pregnancy claim on a breach of contract theory include the possibility that courts will exclude certain elements of damages which would be available under a negligence theory, such as an award for mental anguish, and that coverage may not be available under the physician's professional liability insurance policy. Despite these drawbacks, it might be desirable to make a claim for breach of contract, if the facts support it, where plaintiff cannot prove negligence in the performance of the procedure.

Damages

The major difficulty which courts have had, in wrongful pregnancy claims, is in the area of determining damages. Some courts have felt that any detriment suffered by the parents would be more than compensated by the joys and benefits of parenthood, and have refused to recognize the action at all.[11] The California Supreme Court rejected this argument in Custodio v. Bauer (n. 10, *supra*), however, along with arguments that the child would be adversely emotionally affected later in life when he learned of the lawsuit, and, had the parents truly not wanted the child, they could have aborted it or put it up for adoption.

Since Custodio, most of the courts that have considered wrongful pregnancy claims have granted them recognition, differing only with respect to the elements of damages that they were willing to compensate, although a few have continued to deny all claims for damages for the birth of a healthy, but unwanted, child.[12] The possible damages attributable to the birth of a healthy child following an unsuccessful sterilization or abortion could include the cost of the unsuccessful procedure itself and any attendant pain and suffering associated with it; the medical expenses, pain and suffering, and mental anguish associated with the pregnancy and delivery; any lost wages incurred by the mother during pregnancy and child-rearing; the husband's damages for loss of consortium during the pregnancy and in the postpartum period; the economic costs of rearing the child to maturity; and the emotional costs involved in rearing the child.

The Supreme Court of Arizona provided a comprehensive review of the various positions taken in different jurisdictions with respect to damages in wrongful pregnancy actions in its recent decision in University of Arizona Health Sciences Center v. Superior Court of the State of Arizona.[13] The real parties in interest were Patrick and Jeanne Heimann, who has sued the University medical center, claiming that one of its physician-employees had negligently performed a vasectomy on Patrick, which led to Jeanne's pregnancy and subsequent delivery of a healthy baby girl. The Heimanns claimed they were financially unable to provide for this, their fourth child, and sued both the allegedly negligent physician and his employer. The hospital filed a motion for partial summary judgment in the malpractice suit, asking the trial judge to declare as a matter of law that the Heimanns could not recover for the future costs of raising the child. The judge denied the motion, and the University brought a special action to have the judge's ruling declared improper and vacated. The Arizona Supreme Court accepted jurisdiction to decide the narrow legal issue in order to avoid the costs and delay to the parties that would be caused by utilizing normal appellate procedures.

The majority opinion recognized three distinct views among the cases which have awarded some type of damages in wrongful pregnancy actions; the first limits damages by holding that parents may recover only those damages which occur as the result of pregnancy and birth, and may not recover the cost of rearing the child.[14] The rationale for this view appears to be that it would be inequitable to allow the parents to experience the benefits of parenthood while shifting the economic burden to a third party. The second, which could be characterized as the "full damage" rule, allows the parents to recover all damages and expenses, including the cost of the unsuccessful sterilization procedure, the economic loss from pregnancy, and the economic, physical and emotional cost attendant to birth and rearing the child,[15] but cases espousing this view are a distinct minority. The third view, with substantially more adherents, allows recovery of all damages which flow from the wrongful act but requires consideration of the offsetting benefits. The trier of fact would be instructed to award damages for all past and future damages and expenses incurred by the parents, including the costs of rearing the child, but would also be instructed to deduct the benefits the parents could be expected to receive from having a normal, healthy child.[16] In support of the third view, the court cited section 920 of the Restatement (Second) of Torts, which states: "When the defendant's tortious conduct has caused harm to the plaintiff or to his property and in so doing has conferred a special benefit to the interest of the plaintiff that was harmed, the value of the benefit conferred is considered in mitigation of damages, to the extent that this is equitable."

Reasons given by various courts for adopting the first, "strict," view, which was urged by the University, include the speculative nature of the future emotional and pecuniary costs of raising the child, the argument that the benefit of having the child will necessarily outweigh any of the costs, and the argument that allowing costs for rearing the child would impose an unreasonable burden on the defendant and possibly open the way for fraudulent claims. The major reason, however, is the argument that parents cannot be damaged in any real sense by rearing a normal healthy child. The majority stated that this argument was "based on an emotional premise" and "ignores logical considerations," (i.e., that there may indeed be cases where an unplanned child causes serious emotional or economic problems to the parents). It therefore rejected the view that the costs of educating and rearing an unplanned child can never be compensable elements of damages.

The majority likewise rejected the "full damage" rule urged by the Heimanns. While it agreed that all of the foreseeable damages available under traditional tort principles should, in theory, be compensated, it felt that consideration of the basic values inherent in the parent-child relationship and of the dignity and sanctity of human life required that the foreseeable damages should be offset by the foreseeable benefits of the parent-child relationship.

The majority also expressed the view that a rule which permitted the fact finder to consider all pecuniary and nonpecuniary damages, together with any offsetting pecuniary and nonpecuniary benefits, would place the ultimate decision as to damages with the proper party to reflect the consensus of community values on these issues (i.e., the jury).

In response to the argument that the "benefits rule" of section 920 applies only when the injury and benefit are to the same interest, and that therefore the emotional benefits of child rearing cannot be used to offset the economic costs of same, the court responded with a quotation from Justice Faulkner's concurring opinion in Boone v. Mullendore (n. 14, *supra*), that "the economic burden and emotional distress of rearing an unexpected child are inextricably related to each other."

The majority stated that the danger of juries awarding damages, under this rule, in cases where no real injury exists, would be minimized by giving weight and consideration in each case to the plaintiff's reasons for submitting to the sterilization procedure. Thus, if the parents sought sterilization to prevent the birth of a child with a genetic defect, then the birth of a healthy child would be considered a blessing rather than an injury. The jury should be given sufficient information about all the relevant circumstances of the case to allow it to make a realistic assessment of the benefits and detriments produced by defendant's negligence. The computation of damages in wrongful pregnancy cases would then be consistent with damage rules applicable in all other tort cases. Parents would not be required to mitigate damages by choosing abortion or adoption, however, and their failure to do so would not be considered as an offset, since "the decision not to conceive a child is quite different from the decision to abort or put the child up for adoption once it has been conceived."

A minority opinion written by Vice Chief Justice Gordon, concurring in part and dissenting in part, would not have allowed damages for the costs of rearing a healthy child, stating that the allowance of such damages was contrary to the public policy of the state, since it requires the parents to deny the worth of the child, a fact which would cause emotional harm to at least some children whose parents brought such suits. The majority had mentioned this possibility, but did not seem to think it worthy of serious consideration. (One court attempted to minimize the feared harm by addressing a portion of the opinion to the child himself, in which it stated that it did not understand the complaint to imply any rejection of the parent-child relationship! Rieck v. Medical Protective Co., n. 7, *supra.*)

Justice Gordon also said that the majority was inconsistent in holding that abortion and adoption were unreasonable methods of mitigating damages as a matter of law, and in holding that nonpecuniary benefits could be used to offset pecuniary losses. He may well be correct, yet it may be a wise policy for courts to refrain from espousing any principles that might encourage abortion or adoption.

Justice Gordon's opinion is most noteworthy for its inclusion of a consideration not normally found in such cases, namely, the probable effect of the decision on the availability and costs of the medical procedure in question. He wrote: "It is conceivable that hereafter many health care providers will either refuse to perform these procedures, or they will become so expensive that only the wealthy will be able to afford them. If the intended result of the majority is to lessen the number of unwanted pregnancies by requiring more skill and caution in the performance of sterilization procedures, I believe that this case will be self-defeating. There will probably be an increase in the number of unwanted pregnancies due to the increased cost and relative unavailability of surgical sterilization."

Justice Gordon's attention to the possible effects of the majority's decision on medical practice marks a welcome change from the metaphysical arguments about the sanctity of life and whether or not the emotional pleasures of child rearing outweigh the economic costs. Reports have appeared in the general and medical press recently to the effect that huge damage awards in wrongful life and wrongful birth suits have driven up the cost of malpractice insurance for obstetricians to such an extent in some states that some physicians, such as family practitioners and gynecologist-obstetricians, are abandoning obstetrics entirely rather than pay the additional premiums required.[17] This can only have a detrimental effect on obstetrical care in the long run.

There may be a valuable lesson to be learned from the recent Bendectin controversy, in which Merrell Dow Pharmaceuticals, manufacturer of Bendectin, the only drug effective in combatting extreme nausea due to pregnancy, withdrew the drug from the market, claiming it could no longer afford the expense of defending claims that the drug had caused birth defects in some children of mothers who took the drug during pregnancy. Several such suits had been brought (one resulting in a $750,000 jury verdict which was overturned by the court), despite the fact that no association between the drug and any birth defect has ever been proven.[18] The fear of litigation may likewise deter physicians from practicing in high risk fields such as obstetrics and genetic counseling.

WRONGFUL BIRTH CLAIMS

Wrongful birth claims are perhaps the least problematic of all the ones being considered here, as they typically involve recognizable acts of medical malpractice which result in clearly discernible harm to the parents which, in many cases, will not be offset by the joys attendant upon raising a healthy, normal child. Yet here too courts have been reluctant seemingly to denigrate the worth of the life of even a severely handicapped child by awarding damages to include all the costs of raising that child with no consideration of the offsetting benefits. Thus, one of the principal reasons the New Jersey Supreme Court denied recovery to the parents in Gleitman was the difficulty of measuring the rewards they would receive from parenting a defective child against the emotional and pecuniary injuries they would suffer in raising such a child.

Perhaps the major reason for denying recovery in Gleitman disappeared with the Supreme Court decision in Roe v. Wade, for subsequent cases have had little difficulty in allowing a cause of action on behalf of parents for the birth of a defective child which could have been prevented, but for defendant's negligence.[19] Courts and commentators have described the wrong done to the parents in these cases as the denial of the opportunity to make informed decisions about childbearing. Courts have justified allowing recovery on the grounds that it would deter negligence and elevate the standard of care in the medical profession. They have paid little attention to the possible negative effects on the medical profession from allowing such suits. The argument that damages are speculative and difficult to determine with precision has not been felt to warrant denial of the parents' claim entirely, and damages have been awarded for the costs of raising the child[10] and for the mental anguish suffered by the parents because of the birth of the defective child.[21] A few states have outlawed wrongful birth claims by statute, however.[22]

WRONGFUL LIFE ACTIONS

Allowance of the Claim

The most problematic of all are the wrongful life actions, those brought by the child himself, claiming that but for defendant's negligence he would not have come into the world suffering the burden of his handicap, which may be mental, physical, or social. Courts have seen two main barriers to recognition of this action. The first is the apparent requirement that courts find the plaintiff's very existence to be a net burden to himself. Recognition of the action would seem of necessity to imply recognition of a right on the part of the fetus not to be born, a right which has no precedent. The second barrier is the difficulty of computing damages. Traditional tort principles require that damages be based on a comparison of the condition plaintiff is in because of defendant's negligence with the condition he would have occupied had defendant not been negligent; but, in wrongful life actions, had the defendant not been negligent the plaintiff would never have been born, and most courts have found it impossible to make any meaningful comparison between existence with a defect and nonexistence. These problems have led most courts to deny claims for wrongful life.[23] The author has discussed additional conceptual problems inherent in recognition of the wrongful life action in a previous article.[24]

A few courts have recognized the wrongful life action, however. In Curlender v. Bio-Science Laboratories,[25] the California Court of Appeals allowed a child born with Tay-Sachs disease to sue the laboratory which had erroneously informed its parents that they were not carriers of the gene for the disease. The court was little bothered with the theoretical difficulties of comparing existence with nonexistence. Instead, it stressed the reality that the child both existed and suffered because of the negligence of the defendant, and therefore concluded that the child should be compensated by the defendant for its suffering. The opinion even contained a dictum to the effect that parents who had been accurately informed of the likelihood of producing a defective child and who nevertheless proceeded to give birth to the child might themselves be liable on a claim for wrongful life. The California legislature was quick to respond with a statute forbidding such suits against parents.[26]

In Turpin v. Sortini,[27] the Supreme Court of California allowed a deaf child and her parents to bring suits for wrongful life and wrongful birth, respectively, against a hearing specialist who had negligently failed to diagnose the same genetically-caused deafness in the child's older sister. The parents claimed that it was in reliance on the defendant's erroneous diagnosis that there was nothing wrong with the older child's hearing that they conceived the second child. The court found it foreseeable that a negligent diagnosis could result in the birth of a second, deaf child, and held that the defendant could therefore be liable to both the parents and the child.

California courts have not accepted all wrongful life claims, however. A California appeals court rejected a claim brought by a child who was conceived by an incompetent patient in a mental health facility.[28] The plaintiff claimed the mother's guardian was negligent in supervising her, thus allowing her to become pregnant. The court concluded that the child, who was born healthy, had no cause of action simply because his mother was incompetent and unable to care for him properly. This case could more properly be characterized as a "dissatisfied life" claim, which courts have uniformly disallowed.[29]

The third case to date which has allowed a claim for wrongful life is Harbeson v. Parke-Davis, Inc.,[30] in which the Supreme Court of Washington held that a physician could be liable for wrongful life and wrongful birth claims based on his failure to advise his patient that the drug, Dilantin, which she was taking to control her epilepsy, could cause congenital defects if taken during pregnancy. The woman conceived two children while on the drug, both of whom were afflicted with fetal hydantoin syndrome. The wrongful life claim was upheld on the basis that the woman would not have become pregnant had she been properly informed of the effects of the drug.

It is unclear whether the Washington Supreme Court needed to characterize the child's claim as one for wrongful life, rather than for prenatal negligence.[31] Actions for prenatal injuries, and even for preconception injuries, are now recognized in many jurisdictions, and can be handled under traditional tort principles provided the requirement of foreseeability is met.[32] In all other wrongful life cases, the child plaintiff could only have been born with the defect or not been born at all. In Harbeson, however, the possibility exists that the same child could have been born normal had its mother not been taking the drug while she was pregnant. If, given the proper information, the mother would have gone without Dilantin for the duration of her pregnancy, or substituted some other drug with no teratogenic effects, the child might have been normal. The court may have felt compelled to view the complaint as one for wrongful life rather than wrongful birth because it alleged that the mother would not have conceived the child had she been correctly informed of the effects of the drug, not that she would have stopped taking the drug prior to conceiving the child.

Connecticut recently became the third state to allow a cause of action for wrongful life.[33] A mother sued a physician on her own behalf and on behalf of her infant daughter, who was born with Down's syndrome, alleging that the physician had been negligent in failing to diagnose the mother as a high-risk patient, failing to advise her of the risk of amniocentesis, and failing to refer her for genetic counseling. She sought damages for the daughter's past and future medical expenses, for her own emotional distress caused by her daughter's affliction, and for the suffering of her daughter. The latter would properly be characterized as "wrongful life" damages. Judge Burton J. Jacobson denied defendant's motion to strike the complaint as to all three counts. He found the child's claim for wrongful life to be in accord with generally recognized principles of tort law (a find not concurred in by courts which have declined to recognize the action for wrongful life, and by this author, in the article cited in note 24). Judge Jacobson found that the defendant owed a duty of care to the child which arose out of the physician's duty to obtain informed consent from the mother. He stated that the doctor's duty to disclose encompasses risks of birth defects to the infant, who is within the radius of risk of the physician's negligence. Judge Jacobson was unpersuaded by either of the two arguments usually raised against wrongful life claims: the difficulty of calculating damages, and the argument that life, however impaired, is more precious than nonlife.

The same states that have outlawed wrongful birth actions have outlawed wrongful life actions as well.[34]

Damages

In Curlender, the California Court of Appeal allowed the child to recover both general and special damages for its projected life expectancy, but in Turpin and Harbeson the courts limited damages to the extra expenses the child would have due to its handicap, declining to award damages to the child for the pain and suffering associated with the handicap because of the impossibility of measuring the benefits and drawbacks of existence with a handicap versus nonexistence. If damages are so limited, it is difficult to see why courts had to recognize a separate action on behalf of the child, since these same expenses would be recoverable in the parents' suit for wrongful birth, at least those expenses which would be incurred before the child attained the age of majority. In states (including California) where parents are responsible for the support of an adult child who is unable to support himself, the parents could also recover in the wrongful birth action the expenses to be incurred after the child reached its majority.

The holding in Turpin may have represented a compromise, avoiding metaphysical speculations on the value of existence with a handicap versus nonexistence, but awarding damages of a more readily ascertainable kind. One author has proposed that damages in wrongful life actions include a "sustenance award" to help the plaintiff become self-supporting upon reaching the age of majority, but only after a jury has concluded that the value of plaintiff's existence with the impairment does not outweigh the value of nonexistence.[35] This seems like a sensible limitation on damage awards in wrongful life actions, if indeed such actions need to be recognized at all.

Problems Inherent in Wrongful Life Actions

Should wrongful life actions be treated differently from dissatisfied life actions, which courts have uniformedly disallowed? In Williams v. State (n. 29, *supra*), the court stated that "being born under one set of circumstances rather than another or to one pair of parents rather than another is not a suable wrong that is cognizable in court," presumably a corollary of the notion that there is no "right" to be born under one set of conditions rather than another. Yet some courts and commentators[36] have rashly postulated a "right to be born as a whole functional human being," in justification for recognition of actions for wrongful birth and wrongful life. It is difficult to conceive of a right that no human agency can guarantee. It is also difficult to ascribe precise content to the words "whole" and "functional." Since there are many defective conditions which no human power is capable of curing at this point, who is to decide how severe the defect must be before the child's right not to be born comes into existence?

Courts which have denied actions for wrongful life have done so largely on the basis of theoretical difficulties in computing damages and weighing the value of an impaired life against that of no life at all. Courts which have recognized the action have brushed aside these arguments in their zeal to provide some financial compensation to a plaintiff who is evidently suffering. Both have paid insufficient attention to the many practical reasons for not recognizing the action, in addition to other theoretical reasons based on general principles of tort law.[37]

Recognition of wrongful life implies recognition of the right of a defective fetus not to be born, or not to be conceived (depending on whether the alleged negligence occurred after or before conception). Under what conditions is this right to be recognized? Given that congenital defects fall on a continuum from mild to severe, at what point on the continuum does the fetus' right to life[38] give way to its right to nonlife? What if the fetus' right to nonexistence conflicts with the parents' desires to have children, even handicapped children, or with their scruples against abortion? Whose rights will take precedence over the other's?

Will obstetricians, uncertain of their potential liability, hasten to counsel abortion in situations where the birth of a defective child is a possibility, just to avoid liability to the child in wrongful life suits? It is true that in many jurisdictions they will be potentially liable to the parents for wrongful birth, but a wrongful life suit will hold out the spectre of additional damages, and thus provide added incentive to avoid liability.

After a defective child is born, if a question arises as to the advisability of rendering lifesaving treatment, will the physician who was responsible for the birth of the child have an economic incentive to counsel against such treatment, knowing that if the child survives in an impaired state he may be held responsible to the child, as well as to the parents, for lifelong expenses attributable to the handicap? Such practical consequences of recognizing wrongful birth and wrongful life claims are given little, if any, consideration by the courts.

Where the failure to prevent the birth of a defective child is based on negligence in genetic counseling, there is a real danger that in their desire to compensate a handicapped plaintiff at the expense of the defendant's liability insurer juries will ignore that fact that the field of genetic diagnosis and counseling is in an exponential growth phase at the present time, and apply a standard that exists at the date of judgment to acts that may have taken place years before. Astronomical awards in wrongful life and wrongful birth claims based on negligent genetic counseling may result in people not entering, or leaving, that field, and in higher charges by those who do choose to remain in the field. The higher costs may have the effect of discouraging some parents from seeking genetic counseling. Thus the allowance of wrongful life claims might paradoxically result in the birth of more, not fewer, defective children.

Some tests for genetic defects carry an inherent risk of error which cannot be abolished, other than by not doing the test.[39] If a jury should find that it was negligence to do the test at all, given the rate of erroneous results, an award of damages might lead to abandonment of a test which, in the long run, would benefit many more people than it would harm.

The above are some of the practical reasons for not allowing wrongful life suits. There are also additional theoretical reasons aside from the ones already mentioned. If not for the defendant's negligence in allowing the defective child to be born, that child would not be alive to file a lawsuit against the defendant. It makes no sense to award the child damages for the pain and suffering of its existence because either it is so handicapped that it will be unable to obtain any pleasure from the award, or, it will be able to obtain some pleasure with the money awarded, in which case its existence cannot be all that miserable.

Given the vast number of mental and physical defects which are genetic in origin, allowance of wrongful life claims would truly open the floodgates to litigation. The continuum of defects, from mild to severe, would make it impossible for courts and juries to draw a consistent line between deserving claims and frivolous ones. Some defective children would be the beneficiaries of huge damage awards, while many more children with the same defect would go uncompensated, either because their parents did not seek genetic counseling, and thus have no one to blame for their misfortune, or because they were not sophisticated enough to know they could bring a lawsuit, or for a variety of other reasons. Allowance of such claims would merely exaggerate the existing inequities in the genetic lottery. Any benefits which might accrue to the handicapped individual would be more than offset by the detriment to the medical profession and to other potential handicapped children and their families. In most jurisdictions, parents already have a remedy for the wrong done to them: the wrongful birth action. If a child is seriously handicapped, to the point where it will never be self-supporting, then the expenses of caring for the child for its entire life expectancy should be awarded in the wrongful birth action. This is preferable to recognizing a new form of action with no sensible boundaries and all of the inherent problems stated above.

REFERENCES

1. 410 U.S. 113 (1973).
2. 49 N.J. 22, 227 A.2d 689 (1967).
3. Winborne, W.H., ed. 1983. "Handling Pregnancy and Birth Cases." Chaps. 3 and 6 in *Family Law Series*. Colorado Springs: Shepard's/McGraw-Hill.
4. Furrow, B. 1982. "Diminished Lives and Malpractice: Courts Stalled in Transition." *Law, Medicine, & Health Care* 10(3):100.
5. *See* Holt, D.K. 1982. "Wrongful Pregnancy." *Defense Law Journal* 31(July):370.
6. *See* Griswold v. Connecticut, 381 U.S. 479 (1965).
7. Rieck v. Medical Protective Co., 64 Wis. 2d 514, 219 N.W.2d 224 (1974); Ziemba v. Sternberg, 45 A.D. 2d 230, 357 N.Y.S.2d 265 (1974).
8. Clapham v. Yanga, 102 Mich. App. 47, 300 N.W.2d 727 (1980).
9. Holt, 377, n. 25.
10. Jackson v. Anderson, 230 So. 2d 503 (Fla. Dist. Ct. App. 1970); Custodio v. Bauer, 251 Cal. App. 2d 303, 59 Cal. Rptr. 463 (1967); Green v. Sudakin, 81 Mich. App. 545, 265 N.W.2d 411 (1978).
11. Shaheen v. Knight, 6 Lycoming Rptr. 19, 11 Pa. D.&C. 2d 41 (1957); Christensen v. Thornby, 192 Minn. 123, 255 N.W. 620 (1934).

12. Terrell v. Garcia, 496 S.W.2d 124 (Tex. Civ. App. 1973); Clegg v. Chase, 391 N.Y.S.2d 966 (N.Y. 1977).
13. 667 P.2d 1294 (1983).
14. Boone v. Mullendore, 416 So. 2d 718 (Ala. 1982); Coleman v. Garrison, 327 A.2d 757, aff'd 349 A.2d 8 (Del. 1975); Cockrum v. Baumgartner, 447 N.E.2d 385 (1983); Schork v. Huber, 648 S.W.2d 861 (Ky. 1983); and Sala v. Tomlinson, 422 N.Y.S.2d 506 (1979).
15. Custodio v. Bauer, 251 Cal. App. 2d 303, 59 Cal. Rptr. 463 (1967).
16. Stills v. Gratton, 55 Cal. App. 3d 698, 127 Cal. Rptr. 652 (1976); Ochs v. Borelli, 445 A.2d 883 (Conn. 1982); Troppi v. Scarf, 31 Mich. App. 240, 187 N.W.2d 511 (1971); Sherlock v. Stillwater Clinic, 260 N.W.2d 169 (Minn. 1977). The latest addition to this list is Jones v. Malinowski, Md. Ct. App. No. 29, April 6, 1984, which cited both the Arizona case and section 920 of the Restatement in the opinion.
17. *See* Chapman, S. 1979. "What Are Your Odds In The Prenatal Gamble?" *Legal Aspects of Medical Practice* 7(3):30; and "'Wrongful Birth' Lawsuits Raise Complex Social Issues." 1983. *American Medical News,* October 14, p. 2.
18. Williams, D.A. 1983. "Anatomy of a Consumerist Crusade—The Rise and Fall of Bendectin." *Private Practice,* November, p. 11.
19. *See* Gildiner v. Thomas Jefferson University Hospital, 451 F.Supp. 692 (E.D.Pa. 1978); Phillips v. United States, 508 F.Supp. 544 (D.S.C. 1981); Berman v. Allen, 80 N.J. 421, 404 A.2d 8 (1979); DiNatale v. Lieberman, 409 So. 2d 512 (Fla. 1982); Eisbrenner v. Stanley, 308 N.W.2d 209 (Mich. App. 1981); Schroeder v. Perkel, 432 A.2d 834 (N.J. 1981); Speck v. Finegold, 439 A.2d 110 (Pa. 1981); Becker v. Schwartz, 386 N.E.2d 807 (N.Y. 1978); Moores v. Lucas, 405 So. 2d 1022 (Fla. 1981).
20. *See* Becker v. Schwartz.
21. *See* Gildiner v. Thomas Jefferson University Hospital.
22. 1982 Minn. Laws, Ch. 521, subd. 2; S.D. Codified Laws Ann. sections 21-55-2 through 21-55-4.
23. Gleitman v. Cosgrove; Becker v. Schwartz; Berman v. Allen; DiNatale v. Lieberman; Dorlin v. Providence Hospital, 325 N.W.2d 600 (Mich. App. 1982); Eisbrenner v. Stanley; Speck v. Finegold; Strohmaier v. Associates in Obstetrics and Gynecology, 332 N.W.2d 432 (Mich. App. 1982).
24. Taub, S. 1982. "Wrongful Life—Its Problems Are Not Just Semantic: A Reply to Furrow." *Law, Medicine, & Health Care* 10(5):208.
25. 165 Cal. Rptr. 477 (Ct. App. 1980).
26. Cal. Civil Code section 43.6, West, 1981.
27. 182 Cal. Rptr. 337 (Cal. 1982).
28. Foy v. Greenblott, 190 Cal. Rptr. 84 (Cal. Ct. App. 1982).
29. *See* Zepeda v. Zepeda, 190 N.E.2d 849 (Ill. App. 1963), cert. denied, 379 U.S. 945 (1964); Williams v. State, 223 N.E.2d 343 (N.Y. 1966); Slawek v. Stroh, 215 N.W.2d 9 (Wis. 1974).
30. 656 P.2d 483 (Wash. 1983).
31. *See* VanDerhoef, P.J. 1983. "Washington Recognizes Wrongful Birth and Wrongful Life—A Critical Analysis." *Washington Law Review* 58:649.

32. Renslow v. Mennonite Hospital, 367 N.E.2d 1250 (Ill. 1977); Jorgensen v. Meade Johnson Laboratories, Inc., 483 F.2d 237 (10th Cir. 1973).
33. Woodruf v. Hoffman, —A.2d— (Conn. Super., Dec. 9, 1983); discussed in 27 ATLA L. Rep. (1):6, February, 1984.
34. Minn. Stat. Ann. section 145.424(1), West; S.D. Code L. sections 21-55-1 through 21-55-4.
35. *See* Packer, A.J. 1982. "Wrongful Life: Liability and Damages After Turpin v. Sortini." *Whittier Law Review* 4:639.
36. Park v. Chessin, 60 A.D. 2d at 88, 400 N.Y.S.2d at 114.
37. *See* Taub, n. 24.
38. In Roe v. Wade the Supreme Court implicitly recognized a right to life on the part of a viable fetus, at least, in prohibiting third trimester abortions except where the mother's life or health was threatened.
39. This may have been the source of the erroneous advice in the Curlender case. *See* Annas, G.J. 1981. "Righting the Wrong of 'Wrongful Life.'" *Hastings Center Report* 11(1):8.

Artificial Insemination Donor: A Constitutional Model

Rebecca S. Levine, Esq.

> I worry about the donor's medical history, his family background, his appearance, even the quality of his eyesight. It's funny. This is a major decision in my life and I know less about what I'm getting then when I bought my Cuisinart.

ARTIFICIAL INSEMINATION: THE MEDICAL PERSPECTIVE

The first successful artificial impregnation (AI) of a human being has been reported to have occurred in England in 1799. Estimates of the total number of children conceived in the United States by this method range from 50,000 to more than 250,000, with perhaps another 100,000 in foreign countries.[1] As a result of improved medical technology, declining numbers of adoptive children and a more conducive social atmosphere, an increasing number of couples and single women unable, or unwilling, to procreate naturally are turning to artificial insemination.

The actual technique employed varies but essentially all consist of introducing potent sperm (usually within one hour of ejaculation) into the recipient's vagina or uterine cavity using a syringe or other instrument. A rather high rate of success, measured by the resulting number of full-term pregnancies,[2] has been reported for AI.

The sperm used can be that of a donor (termed artificial insemination heterologous), the recipient's husband (artificial insemination homologous) or a combination of the two. The latter combination is used primarily for psychological reasons, to maintain the fiction that the recipient's husband could be the natural father of the child conceived thereby. Technically, it is possible that if the husband merely had a low sperm count, the insemination technique could boost his ability to fertilize the female ovum. But, normally, when donor sperm is used, it is because of the infertility of the husband. The husband's sperm is used exclusively (AIH) when neither party is infertile but an incapacity of one (for example, the husband's impotence) prevents intercourse.

Another reason for using donor sperm is that the recipient is an unmarried woman—a phenomenon that is occurring more and more frequently (although undocumented) as morality and attitudes toward illegitimacy change. Donor sperm is available through sperm banks or through private physicians, many of them so-called fertility specialists. The doctors obtain the sperm from sperm banks or have a private supply of donors.[3]

Most donors are medical students, interns, or residents, so it could be said they have demonstrated a level of academic achievement, and thus intelligence, that would make them suitable parents, eugenically speaking. But other qualities come into play. Most physicians believe in ethnic matching (i.e., a Jewish donor for a Jewish recipient, a Chinese donor for a Chinese recipient, etc.). Where a husband is involved, some physicians will attempt to match the donor's appearance with that of the husband.

Some states seek to regulate donor selection by statutes, usually under the public health law, which establish criteria such as medical tests for venereal disease as a prerequisite to becoming a donor,[4] but these set only minimal standards.

A study done in 1979,[5] referred to as the Curie-Cohen study, surveyed the practices of 379 physicians performing artificial insemination donor (AID), who accounted for approximately 3,576 births in 1977. Almost 10 percent had used AID to fertilize single women. The study further revealed that even on the basis of simple genetics, physicians administering AID were "not trained for the task" and made many inconsistent decisions. For example, 80 to 95 percent of all respondents said they would reject a donor if he had one of the following traits, and more than 50 percent would reject the same donor if the trait appeared in his immediate family: Tay-Sachs, hemophilia, cystic fibrosis, mental retardation, Huntington's, translocation or trisomy (a genetic disorder), diabetes, sickle-cell trait and alkaptonuria. Yet, donors were not tested for these traits.[6]

Some 96 percent of the doctors did take family histories from donors, but this consisted of nothing more than asking the prospective donor if any genetic diseases existed in his family or presenting him with a short checklist of common familial diseases. Some doctors asked medical students and hospital residents to screen themselves. Clearly, both the AID recipient and her child born of the procedure deserve better, and legislatures of the future will have to deal with the problem.

> The months of my pregnancy were lonely and made me very much aware of how much I would have liked a man in my life. But in the four months since my daughter was born, I've never regretted that I chose to have her.

ARTIFICIAL INSEMINATION DONOR: THE RECIPIENT'S PERSPECTIVE

For the AID recipient, the primary motivation is to have a child of her own. For this privilege, she will push out of her mind the possible inadequacies of donor screening procedures, choose not to know about them or rationalize that if she chose a potential father of her child out of love alone, she would probably not have considered his genetic suitability, either. That this is true must be kept in mind, for as imperfect as the present system may be, it does provide for her impregnation and for the child she so desperately desires.

Whether she is married or not is irrelevant to her desire for motherhood. The times are most definitely changing, and unwed motherhood and illegitimacy no longer carry the stigmas they once did. Divorce has already created many single parent families and the unwed mother is able to blend right in. American society has undergone a fundamental shift in attitude, the key component being the primacy of the individual over the traditional social structure. Even the courts, which decided the fate of the illegitimate and thereby influenced the community's attitude toward them, have changed their outlooks. The distinctions are blurring between legitimates and illegitimates and fewer sins of the parents are being visited on their children.

Many of the women having children today are doing so at older ages. The post-World War II baby boom generation grew up into the singles scene of what journalist Tom Wolfe called the "Me Generation," often deferring marriage and child raising into their late 20s and even 30s. Some never married at all or had brief and unsuccessful marriages, yet their appetites for parenthood were undiminished. As they approach their mid and upper 30s, they become painfully aware that they are up against a biological deadline, and the time to have children—if at all—is at hand. For many who are tired of waiting for the fairy tale prince to marry them and make parenthood "socially acceptable," single parenthood is the only alternative.

While adoption has recently opened up to single adults, the supply of adoptable infants is short of the demand. At one time, applications for adoption outnumbered, by a 10:1 ratio, the supply of babies available.[7] And that was before the legalization of abortion and the tendency of many unwed mothers to keep their babies substantially decreased the supply of adoptive infants for married, as well as for single, prospective adoptive parents. For some single women, the prospect of waiting endlessly on an adoption agency list or even of being able to adopt an older child is less attractive than that of having a baby of their "own."

The option of illicit sex merely for the purpose of getting pregnant is repugnant to some of these women, thought to be immoral by others. Many fear the legal complications that could arise from such a liaison. Should one tell the man that she has conceived a child by him? If she does, will he expect to have visitation rights, or custody? Will his consent be required if she later marries and her husband wishes to adopt the child?[8]

Some single women worry about the psychological effect on their children of having a "sometime" father in their lives, particularly if he is unreliable. This may often be the case since, if the man has merely been selected by the mother to father her child, his ties to her are ephemeral and he may even perceive himself as being used and resent this fact.

Although AID as a method of conception does have legal implications, the donor is most often kept anonymous and that will deter legal issues from arising in most cases.

> I'm scared of having a long-term legal relationship with a man if I don't have a long-term romantic relationship with him.

ARTIFICIAL INSEMINATION DONOR: THE LEGAL PERSPECTIVE

The state, through its *parens patriae* powers, has broad authority to regulate for the safety, health and welfare of its citizens. For example, the state may regulate the incidents of marriage. It is from the same constitutional source that the state—its courts and legislatures—takes its power to regulate certain elements of the artificial insemination process.

And if AID is to operate legally and effectively, some regulation will be needed, for the legal problems that could arise in an AID transaction, particularly where the donor is not kept strictly anonymous, can be numerous. Few cases have yet come before the courts, but as AID becomes more widespread in its usage, there will surely be more.

In the domestic relations area, the key question will be the legitimacy of the child, particularly when the recipient mother is married. To date there has been no resolution of the question, but the following cases have dealt with the subject: Doornbos v. Doornbos, 23 U.S.L.W. 2308 (1954); Strnad v. Strnad, 190 Misc. 786, 78 N.Y.S. 2d 390 (1948); L.v.L., 1 All E.R. 141 (1948); Gursky v. Gursky, 39 Misc. 2d 1083, 242 N.Y.S. 2d 406 (1963); Anonymous v. Anonymous, 246 N.Y.S. 2d 835 (1964); In Re Adoption of

Anonymous, 74 Misc. 2d 99, 345 N.Y.S. 2d 430 (1973), and People v. Sorenson, 68 Cal. 2d 280, 437 P. 2d 495 (1968).

The latter case, a criminal prosecution for nonsupport of a child brought against the ex-husband of an AID recipient, constitutes the first time the highest court within a state (here, the California Supreme Court) has spoken on the subject of AID. The Sorenson court held that the law favors legitimation to protect the integrity of the family unit and that no useful purpose is served by stigmatizing the AID child with the label "illegitimate."

In 1964, Georgia became the first state to pass a statute on the subject. The legislation, Ga. Code 74-101.1 (1973), creates an irrebutable presumption of legitimacy when both the husband and wife consent to the administration of AID. Since then, 18 other states have enacted similar legislation.[9]

Another question apt to face the courts is whether, by having AID performed on her, and by conceiving via AID, a married woman has committed adultery (*see* Orford v. Orford, 49 Ont. L.R. 15 (1921), and Doornbos, *supra*). A related issue is whether a married woman's conception by AID without her husband's consent provides other grounds for divorce, for example, whether it would be sufficient to constitute cruel and inhuman treatment, or separate grounds.

Other issues which have come before the courts in past years, and are likely to again, concern the legal rights and duties of the husband of an AID recipient vis-à-vis the child. Must he support the child? (*See* Strnad v. Strnad, *supra;* Sorenson, *supra;* and Anonymous v. Anonymous, *supra.*) Is the husband entitled to costody or to visitation rights if he and his wife later separate or divorce? (Abajian v. Dennett, 15 Misc. 2d 260, 184 N.Y.S. 2d 178 (1958); C.M. v. C.C., 152 N.J. Super. 160, 377 A. 2d 821 (1977).)

Does the donor have an obligation of support? Is it enforceable? Eight jurisdictions provide by statute[10] that the AID donor has no obligation to support his children conceived by this method. These statutes also provide the children have no interest in the donor's estate and no right to take intestate shares. There have been no cases on this matter as yet. It would seem possible that in a state which has no such statute, if the donor's identity could be learned, the issue of donor support could arise. In such a situation, would a will left by the donor and referring to his "issue" be construed as referring to his issue by AID? Would an AID child be capable of sharing in a wrongful death recovery brought on behalf of his donor father, or vice versa?

Tort actions for medical malpractice are also likely to be generated from the AID procedure. Most of these will center around donor screening procedures where fetus or child is defective or where the mother contracts a venereal disease, for example, from introduction of the donor's sperm. While there have been no reported[11] cases in this area to date, there is speculation that sperm donation might be analogized to donations/transfusions of blood. If sperm, like blood, is held to be an "inherently dangerous" substance, a doctor introducing defective sperm might be held liable on a theory of strict liability.

Some states have enacted donor screening regulations and other requirements to be followed in the practice of AID. New York City Health Code, Article 21, is a good example of these. Article 21 provides that only a licensed physician may perform AI in the area (§21.01); a serological test for syphilis and a smear for gonorrhea be performed on the donor (§21.03A); a serological test to determine the donor's RH factor and that of the recipient must be performed (§21.03B); the doctor must keep records, which must remain confidential to all but city health officials (§21.07).

Other states could do well to follow this model. However, even this model does not go far enough. It does not provide for serological tests for Tay-Sachs and Sickle Cell trait. Nor does it mandate routine genetic screening, or set guidelines for proper medical histories to be taken under the circumstances.

The Georgia statute provides that a doctor performing AID is relieved of liability, except for his own negligence, in performing the procedure (thus, for example, a case like Fitzgerald v. Rueckl could not be brought in Georgia). Other states need such legislation.

Also needed are statutes to clarify the aforementioned gaps in the domestic relations and estate law areas to deal with problems before they arise.

Only two states, Minnesota and Ohio,[12] have attempted to prohibit AID altogether, and neither was successful. In light of Roe v. Wade (*infra*), it is doubtful such statutes would be constitutional.

Outside of what is clearly prohibited as a constitutional violation, there is a need for regulatory legislation to insure the rights of all parties to the AID transaction and to warrant the procedure medically sound. Only through such legislation will the practice be safe from legal controversy and heartbreaking courtroom fights. The transition into a growing, emerging concept of the family demands that protection.

> I just don't have the ability to walk into a singles' bar, pick some attractive guy to come on to, have his baby and never tell him. It just seems immoral.

ARTIFICIAL INSEMINATION DONOR: THE RELIGIOUS PERSPECTIVE

Before making any determination concerning artificial insemination, the courts and legislatures will, by necessity, look to the attitudes of organized religion. Following is a compendium of the views of the three major denominations in the United States regarding AI.

There is no ecclesiastical synod in the Jewish religion that has power over all Jews, so it cannot be said that the entire rabbinate favors artificial insemination as a means of conception. It is for each Jew to weigh the views of the rabbinical authorities and decide for herself.[13]

According to one of two scholars who has studied the subject, Dr. Solomon B. Freehof, Rabbi of Temple Rodef Shalom, Pittsburgh, certain legal problems must be resolved before there can be an answer to the question of whether the Jewish religion permits AID. The first is whether by donating his sperm the donor fulfills or violates the commandment to beget children ("Be fruitful and multiply"). A related concern is whether the donor is guilty of "wasting seed."

A further question is whether a wife, inseminated by a man other than her husband, has committed adultery, and whether a child born of AI is legitimate. A final legal caveat is that of the laws of consanguinity, which forbid an AID child from marrying another child of the same donor.

Concludes Dr. Freehof, "My own opinion would be that the possibility of the child marrying one of his own close blood kin is farfetched, but that since, according to Jewish law, the wife has committed *no sin* and the child is 'kosher,' then the process of artificial insemination should be permitted."[14]

Paradoxically, the orthodox Jewish view is that an AID child is legitimate, but the practice of AID is forbidden.

Like the Jews, no one can speak for all Protestants. However, the religion is open minded about the possibilities of AID.[15] Holding that all life proceeds from God and is, therefore, to be held in reverence, the faith holds no child illegitimate. A second religious tenet is belief about love and the family; a third, concern for fulfillment, and a fourth, emphasis upon freedom combined with responsibility. Many Protestant churchmen would look with favor upon AID for couples who desired it as their only hope of fulfilling these religious sanctions.

Recognizing that children born under these circumstances would certainly be desired and would bring hope to numerous childless couples, the Protestants seem to favor general availability of AID subject to state regulation.

Of the three major denominations in the U.S., only the Catholic religion places firm prohibitions upon AID. The Catholic hierarchy believes it is never morally justifiable to impregnate a woman with the sperm of any man but her own husband and that AID involves the evils of both masturbation and adultery. AIH is prohibited because, while adultery is not involved, masturbation is.[16]

This Catholic position and its strong prohibition of AID and AIH go back to a 1949 discourse of Pope Pius XII to the Fourth International Congress of Catholic Doctors, held in Rome. The Church's position has not changed at all since that time.

One justification for discouraging the practice of AID, and a reason for some opposition to the technique, is that the practice is offensive to the members of certain religions. It is argued by advocates of AID that this is a wholly insufficient ground for state interference with such a fundamental liberty as the ability to conceive a child.

> Why don't you meet a nice guy, instead?

ARTIFICIAL INSEMINATION DONOR: THE OPPOSITION'S PERSPECTIVE

Many segments of the population oppose artificial insemination, particularly of the donor variety and particularly where an unmarried recipient is involved. The reactions range from mild disapproval, expressed by the above quote, to fanatical fervor leading to political activism to have AID prohibited.

Among those who oppose AI are members of the more traditional segments of society, including members of some religious persuasions, many of them represented by the Right to Life movement, which opposes medical intervention to initiate, as well as terminate, pregnancies.

It is unclear just what form their political activism will take in the future. But it is not unrealistic to expect some of this activity will center on the institution of outright bans on AI, or at least on the erection of procedural barriers (such as spousal consent) to discourage certain categories of recipients from seeking the procedure.

Opponents of AID might support civil actions by AID recipients suing for child support from donor-fathers, hoping that the fear of large-scale liability will discourage young men from donating sperm in the future. Such opponents would use donor liability to reach their own ends—ends which may largely be based on cultural stereotypes of the feminine role and of the marital state and are antifeminist in their orientation.

Following are three model briefs dealing with issues of constitutional magnitude arising out of the performance of AID. The first deals with legislation that would prohibit AI from being performed on unmarried recipients, while the second confronts the impact of spousal consent requirements on married potential recipients. The last brief addresses the rights of the AID child to have medical/birth records unsealed in order to learn the identity of the biological father, and examines the relative rights of the parties to the AID transaction.

How the Supreme Court would rule if these issues were to come before it is crucial to the future of AID. The Court is simultaneously capable of following and shaping cultural attitudes, and the degree to which it does each will determine the success of a large number of women aspiring to single (or married) motherhood by way of AID.

What the court does with this issue may have a crucial impact as well on the future form of the American family.

NOTES

1. Silvoso, "Artificial Insemination: A Legislative Remedy," *W. St. U.L. Rev.* 3(1975):48.

2. The rate of spontaneous abortion (miscarriage) for AI is within the 5 to 20 percent range of the general population.

3. The use of the term donor is disputed by some, who claim that, because these young men are paid, they are, in fact, vendors of sperm.

4. For example, see New York City Health Code, Article 21.

5. M. Curie-Cohen, L. Luttrel, and S. Shapiro, "Current Practices of Artificial Insemination by Donor in the United States," *New Eng. J. Med.* 300(1979):585.

6. Fewer than one percent of the surveyed doctors performed a test for the Tay-Sachs carrier state in the donor. The test consists of taking blood from the donor and analyzing it and costs under $30.

7. S. Katz, "Community Decision Makers and the Promotion of Values in the Adoption of Children," *Fam.L.Q.* 4(1964):7, 8.

8. Caban v. Mohammed, 99 S.C. 1760 (1979).

9. Alaska Stat. §20.20.010 (1975); Ark Stat. Ann. §61-141(c) (1971); Cal. Civ. Code §7005 (West 1975); Fla. Stat. Ann. §742.11 (West 1973); Kan. Stat. §23-219 (1977); La. Civ. Code Ann. art. 188 (West 1975); Md. Est. & Trusts Code Ann. §1-206(b) (1975); Mont. Rev. Codes Ann. §61-306 (1975); N.Y. Dom. Rel. Law 75 (McKinney 1974); N.C. Gen. Stat. §49A-1 (1974); Okla. Stat. tilt. 10 §552 (1974); Or. Rev. Stat. 109.243 (1977); Tex. Fam. Code Ann. titd. 2, §12.03 (Vernon 1977); Va. Code §64.1-7.1 (1977); Wash. Rev. Code Ann. §26.26.050(1) (West 1976); Wyo. Stat. §14-2-103(a) (1978).

10. California, Colorado, Connecticut, Montana, Oregon, Texas, Washington and Wyoming.

11. An unreported AID malpractice case, Fitzgerald v. Rueckl, No. 11433, was set for argument before the Nevada Supreme Court as this was going to press. The plaintiff couple sued the defendant doctor for malpractice after he performed AID on the wife without her husband's consent.

12. Minnesota House Bill 1090 (1949) and Ohio Senate Bill 93 (1955). Neither bill passed.

13. "Symposium on Artificial Insemination," *Syracuse L. Rev.* 7(1955):96, 104.

14. *Ibid.,* 105.

15. *Ibid.,* 101.

16. *Ibid.,* 99, 100.

SUPREME COURT OF THE UNITED STATES

---X

THE PEOPLE OF THE STATE OF ORWELL,
Respondent,

—against—

DR. MILES ISAACS,
Appellant,

and

JANE DOE and others similarly situated,
Appellants,

—against—

GERRY FOLWELL, Director, Family Planning of Huxley, and PETER RAND, Secretary of Health, State of Huxley,
Respondents.

---X

APPELLANTS' BRIEF

Rebecca S. Levine
201 East 25 Street
New York, N.Y. 10010
(212) 683-3645

QUESTIONS PRESENTED

1. Whether the criminal statute of the State of Orwell prohibiting physicians from performing AID on single women is an unconstitutional violation of the Equal Protection Clause of the Fourteenth Amendment?
2. Whether the statutory scheme of the State of Huxley which established and administered Huxley Family Planning and the Centers' practice of denying access to AID to unmarried women is a violation of the Equal Protection Clause?
3. Whether Respondents' actions constitute unlawful sex discrimination in violation of the Due Process guarantees of the Fourteenth Amendment?

STATEMENT OF FACTS

In this action, two appeals are combined because of the similarity of the issues presented. Both cases concern the propriety and legality of administering the medical procedure of Artificial Insemination Donor, hereinafter referred to as AID, to unmarried women for the purpose of producing pregnancy.

The State of Orwell prohibits anyone other than a licensed physician from performing the procedure (ORW. Public Health Law §30) and makes it a Class E Felony for a physician to perform AID on an unmarried woman (ORW. Penal Code §582). The statute imposes a $500 fine and a jail sentence of up to two years.

Appellant Isaacs, an obstetrician/gynecologist who has practiced in Orwell for the past 23 years, was convicted under the statute on April 4, 1980, and sentenced to one year in prison for performing AID on one Ella Cutler. He seeks to overturn his conviction on the grounds that ORW. Penal Code §582 is an unconstitutional violation of the Due Process and Equal Protection Clauses (Constitution of the United States, Fifth and Fourteenth Amendments; Orwell State Constitution, Article 1, Section 4).

Dr. Isaacs has been performing artificial insemination for the past 10 years, using either the sperm of donors or that of his patients' husbands, when possible. During that period, he inseminated 36 women, resulting in 25 known pregnancies and 22 live births.[1] Only one of these women, Ms. Cutler, was unmarried.

Dr. Isaacs inseminated Ms. Cutler on five occasions in the three months from September 15, 1979 to December 18, 1979, when her pregnancy was positively diagnosed.

Appellants in the companion case, Doe v. Folwell, were not so fortunate. They are a class of unmarried women seeking to become mothers by AID and precluded from doing so by their domicile's regulatory scheme.

Huxley Public Health Code, §16, is a statutory scheme for regulating access to and the practice of artificial insemination in the state. One of its provisions limits the performance of the procedure to certain state-approved and licensed facilities, and provides for state supervision. The centers collectively operate under the name Family Planning of Huxley and are directed by the Respondent, Folwell.

While nothing in the statutory scheme prohibits the administration of AID to unmarried women, the centers themselves deny unmarried women access to this particular service and have turned away single women *in every known case* where AID was requested. The State's approval, licensing and supervision responsibilities, as well as the existence of its statutory scheme, are sufficient state involvement to subject the practice and the statutes to Constitutional scrutiny. Appellants contend the denial of AID to single women is a violation of the Equal Protection Clause of the Fourteenth Amendment and sex discrimination in violation of both the Equal Protection and Fifth Amendment Due Process guarantees, as well as these guarantees as expressed in the Huxley State Constitution, Article 1, Sections 5 and 14.

The class contends the State's action restricts its members' fundamental right to reproductive freedom and their right to privacy by denying them access to AID. Each of the women went to Family Planning of Huxley and requested AID within the last three years. Each was turned down following one interview with a Family Planning social worker and based on a two-page application. Few were given reasons for the denial, and where reasons were given, they were vague and uninformative.[2]

The Appellant class is, for the most part, within the ages of 28 and 40. It is comprised of widows, divorcees and women who have never been married, with a median income of $23,500 per year.[3] Of the 15 women represented, eight are in the professions. All but two are college graduates and ten hold advanced degrees. All are in good health, physically and emotionally, and all are capable of taking care of a child financially. Most are currently employed and contemplate a variety of household arrangements for the care of the child.

Each of the plaintiffs shares with the others the desire for a child of her own and none wishes to be precluded from motherhood for lack of a husband. Each faces, in varying degrees of proximity, the onset of a biological deadline, after which her childbearing capacity will be greatly diminished and, finally, terminated. Each sought the assistance of one of the six Family Planning centers (of a total of ten throughout the state) involved in the present suit and was denied access to the procedure.

Ms. Doe is a 36-year-old widow who lives alone. After several years of contemplating single parenthood and endless waits on adoption agency lists, Ms. Doe decided on AID because of her shyness about dating and her fear of ongoing legal consequences involved in a casual choice of a father. Ms. Doe is presently employed as an instructor of English at a private college in Huxley but plans to quit working if she has a child. Because of an annuity from her late husband, she is financially able to do so. And if she wishes to work again, she has an occupation to which she can readily return and by which she can readily support herself and her child. Like the others, Ms. Doe submitted her application to a Family Planning center and was denied as an AID recipient.

The women joined together to bring the present Article 78 proceeding in the nature of mandamus against the State Director of Family Planning and the State Secretary of Health to compel the centers to accept unmarried women into its AID program.

The entire scope of the plaintiff class is not determined, but in an earlier action, the plaintiffs argued that notice to the entire class was unnecessary for reasons set forth below and that, alternatively, defendant should be compelled to provide a list of other unmarried women it has turned down and to provide notice to them since the exclusive access to this information is in the control of the defendant.

Because plaintiffs are suing for admission to the facilities' AID programs for *all* single women, whether members of the class or not, they submit that other unidentified class members are represented and their interest in suing for damages not prejudiced. In addition, the plaintiffs hope that the publicity generated by this suit would notify other unmarried women seeking AID of their right to receive it. This would include other women turned down by these same facilities. This motion was argued before the District Court, which held the suit could be maintained without notice to the entire class.

The District Court also held that the State of Huxley could constitutionally limit the right of AID to married women as a means of discouraging single parenthood. The plaintiff class appeals this ruling.

Point 1. Respondents' actions deprive single women of their reproductive freedom as guaranteed by Roe v. Wade and violate the Equal Protection Clause of the United States, and respective state, constitutions.

The criminal statute of Orwell and the practices of Huxley's Family Planning centers are impermissible restrictions on an unmarried woman's right of personal privacy and on her reproductive freedom, both fundamental liberties guaranteed by the United State Constitution. In addition, Dr. Isaacs contends the statute under which he stands convicted is an impermissible restriction upon the practice of medicine and an interference with his First Amendment right to privacy.

The United States Supreme Court, in Griswold v. Connecticut, 381 U.S. 479 (1965), first recognized the fundamental right to privacy as implicitly granted by the various penumbras, or zones of privacy, of the Bill of Rights. The case concerned the right of a physician to administer birth control information to married couples. Seven years later, the Court held the right to personal privacy in the area of contraception was shared by the unmarried, as well, in Eisenstadt v. Baird, 405 U.S. 438 (1972).

In Roe v. Wade, 410 U.S. 113 (1973), the Court struck down a Texas criminal abortion statute as violative of a woman's right to personal privacy protected by the First, Fourth, Fifth, Ninth and Fourteenth Amendments, thus holding that the right to privacy encompassed the right to reproductive freedom. That right of privacy is not absolute and must be balanced with the state's interest in safeguarding the health of the mother and of the fetus.

Doe v. Bolton, 410 U.S. 179 (1973), a companion case to Roe, reiterated Roe's holding that states may not prevent abortions by making their performance a crime, then said that a state may not discourage abortions by making them difficult to obtain by means of elaborate procedural barriers.

Surely, if a state may not unduly restrict a woman's right to terminate her pregnancy, it likewise may not interfere with her right to initiate one. For the right to control one's fertility is synonymous with the reproductive freedom encompassed within the guarantee of privacy and is no less fundamental. Viewed in this manner, a woman's right to conceive a child—by artificial insemination or other means—is one with which the state may not interfere, unless such interference is justified by a compelling state purpose.

While it is permissible for a state to attempt to achieve its purpose or solve some social problem by means of piecemeal legislation aimed at solving just part of the problem, the Equal Protection Clause prohibits such legislation if it does not treat those similarly situated in similar ways, or have compelling reason not to.

Thus, it was held in Skinner v. Oklahoma, 316 U.S. 535 (1942), that compulsory sterilization statutes (requiring sterilization of persons convicted of certain felonies) must not arbitrarily single out particular individuals for treatment. To do so was held a violation of the prisoners' Equal Protection rights.

Similarly, to single out unmarried women and regulate only their ability to conceive children (that is, to use marital status as the basis for a statutory scheme) is a violation of Equal Protection.

Under traditional Equal Protection analysis, the Court will look to whether the legislation is aimed at a "suspect classification," one which is either a "discrete and insular minority," which is set apart by an "immutable characteristic determined solely by the accident of birth" and, often, which has been the subject of historic discrimination.

When the legislation is found to be aimed at a suspect classification, the Court will apply strict scrutiny—its highest standard—to determine whether the state's interest is sufficiently compelling to justify use of the classification. If not, the legislation is held to be unconstitutional as a violation of Equal Protection.

Neither marital status nor professional status (i.e., neither single women nor physicians) have previously been held by the Court to be suspect classifications. Only once has the Court held gender to be such a category[4] and it has since retreated from that position. In light of this fact, it is doubtful that appellants would be held to constitute suspect classifications for the purposes of invalidating the legislation before the Court.

However, suspect classifications are not the only triggers to strict scrutiny. When the issue presented involves a fundamental liberty—on the order of privacy and reproductive freedom—the Court will apply the same strict scrutiny standard. For when an individual's interest is fundamental, the state's interest must be compelling enough to warrant the intrusion upon it.

Appellants contend that, because women's fundamental liberties are involved in the present actions, the strict standard should be applied. It is also contended that the interests of Huxley and Orwell are not sufficiently compelling and that the legislation at issue is not well tailored to effect the States' purposes, that is, is both underinclusive and overinclusive. Appellants further contend that a liberal reading of Roe v. Wade mandates that unmarried women have the right of access to AID.

The States' Purposes Are Not Sufficiently Compelling

The Respondent States submit that their interest in population control justifies their prohibitions on AID for unmarried women. It is conceded that government presently has a compelling state interest in population control, that maximum time is needed to find substitutes for nonrenewable resources during which population increases should be kept to a minimum in order to preserve what supplies of these resources still exist. It is conceded constitutional authority for population control legislation may be found within Congress' specific powers[5] and powers designated to the States.

Nevertheless, while the state purpose may be compelling, the analysis doesn't stop there. The next inquiry must be into *how* the regulation is instituted. If it seeks to address itself to a problem affecting the entire populace by irrationally focusing on one class, it is underinclusive (i.e., too narrowly tailored to fit the intended purpose). Such is the case with the criminal statute of Orwell and the procedure carried out by Huxley's Family Planning centers, and as such, the legislation cannot stand. Limiting tax deductions for dependents might be a less restrictive method of accomplishing the same goal.

Encouraging Two-Parent Families Is Unrealistic

The State's interest in the upbringing of its future citizens, and therefore in encouraging two-parent families, is insufficient in light of the impact of societal changes on the American family to justify interference with the right of single women to bear children.

The States' argument is undercut by the fact that the two-parent family is disappearing rapidly across the United States due to the rising rates of illegitimacy and divorce. Last year, there were one million divorces in this country, with some 1.3 million children involved.[6] Women who never planned or prepared to be single parents (some with no work skills or means of support) are being forced to play that role, while the disputed legislation and practices here would deny women who had prepared for the experience the opportunity for single motherhood. Also undermining Respondents' point of view is the recognition by adoption agencies that single parents can provide excellent homelives for adoptive children. This recognition is reflected in the growing number of single parent adoptions in recent years.[7]

The American family is changing. The middle-class nuclear family of four safely tucked away in the suburbs is no longer the model for the coming decades. It is hinted that family disintegration threatens social well-being, but demise of the family as we know it does not necessarily mean doom. AID and other developments in medical technology will change the meaning of parenthood and the definition of the phrase "a child of one's own," but that change does not mean the weakening of parent-child bonds.

To deny a single woman the experience of parenthood to preserve, temporarily, the traditional structure of the American family is neither effective not fair.

Evidence has emerged in recent years that shows single parents, particularly those who planned this situation, can do an equally effective job of child raising as two-parent families. One thing they have going for them in an AID situation is that the child is planned, and that usually translates into "wanted." This is an important consideration in determining whether the state's interest in fostering the child's best interest is served by a statute prohibiting AID to single women.

Psychological studies support the view that single women can be excellent parents and that loving single mothers raise healthy, well-adjusted children—even if the mothers work.[8]

This is contrary to the view, particularly as represented in the media of the 1950s, that a working mother left permanent scars on her child's psyche. It must be remembered that this was a convenient social philosophy given the economic pressures of the times. During World War II when there was a shortage of men to operate industry at home, women were encouraged to take to the factories. When the war ended and the men returned to the homefront, women were encouraged to leave the factories to make way for returning veterans. Popular literature reinforced the message that a working mother was hazardous to her child's health. The guilt that was fostered was economically convenient.[9] Such is not the case in the 1980s. The working mother has gone from oddity to economic necessity as inflation puts added pressure on the husband's income, even in the most traditional families.

But, if the psychological theories of the day are unreliable gauges of the child's best interests, so are the determinations of an individual judge. Such a determination is inherently subjective: It is possible for a judge to award custody based on the determination that living on a farm, or in the city, was in a child's "best interest."

The best interest of a child may very well be served by being in a home where it is loved and wanted and where economic resources are present and largely available for the child's needs. The decision cannot be made on a mass level by state legislatures based on stereotypes of single parents. The presumption that single parents are inferior, and legislation based on that presumption, are overbroad, in that not all single women are poor parents; they are likewise underinclusive, in that inadequate married parents do not face restrictions on their liberty to reproduce.

Discouraging Illegitimacy Is a State Goal

Huxley and Orwell's goal of discouraging illegitimacy is an impermissible basis for restricting Appellants' fundamental rights of privacy and reproductive freedom. Recent Supreme Court decisions have meant the breakdown of stereotypes about and discrimination against illegitimates (Levy v. Louisiana, 391 U.S. 68 (1968); Glona v. American Guar. & Liab. Ins. Co., 391 U.S. 73 (1968); Weber v. Aetna Casualty & Surety Co., 406 U.S. 164 (1972)).

Part of the States' rationale for discouraging illegitimacy is the apprehension that such children will become dependent upon the state for economic support. Such a stereotype is not always true, as evidenced by the plaintiff class. Each member has the means to support her child and has plans for the child in the event of her own death (with life insurance, wills, and/or trusts).

More important, the right to conceive by natural means is not conditioned on the financial ability to pay for one's children. To demand a higher standard of single women desiring motherhood is underinclusive, and the possibility that the burden to support the children of such conceptions would fall to the State is not enough to outweigh the Appellant's constitutional right to privacy. Even if the interest were more compelling, it is doubtful that prohibiting moral single women, many of them economically advantaged, from reproducing is the means best tailored to achieving the desired end.

The States' goal of regulating moral standards, and hence its disapproval of illegitimacy, are inadequate to justify infringement of fundamental liberties. It cannot be justified on grounds that the state—in the exercise of its *parens patriae* authority to regulate health and welfare of its citizens—is protecting the individual from self-inflicted harm. This paternalistic rationale cannot hold up.

If the state seeks to curtail activities that offend the public, the relevant inquiry would seem to be an objective one: Would a reasonable person be offended by this behavior? The State's power to foster a particular view of morality is less broad than its powers in the health and welfare area, and it must be particularly careful about restrictions in the area of sexual morality, lest it run afoul of Griswold v. Connecticut (*supra*).

Avoiding offense to others and vague goals concerning "preserving a decent society" are insufficient to justify state intervention into a single woman's reproductive freedom.

States Seek to Prevent Incestuous Marriages

Huxley claims that its interest in preventing incestuous marriages is served by the prohibition of AID to unmarried women. Unmarried women are more likely, naturally, to have AID, thus increasing the number of children born of donors, and hence of any one donor. Since the donors remain anonymous, the State argues, children of the same father would be unable to identify each other and could marry each other without realizing they were committing incest.

The State's argument borders on the fanciful. The likelihood that (particularly in a large city) two AID children of the same donor would meet and marry is small. Even admitting the possibility of such an occurrence, the State has other, less restrictive, means of guarding against incestuous marriages. A statute regulating donor screening procedures and limiting donors to a fixed number of inseminations or pregnancies would solve the problem by making the chance of such an occurrence less likely.

A clearinghouse system for AID records could also be established. If two AID children wished to marry, they could go to such a clearinghouse and be reassured that they are the children of different donors, without the identity of the donors being revealed.

The State of Orwell claims an interest in promoting adoptions, particularly of black and handicapped children. By reducing the pool of potential adoptive parents, the State claims, AID impedes the adoption process. This would seem to be true of all artificial insemination, even where the husband's sperm is utilized.[10] To restrict only an unmarried woman's access to the procedure unfairly places the burden on her to solve the entire problem. This is unconstitutional discrimination.

Additionally, some of the women who seek AID—and particularly those who seek AIH—want children of their "own" and would not be likely to adopt if artificial insemination were denied to them.

Orwell's argument unrealistically assumes an umlimited pool of adoptable children. Even if such a pool presently existed, which it does not,[11] it could not continue to meet the demand of adoptive parents, particularly if abortions continue to be performed in their present numbers.

Many contemplating single parenthood have previously tried the adoption agencies,[12] only to be turned away or placed on waiting lists that stretch on for years. Single parents have traditionally been a class disfavored by adoption agencies. It is only lately that the agencies are recognizing the advantages offered by single parents. Despite this shift in attitudes, two-parent families are still preferred, and if the single woman is prohibited from AID and then turned down by an adoption agency, she is denied all chances to become a parent, or forced to take on the complications of illicit sex.

In light of the seriousness of this denial, the State's interest in making an adoption market is insufficient and insufficiently tailored to warrant the intrusion on individual liberties.

None of the stated purposes of Orwell and Huxley warrant such an intrusion.

Point 2. Respondents' actions are based on, and perpetuate, antiquated stereotypes of single women and of women in general and constitute unlawful sex discrimination in violation of the Fourteenth Amendment's Due Process clause.

Respondents' legislation and practices, which serve to prohibit unmarried women from conceiving by means of artificial insemination, are based on archaic and overbroad generalizations of female dependency (Frontiero v. Richardson, *supra*). On these stereotypes, the respective legislatures have premised irrebutable presumptions that women seeking AID will be unable to overcome.

Thus, the determination of whether a woman qualifies for the procedure is based not on individual treatment and consideration, but rather upon criteria thought to be applicable to *all* single women and, even, to *all* women. To deny an unmarried woman the right to parenthood on the basis of outdated sexual stereotypes is to discriminate in an invidious manner[13] (Frontiero, *supra;* Weinberger v. Wiesenfeld, 420 U.S. 636 (1975); Califano v. Goldfarb, 97 S.C. 1021 (1977)).

The following stereotypes are operative in the present case:

1. Women are economically dependent on men, so single women will be particularly needy.
2. Single parent families will be economically dependent, perhaps even, on the state.
3. Single parents are inherently not as effective as two-parent families.
4. Single women who want to be unwed mothers are immoral,[14] selfish and irresponsible.

Such stereotypes are self-perpetuating and self-regulating. A woman, whose upbringing and every contact tells her these things are so, will disqualify herself from so-called inappropriate activities. To a large extent, these notions also foster in state legislators a sense of "romantic paternalism"[15] destructive to the rights of women, for the "protections" they shackle women with do not apply to men. It is clear the State's real reason for "protecting" women is to keep the status quo intact.

By perpetuating the myth of feminine dependency, the legislatures keep women in their traditional home-centered roles and out of the breadwinner role, *out of the labor force* where they will compete with men for needed jobs. By forcing women into the marital state in order to fulfill their desires to procreate, the state hands over to men the control of female procreative freedom and denies women the freedom over even their own bodies.

The States of Huxley and Orwell go even farther. They limit her ability to arrange with a doctor or donor to have AID performed, thus impairing the unmarried woman's freedom of contract. Women are thus kept in a subordinate position on the homefront, as well as in the workplace.

In Stanley v. Illinois, 405 U.S. 645 (1972), dealing with the rights of the putative father of illegitimate children to block their adoption, the Court held a father's right to raise his children is not defeated because he chooses to remain unmarried. To deny the same right to women is invidious discrimination based on gender and a violation of the Equal Protection guarantee of the Fourteenth Amendment.

The Supreme Court held gender a suspect classification subject to strict judicial scrutiny in Frontiero v. Richardson, in which the husband of a servicewoman was denied benefits on the basis of a presumption that only service *wives* would be dependent on their spouses' incomes. It has since retreated from that position and views gender with either heightened scrutiny[16] or under the rational relationship test.

It is doubtful that the States' purposes, analyzed within, could outweigh the fundamental interests at stake for women even under the most minimal scrutiny.

A legislature that forecloses reproductive freedom on the basis of gender or marital status is also in violation of the Fifth and Fourteenth Amendments' Due Process guarantees. Under Substantive Due Process analysis, a state's ability to deprive a person of liberties guaranteed by the Bill of Rights is subject to limits, regardless of the adequacy of procedures employed (Lochner v. New York, 198 U.S. 45 (1905)).

Under Due Process analysis, a more flexible balancing standard will be employed than that used under Equal Protection. If the impact on the right is of such nature as to merit extraordinary review, strict scrutiny will be applied and the state purpose will have to be compelling, rather than merely rationally related, to a permissible state objective.

In the present cases, the rights of unmarried women in Huxley and Orwell to sexual privacy and reproductive freedom are encroached on by statutes that are facially gender neutral. These statutes, however, have an impermissible discriminatory impact (Griggs v. Duke Power Co., 401 U.S. 424 (1971)). They restrict the reproductive rights and freedoms of women on the basis of marital status, while not doing the same to men.

The denial of these Due Process rights, based on worn-out stereotypes and presumptions, are not justified by the States' objectives, real or purported. And the limitation of opportunities for women based on marital status alone, when such limitations serve no permissible state end, and when they do not apply to men with equal force, cannot be tolerated.

CONCLUSION

For all the aforementioned reasons, the criminal statute of the State of Orwell (ORW. Penal Code §582) should be declared unconstitutional and Appellant Isaacs' conviction reversed. The State of Huxley should be required to adopt procedures for the immediate admission of the Appellants and other unmarried women as AID recipients at its Family Planning centers.

To continue to make AID illegal for, and inaccessible to, unmarried women serves only to drive the practice underground and beyond the control of responsible medical practitioners. Such a prohibitory scheme is unenforceable and self-defeating. Its presence merely forces unmarried women, eager to conceive, to engage in illicit sex, to have AID performed in another state or to inseminate themselves.[17]

If these women choose illicit sex, the legal problems concerning paternity, custody, support and inheritance rights could burden the courts. If women choose marriage merely as a way of fulfilling the desire for children, the impact on the divorce rate and the resultant upsurge in domestic and related litigation would also add to the courts' burdens while undermining the strength and harmony of the family.

By upholding the rights of women to their freedom in making reproductive decisions, the Court would be recognizing the changes the past decades have wrought on the American family and would be taking the lead in shaping the family for future decades.

Dated: New York, New York
December 17, 1981

Respectfully submitted,

REBECCA S. LEVINE
Attorney for Appellants
201 East 25 Street
New York, New York 10010
(212) 683-3645

NOTES

1. The figures represent a rate of spontaneous abortion (miscarriage) close to that of the female population in general. Also represented is the fact that several of Dr. Isaacs' patients chose to conceive two or more children by this method.

2. See Trial Transcript, p. 12.

3. Two lesbian couples also applied during the period but chose to opt out of the present suit. Another woman recently opted out of the class after getting married.

4. Justice Powell's majority opinion in Frontiero v. Richardson, 411 U.S. 677 (1973).

5. For example, authority could be found within the Commerce Clause, since many of the effects of population growth are harmful to interstate commerce (pollution which spreads across state lines, deterioration of national parks and increased pressure on resource supplies).

6. Bureau of the Census.

7. Trial Transcript, p. 44.

8. It is presumed the single mother will work at some time during her child's minority.

9. During this period, one commentator supported AID based on a possible future shortage of men (a result of wartime depletion) and surplus of young women who desire children. Levisohn, "Dilemma in Parenthood," *J. For. Med.* 4(1957): 147, 168.

10. By preventing medical intervention in infertility cases, the State would be expanding the pool of potential adoptive parents. These people would be forced into the adoption market to fulfill their desire for parenthood. It is not suggested here that this should be done.

11. Trial Transcript, p. 67.

12. Statement, Jane Doe, Trial Transcript, p. 68.

13. If parenthood could be equated with employment in a way which would make it subject to the regulations of Title VII of the Civil Rights Act of 1964, it could be said that a marital status qualification is irrational and constitutes unlawful discrimination. It is doubtful the state could argue married status was a Bona Fide Occupational Qualification for parenthood in 1981 America.

14. Actually, the unmarried woman seeking AID is refusing to engage in illicit sex, an adherence to a traditional standard of morality.

15. Frontiero v. Richardson, *supra,* p. 684.

16. Craig v. Boren, 429 U.S. 190 (1976).

17. C.M. v. C.C., 152 N.J.Super. 160, 377 A. 2d 821 (1977).

SUPREME COURT OF THE UNITED STATES

———————————————————————X

IRWIN and EVA SUTTER,
Respondents

—against—

DR. VERONICA MOORSE and PLANNED PARENTHOOD OF NEW MORALITY,
Appellants

and

MARY YVONNE BLISS,
Appellant

—against—

JESSE HELLMAN, Attory General, State of Harmony,
Respondent.

———————————————————————X

APPELLANTS' BRIEF

Rebecca S. Levine
201 East 25 Street
New York, New York 10010
(212) 683-3645

QUESTIONS PRESENTED

1. Whether a requirement of written spousal consent as a condition precedent to the administration of AID to a married woman violates her constitutional rights of sexual privacy and reproductive freedom?
2. Whether a statute which promulgates such a requirement is a violation of the Fourteenth Amendment Equal Protection Clause?
3. Whether a court ruling that a doctor's failure to obtain such a consent form prior to performing AID on a married patient is prima facie negligence violates Fourteenth Amendment guarantees and deprives the doctor of his First Amendment right to free speech?
4. Whether a spousal consent requirement promulgated by a state constitutes unlawful sex discrimination?

STATEMENT OF FACTS

The issue presented by this combined appeal is whether a wife who is required to obtain the written consent of her husband as a condition of administration of a particular medical procedure—that of Artificial Insemination Donor, hereinafter referred to as AID, for the purpose of producing pregnancy—is being deprived of her rights in violation of the Equal Protection Clause of the Fourteenth Amendment.

Sutter v. Moorse is an appeal from the State Court of Appeals of New Morality, which granted judgment for the plaintiffs, Mr. and the ex-Mrs. Sutter, for emotional injuries allegedly arising out of Dr. Moorse's medical malpractice. The learned Trial Judge held that Dr. Moorse's administration of AID to Mrs. Sutter, without her husband's prior written consent, was prima facie malpractice. Appellant Moorse disputes that such action constituted malpractice on her part; contends that a written consent requirement unconstitutionally deprives women of their right to privacy, and asks that the judgment of the court below be reversed.

Bliss v. Hellman, an appeal from the Federal District Court of Harmony, challenges the constitutionality of a statute requiring written spousal consent as a condition precedent to the administration of AID to a married woman (see Figure 1 for a sample of Harmony's spousal consent form).

Appellant is a 25-year-old Catholic woman, who has been separated from her husband for five years after an extremely brief marriage. For religious reasons, neither wishes to divorce. The couple have one child, 6-year-old Elizabeth, who is supported entirely by her mother's earnings as an elementary school teacher. Mrs. Bliss receives no support from her husband, who is unemployed.

Mrs. Bliss would like another child ("a brother or sister for Elizabeth")[1] but does not wish to engage in illicit sexual intercourse or commit adultery. A year ago, Mrs. Bliss consulted her physician regarding AID and, despite her Church's prohibition of the practice, decided to attempt to become pregnant by that method.

Mrs. Bliss' doctor informed her that the state in which she lived and he practiced, Harmony, had a statutory requirement of written spousal consent and that he could not perform the procedure until he had the consent of Mr. Bliss on file in his office records. Mr. Bliss is vehemently opposed to the idea ("I don't want to end up having to take care of two of 'em one day")[2] and has refused to sign the consent form.

Mrs. Bliss brought the present action against the State's Attorney General seeking to enjoin enforcement of the requirement and to have the statute (Har. Public Health, Art. 21) declared unconstitutional. She brought an appeal to this court after the Federal Court, applying Harmony substantive law, upheld the statute.

AGREEMENT FOR ARTIFICIAL INSEMINATION

The undersigned, ______________________________, and ______________________________, both being of legal age, represent that they were married on ______________, 19____, at ______________, and that they have continuously cohabited together as husband and wife since the aforementioned date. The undersigned request and authorize Dr. ______________ and such assistants as he may designate, to inseminate the wife, artificially, subject to the following conditions and agreements.

1. The insemination may be repeated at times recommended by the physician until the wife becomes pregnant.

2a. The physician shall use only semen collected from the husband.

2b. The physician shall use pooled semen from the husband and a donor or donors whose name or names shall not be required to be disclosed to the husband and the wife.

2c. The physician shall use the semen of a donor or donors whose name or names shall not be required to be disclosed to the husband and wife.

3. The husband and the wife agree to cooperate fully with the physician in all phases of this procedure and never to seek to discover the identity of any unknown donor or donors.

4. The husband and the wife have been fully informed by the physician of the hazards, risks and possible consequences involved, and nevertheless, individually and jointly agree to hold the physician and such assistants whose services he may utilize, and the donor or donors, free and harmless for any claims, demands, or suits for damages for any injury or complications whatever which may result directly or indirectly from any treatment or artificial insemination performed pursuant to this agreement.

Signed______________________(husband)

Signed______________________ (wife)

Date______________

Accepted:

Signed______________________M.D. Witness______________

NOTE: Use the applicable paragraphs under 2. Paragraphs 3 and 4 would also be altered in cases where the husband is the donor.

FIGURE 1. Consent Form Required in State of Harmony.

The Appellant physician in the first action does not believe that a woman's right to control her own reproductivity should be restricted by spousal consent requirements. That is why she accepted her present employment at a Planned Parenthood clinic in a state (New Morality) which has no legislation on the subject. Unlike most private physicians in the area, Dr.

Moorse has been performing AID on married women, when requested, without consent of their husbands.

Prior to her experience with the Sutters, it worked out well. The couples were enormously grateful for the opportunity to have a child at last, and about 20 percent have returned to have second and even third children this way.

The case of the Sutters is a sad one, the doctor admits, but denies it was a result of her own negligence. The couple came to her in June of 1976 after Mr. Sutter had been diagnosed as sterile. They asked about AID as a means of conceiving. Both seemed eager to have a child that was at least *Mrs.* Sutter's, biologically, and Mr. Sutter seemed undisturbed at the prospect of raising another man's child—even after several interviews over a period of three months. The treatments began in November and continued for six months, after which Mrs. Sutter was positively diagnosed as pregnant.

The Sutters contend that late in Mrs. Sutter's pregnancy, Mr. Sutter became emotionally disturbed about what he came to call his "wife's infidelity." He became preoccupied and had to be hospitalized intermittently during the subsequent months at great expense.

Mrs. Sutter gave birth in January, 1978, to a six-pound son, delivered by her private obstetrician.[3] The child died during delivery due to complications surrounding that delivery.[4] Mr. Sutter's emotional condition worsened. Mrs. Sutter began undergoing psychiatric treatment, as well, and the couple's financial condition suffered as a result. The couple has since divorced.

As noted, the Trial Court found Appellant liable on the basis of her failure to demand a signed, written consent from Mr. Sutter. The outcome of this case will determine a standard of care to be exercised by New Morality physicians in performing AID[5] and the Appellant does not wish to be forced to ask future patients to sign such consent forms with their husbands. If she loses this case, she will be required to do just that, since her malpractice insurer has indicated that—absent a clear showing in the Court that a doctor won't be held liable for anything but his own negligence in performing AID—the consent form will be a requisite to coverage for the procedure. The doctor contends that this form of regulation is not a proper function of the medical profession and is an intrusion into the physician-patient relationship.

Point 1. The Harmony statutory spousal consent requirement for AID and the New Morality State Court's malpractice ruling infringe on women's fundamental freedoms in violation of the Equal Protection Clause of the United States and respective state constitutions.

A spousal consent requirement unduly burdens a woman's ability to become pregnant by AID, interfering with her privacy and her reproductive freedom, just as analogous cases have held such a requirement restricts a woman's right to have an abortion (Planned Parenthood of Central Missouri v. Danforth, 428 U.S. 52 (1976); Doe v. Bolton, 410 U.S. 179 (1973)). Such restrictions of fundamental liberties, absent a compelling state objective served by the disputed legislation or state action, are violative of Equal Protection guarantees. For this reason, Harmony's statutory requirement of spousal consent as a condition precedent to receiving AID, and New Morality's common law as reflected by the Sutter malpractice ruling, are unconstitutional (Constitution of the United States, Fourteenth Amendment; Constitution of the State of Harmony, Article 1, Section 6; Constitution of the State of New Morality, Article 12, Section 4).

Certainly, a husband has an interest in his wife's plans to either have an abortion or become pregnant by AID. In the example of the abortion, the husband's right to parenthood is involved. Yet, the Supreme Court has held that, as crucial as that right is, it cannot override the right of the wife to control of her own body and reproductive functions (Planned Parenthood v. Danforth, *supra*). Where the decision is to conceive a child, the husband's interest is slightly different. Statutory presumptions in the domestic relations[6] law of most states hold that a child born within wedlock is presumed to be the natural child of the husband, and it is he who is responsible for the support of the child.

It is not suggested that any man be forced to be responsible for children he never wanted and had no role in conceiving. It would be immoral to forbid a married man any element of control over his wife's decision to carry and bear another man's child and then hold the husband responsible for that child's support through majority. Statutes in a growing number of states deal with this problem. Such legislation provides that written consent to AID must be supplied by the husband of a married recipient in order for the child of the resultant pregnancy to be deemed legitimate and to be entitled to support and inheritance from the husband.[7]

This is quite different from taking the right to control the decision away from a woman and turning it over to her husband. The right is not the state's to give (Planned Parenthood v. Danforth, *supra*).

Right to Privacy Established

In Griswold v. Connecticut, 381 U.S. 479 (1965), the Court found, in the penumbras of the Bill of Rights, the right to sexual and marital privacy and held that right to be "fundamental." The case concerned the right of a physician to dispense birth control information to married couples, and it paved the way for a series of liberal opinions to follow in the area of privacy and reproductive freedom, including the landmark abortion decision in Roe v. Wade, 410 U.S. 113 (1973).

In striking down state criminal abortion statutes, the Roe Court held a woman's decision whether or not to terminate her pregnancy was encompassed within the broad right to privacy cited by Griswold. Appellants contend, by analogy, that the right to terminate a pregnancy encompasses the right to initiate a pregnancy, as well. Doe v. Bolton, 410 U.S. 179 (1973), decided at the same time as Roe, declared unconstitutional a Georgia statute to regulate abortion on the ground that the scheme placed an impermissible burden on the abortion decision and on a woman's right to terminate her pregnancy. Appellants contend that a spousal consent requirement constitutes the sort of elaborate procedural barrier contemplated by the Court in Doe.

Appellant, Doctor Moorse, further contends that the consent requirement is an encroachment on her right of free speech (Constitution of the United States, First Amendment), for in compelling the female patient to consult with her husband on the AID decision, the court has interfered with the physician-patient relationship.

Neither of the Respondent states demonstrates a sufficiently compelling purpose to justify the intrusion into fundamental rights. Harmony argues that it has an interest in promoting the marital relationship. This very contention inheres from a mythical notion: Where a husband and wife disagree on so fundamental an issue as whether to conceive a child and how to conceive that child when the husband's sterility precludes the normal methods, harmony can no longer exist. In such a situation (for example, the marriage of Appellant Bliss), marital discord is unlikely to be avoided by the State's requirement of a consent form. Nor is the requirement likely to promote the couple's agreement. And, where the couple is in agreement concerning their mutual desire for AID, the consent requirement is a mere formality that reiterates this agreement. It lacks substantive value, so is not well-tailored to fit the state's objective.

The husband's interest in procreative potential of the marriage must be protected, according to New Morality, and it is the State's function to take on the protective role. As the Court so wisely recognized in Planned Parenthood v. Danforth, despite the importance of the husband's interest in this area, where a conflict exists, the rights of the two parties cannot be reconciled to the satisfaction of each. One view must prevail and, because it is the wife who must bear any children of the marriage, it must be her view. Appellants contend the inquiry is the same whether dealing with abortion or conception by AID.

This is particularly true where AID is at issue. When AID is to be used, it is because the husband is already incapable of procreation. There is *no* restriction on his right not to parent because he has been biologically deprived of that right. It would not restore his ability to procreate to give him an absolute veto over his wife's decision to use AID, thus depriving her of her own reproductive freedom.

The States' spousal consent requirement is not well-suited to achieving the ends Respondents seek to achieve and does not warrant infringement on the fundamental rights of women.

Point 2. The Respondent states' actions in the instant cases treat women differently than men in their abilities to consent to medical treatments performed upon them. This constitutes unlawful discrimination based on gender classifications and on outdated stereotypes.

Spousal consent requirements as a prerequisite to AID for married women have no counterparts in the medical treatment of men. The Appellants cannot think of one medical procedure performed on males that would require the consent of anyone other than the patient himself. Certainly, no such medical procedure (including voluntary sterilization procedures) requires the consent of a married patient's wife. Why, then, is spousal consent required for medical procedures performed on female patients?

Appellants contend the requirement is based on outdated notions of female incompetency to contract and to hold property. The law and society have changed since this incapacity was a tenet of the early common law and statutory schemes of most states, and statutes based on this presumption of incapacity have long since been abandoned.

It is time the presumption of incapacity as a decision making tool of the courts and legislatures is also abandoned. It is not a sufficient basis for laws which treat men and women unequally, or for those which have an unequal impact (Griggs v. Duke Power Co., 401 U.S. 424 (1971)).

CONCLUSION

Appellant Moorse, contending the conclusion of the District Court was erroneous and that failure to obtain spousal consent to AID was not prima facie malpractice, asks that the judgment against her be reversed and that the Court clearly declare such requirements unconstitutional.

Appellant Bliss also seeks a declaration of unconstitutionality of her state's spousal consent requirement and that access to AID facilities be provided without any such prerequisite. She contends that the sacrifice of her reproductive freedom is too high a price to pay for merely "being married,"[8] particularly when that marriage is one in form only and provides its partners with none of the satisfactions, protection, economic security or other advantages that a better union would offer.

Dated: New York, New York
December 17, 1981

Respectfully submitted,

Rebecca S. Levine
Attorney for Appellants
201 East 25 Street
New York, New York 10010
(212) 683-3645

NOTES

1. Trial Transcript, p. 27.
2. Trial Transcript, p. 43.
3. There is evidence in the Record that the obstetrician, Dr. Carl Schultz, was unaware that the child was not that of Mr. Sutter. Trial Transcript, p. 64.
4. In a separate action, Dr. Schultz, was adjudged not guilty of negligence in that delivery (Sutter v. Schultz, 92 N.Mor. 2d 762 (1980)).
5. It is rumored in insurance company circles that the doctor's carrier may, depending on the outcome of this case, forbid its insureds to perform AID or will refuse to provide coverage for suits arising out of the procedure and related incidents.
6. HAR. DOM. REL. LAW, §75; N. MOR. DOM. REL. LAW, §42.
7. N. MOR. DOM. REL. LAW, §47B.
8. Trial Transcript, p. 82.

SUPREME COURT OF THE UNITED STATES

———————————————————————————X

DR. SEYMOUR FROOD,
Appellant,

—against—

CARL JUNGER, Registrar, State of Psychosis,
Dept. of Vital Statistics,
Respondent,

and

CLARK KANT,
Respondent,

—against—

PERRY BLACK, Registrar, State of Identity,
Dept. of Vital Statistics,
Appellant,

and

ROBERT KING, ESQ., as Guardian ad litem
for Jamie Parker, a minor,
Respondent,

—against—

CHRISTINA BARNARD, Registrar, State of Emergency,
Dept. of Vital Statistics,
Appellant.

———————————————————————————X

APPELLANT/RESPONDENTS' BRIEF

Rebecca S. Levine
201 East 25 Street
New York, New York 10010
(212) 683-3645

QUESTIONS PRESENTED

1. Whether an AID-conceived child is denied equal treatment in violation to her Fourteenth Amendment rights by statutes which seal her birth records and deny her access to the identity of her natural father?

2. Whether an AID child, thus denied his genetic heritage and sense of identity, has been deprived of fundamental liberties without Due Process of law?
3. Whether the States' interests in preserving the donor's privacy and the harmony within his and the AID child's family is sufficiently compelling to justify the challenged statutes?
4. Whether the States' interest in encouraging and regulating AID sufficiently outweighs the interests of AID children and donors who seek access to their natural fathers/children?

STATEMENT OF FACTS

The three parties to these combined appeals, the Appellant Frood and the Respondents King and Kant, seek to break the seal of secrecy and gain access to certain birth records on file with their respective states.[1] They contend that statutes which require a state registrar to place, under seal, the original medical records and birth certificates of AID (Artificial Insemination Donor) children and which provide that the seal will be broken only for good cause shown[2] exist in a majority of states, as do analogous laws on adoptees' records. These statutes, the parties say, unconstitutionally deprive the AID child of her/his Due Process rights and are violative of the Equal Protection Clause.

Two of the parties, Respondents Parker (represented by Mr. King, her Guardian *ad litem* in the present action) and Kant were conceived by artificial insemination between male donor and recipient mother. The Appellant Frood was himself an AI donor while attending medical school and attempts, now, to learn the identity(ies) of his biological child(ren). All were plaintiffs in the original actions against defendant state registrars.

Plaintiff/Respondent Parker is a four-year-old girl, who suffers from leukemia and has been in and out of the hospital intermittently during the past 17 months. She is currently in remission and apparently responding well to medication, but she has had setbacks in the past and could have one again at any time. Jamie's mother conceived her by AID while an unmarried woman. Now married to a man who has adopted Jamie, she and her daughter live a comfortable life and do not want economically.

The family seeks to find Jamie's biological father, the AID donor, to obtain needed medical information and because someday Jamie may need a bone marrow transplant from him.[3] In order to learn the donor's identity, the family was forced to bring suit against the State's Dept. of Vital Statistics in Federal District Court. After a ruling in Parker's favor for "good cause shown," the State brought this appeal.

Respondent Kant, a 22-year-old graduate student in journalism, seeks to find his AI-donor father in hopes of establishing a relationship with him, of learning his historical and biological heritage. Kant, who has participated in both individual and group psychotherapy[4] for the past five years and who has a history of minor disciplinary problems in school, has been described by his psychiatrist as suffering from anxiety neurosis centering on lack of well-formulated sense of identity and personal worth.[5] It is at his psychiatrist's urging that Kant initiated the search for his natural father, which has led him to the Supreme Court.

The lower court held in Kant's favor for good cause shown, and the State of Identity brought this appeal.

Appellant Frood was a senior in medical school when he donated his sperm, several times a month during a five-month interval, to a gynecologist near his school's campus. He is now a 32-year-old psychiatric resident at Psychosis State Hospital and wishes to learn his children's identities and whereabouts so he can get to know them. Dr. Frood's own father recently died, a reason Dr. Frood cites for his desire to establish a relationship with his own children. Since the death, Dr. Frood can't bear the thought that he will never see his children, that someone else might adopt them and that he will be unable to trace them so they will be lost to him forever.

Dr. Frood's father, an industrialist, left him a considerable fortune, so it is obvious he plans to make no claims on his children or their families. In fact, one of the motivations for his search is the desire to share his wealth with his issue.

The Federal Court rejected Plaintiff Frood's claim that he had shown sufficiently good cause to warrant unsealing the records. He brings this appeal based on the contention that secrecy statutes are inherently unconstitutional.

Point 1. Statutes which mandate sealing medical records in AID cases, thus denying AID children their biological heritages, violate the constitution's Equal Protection guarantees.

The challenged statutes, which require sealing of the medical records in AID cases, and which provide for the seal to be broken only for good cause shown, infringe on fundamental rights of AID children. By treating children conceived by AID differently from other children, for less than compelling state reasons, the Defendant States violate the Equal Protection Clause of the Fourteenth Amendment of the United States Constitution.

When AID children, like adoptees, seek access to sealed medical records in order to learn the identity of their biological fathers, many rights depend upon their success. First among these is the children's right to know their genetic inheritance and medical history in order to learn if there are genetic or medical risks to which they might be exposed by virtue of their parentage. In Plaintiff Parker's case, that right may encompass the right to life, itself.

Dicta in a New Jersey adoption records case, Mills v. Atlantic City Dept. of Vit. Stat., 372 A. 2d 646, 654 (1977), might be relevant to Parker's situation. In that case, the court said the child's need to have access to family medical histories or information may constitute good cause shown where evidence presented in court demonstrates a valid, justifiable need. The court below in Parker also recognized the importance of this right by holding that Parker had shown good cause to unseal the records.

As in Kant, the AID children's psychological need to know their identity in order to promote social adjustment is no less significant than their need for medical information. Frequently, the children's lack of information about their biological parents leaves them with a gap in self-image or a feeling that there is something vaguely unacceptable about them and their origins.[6] The need to fill this gap should constitute good cause shown.

AID children also have a right to a relationship with their biological fathers and to have the opportunity to inherit from them. Appellant Frood claims his children have this right and that it is being breached by the State's policy of sealing AID records.

An additional interest of the AID children is that of avoiding incest. That children of the same AID donor-father would meet and marry was a widespread fear when AID began being performed in greater numbers. The availability of information to the AID child contemplating marriage could avoid this possibility.

All of these aforementioned rights fall within the broader, First Amendment right to receive information, upheld in Time, Inc. v. Hill, 385 U.S. 374 (1967), and New York Times Co. v. Sullivan, 376 U.S. 254 (1964).

To the extent that it is true that only people who have developed fully and healthily are capable of intelligent decision making, the protection of the First Amendment would seem to extend to information which affects that development.[7] AID children's right of privacy, as guaranteed by the Fourteenth Amendment and interpreted in the line of cases beginning with Griswold v. Connecticut, 381 U.S. 479 (1965), must also protect the individual's control over the development of identity. Although adult AID children will not always be able to assert that access to information about their origins is necessary to any particular decision, they may assert that the protection of their right to make fundamental decisions is of little worth unless they are provided with access to the same information about themselves as others enjoy.[8].

These interests of the child must be balanced against those of other parties to the conception, that is, the donor and the recipient mother. The donor may wish to keep the records sealed to keep his role in the transaction a secret. In order to do so, he may assert his own right to privacy and to the integrity of his expectations (when he donated his sperm) regarding anonymity. A donor such as Dr. Frood, who wishes access to his children, and therefore favors unsealing the records, asserts his interest in his children and rights to parent them free of state interference. The mother may have an interest in keeping the donor anonymous so as not to disrupt her family's harmony and her AID child's life.

Each party has weighty interests in the outcome and those competing interests must be weighed. Under Equal Protection analysis, the Court does not speak in terms of balancing but instead applies strict scrutiny to the competing interests as they are represented by the state's objectives. Where it is contended that the AID child is being denied equal treatment (as compared to other children), and being deprived of fundamental liberties, the Court must apply strict scrutiny to the state purposes. Here, it must conclude those purposes are not sufficiently compelling to justify interference with the AID child's fundamental liberties.

No AID records or analogous adoption records case has yet come before this Court, but the lower courts have been dealing with the problem in the area of adoption records for years. A judge may allow disclosure in exceptional circumstances and for good cause shown, and the courts are getting increasingly liberal in interpreting good cause showing. The trend is in favor of disclosure.[9] In some cases, the courts have allowed partial disclosures. In Chattman v. Bennett, 57 AD 2d 618 (1977), the plaintiff was an adult adoptee who was contemplating starting her own family and wanted medical information about her biological parents. The New York court held that the records could be unsealed to provide plaintiff the medical information she sought but the parents' identities could not be revealed.

State Purposes Are Not Compelling

The purposes cited by the States of Psychosis, Identity and Emergency are not compelling enough to warrant an interference of this magnitude with the rights of the AID child. The State expresses an interest in safeguarding the donor's right to privacy. This right, as derived from the Bill of Rights[10] and guaranteed by the Fourteenth Amendment Equal Protection Clause, can refer to decision making in the area of family and sexuality. The right to privacy referred to here derives from early guarantees of freeing citizens from the necessity of quartering soldiers in their homes and is of a different character.

Interference with privacy of this type can be remedied by bringing a civil action for invasion of privacy. An AID donor who suffered damage as a result of his child's intrusion on his life could bring such an action for damages. Such actions might also have a deterrent effect on parent searches.

The State's interest in preserving the integrity of the family unit is closely related to the above, for it encompasses protecting the donor and his family from intrusions by the child, as well as protecting the AID child, its recipient mother, her husband, and others, from intrusions into their lives by the donor. This interest is significant but not compelling. It is not particularly pertinent, either, in cases where the AID child is an adult or where, as in Parker, the AID child and the child's family waive their right to be free from intrusion in order to locate the donor father for medical reasons.

Finally, the States rely on their interests in preserving the integrity of the AID procedure. If donor anonymity is breached, they argue, other young men will be discouraged from becoming donors for fear of later invasion of privacy, or even of being held liable for support of their AID children. This could sound the death knell for AID programs, eliminating a medical solution for millions suffering from infertility, say the States.

This is a worthy argument, but it is unsupported by the evidence. There is nothing in the record to indicate, nor is it a fact that, fear of these consequences has to date discouraged potential donors. In fact, there is currently a healthy supply of donors (including Nobel prize winners) to meet the current demand.

It can be argued that AID children comprise a suspect classification at which the challenged legislation is addressed. Even if this were not so, the rights encroached upon by the legislation are fundamental. The State objectives expressed do not warrant the unequal treatment or the intrusion into the rights of these children.

Point 2. The sealed records statutes challenged here deprive AID children of fundamental liberties without Due Process of law.

The AID children involved in the present case complain that the challenged statutes deprive them of their privacy, their genetic heritage and their right to receive information, all interests of Constitutional magnitude. The Appellant donor contends he is denied the "companionship, care, custody and management" of his children (Stanley v. Illinois, 405 U.S. 645 (1972)). The statutory sealing of AID records, with access only for good cause shown, works to deprive plaintiffs of the aforementioned rights in violation of the Due Process clause (U.S. Constitution, Fifth Amendment; Caban v. Mohammed, 99 S.C. 1760 (1979)).

In Stanley, the Court recognized the "warm, enduring bonds" that exist between parent and child[11] in holding that the state's practice of denying an unwed father custody of his children without first providing a hearing on his fitness as a parent was unconstitutional. The Court said it applied an Equal Protection standard but its reasoning is more properly viewed in terms of Due Process.

In Due Process analysis, the Court utilizes a balancing test, weighing the rights of the respective claimants. As already demonstrated, the rights of the child must be placed on the scale against those of the donor; the rights of the child balanced against the interests of the State.

Appellant Frood and Respondents Parker and Kant argue that liberties at stake are so fundamental that the States' objectives can't possibly compete.

Where the child is merely curious, his interests take on less weight in the balance, but where the child's need is medical or psychological, the donor's need for privacy takes on less importance by comparison.

CONCLUSION

The plaintiffs demand a halt to the enforcement of the unconstitutional AID records statutes and ask that the respective state registrars be compelled to open plaintiffs' files.

Alternatively, they suggest intermediate-level measures that could be utilized in cases where the interests are not so strong. A clearinghouse could be established to store these records and to serve as liaison between willing donor and willing child. If one party were not willing to have his anonymity breached, the clearinghouse could process that information. In the absence of a clearinghouse, a trial judge could appoint a guardian *ad litem* to represent the interests of the absent natural parent. That guardian could be in contact with the parent, and if the parent did not object to a meeting with his child, the guardian would serve the clearinghouse function.

Another method was supplied by an analogous adoption case, Chattman v. Bennett, *supra,* which provided the plaintiff adoptee information about her biological parents but did not reveal their names. Or, the trial judge could do an *in camera* examination of the records, possibly in conjunction with a geneticist, and decide which (or whether all) information should be released to the plaintiff.

Each of these methods is better suited to the state objectives of promoting family harmony and preserving privacy than the existing statutes, with the advantage of being less burdensome and restrictive of individual rights.

Dated: New York, New York
December 17, 1981

Respectfully submitted,

Rebecca S. Levine
Attorney for Plaintiffs
201 East 25 Street
New York, New York 10010
(212) 683-3645

NOTES

1. Frood donor record file No. 4603; Recipient Kant, No. 38597; Recipient Parker.

2. The Parties challenge, respectively, Psychosis Statistics Act 9:3–9; Identity Records Act §56; State of Emergency Public Records Act §12.

3. Jamie's mother has already been ruled out as a possible transplant donor, for medical reasons.

4. One of Kant's groups dealt exclusively with the problems of adult adoptees.

5. See testimony of Dr. Francine Gregory, Trial Transcript, p. 174.

6. Carolyn Burke, "The Adult Adoptee's Constitutional Right to Know His Origins," *S.Cal.L.Rev.* 48(1975):1196, 1201.

7. *Ibid.*, p. 1205.

8. *Ibid.*, pp. 1208, 1209.

9. In Re Adoption of Female Infant, *Fam. L. Rep.* 5(1979):2311; In Re Adoption of Spinks, *N.C. App.* 32(1977):422; In Re Ann Carol S., 172 *N.Y.L.J.* 31, Aug. 13 1974, at 12, col. 6; Spillman v. Parker, 332 So. 2d 573 (1976).

10. As interpreted by Griswold v. Connecticut, *supra.*

11. Stanley, *supra,* p. 652.

REFERENCES

Books

Decker, Albert, M.D., and Suzanne Loebl. 1978. *Why Can't We Have a Baby?* The Dial Press.

Dowling, Colette. 1981. *The Cinderella Complex.* Summit Books.

Fabe, Marilyn, and Norma Wikler. 1979. *Up Against the Clock.* Warner Books.

Fisher, Florence. 1973. *The Search for Anna Fisher.* Fawcett Crest.

Greenleaf, Barbara Kay. 1980. *Help: A Handbook for Working Mothers.* Berkley Publishing.

Hope, Karol, and Nancy Young, eds. 1976. *MOMMA, The Sourcebook for Single Mothers.* The New American Library.

Jones, Landon Y. 1980. *Great Expectations, America and the Baby Boom Generation.* Ballantine Books.

Kaufman, Sherwin A., M.D. 1978. *You Can Have a Baby.* Bantam Books.

Klein, Carole. 1973. *The Single Parent Experience.* Avon.

Nickles, Elizabeth, with Laura Ashcraft. 1981. *The Coming Matriarchy, How Women Will Gain the Balance of Power.* Seaview Books.

Putterman, Ron. 1981. *To Find My Son.* Avon Books.

Silber, Sherman J., M.D. 1980. *How To Get Pregnant.* Warner Books.

Toffler, Alvin. 1981. *The Third Wave.* Bantam Books.

Articles

Annas, George J. 1980. "Fathers Anonymous: Beyond the Best Interests of the Sperm Donor." *Fam. L.Q.* 14(Spring):1.

Beck, Phyllis W. 1978–79. "Nontraditional Lifestyles and The Law." *J. Fam. L.* 17:685.

Berger, Victor M. 1963–64. "Artificial Insemination." *Brooklyn L. Rev.* 30:302.

Burke, Carolyn. 1975. "The Adult Adoptee's Constitutional Right to Know His Origins." *S. Cal. L. Rev.* 48:1196.

Chamberlain, William M. 1971. "Population Control—The Legal Approach to a Biological Imperative." *Ecol. L.Q.* 1:143.

Chandler, Harry S. 1968. "A Legislative Approach to Artificial Insemination." *Cornell L. Rev.* 53:497.

__________. 1980. "Developments in the Law: The Constitution and the Family." *HarvardL.Rev.* 93:1156.

Dienes, C. Thomas. 1968. "Artificial Donor Insemination: Perspectives on Legal and Social Change." *Iowa L. Rev.* 54:253.

Erikson. 1974. "Women and the Supreme Court." *Brooklyn L. Rev.* 41:209.

__________. 1981. "Eugenic Artificial Insemination: A Cure for Mediocrity?" *HarvardL.Rev.* 94(June):1850.

Isaacs, Stephen L. 1980–81. "The Law of Fertility Regulation in the United States: A 1980 Review." *J. Family L.* 19:65.

Jacobs, Ronald S., and J. Peter Luedtke. 1965. "Notes: Social and Legal Aspects of Human Artificial Insemination." *Wisconsin L. Rev.* 1965:859.

Kass, Leon R. 1979. "Making Babies Revisited." *Pub. Int.* 54:32.

Kindregan, Charles P. 1979. "State Power Over Human Fertility and Individual Liberty." *Hastings L.J.* 23:1401.

Paul, Eve W., and Paula Schaap. 1980. "Abortion and the Law in 1980." *New York L.R.* 25:497.

Rice, Charles E. 1959. "A.I.D.—An Heir to Controversy." *Notre Dame Law* 34:510.

Sergeant, David A. 1970. "Notes: The Legal Status of Artifical Insemination: A Need for Policy Formulation." *Drake L. Rev.* 19:409.

Shaman, Jeffrey M. 1979–80. "Legal Aspects of Artificial Insemination." *J. Fam. L.* 18:331.

Silvoso, Joseph A., II. 1975. "Artificial Insemination: A Legislative Remedy." *W. St. U.L. Rev.* 3:48.

Smith, George P., II. 1978–79. "A Close Encounter of the First Kind: Artificial Insemination and an Enlightened Judiciary." *J. Family L.* 17.

__________. 1981. "Artificial Insemination Redivivus, Permutations Within a Penumbra." *J. Legal Med.* 2:113.

__________. 1977. "The Medicolegal Challenge of Preparing for a Brave Yet Somewhat Frightening New World." *J. Legal Med.* 5(4, April):9.

__________. 1955. "Symposium on Artificial Insemination." *Syracuse L. Rev.* 7:96.

Uviller, Rena K. 1978. "Father's Rights and Feminism: The Maternal Presumption Revisited." *Harvard Women's Law J.* 1:107.

Wadlington, W. 1970. "Artificial Insemination: The Dangers of a Poorly Kept Secret." *Nw. U.L.J.* 64:777.

Weinhaus, Lisa. . "Substantive Rights of the Unwed Father: The Boundaries Are Defined." *J. Family L.* 19:445.

Weinstock, Neal. 1971. "Artificial Insemination—The Problem and the Solution." *Fam. L.Q.* 5:369.

Wellens, David R. 1968. "Human Artificial Insemination: An Analysis and Proposal for Florida." *U. Miami L. Rev.* 22:952.

Wheeler, Louisa A., and Shirley L. Kovar. 1973. "Roe v. Wade: The Right of Privacy Revisited." *Kansas L. Rev.* 21:527.

Wilkinson, J. Harvie, III, and G. Edward White. 1977. "Constitutional Protection for Personal Lifestyles." *Cornell L. Rev.* 62:563.

Wolff, Morris H., and Stephen Cirillo. 1980–81. "The Bastard's Cause of Action: A Statutory Cause of Action for Illegitimate Children." *J. Family L.* 19:463.

Iatrogenic Surgical Liability

Bernard J. Ficarra, M.D., and
Frank Mitchell Corso, Esq.

> There was once, in a remote part of the East, a man who was altogether void of knowledge and experience, yet he presumed to call himself a physician.
>
> Fable 8, The Ignorant Physician, by Pilpay (circa 326, B.C.)

The noun of iatrogenic is iatrogenesis. It is derived from the Greek word *iatros,* meaning medicine, plus *genesis,* which is translated as "caused by." When the ancient citizens of classical Greece employed this term, they did not realize it would gravitate into the lexicon for medical liability in the twentieth century. The ancient Greek word *gignesthai* is the etymological origin of *genesthai* from which the Latinized genesis is derived. Literally, the word is translated as "to be produced."

Prior to its popularity in medico-legal usage, iatrogenic was an adjective limited to the vocabulary of neuropsychiatrists. To them it meant "induced by a physician." Reference was made to a nervous or mental state occurring in a patient as a result of a physician's diagnosis of a physical disease. In a similar concept legal actions have been sustained when negligent medical treatment allegedly causes mental anguish.[1] When the result of negligence is mental anguish that causes illness, some states permit recovery although the tortfeasor caused no physical harm to the plaintiff.[2,3] A physician must be alert at all times as to what is said to a patient during discussions, conversations or expressions concerning the course of disease treatment as well as while rendering a prognosis.[4] This presentation is the clinical record of a person who suffered mental anguish due to iatrogenic negligence. The cause of action was not founded upon the mental disquietude but was based upon the iatrogenesis.

CASE PRESENTATION

The medical history of the patient-plaintiff is that of a 72-year-old widow who was admitted into a hospital with an admission diagnosis of a sigmoid polyp. The discharge diagnosis was perforation of the rectosigmoid. A resumé of the hospital discharge summary record is recounted as to its pertinency. It is noted that the patient was admitted into the hospital on April 2, 1979 and was discharged on April 28, 1979.

History: This is the first admission for this 72-year-old female who complained of rectal bleeding of three months duration. The patient had a work-up which included sigmoidoscopy that revealed a rectal polyp. Barium enema was negative. No change was found in the bowel movement. No complaints of abdominal pain.

Past Medical History: Mild hypertension treated with aldomet. A pinning of the left femur in 1951. The patient denies any other disease or operations in the past.

Physical Examination: The patient was in good general condition, alert and cooperative. Head, neck, chest, and heart were normal. The abdomen was soft, nontender, no masses or organomegaly. Extremities were negative. All peripheral pulses were palpable except the popliteal and pedal. No lymph nodes were palpated. Breasts were negative. Rectal examination was negative.

Laboratory Data: EKG showed atrial fibrillation with marked ST segment depression of ischemic type. Chest x ray was negative.

Hospital Course: On April 3, 1979, the patient underwent sigmoidoscopy and polypectomy.

On the following day the patient started to complain of diffuse abdominal pain and was found to have a markedly distended abdomen. Abdominal x rays which were taken subsequently showed free air under the diaphram. At this point, a perforation of the sigmoid colon of iatrogenic origin was diagnosed. The patient was taken to the operating room where an exploratory laparotomy was performed. Perforation of the rectosigmoid was found. A diverting transverse colostomy with drainage of the pelvic cavity was performed. The patient tolerated the procedure well.

On the first postoperative day, the patient was found to have atrial fibrillation and was administered digoxin and quinidine. The subsequent postoperative period was essentially uneventful. The patient had a low grade temperature over the first postoperative day. She was treated with wide range antibiotics and her fever subsequently subsided.

On the fourth postoperative day, the patient was started on a low residue diet which she tolerated well. On the seventh postoperative day, the patient was transferred to the floor from the Intensive Care Unit. She continued to improve until her hospital discharge.

The operative report dated April 3, 1979 indicates that the postoperative diagnosis was polyp of the sigmoid. The preoperative diagnosis was the same. The title of the operation was written as a sigmoidoscopy with electrofulguration of the polyp. The operative procedure is quoted in toto:

> The patient without anesthesia was placed in the jack-knife position. Sigmoidoscope passed readily to approximately 6". At this point there was in the posterior wall a cherry red polyp which appeared to be on a short pedicle. The polyp measured about 0.5 cm by approximately 3/10th cm. x 3/10th cm. in depth. A snare was encircled around the base of the polyp and using the electrocoagulation current, the polyp was snared off and fulgurated at the same time with electrocoagulation. Some bleeding occurred which was controlled.
>
> The postoperative condition was satisfactory, except that it was noted that the patient had a slightly rapid pulse. No drains. Wound expectancy is usual anorectal healing.

On July 9, 1979 the second operation was performed by an abdominal surgeon. His preoperative diagnosis which was the indication for the operation was "perforating rectosigmoid." The procedure performed was a diverting transverse colostomy with drainage via a sump drain to the pelvic cavity. The dictated operative report is quoted:

> Operative findings: This patient underwent sigmoidoscopy and polypectomy one day prior to this surgery. Almost right after surgery, patient started complaining of diffuse abdominal pain with abdominal distention. Abdominal x rays showed marked pneumoperitoneum with a diagnosis of perforated sigmoid as a result of polypectomy. The patient was taken to the OR for exploratory laparotomy. Upon exploration, there was a small amount of purulent material in the pelvic cavity. The peritoneum appeared to be moderately swollen with some fibrin deposits over it. The ileum appeared to be slightly dilated. There was a hole about 1–1½ cm in diameter in the rectosigmoid at the level of the peritoneal reflection in the posterior wall of the large bowel. The surrounding area appeared to be infected with fibrin deposits. Culture was taken.
>
> Procedure: With the patient in supine position, the operative area was prepped and draped in the usual manner. A left paramedian incision was made and was carried down through subcutaneous tissue and anterior fascia. The muscle was then retracted laterally. Hemostasis was then achieved using clamps and 3-0 plain ties. The peritoneum was then grasped and opened. Hemostasis exploration was then begun, retracting the small bowel cephalad and exploring in this manner the pelvic cavity. The findings were as indicated above. The sigmoid was slightly mobilized by cutting the peritoneal reflection. However, it was evident that the only operation that is feasible in terms of resection is an anterior resection. At this point, it was decided to do a right transverse diverting colostomy. This was performed by making a skin incision at the right upper quadrant in an adequate position for placement of the colostomy bag. The incision was deepened through subcutaneous tissue. The superficial fascia was cut, and the muscle was split and cut transversely using electrocautery. A segment of right transverse colon was brought as a loop through the colostomy, a

Hollister rod was passed under it and it was secured to the skin with 3-0 silk sutures. A vaseline gauze was placed around the colostomy.

The pelvic cavity was then drained using 2 Penrose drains and 1 sump drain. The incision was then closed using No. 30 wires in a Tom Jones type closure. The skin itself was left open and was packed with 2 in. iodoform gauze; to close in primary intention.

The patient tolerated the procedure well and was taken to the recovery room. (The colostomy was closed via a surgical procedure performed six to eight weeks after her hospital discharge: It was done in July, 1979.)

The hospital pathologist's report on the specimen removed initially is the following quotation: "Specimen date is April 4, 1979. Specimen labeled sigmoid polyp. Received in formalin are fragments of polypoid, rubbery, slightly granular, reddish tan tissue totalling 2.2 x 2 x 0.7 cm.

DIAGNOSIS: Fragments of adenomatous polyp;
Fragments of colonic mucosa, muscularis and fat.

A most significant finding by the pathologist upon microscopic review of the histologic specimen was the presence of muscularis and fat. The presence of both these tissues indicated that the removed specimen contained more than mucosa of the colon.[5]

THE LEGAL ACTION

When the plaintiff instituted a cause of action for medical malpractice against the original physician, it became a lesson in fundamental surgical principles as well as an anatomical review of the lower intestinal tract. The pathologist's testimony was a restatement of the clinicopathologic knowledge currently available on the subject of large bowel single polyps.

Prior to recalling the testimony of the medical experts, it is fitting to present some of the salient features of the examination before trial of the defendant. Some of the questions asked and the answers given are taken verbatim from the stenographic recording.

Q. Can you tell me, sir, what complaints the patient exhibited, if any, at the occasion of your first examination of this patient?

A. I will read from the record: She had slight anal rectal bleeding and a protrusion recently.

Q. Can you tell me what you mean by the word "protrusion," doctor?

A. Something coming out of the anal canal.

Q. Did you conduct a physical examination of the patient, doctor, on the occasion of her first visit with you?

A. I conducted the examination that I do especially—an anorectal examination.

Q. What did the examination entail, doctor?

A. It entailed examining her externally around the anus, putting my finger in the anal canal and then following that with an instrument called the sigmoidoscope.

Q. And, doctor, did that examination reveal the presence of anything in the anal canal?

A. Yes.

Q. What did that examination reveal, doctor?

A. It revealed the following: She had slightly ulcerated internal hemorrhoids moderate in size, and at six inches up from the anal canal there was a crimson red polyp measuring about 0.5 centimeters by 0.3 centimeters by 0.3 centimeters on a very small pedicle.

Q. Did you make that determination by use of the sigmoidoscope?

A. Yes.

Q. Can you describe for the record what a sigmoidoscope looks like and also how it works?

A. It's a very simple instrument similar to a telescope with a light at its proximal end. The light is reflected through the tube. At the end of the tube the light can be seen and whatever is in the area that you can visualize at the end of the tube you see. Simply a small telescope.

Q. Did you discuss your findings with the patient?

A. Yes.

Q. What was the substance of that discussion?

A. The substance of the discussion was that she had this polyp, that the hemorrhoids could be left alone for the time being and that she had this polyp which should be removed, that it might become malignant or might be malignant, very difficult to say, and the procedure was discussed with her.

Q. When you say procedure, meaning removal through operation, the surgical procedure, doctor?

A. Right.

Q. Did you discuss anything else with her? I am talking about the risks, if any, in connection with this procedure.

A. The thing was discussed with her in general. I discussed what had to be done.

Q. What did you discuss with the patient about the procedure, doctor?

A. I discussed in general what it means, what the possibilities are, what it would take to remove it. I mentioned, of course, like any procedure in surgery there is some difficulty sometimes, but we did not anticipate them. According to my previous experience that they usually were done without any great problems, but the fact was mentioned in general and in specific that there are risks, there are dangers to any procedure.

Q. Did you tell the patient what specific risks there were?

A. No. It was mentioned that there were hazards attached to this procedure.

Q. Did you recommend a barium enema procedure prior to February 27, 1979?

A. Yes, the previous time.

Q. Where was the barium enema conducted?

A. At the medical center.

Q. Can you tell me, did you have the results of those films on the occasion of the February 27, 1979 visit?

A. Yes.

Q. Can you tell me for the record what those films showed?

A. The barium enema was reported as negative by the radiologist.

Q. Can you tell me the purpose, doctor, that you recommended a barium enema for the patient?

A. It is routine if a patient has a polyp to see whether there are other polyps present in the colon or other problems.

Q. Did the results of the barium enema change or alter your opinion as to the advisability of the sigmoidoscopy with electrofulguration of the polyp, the procedure that you recommended to her on the occasion of her first visit?

A. It altered it temporarily for the following explanation. I looked at the films and I was not satisfied with the radiologist's interpretation and he reviewed the films. I will read this to you:

At my suggestion...

Q. OK.

A. ...I have reviewed the radiographs of your patient who had a barium enema done on 2-9-79. Further history and resume of the physical findings would have been helpful at the time the films were read. The patient probably has a congenital anomaly of rotation with most of the large bowel in the right abdomen and the left abdomen containing loops of ileum that are pacified by reflex. I do not see evidence of an intrinsic lesion in the colon nor is there any mass in the left abdomen that could account for a displaced splenic flexure. I would suggest an IVP to further evaluate the retroperitoneal structures, but still feel that an anomaly of rotation is probably the best explanation.

Q. What did you do after reading that report?

A. I sent the patient for an IVP.

Q. Did you know whether the IVP took place?

A. I cannot say.

Q. Doctor, did you recommend anything else between February 27 and her entry into the hospital in April of 1979?

A. Yes.

Q. What did you recommend?

A. A medical examination by our internist for clearnace for surgery.

Q. Do you know whether or not that took place, doctor?

A. Yes, it was done.

Q. What were the results of that examination, doctor?

A. Cleared for surgery, preoperative medical classification class two.

Q. What does that mean? "Cleared for surgery, preoperative class two"?

A. Pre-op class two means that she's not a prime operative candidate for the procedure, that she has some problem which makes it a greater risk to be operated on medically.

Q. Do you know what problems she had which made her a greater risk to be operated on, doctor?

A. Yes.

Q. What were they?

A. One, hypertension and two, a mild aortic incompetence.

Q. Did you ever discuss the results of this examination with the patient?

A. Yes, on the phone.

Q. Can you tell me what you said to her and what she said to you?

A. I cannot tell you the details of the conversation.

Q. Just the substance, the general substance.

A. The substance was that she could be operated upon.

Q. When for the first time did you see the patient in the hospital, doctor?

A. On the 3rd of April, '79. [Patient admitted to hospital on April 2, 1979.]

Q. What did you do for her on the 3rd day of April of 1979? Did you examine her on April 3, 1979?

A. Yes. Just partially.

Q. What type of examination did you conduct on that date?

A. I spoke to her and then looked at the anorectal part just myself, but I did not do any medical examination on her.

Q. When did the operative procedure take place, doctor?

A. In the afternoon of April 3, 1979.

Q. There came a time when you did the operation on April 3, 1979; is that correct?

A. Yes.

Q. Can you tell me your preoperative diagnosis as contained on the record? It was polyp of the sigmoid; am I correct?

A. Yes.

Q. Can you tell me what the operative procedure consisted of?

[The answer was a reading of the operative procedure as presented previously.]

Q. What is electrofulguration, doctor?

A. Electrofulguration means using an electrical current to burn through the tissue that was being removed.

Q. Is there a specific type of instrument that uses the electrofulguration that is used in that procedure?

A. Yes, it's called a snare.

Q. Did you use a snare in this operative procedure, doctor?

A. Yes.

Q. What does a snare look like and how is it used?

A. A snare is simply a little loop, a metal loop, through which the current is passing which can, by properly using the handle, pull into the neck of the instrument, the long tube, and both cut and burn the tissue that it's snared around.

Q. Can you tell me what is meant by "sigmoidoscope passed readily to approximately six inches," which is contained in the second sentence of the operative procedure?

A. Sigmoidoscope was passed easily without any difficulty to six inches. Six inches up from the anal canal.

Q. And at that point you viewed the polyp, am I correct?

A. Yes.

Q. What did you then do?

A. Put in the snare around the polyp and proceeded to snare it off while the current was activated.

Q. Was it removed in one piece, doctor, or in fragments?

A. It was actually removed in...

[There was an objection to the form of the question.]

Q. Was the entire polyp removed, doctor?

A. As far as I know, yes.

Q. During this procedure, did you observe the rectosigmoid colon, doctor?

A. The rectosigmoid colon? Yes.

Q. Doctor, during this procedure, did you at any time while using any of the instruments, the sigmoidoscope together with the electrofulguration, perforate the rectosigmoid colon of this patient?

[There was an objection to the form of the question.]

Q. Did you on the day of the operation determine or did you find out the results of the pathology report? Do you know the results of the report, doctor?

A. Yes.

Q. Did you on April 3, 1979 make out a postoperative note?

A. Yes.

Q. Can you read what the prognosis was?

A. Guarded.

Q. Do you know what led you to record the prognosis as guarded? What about the patient's condition that led you to record a guarded prognosis? What did you base that prognosis on?

A. Two reasons. First, the possibility that the polyp might be malignant in the pathological section. Two, that there might be some postoperative complication not at that moment envisioned.

Q. Was there anything conducted in the operation which led you to believe that there would be a postoperative complication? Did anything occur during the operation that led you to believe that there would be postoperative complications?

A. No.

Q. When for the first time did you see the written pathology report?

A. The written report was not available until approximately Thursday.

Q. Do you know what day of the week this operation took place?

A. Tuesday.

Q. Can you tell me, where did you review the pathology report?

A. In the hospital, on the chart.

Q. What did that report reveal? What did it say?

A. Fragment of adenomatous polyp, fragment of colonic mucosa, muscularis and fat.

Q. What did those findings indicate to you?

A. The possibility that there was a perforation into the peritoneum.

Q. Was that during the operative procedure, doctor?

[There was an objection to the form of the question. The question was withdrawn.]

Q. Did you ever confirm that possibility, doctor? How did you confirm it?

A. I had a flat upright abdominal plate taken in which there was gas in the peritoneal cavity.

Q. When was that done, doctor?

A. The next day after the operation.

[The subsequent questioning centered about the preoperative diagnosis of a colonic perforation for which a laparotomy was performed by an abdominal surgeon. The operative procedure was admitted into evidence previously as part of the total hospital record. The questioning continued.]

Q. Based on the operative report, what did he do?

A. Based on the operative report, she had a diverting transverse colostomy, laparotomy, drainage.

Q. Did you ever discuss the nature of that operation with the operating surgeon after it was performed on April 4, 1979.?

A. Yes.

Q. What did you say to the surgeon?

A. Very little.

Q. Do you remember anything about what you said to the doctor?

A. I said I hoped that she recovers after his surgery.

Q. Have you ever heard of the term "iatrogenic," doctor?

A. Yes.

Q. Do you know what the term means, doctor?

[There was an objection with the comment: "He is not here as a dictionary."]

Q. Would you return, doctor, to your operative report?

Q. You have written the words "polyp measured 0.5 centimeters by approximately 3/10 centimeters by 3/10 centimeters in depth." Can you tell me when you made the determination as to size of the polyp, doctor?

A. When you see it.

Q. And can you tell me when you passed the sigmoidoscope approximately six inches into the rectum, did it stop at that point or did it extend beyond the six inches? The polyp was located approximately six inches into the rectum; is that correct?

A. Yes.

Q. How far did you pass the sigmoidoscope into the rectum during the operative procedure?

A. Six inches.

Q. In the second sentence you say at this point there was in the posterior a cherry red polyp which appeared to be on a short pedicle. Can you tell me when you mention posterior which part of the rectum you were talking about?

A. Posterior by definition means back, doesn't it?

Q. During the operative procedure, doctor, by use of the sigmoidoscope, do you remember ever coming in contact with the rectosigmoid colon?

A. You have to come in contact with it if you are in that area?

Q. Do you remember perforating the rectosigmoid colon during that procedure?

[Objection by defendant's attorney.]

Q. During the operative procedure, did the patient make any complaints of pain?

A. I don't recall.

Q. Can you tell me, doctor, you say she was placed in a jack-knife position in the operative record. What do you mean by that?

A. The patient is bent at the hips so that her forward part of her body, while she is lying on her stomach, goes down and the posterior part goes down so she is broken as a jack-knife. This is the jack-knife position [indication]. Simply a position.

Q. Was any lubricant used, doctor, to allow the sigmoidoscope to make entry into the rectal area?

A. Yes.

Q. The sigmoidoscope has attached to it mechanisms which allow you to use electrofulguration; am I correct? The sigmoidoscope, does it have attached to it a mechanism which allows current to pass through so that the polyp can be removed?

[Question withdrawn upon objection by defendant's attorney.]

Q. You have written here, doctor, some bleeding occurred which was controlled. [Referring to hospital record.] Did you ever estimate the amount of bleeding?

A. No. Some.

After several other questions pertaining to the laparotomy for which a transverse colostomy was performed the testimony session was terminated.

PATHOLOGY OF POLYPS

The hospital pathologist who examined the macroscopic surgical specimen prior to reading the microscopic section of the polyp was called to testify in court. His testimony as a medical expert is written in narrative form rather than in the question-and-answer format. Initially a request was made to discuss the anatomic and pathologic structure of polyps.

A polyp is a cauliflower-like tissue attached to the lining (mucosa) of the intestinal tract. If the base is broad it is called a sessile polyp (from the Latin derivative meaning "sitting"). When the polyp is attached to the mucosa by means of a slender stem or stalk (as in this patient under discussion), it is termed a pedunculated polyp.

Polyps are encountered frequently in the gastrointestinal tract. They may be found in any portion of the stomach, small intestine, colon, rectum or anus. Symptoms may be absent, or may vary with the location site. Most polyps are single, but they may be multiple. Polyps may form a cluster or a small group within a short segment of the intestine. When many polypoid growths are present the word *polyposis* is used by physicians to describe this disease entity. When the entire colon is involved by polypoid disease, sometimes as a congenital disease, reference is made to this condition as "multiple polyposis." It seems to be a reduplication of meaning. For this reason some authorities on this disease entity have preferred the descriptive phrase "multiple polypoid disease of the colon."[6] The identification of a polyp in one site implies the possibility of others being present elsewhere in the intestinal tract, hence the necessity for x-ray studies of the gastrointestinal tract, including a barium enema.

Gross anatomic description of a polyp verifies that the size thereof may vary from a few millimeters to several centimeters in diameter. The average size is one centimeter. Polyps result from either a hypertrophy of the mucous membrane of the intestine or are true tumors. They are soft and friable. When a polyp has a broad base (sessile polyp) at the point of attachment to the intestinal wall it becomes pedunculated as the weight of the suspended mass (tissue) pulls away from the wall of the intestine. The enlarging mass (growing tissue) is pulled upon by the fecal current, increasing the length of the pedicle. As a general statement, it is believed that most polyps start with a sessile base which later becomes pedunculated. If this belief is accurate, sessile polyps are younger than those with a stalk, or pedicle. On many occasions the intestinal mucosa extends over the stalk onto the polyps so that some polyps appear to be a mucosal flap. All polyps that have existed for a long time show some degree of edema, hemorrhage or chronic inflammation. Surface ulcerations with granulation tissue formations are described as common accompanying macroscopic findings. These surface changes are due to the irritation caused by the fecal stream and the normal peristaltic activity.

Microscopically, polyps may have a papillomatous or fibromatous architecture. Other histologic characteristics may be present, such as the features of an adenoma. When malignant changes occur in a polyp these cell alterations are seen under the microscope. The most common locations for polyp formation are the rectum, the sigmoid, the descending transverse and ascending colon. They may form in other anatomic areas where a mucous membrane exists, such as the nose, vagina or urinary bladder.[7]

Concerning the complications attributed to a polyp, three major ones were discussed. The first is surface erosion of the polyp that may result in hemorrhage. The larger the surface involved, the greater the volume of blood loss with or without visible bleeding. The second complication is the possibility of a polyp's being an irritant leading to the development of an intussusception (invagination) of the intestine. Thirdly, consideration is given to malignant alteration in a polyp as a serious complication that occurs in 50 percent of colonic polyps.[8]

The testimony of the pathologist brought forth the facts that the surgical specimen as measured by the defendant was 0.5 cm. by 3/10 cm. by 3/10 cm. in depth. The pathologist's measurements were much greater. The specimen was reported to be 2.2 cm. by 2 cm. by 0.7 cm. The microscopic report was reread to find the pathologic diagnosis ("fragments of adenomatous polyp, fragments of colonic mucosa, muscularis and fat"). When asked about the size of the specimen and the pathologic diagnosis, the pathologist said that the specimen was larger than the described polyp because it contained tissue other than the polyp. The tissues were colonic mucosa, muscularis and fat. The critical significance of the extra tissue was that it indicated to the pathologist that part of the normal wall of the colon was removed in addition to the fragments of the polyp.

SURGICAL EXPERT WITNESS

A board-certified surgeon testified in behalf of the plaintiff. He was asked to discuss the pathologic diagnosis which was in the hospital record. The testimony verified that colonic mucosa, muscularis and fat proved that some of the wall of the large intestine was removed, which would mean that perforation resulted from the removal of these tissues. The presence of serosal fat meant that the outer layer of the colon was pierced, since the fat is attached to this exterior, or serosal, surface.

To clarify this opinion the surgeon was asked to describe the anatomic structure of the sigmoid colon. His description is summarized herewith. The sigmoid colon is S-shaped. It is 40 centimeters in length as it lies in the bony pelvis. Four layers compose the wall of the colon. These four coats from the outside inward are called the serous, muscular, areolar and mucous layers. The exterior serous layer completely surrounds the rectosigmoid. In the course of its distribution this peritoneal, or serosal, covering forms a number of small pouches with indentations. These are filled with fat, termed fat tags, which anatomically are identified as *appendices epiploicae.* Some of this fat tissue was contained in the operative specimen sent to the pathology laboratory.

The next layer beneath the serosa is the muscular coat (muscularis). This coat is composed of external longitudinal muscle fibers (going up and down) and an inner circular group of muscle fibers which are more numerous, since they have a squeezing function in the peristaltic mechanism. The circular muscle fibers are more numerous in the sigmoid, rectum and anus. These circular fibers form the internal sphincter muscle of the anus.

The areolar layer connects the muscular layer below and the mucous layer above it. Because of its holding position below the mucosa it is referred to as the submucosa. The mucous membrane is the lining surface of the colonic lumen. For the sake of brevity, it is called the mucosa. It contains the blood supply, lympathic drainage and solitary lymph nodes. In view of its vascularity, because it contains the blood vessels, the polyp that forms in the mucosa *ipso facto* is vascular and bleeds briskly when incised.

Strict emphasis was placed upon the procedure of proctosigmoidoscopy during the court trial. Therefore, at this point the medical witness was asked to describe the technique for performing a sigmoidoscopy. Prior to rendering this testimony a clarification of terminology was required. The words sigmoidoscopy, colonoscopy, proctosigmoidoscopy, coloprotoscopy and proctocolonoscopy are used interchangeably. All mean the insertion of an instrument through the anal opening for the purpose of endoscopic diagnosis of colonic diseases.[9]

Almost always an endoscopic procedure is preceded by a digital examination. Digital and sigmoidoscopic examinations are diagnostic procedures carried out as part of a complete, total physical evaluation. When performed with gentleness, caution and care, they are safe and relatively painless to the patient. For endoscopic study the position assumed by the patient during this examination is the physician's choice.[10] However, on the record of the sigmoidoscopic procedure, the position of the patient should be mentioned. Thus the reviewer of the procedure will be able to determine the exact location when the disease process is described as being present on the anterior or posterior wall of the colon. The positions in which the patient is placed may be the knee-chest, the knee-elbow, the lithotomy or jack-knife position. The inverted position is known as the jack-knife position.

The patient who is the plaintiff in this lawsuit was placed in the lithotomy position at the first examination. During the hospital procedure for the removal of the polyp she was in the jack-knife position. Hence, during the direct questioning the defendant was confused about the location of the polyp in the plaintiff-patient. It is self-evident that the position of the patient during endoscopy should be known and recorded.

PROCTOSIGMOIDOSCOPY PROCEDURE

Prior to an endoscopic examination a cleansing enema is mandatory. Enemata should be given until the liquid returns are clear. The patient is placed in the position selected. A well-lubricated finger is inserted into the anal canal; this digital examination assures the patient that no unbearable pain is associated with the insertion of a finger or instrument into the anorectal canal. Not only does digitation allay the fear of the contemplated procedure, but it relaxes the anal sphincters, allowing an easier insertion of the endoscopic instrument. Simultaneously, within the realm of the palpating finger, it allows the identification of any obstruction (fecal impaction, inspissated barium or tumor) or extraordinary tenderness that would contraindicate the passage of an instrument.

The lubricated instrument to be inserted is grasped firmly, so that the instrument and the hand form a working unit. The endoscope is inserted slowly; its progress is monitored via direct observation. The instrument is inserted 5 cm. from the anal verge in direction of the patient's umbilicus using the jack-knife (inverted) position. The tip of the instrument by this time is distal to the anal ring. The obturator is removed as the sigmoidoscope is advanced under direct visualization. The instrument is not to be allowed to progress as far as it can go if undue pressure is necessary. Force can perforate the bowel easily.

Insufflation may be used to distend the intestine in the path of the instrument. When the patient is in the jack-knife position less insufflation is necessary because the inverted position allows the small intestine to fall out of the pelvis. Thus, the pressure of the small bowel on the rectosigmoid is relieved, allowing the colonic lumen to expand. An inflating bulb is used to balloon the colon. This ballooning permits the visualization of several more inches of the sigmoid. At the same time, it smoothes out the accordionlike mucosa of the colon so that the crevices can be visualized. Excessive insufflation with increasing pressure can cause a bowel segment to burst with subsequent peritoneal contamination. The examiner conducts a major portion of the colonoscopic examination under direct vision while inserting the instrument. This is extremely advantageous in patients with polyps, carcinoma or colitis because the danger of bleeding or perforation can be avoided.

When the endoscope passes the rectosigmoid it then enters the lower sigmoid. At this point there is a tugging effect on the mesosigmoid, which may cause an abdominal cramp. Informing the patient of this anticipated occurrence not only augments confidence, but assures the patient that the endoscopist is experienced in the procedure. With the withdrawal of the instrument direct visualization continues as part of the conducted examination. Often a missed diagnosis upon entry is discerned during the egress of the endoscope. Moreover, while removing the instrument, any complication such as bleeding or perforation may be identified.

The defendant testified that he had used a Welch-Allen Fiberoptic Sigmoidoscope that was 10 inches long. However, the sigmoidoscope on view in the courtroom was a rigid metal instrument made of aluminum without an obturator. The surgical expert was asked concerning the currently available sigmoido/colonoscopes used in the United States. The answer given was that the foremost endoscopic instruments whose technical data are considered outstanding are four in number. These instruments are the Olympus, the ACM-Wappler, the Wolf and the Fujinon.[10]

The subject turned to the known complications associated with sigmoidoscopy. The gamut of complications in colonoscopy have been listed in the order of occurrence as bowel perforations, intraluminal bleeding, mesenteric bleeding and death due to shock.[11] Perforation of the large intestine can occur as a complication of sigmoidoscopy, rectal or sigmoid biopsy. A simple cleansing enema in the presence of an inflammatory or necrotizing state of the bowel can cause a rent in the intestinal wall, if the perforation is extraperitoneal there may be no immediate sign or symptom of this. Consequently, a delay in diagnosis is understandable. The risk of a colonic perforation while administering an enema prior to endoscopy is a rarity; nevertheless it should not be ignored when thought is given to forceful enemata. Likewise, the performance of a barium enema soon after a rectal or a sigmoid biopsy may convert an incomplete bowel perforation into a complete perforation.[12]

The manner in which a perforation may occur varies greatly. Some of these incidents occur during a simple diagnostic procedure. Other perforations are associated with the therapeutic procedure using a biopsy forceps or a snare. Any maneuver such as forcing an instrument past an organic structure or continual colonic spasm, extracting too much tissue during a biopsy or excision of tissue, or pulling a polyp too far downward before removing it with a snare can perforate the intestine. This last mechanism brings the full thickness of the colon wall into the cutting grasp of the snare. The performance of a biopsy on ulcerated tissue (colitis, diverticulitis, carcinoma or necrotic polyp) which has caused an attenuation (thinning) of the intestinal wall can also result in a perforation.[13]

The medical literature contains a history in which a perforation of the sigmoid occurred three days after a simple diagnostic colonoscope examination. In order to prevent perforations of this classification, it has been suggested that a stool softener and a low residue diet be administered following all diagnostic and therapeutic colonoscopies.[14,15] With the advent of the modern fiberoptic colonoscope, the incidence of perforations has declined markedly.[16] Endoscopic colonic procedures are assuming a valuable role as an evalutory technique in the management of colonic polyps. Colonoscopy has found a place in the surgeon's therapeutic armanentarium. Although most endoscopists are gastroenterologists, an increasing number of general surgeons have become enamored of this technology.[17]

THE MEDICO-LEGAL DEFICIENCIES

During the course of litigation for medico-surgical malpractice, certain weaknesses in the defense position became evident with definitive clarity. These debilitating facts could be classified into several categories:

- not informing the patient of the risks involved in the sigmoidoscopic removal of the polyp
- the defendant displayed a lack of knowledge
- the endoscopist failed to perform certain safeguarding, preventive surgical pursuits
- the defendant-physician deviated from the accepted standard of colonoscopy (i.e., the patient was not informed that complications of the procedure may be hemorrhage or perforation
- the defendant did not obtain a proper informed consent

The defense argued that the patient was a 72-year-old widow with some cardiac irregularity. The physician stated he did not desire to worry her because she might think she could bleed to death from the procedure. It was recalled that the plaintiff was familiar with hospitals and operations, since she had a prior major operation for a fracture of the hip which necessitated the insertion of a vitallium pin into her femoral bone. There was no logical reason presented for not obtaining a proper informed consent. The physician admitted that he did not inform the patient concerning the possibility of a perforation. The reason given was that he thought the patient might refuse the procedure, which he did not want because he suspected the presence of cancer. When the patient-plaintiff was in the witness box, she had a pleasant appearance. She was alert, intelligently articulate, responsive, and readily admitted that she had no fear of surgery, even with full understanding of the possible risks.

Lack of medico-surgical knowledge was displayed when the defendant could not recall whether, prior to removing the polyp, it was on the anterior or posterior wall of the colon. The confusion was clarified later by the medical expert witness and the plaintiff. In the operating room the patient was placed in the jack-knife position, whereas in the physician's office at the time of the first examination the patient was in the lithotomy position. Thus, in one position the polyp would be visualized as being anterior; with a reversal of the patient's position the polyp would be posterior in location. In addition, when discussing his own methodology of performing a sigmoidoscopy, the defendant offered incomplete information; his presentation was not half so thorough as that of the medical expert witness. Moreover, he had limited knowledge of the more modern colonoscopes. When discussing the specimen removed, his identification of the tissue was different from the preoperative description. The removed tissue was described as being charred. A measurable discrepancy existed between the size of the cherry red polyp *in situ* and that recorded by the pathologist.

The defendant's failure to perform or have available certain equipment consistent with colonoscopy were medical inadequacies. Among these are the following:

1. He had no bulb or other means of inflating or ballooning the

intestine for adequate visualization of the polyp. (An admission of an unsatisfactory view of the specimen was made during the defendant's testimony.) An inflation of the sigmoid enlarges the lumen, eliminates the mucosal crevices and places the mucosa under tension. With these changes in the mucosal surface, the redundancy that overlies the polyp is stretched, allowing identification of the distal curvature of the polyp as well as the stalk or pedicle with which it is attached to the sigmoid. At the same time the distention throws the polyp into the lumen of the bowel, facilitating its detection.

2. No forceps were available with which to grasp the specimen prior to its removal. The defendant admitted to the absence of forceps, stating that he used the suction tip (with the suction on) to hold the specimen during the snaring activity. The uncontrollable active suction pulled the specimen beyond the level of the mucosal attachment, tenting the mucosa. The snare was placed beyond the pedicle, grasping the tented normal mucosa. The electrofulgurating snare cut through the four layers of the intestinal wall, causing an aperture.

The deviations from the medico-surgical standards of performing a routine removal of an uncomplicated polyp through a sigmoidoscope were as follows:

1. The removed specimen was charred, according to the defendant. If the specimen was charred, then the site of removal was charred as well. This is actual notice that the intestinal wall is perforated or weakened to a point of probable perforation. The charring indicates that the volume of electricity in the electrocoagulation current was greater than that needed to transect the stalk of the polyp. This charring would increase the diameter of the perforation previously presented at the tented mucosal site.

2. Postoperative examination of the specimen was inadequate. Proper review of the specimen would have indicated to the physician that the removed tissue was much larger than the size of the polyp. A satisfactory examination of the tissue removed via fulguration would have revealed the presence of the section of the bowel wall that was described by the pathologist.

3. It is standard technique to reinsert the sigmoidoscopy following a biopsy or polypectomy to police the area of surgery for bleeding, a tear or perforation. This reinsertion was not done. After the removal of a polyp by a snare, a perforation can be identified, sometimes, by the protrusion of omental or epiploic fat or small bowel at the perforation site, in addition to seeing the actual perforation. The presence of smoke in the bowel lumen is no excuse for lack of proper visualization. The active suction pipe can be used to exhaust any smoke that is present following fulguration.

The plaintiff's attorney accentuated the delay between the time of perforation in the operating room and the delayed performance of the colostomy. This delay caused the patient pain and suffering for which compensatory damages were demanded. This delay could have been avoided if the defendant had requested a consultation at any time, even in the operating room during the polypectomy. Every hospital has a full staff of consultants in every specialty who are available 24 hours a day. Failure to seek a consultation has been found to be negligence.[18,19,20] This memorandum of the law was brought forth as an addendum upon which medical malpractice was supported.

Additional compensatory damages were requested because of the failure to diagnose the perforation and to seek the services of a consultant. This lack of due care resulted in the peritonitis described at the laparotomy procedures. Additional compensation was demanded for the inconvenience plus the mental anguish produced by the colostomy. Further compensatory damages were requested for the persistent postoperative laparotomy scar and the probability of peritoneal adhesion formation that is a competent producing cause for an intestinal obstruction at any time in the future.

CONCLUSIONS

The jury rendered a verdict in favor of the plaintiff for $125,000. It is a high price to pay for an error in a procedure that is performed universally as a daily routine. With the new endoscopic equipment, proper hospital surroundings and assistance, no complication should arise from colonoscopy. The redhibitory defects brought forth and discussed during the court trial could only lead to a verdict favoring the plaintiff's bar.

Multiple medico-legal lessons have been learned from this case presentation. Among these is the necessity for the physician to be a truthful informant, allowing the responsibility for decision making to go to the patient. Prior to the sigmoidoscopy and polypectomy, the physician did not inform the patient on the hazards or complications of the contemplated procedure. The reason was that he did not desire to frighten her into refusing the procedures. This restrained communication, for whatever reason, is no excuse. It remains negligence since it appears to be an error, a mistake, or an oversight to another interpreter.[21]

The conceptual essence of negligence implies that no malice is intended or involved. Negligence is a neglect, a failure to do a thing properly, or a failure to do it all, as required by the applicable standard of care.[22,23] Interpolated additions to the interpretation of negligence are derived from the verb neglect, meaning to fail to treat with attention, to ignore, to fail to perform through carelessness or oversight. Habitual want of attention also is termed neglect. Notwithstanding the noble intentions the defendant may or may not have possessed, the physician was negligent in failing to inform the patient or her family of the risks involved in performing a polypectomy via a sigmoidoscope.

No one should attempt to perform any medico-surgical procedure without the skill necessary to be the master of the proposed instrumentation or technique. Commensurate with the skill is the necessary experience to manage and treat any complication that may eventuate from the proposed procedure or operation. In the absence of these virtues, the dignity of the learned medical discipline will diminish or perish. When a specialized profession is failing in esteem, the bolstering advice to give those who would restore it is to refurbish it to the principles from whence it sprung.

Prevention against iatrogenic medical malpractice is a pathway to a triumph over medical negligence in general. It is a basis for curative measures against medical liability. Prevention is an urgent necessity in the medico-surgical practitioner's struggle to decelerate the momentum of the geometric rise in causes of legal action founded upon alleged medical negligence.

The laity should be made aware that medical liability is the greatest of all the hazards that are destroying the desire for excellence and perfection in the medical profession. The legal impediment of alleged malpractice has risen to a position of major consternation to those engaged in the healing art. In the light of past and present experience, this legal embarrassment is becoming more perturbing. The pursuit of modern medicine and surgery is sufficiently complex without the additional burden of threatening legal pitfalls.

REFERENCES

1. Henry v. U.S., 280 F.Supp. 27, D.C., N.Y. (1968).
2. Dillon v. Legg, 441 P.2d 513 Cal. (1968).
3. Haight v. McEween, 251 N.Y.S.2d 839 (1964).
4. Ficarra, B.J. 1980. "Medical Negligence Based on Bad Faith, Breach of Contract or Mental Anguish." In *Annals of Legal Medicine*. Philadelphia: W.B. Saunders.
5. Pauline Seabury v. S. Levy and La Guardia Hospital, Supreme Court, N.Y.S., Queens County, (Jan.) 1982.
6. Buie, L.A. 1938. *Practical Proctology*. Philadelphia: W.B. Saunders.
7. Rohertson, H.E. 1934. "Polyps of the Colon and Their Possible Significance." *Bulletin Am. Soc. Control of Cancer* 16(1):6, 7.
8. Goligher, Duthrie, and Nixon. 1977. *Surgery of Anus, Rectum and Colon*. London: Bailliere Tindall.
9. Shinya, Hiromi. 1981. *Colonoscopy*. New York: Igaku-Shoin Medical Publishers.
10. Skandalakis, J.E., S.W. Gray, and R.P. Olafson. 1976. "Anorectal Landmarks for Digital and Sigmoidoscopic Examination." *Contemporary Surgery* 6(2):65, 68.
11. 1981. *Journal of Colo-Proctology* (International Issue) 3(1):40–41. Munich: Gmbh and Co.

12. Smith, L.E., and S. Nivatvongs. 1975. "Complications in Colonoscopy." *Diseases of the Colon and Rectum* 8(3):214, 220.
13. Fielding, J.F., and K. Lumsden. 1973. "Large Bowel Perforations in Patients Undergoing Sigmoidoscopy and Barium Enema." (From the Radcliffe Infirmary, Oxford University.) *British Med. Journal* 1:471–473.
14. Thorbjarnarson, B. 1962. "Iatrogenic and Related Perforations of the Large Bowel." *AMA Archives of Surgery* 84(6):28, 34.
15. Dagradi, A.E., M.E. Norris, and Z.C. Weingarten. 1978. "Delayed ("Blow-out") Perforation of the Sigmoid following Diagnostic Colonoscopy." *Am. Jour. Gastroenterology* 70(3):317, 320.
16. Adair, H.M., and S. Hirshon. 1981. "The Management of Colonoscopic and Sigmoidoscopic Perforation of the Large Bowel." *British Jour. Surgery* 68(1):415, 416.
17. Forde, K.A. 1977. "Colonoscopy for the General Surgeon." *Contemporary Surgery* 10(3):21, 25.
18. King v. Flamn, 422 S.W.2d 679, Texas.
19. Largess v. Tatem, 291 A.2d 398, Vt. (1972).
20. Forde, K.A. 1977. "Colonoscopy for the General Surgeon." *Contemporary Surgery* 10(3):21, 25.
21. Oppenheim, E.B., and C. Youmans. 1981. "Deadly Omission: When Must the Doctor Talk?" *Legal Aspects of Medical Practice* (Special Issue) 9(10):1, 3.
22. Seattle First National Bank v. Rankin, 59 Wash. 2d 288, 367 P.2d 835 (1962).
23. Hoglin v. Brown, 4 Wash. App. 366, 481 P.2d 458 (1971).

The Limits of Liability for Psychiatric Malpractice

Sheila Taub, J.D.

INTRODUCTION

Psychiatrists are sued for malpractice less frequently than physicians in most other specialties, but they may soon lose this distinction, if the current trend continues.[1] In the past, several factors combined to minimize the number of lawsuits against psychiatrists: the stigma attached to psychiatric treatment, the difficulty of proving a causal relationship between improper treatment and the patient's deterioration or failure to improve (especially where the treatment was mainly verbal), and the difficulty of proving the applicable standard of care, to name just a few. Today much of the stigma attached to psychiatric treatment has dissipated, leaving patients less reluctant to publicize the fact that they have been in therapy by filing a lawsuit against the therapist. Patients may also have greater expectations of psychiatric treatment, as they do of medical treatment in general, leading to greater dissatisfaction if the results are not what they anticipate. The publicity given to large verdicts in a few sensational suits no doubt encourages other patients who are already dissatisfied with the results of their treatment to file suit.

Until now it has been impossible to state definitively whether malpractice claims against psychiatrists were rising disproportionately to claims against other medical specialists, or what activities by psychiatrists were most likely to generate malpractice claims.[2] An analysis currently in progress of 1,000 closed claim files accumulated over the past decade by the American Psychiatric Association (the largest liability insurer for the psychiatric profession in America) has begun to answer these questions.[3] About 80 percent of the files were closed without payment to the claimant, and another 10 percent were settled for less than $5,000,[4] suggesting that in most of these cases liability was doubtful, the patient could not demonstrate causation or damages, or both. While the types of claims have not changed much over the past five years, their frequency and cost have doubled during that period of time. The average physician, however, is still six times more likely to be sued than a psychiatrist.

Claims were grouped into the following categories, listed in order of decreasing frequency of occurrence:[5]

1. Improper treatment (many of these cases involved sexual relations between the patient and the therapist) 27%
2. Drug reactions (these include cases where the drug was ineffective or produced unwanted side effects) 18%
3. Patient suicides 18%
4. Failure to prevent harm to a third party 13%
5. Improper diagnosis 12%
6. Improper commitment 4%
7. Breach of confidentiality 3%
8. Libel and slander 2%
9. Lack of informed consent 2%
10. Improper use of electroshock therapy 1%

Slightly different, but comparable, figures were obtained from an analysis of 1,600 claims filed with the A.P.A. from 1972, when it began its liability insurance program, to March, 1983.[6] The claims fell into the following categories:

1. Improper treatment 25%
2. Drug reactions 20%
3. Suicide 20%
4. Failure to restrain (a few of these involved failure to protect third parties from the patient) 14%
5. Failure to diagnose 12%
6. Improper commitment .... <5%
7. Breach of confidentiality 3%

Of the 1,600 claims filed, a committee of psychiatrists found 410 to be "serious," as defined by the potential liability in dollars. Within this group, the committe found no negligence in 242, or 59 percent, some deviation from the standard of care in 139, and questionable liability in the remainder.

It is evident from these figures that a substantial proportion of malpractice claims against psychiatrists differ in kind from the vast majority of claims against other kinds of physicians. Claims based on patient suicide or violence committed by the patient against a third person would rarely be made against physicians in other specialties. Claims based on sexual relations between the physician and his patient do occur in other medical specialties, and in dentistry as well, but probably not as frequently. Together these three categories of claims (suicide, violence toward a third person, and sexual relations with the therapist) comprise nearly half the total number of claims. The remarkable aspect of that is that all three are triggered by the patient's own voluntary acts (the patient is usually not physically forced to engage in sexual relations with the therapist). This raises legal questions concerning the patient's ability to prove the essential elements of a negligence claim of duty and causation, and philosophical questions regarding how one individual, the physician, can be held accountable for the voluntary act of another, his patient. This article will discuss some recent cases that suggest tentative answers to these questions, the answers varying according to the nature of the action.

Cases Based on Patient Suicide or Attempted Suicide

A therapist's liability for a patient's suicide or attempted suicide can only be predicated on negligence, as opposed to strict liability. That is, to succeed with a claim the plaintiff must establish in court that the therapist either knew or should have known that there was a likelihood that the patient would attempt to commit suicide, and that the psychiatrist should have taken all reasonable precautions to prevent it. Generally speaking, the therapist's conduct will be measured against the standard of the reasonable prudent person practicing the same specialty under comparable circumstances (the precise standard of care may vary somewhat in different jurisdictions). A number of cases have found liability for patient suicide on these grounds.[7] Thus, in Breese v. Indiana,[8] where the father of a patient who committed suicide brought a wrongful death action against the hospital in which he hung himself, the trial court dismissed a claim based on *res ipsa loquitur* (a legal doctrine which holds, in essence, that the act itself is evidence of negligence), despite the fact that the son had a history of numerous suicide attempts. The court of appeals affirmed, saying that to hold otherwise would be to say that suicide by a person with a history of prior suicide attempts establishes liability on the part of the custodian. The father had also pleaded negligence in failing to properly guard and restrain the son, as well as breach of contract, and the court of appeals remanded for a new trial based on those counts.

Even with no history of prior suicide attempts, if the patient shows other behavior patterns that are statistically correlated with suicide, that may be enough to impose a duty on the therapist either to restrain the patient or to issue a warning to the patient's family, if the patient is not in custody. The psychiatrist's potential liability for patient suicides may increase as more becomes known about behavior factors associated with suicide.[9]

Cases Based on Unintentional Self-Inflicted Injury to Patients

If the psychiatrist knows, or should know, that the patient is not in a condition to protect himself from common hazards he may be under a duty to take additional precautions to prevent the patient from injuring himself. Thus in Gunnarson v. State,[10] a New York appellate court said that the state was properly held liable in damages to a paranoid schizophrenic who burned herself while lighting a cigarette in a coatroom at the state psychiatric hospital to which she had been involuntarily committed. The hospital employees were held negligent because she had been heavily sedated, she had not been searched on admission, and she had been allowed to retain possession of cigarettes and a lighter, in violation of hospital rules.

Cases Based on the Patient's Violence Toward a Third Person

The leading case in this area is the well-known Tarasoff v. Regents of the University of California.[11] The California Supreme Court held that a therapist who determines, or should determine, that a patient presents a serious threat of violence to another incurs an obligation to use reasonable care to protect the intended victim. The therapist may satisfy that obligation by warning the potential victim or those in a position to protect the intended victim, by notifying the police, or by taking any other steps that are reasonably necessary under the circumstances. Tarasoff broke new ground in finding that the duty to protect intended victims was inherent in the therapist-patient relationship, and independent of any contractual agreement or any relationship between the therapist and the potential victim. The case evoked a largely hostile response from the psychiatric community, whose members charged that the decision would lead to the overprediction of dangerousness, engender distrust between therapist and patient, deter dangerous patients from seeking therapy, and impair the effectiveness of therapy.[12] Some psychiatrists take a less jaundiced view of Tarasoff, stating that the duty to inform and protect third parties is an extension of the physician's traditional responsibility to alert the public to danger.[13]

The major controversy surrounding the Tarasoff decision concerns the ability of psychiatrists to predict dangerous behavior. Psychiatric patients will often voice desires to harm others without having any intent of fulfilling them. Giving a warning to the potential victim entails a breach of the psychiatrist's ethical duty to maintain the patient's confidences, and should therefore be done only when the threat appears to be genuine. Thus, the proper implementation of the Tarasoff duty to warn requires the ability to distinguish genuine threats from idle ones, and to predict which patients do indeed present a danger to an individual or to society. At one time psychiatrists believed that professionals with the proper training could make accurate predictions of dangerousness. About 10 years ago, however, the American Psychiatric Association stated that psychiatrists were no better at predicting dangerousness than anyone else.[14] Today, the pendulum shows signs of a slight shift in the opposite direction, with a few psychiatrists claiming that accurate predictions can be made under certain conditions.

Two recent legal decisions come out on opposite sides of this controversy. In the Matter of William Wilson[15] the court upheld a motion to exclude psychiatric testimony on the future dangerousness of an individual at his civil commitment hearing, on the grounds that there is no established area of expertise in the fields of psychiatry or psychology in predicting dangerousness, and that the current state of scientific knowledge does not permit the assertion of a reasonable psychiatric opinion on the issue of whether or not a person is likely to injure himself or others. However, less than three months later, a majority on the United States Supreme Court ruled[16] that psychiatric testimony about a defendant's long-term dangerousness could be used when a death sentence is being considered, even if the psychiatrist had never examined the defendant. The cases may be reconcilable if different definitions of "dangerousness" are involved when the issue is civil commitment as opposed to imposition of the death penalty on a convicted criminal, and it may be that some predictions of dangerousness are more valid than others.[17]

Whatever the actual ability of psychiatrists to predict dangerousness, a long line of cases subsequent to Tarasoff, arising in a number of different jurisdictions, has confirmed the existence of a legal duty to protect third parties from violent acts committed by psychiatric patients, at least under certain circumstances.[18] From the widely varying factual situations which gave rise to these cases, the limitations that the law will place on this duty are beginning to be discernible. The therapist will not be liable to the victim for failure to issue a warning where the patient made no explicit threat to kill the victim or where the issuance of a warning would have been in violation of a statute.[19] Where the patient is known to be dangerous, but the identity of the potential victim is unknown, the therapist will not be obliged to issue a warning, but may be held liable by failing to take other steps to mitigate the danger, which may include confining or restraining the patient.[20] Liability may be based on the negligent release from confinement of a patient who the psychiatrist knows, or should know, has dangerous propensities,[21] or on the general duty to confine or otherwise control such patients.[22] Liability will not be imposed where the defendant had no legal right to restrain the patient.[23] There is no duty to warn a potential victim who is already aware of the danger the patient poses.[24]

A recent decision rendered by the U.S. District Court in Maryland took account of the practical difficulties involved in implementing the duty to restrain a potentially violent patient.[25] The plaintiffs were injured when their car collided with one driven by the patient on the wrong side of the road with its headlights off. The patient, who suffered from alcoholism and schizophrenia, and was legally intoxicated at the time of the accident, had been seen as an outpatient 12 days before. At that time the psychiatrist concluded that he was not in need of hospitalization, changed the patient's medication from Thorazine to Mellaril, and scheduled a follow-up visit for one month later. The plaintiffs claimed the psychiatrist was negligent in failing to hospitalize the patient, in changing his medication, in not scheduling a follow-up appointment sooner, and in not notifying the department of motor vehicles that he was incapable of operating an automobile safely. The district court found that under the circumstances of the case the psychiatrist lacked the legal right, much less the duty, to hospitalize the patient or to notify the motor vehicle department, and that his decisions regarding the medication and the follow-up appointment were not grossly negligent (which the plaintiff would have had to prove in order to prevail, as suit was brought under the Federal Tort Claims Act). The court noted that a duty to protect third parties from the patient cannot be imposed where the psychiatrist has no right to control the patient, which is usually the case with voluntary outpatients. The court also recognized the impossibility of preventing the patient from driving if he was determined to do so. It cited the literature on the unreliability of psychiatric predictions of dangerousness and the absence of notice to the psychiatrist that the patient did pose a danger to other drivers.

Another recent case in which the plaintiff was injured by the negligent driving of a psychiatric patient had a different outcome, but is readily distinguishable from Hasenei on its facts. In Petersen v. State of Washington,[26] the driver was under the influence of drugs at the time of the accident. He had been released from a Washington state hospital a few days before, despite the fact that he was apprehended for reckless driving on the hospital grounds just prior to his discharge. The Washington Supreme Court found that the circumstances presented sufficient evidence of gross negligence to state a cause of action.

In other recent cases courts have held that the failure to issue a warning or take other measures to prevent threatened harm to third parties could serve as a basis for liability. Some of the more pertinent cases are discussed below.

In Chrite v. United States,[27] the plaintiff alleged that the hospital was negligent in releasing a patient who, six months later, murdered his mother-in-law. The court denied defendant V.A. Hospital's motion for summary judgment, stating that, although it had no duty to restrain the patient once it found him to be no longer a person requiring treatment, it could be liable for failing to warn the mother-in-law of his dangerous tendencies, since she was a readily identifiable potential victim.

Jablonski v. U.S. [28] held that a minor could recover for the wrongful death of her mother, who was killed by the man she lived with after he was released from the V.A. Hospital. The hospital had failed to record and transmit information obtained from the police regarding his dangerousness, had failed to obtain his past medical records, which showed his homicidal tendencies, and had failed to warn the woman adequately of his dangerousness. The man had not explicitly threatened the woman, but the V.A. psychiatrist had diagnosed him as an antisocial personality and potentially dangerous.

In Davis v. Lhim,[29] a state hospital and a psychiatrist employed there were sued for authorizing the release of a voluntarily-committed schizophrenic patient into the care of his mother, whom he shot and killed two months later. The appellate court affirmed a $500,000 jury verdict for the plaintiff based on defendants' negligence in failing to warn the mother that the son presented a threat to her safety.

In Durflinger v. Artiles,[30] a lower court ruled that psychiatrists at a Kansas state facility had improperly diagnosed and prematurely released a patient who murdered his mother and brother six days after leaving the hospital. An appeal was scheduled for September 14 at the 10th Circuit Court of Appeals in Denver. The Kansas State Psychiatric Association had submitted a brief to the court stating there should be no duty to protect the family members, since (1) they were already aware of the patient's mental history and condition, (2) he had committed previous violent acts, and (3) he had not specifically threatened the deceased family members.

However, in Sherrill v. Wilson,[31] the Missouri Supreme Court held that psychiatrists could not be sued by members of the general public for negligently releasing an involuntary patient on a pass, or for negligently failing to secure his return after he overstayed his pass. The patient shot a third party while on release, but there was no evidence that he posed a particular danger to the decedent, a fact which distinguished the case from Tarasoff, in the court's eyes.

Probably the most publicized of the recent Tarasoff-type cases is that of Brady v. Hopper,[32] brought by three of the victims of John Hinckley, President Reagan's would-be assassin, against the psychiatrist who treated Hinckley prior to the shootings. The Colorado district court judge granted the defendant's motion to dismiss the complaint on the grounds that Hinckley had not made any specific threat toward the victims, or anyone else for that matter, and therefore their injuries were not foreseeable and were outside the scope of defendant's duty. The plaintiffs had argued that if Hopper had interviewed Hinckley more carefully he would have discovered that Hinckley was obsessed with Jody Foster, that he collected books on Ronald Reagan and political assassination, and that he practiced with guns. They charged

Hopper, in addition, with improper treatment of Hinckley and failure to warn his parents to watch him more closely. The judge did not rule on the appropriateness of Dr. Hopper's treatment of Hinckley, basing the decision instead on the desirability of limiting the Tarasoff holding to clearly identifiable victims, given the unpredictability of human behavior.

One can conclude from the above decisions that the more obvious and explicit the threat, the more likely a court is to impose a duty on the therapist either to warn the potential victim or to take other precautions to eliminate the danger. Where a psychiatrist has acted reasonably and has no notice that the patient presents a threat to third persons, he is unlikely to be held liable to the patient's victim. According to Brady v. Hopper, the psychiatrist will not be liable even if his lack of knowledge was due to the failure to conduct a careful examination of the patient. This case will no doubt be appealed, and thus the issue remains open.

The outer limits of Tarasoff-style liability were tested in the case of Cole v. Taylor.[33] The psychiatrist was sued, not by the patient's victim, but by the patient, who claimed the psychiatrist had negligently failed to prevent her from killing her former husband, either by hospitalizing her or by warning the husband, after she had disclosed to the psychiatrist her intention to kill him. The woman's current husband joined in the suit, asking damages for loss of consortium (the woman having been convicted of murder after unsuccessfully pleading the insanity defense). The District Court refused to dismiss the complaint, but the Iowa Supreme Court did so on an interlocutory appeal, on the grounds that a person cannot maintain an action which he can only establish by relying in whole or in part on his own illegal or immoral act. Tarasoff was not controlling, said the court, since the duty to warn established by that case runs only to the intended victim, not to the patient.

The result in Cole seems sensible, for the reason that the court gave: It seems an unwise policy to hold psychiatrists legally accountable to the patient for the patient's own voluntary, illegal acts. Yet, if psychiatrists are to be held liable to their patients' victims, the unspoken premise is that the patients' acts are to some extent predictable and beyond the patient's voluntary control. If that premise is true, and if the patient has, by entering treatment, placed his trust in the therapist to protect him from his own dangerous impulses, it does not seem a very great step forward to hold the therapist liable to the patient as well. Cole may not have been an ideal case for finding liability to the patient; doubtless other cases will arise in the future to test the viability of this theory of liability.

Cases Involving Sexual Exploitation of Patients

A patient who consults a sex therapist for a specific sexual problem may expect the treatment to involve some form of sexual encounter, but a patient who consults a psychotherapist for treatment of mental or emotional problems normally does not expect that sexual relations with the therapist will be a part of the treatment. Indeed, the psychiatric profession as a whole has frowned on sexual relations between therapist and patient from its beginnings.[34] One or two psychiatrists have openly advocated sexual relations with patients as a form of treatment,[35] but in the majority of cases studied where therapists engaged in sex with their patients they did so in response to their own needs, not out of the belief that the patient would be benefited.[36] A therapist who engages in sex with his patient will be unable to retain his objectivity.[37] He risks exploiting the patient, who is often emotionally vulnerable. The fulfillment of the patient's fantasies of having sex with the therapist may lead to further confusion of fact with fantasy in the patient's mind.

Sex between therapist and patient may be unethical, but is it malpractice? Numerous legal decisions state that it is, citing the mishandling of the "transference" relationship that develops between patient and therapist during the course of therapy as the specific deviation from the standard of care.[38] The transference phenomenon is one in which the patient relates to the therapist as she did to key figures from her childhood, especially her father. She may actually believe that she is falling in love with the therapist. It is crucial that the therapist maintain his objectivity, for it is only by working through the transference relationship with the patient that the patient will be helped to understand and change her faulty ways of relating to other people.

Besides subjecting the therapist to liability for malpractice, having sex with patients can result in license revocation or prosecution for rape.[39] Some states have statutes making sexual relations with a patient under the guise of treatment a criminal offense.[40]

Is sex between patient and therapist necessarily harmful to the patient? For obvious reasons, there are no reliable statistics on the outcome of therapist-patient sexual encounters. The available information on the subject consists of anecdotal reports, the results of questionnaires addressed to therapists,[41] and, of course, the cases that have been litigated. There are also many theoretical discussions stating why such relationships are likely to be detrimental to patients. Controlled studies are highly unlikely to be permitted in this area, given the current climate of opinion regarding human experimentation, nor should they be, when the professional consensus is that such relationships are most likely to be harmful.[42] The harm consists not only in the patient's subjective sense of having been betrayed by the therapist, but in the documented difficulty which these patients have in establishing relationships with subsequent therapists.[43]

A recently published study has confirmed that therapist-patient sex is harmful to the great majority (90 percent) of patients.[44] The authors sent questionnaires to every licensed psychologist in California requesting information about patients who reported having engaged in sexual relations with previous therapists. The results, based on responses obtained from 704 psychologists, were consistent with prior studies in that the vast majority of patients (92 percent) involved in these relationships were female. Almost half had problems resuming therapy with a new therapist, and more than half (64 percent) reported problems in their personal adjustment as a result of the sexual relationship. Although many were aware that the therapist's behavior was unethical and illegal, only about 10 percent took some form of action against the therapist (either bringing a lawsuit, notifying the state licensing board, or a professional ethics committee). This substantiates the notion that the number of patient-therapist sex cases litigated represents only the tip of the iceberg. Indeed, based on the results of various questionnaires addressed to therapists, it has been estimated that between 5 and 13 percent engage in sex with their patients.[45]

Damage awards can be high in malpractice suits based on therapist-patient sex because the plaintiff often succeeds in proving that the sexual relationship deprived her of necessary treatment and made her condition worse. In many cases the relationship destroyed the patient's marriage as well, and, in a few, the patient became suicidal. The largest such award was the $4.6 million jury verdict in Walker v. Parzen,[46] which was reduced by settlement, while an appeal was pending, to $2.5 million. A 19-year-old woman who started seeing a psychiatrist at the age of 15 for schizophrenia was awarded $650,000 by a jury in Virginia, based on allegations that his engaging in sex with her on numerous occasions caused her condition to deteriorate, necessitating years of additional hospitalization.[47] A Florida woman who claimed a psychologist whom she had consulted for depression engaged in sexual relations with her for a year, under the guise of treatment, received a $135,000 settlement,[48] and a New York woman received a $175,000 jury award for a single act of intercourse which had taken place with her psychiatrist 10 years before.[49] In the latter case, the state supreme court upheld the trial court in its refusal to submit the issue of contributory negligence to the jury, stating: "The relationship of therapist and analysand is one of trust and confidence—a confidence which was abused in this case. . . ." The same New York psychiatrist was the subject of two other lawsuits by patients who alleged that he had sexual relations with them over an extended period under the guise of therapy. The suits were settled for $100,000 and $150,000, respectively.[50]

Insurance companies have been held liable for malpractice awards based on having sexual relations with patients in psychotherapy,[51] and where the therapist was employed by the defendant, courts have held that having sexual relations with the patient could be considered within the scope of employment, so as to hold the employer liable under the doctrine of *respondeat superior.*[52]

The case which tests the current limits of a psychotherapist's liability in this area is Mazza v. Huffaker,[53] where the psychiatrist had sexual relations not with the patient but with the patient's wife. The patient, a manic-depressive, had separated from his wife during the course of therapy. He subsequently discovered that the therapist was having sex with his wife. The court rejected the psychiatrist's argument that this was not malpractice, saying that the physician owes a duty to his patient which extends beyond the consulting room. The psychiatrist's actions had destroyed the patient's trust in him, harmed his well-being, and made it difficult for him to establish a trusting relationship with any other physician. The court likewise rejected the psychiatrist's argument that the patient was contributorily negligent in breaking down the door of his wife's bedroom when he had reason to know that the psychiatrist was there. He had seen the psychiatrist's car parked in front of the house and some of his clothes in the living room. The jury awarded the patient $649,585 in compensatory and punitive damages, and said that he was entitled to recover the $17,000 in fees paid to the psychiatrist since the latter had undone all the benefits of the previous treatment by going to bed with the patient's wife.

Mazza represents more than a slight departure from cases involving patient-therapist sex. In those cases, the act which was deemed to be malpractice occurred between patient and therapist while therapy was supposedly being administered, whereas in Mazza the act did not directly involve the patient or even take place in the physician's office. If Mazza is good law, then almost anything the therapist does which upsets the patient could conceivably be viewed as malpractice. Going to bed with the patient's wife is certainly a breach of trust, unethical, and quite possibly tortious, but calling it malpractice seems to this author to set a dangerous precedent. If Mazza is followed, there may be no limit on the potential liability of psychiatrists for malpractice.

REFERENCES

1. *See* Nieland, R. 1979. "Malpractice Liability of Psychiatric Professionals." *American Journal of Forensic Psychiatry* 1(2):22; Wilkinson, A. 1981–1982. "Psychiatric Malpractice." *American Journal of Forensic Psychiatry* 2(3):3; Twardy, S. 1978. "The Issue of Malpractice in Psychiatry." *Medical Trial Technique Quarterly* 25(2):161; Appleson, G. 1982. "More Patients Are Suing Their Psychiatrists." *American Bar Association Journal* 68:1353; Berreby, D. 1983. "Forcing Therapists To Pay." *National Law Journal* 5(19, January 17):1.
2. *See* Schaeffer, P. 1981. "Psychiatrists Still At Low Risk For Malpractice Suit." *Clinical Psychiatry News* (September):1.
3. "APA Malpractice Claim Types Constant, But Frequency, Costs Have Doubled." *Psychiatric News* (November 4, 1983):3.

4. Personal communication from Joseph Deacon, Director, Office of Benefits, American Psychiatric Association, December 10, 1982.
5. Table was constructed from figures cited in article at n. 3, *supra.*
6. "No Signs of Negligence Found in Over Half of 410 Malpractice Cases Reviewed." *Clinical Psychiatry News* (October, 1983):1.
7. *See* Payne v. Milwaukee Sanitarium Foundation, Inc., 260 N.W.2d.386 (1977); Farrow v. Health Services Corp., 604 P.2d. 474 (Utah 1979); Bell v. New York City Health and Hospitals Corp., 456 N.Y.S.2d 787 (N.Y. App. Div. 1982).
8. 449 N.E.2d. 1098 (Ind. Ct. App. 1983).
9. "Efforts At Prevention Of Suicide Could Reduce Incidence." *Clinical Psychiatric News* (October, 1983):2.
10. 463 N.Y.S.2d 853 (N.Y. App. Div. 1983).
11. 131 Cal. Rptr. 14 (Cal. 1976).
12. *See* Stone, A. 1976. "The Tarasoff Decisions: Suing Psychotherapists to Safeguard Society." *Harvard Law Review* 90:358; Stone, A. 1982. "Psychiatric Abuse and Legal Reform—Two Ways To Make A Bad Situation Worse." *International Journal of Law and Psychiatry* 5(1):9; and Schimel, J. 1980. "Accountability in Psychiatry." *Journal of Psychiatry and Law* 8:191.
13. Feldstein, R. 1983. "Medicine, Not Law." Letter to the Editor, *Psychiatric News* (October 21):2.
14. *Mental Disability Law Reporter* (July/August 1983):295.
15. M. H. No. 1124-82, Superior Court of the District of Columbia, April 14, 1983.
16. Barefoot v. Estelle, No. 82-6080, 52 U.S.L.W. 3267, July 6, 1983.
17. *See* Arneson, G.A. 1983. "Predicting Dangerousness." Letter to the Editor, *Clinical Psychiatry News* (August):6.
18. *See* Roth, M.D., and L.J. Levin. 1983. "Dilemma of Tarasoff: Must Physicians Protect The Public Or Their Patients?" *Law, Medicine & Health Care* 10(3, June):104.
19. Shaw v. Glickman, 415 A.2d. 625 (Md. App. 1980).
20. Lipari v. Sears, 497 F.Supp. 185 (D. Neb. 1980); Thompson v. County of Alameda, 167 Cal. Rptr. 70 (Cal. 1980).
21. Bradley Center, Inc. v. Wessner, 296 S.E.2d. 693 (Ga. 1982).
22. Semler v. Psychiatric Institute of Washington, D.C., 538 F.2d. 121 (4th Cir.), cert. denied, 429 U.S. 827 (1976).
23. *See* Furr v. Spring Grove State Hospital, 454 A.2d. 414 (Md. Ct. Spec. App. 1983).
24. Cairl v. Minnesota, 323 N.W.2d. 20 (Minn. 1982); Heltsley v. Votteler, 327 N.W.2d. 759 (Iowa 1982).
25. Hasenei v. United States, 541 F.Supp. 999 (D. Md. 1982).
26. 100 Wn.2d 421 (Wash. 1983).
27. 564 F.Supp. 341 (D.C. E.D. Mich. 1983).
28. 712 F.2d. 391 (C.A.9 1983).
29. 335 N.W.2d. 481 (Mich. Ct. App. 1983).
30. 563 F.Supp. 322 (D. Kan. 1983).
31. 653 S.W.2d. 661 (Mo. 1983).
32. 570 F.Supp. 1333 (1983).
33. 301 N.W.2d. 766 (Iowa 1981).

34. *See* Nelson, B. 1982. "Efforts Widen To Curb Sexual Abuse In Therapy." *New York Times* (November 23):p.C1, col. 5; Solloway v. Dept. of Professional Regulation, 421 So.2d. 573 (Fla. Dist. Ct. App. 1982).
35. *See* Marmor, J. 1970. "The Seductive Psychotherapist." *Psychiatry Digest* 31:10.
36. Butler, S., and S. Zelen. 1977. "Sexual Intimacies Between Therapists And Patients." *Psychotherapy: Theory, Research and Practice* 14(2, Summer):139.
37. Cohen, R.J., and W.E. Mariano. 1982. *Legal Guidebook In Mental Health,* at 252. New York: Free Press.
38. Zipkin v. Freeman, 436 S.W.2d. 753 (Mo. 1968); St. Paul Fire and Marine Ins. Co. v. Mitchell, 296 S.E.2d. 126 (Ga. App. 1982); *See also* Solloway v. Dept. of Professional Regulation, 421 So.2d. 573 (Fla. Dist. Ct. App. 1982).
39. *See* Morra v. Kansas Board of Examiners of Psychologists, 510 P.2d. 614 (Kan. 1973); Clark v. Michigan Board of Registration in Medicine, 116 N.W.2d. 797 (Mich. 1962); Jacobi v. Texas Board of Medical Examiners, 308 S.W.2d. 261 (Tex. Civ. App. 1958); Bernstein v. Board of Medical Examiners, 22 Cal. Rptr. 419 (Cal. App. 1962); and Solloway, no. 37, *supra.*
40. Mich. Stat. Ann. sec. 28.285 (1981); Ohio Rev. Code Ann. sec. 2907.03 (1982).
41. Voth, H.M. 1972. "Love Affair Between Doctor and Patient." *American Journal of Psychotherapy* 26:394; Kardener, S.H., et al. 1973. "A Survey of Physicians' Attitudes and Practices Regarding Erotic and Non-erotic Contact With Patients." *American Journal of Psychiatry* 130:10.
42. Taylor, B.J., and N.N. Wagner. 1976. "Sex Between Therapists and Clients: A Review and Analysis." *Professional Psychology* 2(4, November):593.
43. Burgess, A.W. 1981. "Physician Sexual Misconduct and Patients' Responses." *American Journal of Psychiatry* 138(10, October):1335.
44. Bouhoutsos, J., et al. 1983. "Sexual Intimacy Between Psychotherapists and Patients." *Professional Psychology: Research and Practice* 14(2, April):185.
45. Nelson, n. 33, *supra.*
46. *See* Wilkinson, A. 1982. "Psychiatric Malpractice: Identifying Areas of Liability." *Trial* 18(10, October):72.
47. Combs v. Silverman, No. LE596 (Richmond, Virginia Circuit Court, February 5, 1982), cited in *ATLA Law Reporter* 25(December, 1982):475.
48. Lopez v. Avent, No. 81-829 (Okaloosa County Circuit Court, Florida, February 25, 1982), cited in *ATLA Law Reporter* 25(December, 1982):475.
49. *See* Breitbard v. Leonard, cited in *New York Law Journal* 189(9, January 13, 1983):1, 28.
50. Osborne v. Leonard, N.Y. County Supreme Court, Index No. 21788/77, November 5, 1982; and Postmantier v. Leonard, N.Y. County Supreme Court, Index No. 21789/77, November 5, 1982.
51. Aetna Life and Casualty Co. v. McCabe, 556 F.Supp. 1342 (D.C. Pa. 1983).
52. Marston v. Minneapolis Clinic of Psychiatry and Neurology, Ltd., 329 N.W.2d. 306 (Minn. 1982).
53. 300 S.E.2d. 833 (N.C. Ct. App. 1983).

A Model for Making Medical Consent Forms More Comprehensible

David S. Kaufer, Erwin R. Steinberg, Ph.D., and
Sarah D. Toney, M.A.

INTRODUCTION

The concept of informed consent, now over 200 years old, is firmly seated in American law:

> Anglo-American law starts with the premise of thoroughgoing self-determination, each man considered to be his own master. This law does not permit a physician to substitute his judgment for that of the patient by any form of artifice. This doctrine of informed consent arises out of this premise.[1]

The classic ruling on the consent doctrine in this century was made by Judge Cardozo, who wrote in 1914:

> Every human being of adult years and sound mind has a right to determine what shall be done with his own body; and a surgeon who performs an operation without his patient's consent commits an assault, for which he is liable in damages.... This is true, except in cases of emergency where the patient is unconscious, and where it is necessary to operate before consent can be obtained.[2]

Various administrative bodies and legislatures have joined the courts in defining and affirming the concept of informed consent. In Pennsylvania, for example, the "Patient's Bill of Rights" directs that, "The patient has the right to full information in layman's terms, concerning his diagnosis, treatment, and prognosis, including information about alternative treatments and possible complications." The Patient's Bill of Rights goes on to make this important stipulation: "When it is not medically advisable to give such information to the patient, the information shall be given on his behalf to the patient's next of kin or to other appropriate persons."[3] The state legislature, as well, has formally defined informed consent and explored a few of its implications:

> "Informed consent" means for the purposes of this act or any proceedings arising under the provisions of this act, the consent of a patient to the performance of health care services by a physician or podiatrist: Provided, that prior to the consent having been given, the physician or podiatrist has informed the patient of the nature of the proposed procedure or treatment and of those risks and alternative to treatment of diagnoses that a reasonable patient would consider material to the decision whether or not to undergo treatment or diagnoses.[4]

Furthermore, courts are insisting that a patient's signature on a consent form is no assurance that that patient was informed. Only a patient who has received sufficient information in language he or she can understand is truly informed. One court held, for example:

> [S]ince the patient must rely on the physician to tell her of all the appropriate risks, the physician cannot discharge this duty by having the patient execute a form which states that the risks have been explained.... The courts will look beyond forms signed by patients to determine if the duty to inform has been discharged.[5]

Although the principle of informed consent is reasonably clear and has been accepted by the court, its application is still being widely debated. At a recent meeting of the President's Commission for the Study of Ethical Problems in Medicine and Biomedical and Behavioral Research, for example, the Commissioners had a spirited debate on the argument that "health care professionals have an ethical obligation to provide patients with information and other assistance responsive to their particular concerns and values in order to enable patients to participate effectively in decision making about their care." Several Commissioners expressed their concern "about any categorical statements regarding such delicate matters, and in particular, about statements enshrining autonomy as the paramount value in health care." Another "stressed the desirability of moving the debate beyond an arid confrontation between absolutist notions of autonomy and paternalism." And several others stressed the need for a balance between "the values of patient self-determination and patient welfare."[6]

For those responsible for writing, revising, filling in, or signing medical or surgical consent forms, however, there is a further question. When the physician has determined how much, given a patient's physical and psychological state, he or she should tell that patient, there is still the problem of providing that information "in layman's terms," to quote the Pennsylvania "Patient's Bill of Rights."[7] Traditionally, consent forms have been so full of medical and legal jargon that they have been impossible for even the educated layperson to understand; and, for most people, signing them has been a meaningless ritual.

A study of 60 consent forms from five national cancer clinical trial groups, for example, concluded:

> The forms were found slightly less difficult to comprehend than medical journals but substantially more difficult than comparable materials from the popular press. Three of four passages describing treatment methods, procedures, discomforts, and risks required a college level or greater reading ability to comprehend. Informed consent documents may not be understood by a substantial portion of patients who sign them. And so, the very regulations designed to ensure a patient's informed cooperation may inadvertently lead to forms so complex as to make informed cooperation virtually impossible.[8]

Other studies support those findings.[9]

Recent years have brought increasing pressure from the public and the courts for truly informed patient consent to medical treatment and surgical procedures. The experience of the members of the Communication Design Center at Carnegie-Mellon University over several years in revising consent forms has led to the development of a model for such revision.[10] In this article, we present the model, explain each step, and give examples of each from many of the consent forms we have revised. Finally, we revise a single form according to the model and test it for improved readability (via readability indices and computerized syntactic and lexical analyses) and comprehensibility (as assessed by number of correct responses to questions and response time). This article is, in effect, a manual for revising medical consent forms to make them easier to understand.

Before embarking directly into our model, we wish to offer an important caveat. We are specialists in communication, not law or medicine. As a result, our model for revising consent forms is intended to increase the comprehensibility of forms that are already judged to be legally sound and medically prudent. We have nothing to say about how to make medical consent forms sound and prudent in the first place. In this regard, the techniques we describe below should be undertaken under the close supervision of legal and medical personnel. It will be of little comfort to know that a medical consent form has been made more comprehensible—and to find out it has also been made less viable on grounds of law or prudence.

A MODEL FOR REVISING CONSENT FORMS

The outline below is intended as a model for the revision of medical consent forms. At first blush, this model may seem little more than a "laundry list" of unrelated, though commonsensical, stylistic do's and don'ts. However, unlike such a random list, the questions raised by the model and the order in which they are raised reflect our theory of the interactive contribution of verbal and visual cues to the comprehension of medical consent forms. One could imagine a professional editor appealing to some or all of these questions on an ad hoc basis, without a clear understanding of how the information provided by these questions is ordered and mutually reinforcing. In fact, in a later section, we show how the results of our model fare against an expert revision undertaken in an ad hoc manner.

I. Duplication
  a. Can two forms be combined?
  b. Can a single form be rewritten as two?
II. Information
  a. What information is essential for the patient to understand before he or she signs the form?
    1. Is any necessary information missing?
    2. Is unnecessary information included?
  b. Is the information under each heading comprehensible?
    1. Is the language wordy or unnecessarily technical?
    2. Are the principal parties to the agreement placed in syntactically prominent positions?
    3. Are the clauses coherently combined?
    4. Do the sentences vary by type and length?
    5. Do the sentences get quickly to the point?
III. Layout
  a. Does the layout highlight the essential information?
  b. Does it reflect the structure of the message?

Using the Model

Duplication

In revising, one should think about the set of consent forms in use, not single forms in isolation.

Can two forms be combined? For example, consent to release information from alcohol treatment programs and drug abuse programs can be covered in a single form. Similarly, we combined a patient's release form for refusal of blood or treatment on religious grounds with a similar release form for a spouse or relative (where the patient was not competent to sign).

Should a single form be rewritten as two? We found a consent to ambulatory care (see below) which required a patient to consent to both examination and treatment at the same time. Before examination and diagnosis, however, a physician often cannot say very much about treatment. Any such consent form that a patient signs, therefore, could well be challenged later in court. We wrote two consent forms, therefore: one for examination and one for treatment. In another instance we found in an authorization for autopsy a section on donation of organs and tissue, even though there was a separate form available for that purpose.

Information

Is all necessary information included? As we have indicated, a statement like "The doctor has explained the possible risks to me" is not specific enough. Such sections should read:

The doctor has explained to me the nature of these anesthetics, the way they will be given to me, and their usual effects. He has also explained the following risks connected with their use:

____

____

____

(blanks to be filled in by anesthesiologist)

Is any unnecessary information included? A family consent to "no extraordinary measures" listed: "arrhythmia control, life support with existing devices, use of artificial or mechanical organs, transplantation of organs and tissues (including blood and blood byproducts), invasive monitoring, parentoral, nutrition, and IV infusion of potent vasoactive drugs." We recommend that this form be combined with a form for family consent "for all but CPR" into a new form consenting to or refusing life support treatment. We also recommend that the "extraordinary measures" section read:

I request that (check one):
__________the patient receive all appropriate means of treatment.
__________the patient receive all appropriate means of treatment except Cardio-Pulmonary Resuscitation (CPR).
__________no "Extraordinary Measures" be initiated.
__________"Extraordinary Measures" in effect be discontinued.
Other: ________________________________

____

____

(Specify Restrictions on Treatment)

We further recommend that a separate checklist and glossary regularly updated be prepared for doctors to consult when explaining the meaning of "extraordinary measures" and filling in the consent form. Since no such list would be current for long, we felt that including it on the form would be inefficient because it would have to be updated—and thus reprinted—frequently. We also felt that the doctor should explain each term in layperson's language. Providing such explanations in the glossary, therefore, would prove helpful to both doctor and patient.

Is the information expressed in wordy or unduly technical terms? Here are some examples of passages revised to make them more comprehensible to the layperson.

ORIGINAL	REVISION
I, ________________, request and authorize ________________, M.D., his assistants and associates and the hospital and its personnel to conduct an examination to determine the medical implications of an alleged sexual assault made upon me.	I am asking Dr. ________________, his assistants and associates and the hospital and its personnel to examine me for medical evidence that I have been sexually assaulted.

In the revision, it may be useful to add the word "alleged" or "allegedly" to divest the hospital of liability.

I understand that this examination will include tests for presence of sperm as well as clinical observations for physical evidence of penetration....	I permit them to test for presence of sperm and to examine me for physical evidence of penetration....
This consent is expressly intended to release the hospital, its personnel, the operating physician or physicians, and any other participating in my care for any and all liability that could result from the taking and authorized use of such photographs or films.	I release the hospital, its personnel, and any other persons from any liability connected with the taking or authorized use of the photographs.

The principle is simple: remove as much legal and medical jargon as possible, and avoid as many words of Latin origin as possible.

Are the principal parties to the agreement placed in syntactically prominent positions? A consent form records agreements between a doctor and a patient; these agreements refer to real or conceivable actions, the consequences of these actions, and who is responsible for them. One way to insure that a consent form does all these clearly is to put human beings (the parties to the agreement) in subject and direct object positions—syntactically prominent slots.

ORIGINAL	REVISION
The following attendant risks were explained by the doctor.	The doctor explained the following risks to me.
It is the express intent of this agreement to release the hospital....	This agreement releases the hospital ... *or* I release the hospital....

Whenever possible, grammatical subjects should be linked to direct objects with simple and concise action verbs: "I release the hospital...." In the original example, the words "the doctor" do not appear in subject position as they should, but are buried at the end in a prepositional phrase; the patient does not appear at all. In the second example, an empty "it" fills the subject slot and a long introductory phrase needlessly postpones the key words in the sentence: "agreement" and "release."

Are the clauses coherently combined? A text is easier to follow if it highlights a single topic from sentence to sentence and if the grammatical relationships among the people and things involved are also sustained, whenever possible, across sentences. In the first sentence of the following example, the topical focus seems to be on methods of delivery, procedures, risks, etc.; the patient, and then the doctor, are introduced later. In the second sentence the focus is on the patient ("I") and the doctor seems to have disappeared from view:

The nature of various methods of delivery and procedures available in my case, the risks involved, the possible consequences and the possibility of complications have been explained to me by ______________________, who has also explained possible alternate methods of delivery or treatment, their nature, risks, or consequences and possible complications. I have been given an opportunity to ask questions about my delivery and I have no further questions at this time, but I have been informed that I may ask additional questions at any time.

A revision of this passage appears below.

Do the sentences vary by length and type? One of the surest signs of bureaucratic prose is sentences that are consistently long, unwieldy, contain many levels of coordination (and, or, but) and subordination (if... then, that, because, hence, wherefore, etc.). Sentences that contain both coordination and subordination are called compound-complex. Long complex-compound sentences give official forms a tone of authoritative incomprehensibility, as in the following:

Dr. ______________________ has explained to me that transfusions of blood and blood components are not always successful in producing a desirable result and that there is a possibility of ill effects from transfusions, such as the transmission of infectious hepatitis or other diseases, blood impairments, or untoward blood reactions.

In consideration of this transfusion of blood and blood components, I release my physician, his associates or assistants, the hospital, its personnel and any other persons participating in my care from any responsibility whatsoever from any resulting illness or ill-effects, or reactions.

A revision should not only simplify and break the sentences into smaller units, but should also reduce compound/complex sentences into a wider variety of simple (without coordination or subordination), compound (coordination only) and complex (subordination only) sentences.

The doctor has explained to me in general what a transfusion is and the procedures that will be used. He has also explained to me that there are possible risks involved with this blood transfusion, including infectious hepatitis, unexpected blood reactions and....

I therefore permit the doctor or such other doctors or persons as may be needed to assist him to give me the transfusion.

The first sentence of the original has been broken into two sentences in the revised form. The first sentence of the revision expresses the information contained in the original's coordinating clauses. The second sentence expresses the information contained in the original's subordinate clauses. In general, the sentences of a consent form should comprise a healthy assortment of simple, compound, and complex sentences. Whenever possible, the reviser should eliminate compound/complex sentences; such sentences are likely to pack too much information in too compact a space to process effectively.

Do the sentences get to the point quickly? Another mark of bureaucratic prose is its long wind-ups, its tendency to delay (and obscure) important information with canned introductions and verbal formulas. A frequent offender in medical consent forms is the expletive "it" as in "it is agreed that..." or "it is acknowledged that...." The force of this phrase is to depersonalize the doctor/patient relation, to put into the mouth of the patient an easily disavowable pontifical decree instead of a very human and very personal contract. But the phrase can also be used to obscure the responsibilities of parties since it is a way of keeping human agents out of subject slots. Often times, if a reviser takes care to start the sentence with a relevant party, he or she will also eliminate any digressive wind-ups.

Layout

Does the layout reflect and reinforce the structure of the message? Even if the grammatical structure in the consent to delivery form were revised to improve coherence, the resultant paragraph would be dense because of the length and complexity of the sentences. In the revision below the passage has been "opened up" by attention to layout:

Dr. ______________________ has:

a. explained to me the various possible methods of delivery in my case;
b. explained to me the risks involved, the possible consequences, and the possibility of complications, including

____

____

____

c. given me the chance to ask questions, and I have no further questions at this time; and
d. told me that I can ask more questions at any time.

The revision uses fewer words, is built on a series of grammatically parallel clauses to keep consistent the relationship among the doctor, the patient, and the ideas communicated, and is laid out on the page to show the reader visually the relationship of the ideas presented: "The doctor has: explained to me. . .; explained to me. . .; given me. . .; and shown me. . . ." Furthermore, even though the revision is a single long and quite complex sentence, laying it out on the page in such a way as to emphasize essential points and to allow the reader to absorb it a piece at a time improves comprehensibility. Thus, although the revision above contains 58 words, it is much more comprehensible than a 58-word sentence would be. It probably is almost as comprehensible as if it were written as four sentences rather than one.

The last example shows how the improvements resulting from responding to all of the questions above interact and reinforce each other to improve comprehensibility radically. Making consent forms easy to read, understand, and assimilate is particularly important, since people who are called upon to sign them are often under considerable stress.

A SPECIFIC APPLICATION ON FORM P-43

This section reports on how our model took us from the original consent form P-43 (Figure 1) to the revised P-43 (Figure 2). The original P-43, a severely flawed consent form, had itself undergone several revisions by professional writers *before* we laid hands on it. It seems that the "technically correct" revisions of expert writers, when not also guided by a theoretical understanding of what consent forms are used for, are insufficient to bring a form to functional standards. Our model was designed to help writers make technical revisions of forms under the direction of these functional standards.

Duplication

Should P-43 be generalized so as to cover consent to treatment beyond blood transfusions? Should it be limited in its application so as to cover only part of the transfusion process? For the purposes of our revision of the original P-43 we decided not to try to answer this question, because an answer would require a full-scale analysis of the institution using P-43 and the clientele it serves. Suffice it to say that questions of combining or multiplying consent forms can hinge on such institutional variables as storage space, printing costs, time, the patience and attention span of clients, the importance of distinguishing treatments, the consequences of failing to make such distinctions, and so on.

FORM P-43

AGREEMENT FOR BLOOD TRANSFUSION

To: Dr. ______________________ and ______________________ Hospital
(attending physician)

Date: ______________________ Time: ______________________ A.M. P.M.

1. I authorize the administration of a blood transfusion to

______________________ and such additional
(myself or name of patient)
transfusions as may be deemed advisable in the judgment of the attending physician, or his associates or assistants.

2. It is understood and agreed that the attending physician or his associates or assistants shall be responsible only for the performance of their own individual professional acts, and that the blood typing and the selection of compatible blood are the responsibilities of those who actually perform the necessary laboratory tests.

3. It has been explained that blood transfusions are not always successful in producing a desirable result and that there is a possibility of ill effects, including but not limited to the transmission of infectious hepatitis, or other diseases or blood impairments.

4. Also, it has been explained that emergencies may arise when it may not be possible to make adequate cross-matching tests, and that immediate need may make it necessary to use existing stocks of blood which may not include the most compatible blood types.

5. It is understood and expressly agreed that the blood supplied in accordance with this agreement is incidental to the rendition of services and that no requirement, guarantee, or warranty of fitness or quality shall apply.

Signed ______________________
(Patient or person authorized to consent for patient)

Witness ______________________

FIGURE 1. Original Form P-43.

FORM P-43

AGREEMENT FOR BLOOD TRANSFUSIONS

To: Dr. ______________________________ and ____________________________ Hospital
(attending physician)

Date: ______________________________ Time: ____________________________ A.M. P.M.

1. What my doctor has explained to me.

   My doctor has explained:

   a. the procedure to be performed.

   b. the risks involved if I undergo this procedure.

   c. the risks involved if I do not undergo this procedure.

   d. that the choice to undergo or not to undergo this procedure is mine alone.

2. What I consent to have done — one or more blood transfusions.

   I agree to allow authorized members of the hospital staff to give me a blood transfusion or as many transfusions as they think I need.

3. Who is responsible for making sure the blood given to me matches my own in non-emergency (routine) situations?

   I understand that in non-emergency situations the lab technicians who perform the blood tests are responsible for determining my blood-type and for making sure I am given blood that matches my blood-type. The attending doctor, his associates or assistants are not responsible for these actions but only for their own actions toward my care.

FIGURE 2. Revised Form P-43.

Information

Essential and Unnecessary Information

Lawyers stipulated that all of the propositional information in the original P-43 was needed, but we felt that the information was not presented as clearly or concisely as it could be. In particular, we found that there were four essential points of information in the original which the patient should understand.

1. The doctor has explained all relevant information about the procedure, including benefits, risks, and the patient's right to refuse. This, we believe, is information essential to any medical consent form.
2. The client has consented to one or as many transfusions as the attending physician deems advisable.
3. The lab technicians, not the attending doctors, are responsible for blood-typing and lab tests in non-emergency situations.
4. There are other risks, involving side-effects, emergency situations, and poor blood quality associated with blood transfusions.

These clauses were separated and given visual prominence in the revised form.

Unnecessary words.. In paragraph 1 of the original, the word "administration" adds no information: to authorize a blood transfusion is to authorize the administration of one. An efficient writer should just use "administer" or "authorize" but not both. Also, in that paragraph, the words "advisable" and "in the judgment" are redundant and the embedding sentence could be recast as sentence 2 in the revised form. We leave it to the reader to determine other examples of wordiness by comparing our revised and the original form.

Parties to the agreement in prominent syntactic slots. The original form obscures the parties to the agreement and their relation to one another. Only the first paragraph contains a human subject and, even there, mention of the doctor (the other party involved) does not follow the verb as direct object but is buried in a prepositional phrase. The remaining four paragraphs use an expletive "it" as subject and an inactive form of the verb "to be" followed by a long compound-complex "that" clause. The effect is to obscure the reader's understanding of the question "who is doing what to whom?" Our revision puts a human agent in every subject slot. We also revised nonactive "to be" verbs into active ones.

Coherent progression of topical information. Topic prominent information should ideally be cast in subject or direct object position. Unfortunately, all the paragraphs of the original seem to shift topics abruptly because the referents of subjects and objects abruptly shift. In paragraph 2, for example, the topic seems to be "attending physician" and then it shifts abruptly to "blood-typing"; in paragraph 3, the topic at first seems to be "blood transfusions" and then shifts to "possibility." In the revised version, topics are maintained as subjects and objects and the subjects and objects change reference only when the topics are designed to change.

Varied sentence types and lengths. Most sentences of the original are of one difficult type (i.e., compound-complex) and one difficult length (very long, approximately 30 words each). As we explained above, sentences that are unremittingly long and compound-complex stand a good chance of seeming convoluted. We revised the sentences in the original so to span more sentence types (viz., simple, complex, or compound) and lengths (viz., 10–15 word sentences as well as 30–50 worders).

Getting quickly to the point. Most sentences in the original start with the empty expletive: "it is agreed that. . . ." We deleted these expletives and began each sentence with a noun prase subject.

Layout

Every essential point should be visually prominent. The layout of the original, however, did not give visual prominence to each essential point. Point 1, a sina non qua of any consent form, is missing from the original version. Point 2 is buried in the first paragraph. Point 3 is visually prominent (in paragraph 2 of the original) and thus needs no revision on this step. Point 4 is spread across the third, fourth, and fifth paragraphs of the original in no logical order. Furthermore, although the numbered paragraphs lead the reader to five specific references, they do not lead the reader to see how these references fit together. To highlight this essential information in the revised form we gave a separate heading to each point. Point 4 received three subheadings corresponding with the third, fourth, and fifth paragraphs of the original. Generally, the numbered, lettered, and underlined headings affect the reader's ease of comprehension by (1) providing an apparent structure for locating and integrating information, (2) signalling the reader to adjust his or her reading speed to the amount of information presented, and (3) breaking/shortening these items into easily assimilated units. The horizontal line is a factor that distinguishes the headings and subheadings from the regular text. Horizontal lines are among the most useful means for separating information, and separating information is, in turn, among the most effective ways to highlight it visually.

BEFORE AND AFTER TESTS

Once a revision has been made along the guidelines of our model, how does one know it enhances comprehensibility? We offer three tests to answer this question: (1) readability formulas, (2) computer-based text evaluation programs, and (3) user tests.

Before we proceed, however, we should explain the concept of testing we employed. Evaluators frequently distinguish *formative* and *summative* testing:[11]

> If the evaluation is performed to determine how well students have mastered various elements in a postulated hierarchy so that decisions can be made on how instruction should best proceed, then it is formative in nature.... However,... if the purpose is simply to grade the student at the end of one unit before proceeding to the next, then the evaluation is summative.

Formative evaluation goes on while a unit of instruction proceeds so that the teacher can learn how to adjust to the needs of the students. Summative evaluation occurs at the end of a unit so that the teachers can discover what the students have learned.

Documents can be evaluated similarly. If a document designer wants to find out what parts of a draft may cause trouble, or has reason to believe that a document has many trouble spots or interesting problems, or is relatively inexperienced, he or she may want to do a formative evaluation on a draft or on a document to be revised—a "user edit." The technique calls for giving someone who might reasonably be expected to use the final document a copy of the draft and have him or her read it out loud and use it, commenting along the way on things that are unclear. It is simple to do a user edit of a manual, for example, for with such a document all one has to do is ask a potential user to follow the instructions:[12]

> The user edit is based on a very simple idea: find someone who knows nothing about your machine and have him work with it, using only your manual as a guide; his errors and hesitations should tell you where the weak points are. To get more detailed information, it is also a good idea to ask users to talk while they work, telling what they are trying to do, what they are looking for, what gives them trouble, and what they would suggest to make the manual better.

Since one does not "use" a consent form in the same sense or way that one "uses" a manual, a user edit of a consent form calls for a slightly different technique—reading the document out loud and saying *everything* that is on one's mind as one reads:[13]

> It is understood and agreed that... hmm, why both understood and agreed?... and who is agreeing, me?... so if I sign this it means that I understand and agree that...

The evaluator normally tapes such a monologue so as to have a record to examine for trouble spots.

Since the issues in this form were fairly simple and we were quite experienced in revising consent forms, and thus knew what was most likely to cause problems, we did only "summative" evaluations, "before and after" tests. Still, many revisors of medical consent forms, faced with forms that contain difficult medical concepts and terminology and uncertain as to how a target population will try to make sense of them, will probably want to use formative as well as summative evaluations.

Readability Formulas

Inspired by the work of Flesch,[14] readability formulas are attempts to quantify the readability of a text. Although there now exist many formulas that measure readability, all such formulas are especially sensitive to the number of words per sentence and the number of syllables per word. Thus, the more words per sentence and the more syllables per word, the more difficult readability is presumed to become.

As one can guess, readability formulas are highly corrigible instruments. They do not take into account, for example, the occasions on which adding longer words and longer sentences to a text can improve its comprehensibility (e.g., when a text is unduly terse and abbreviated). The Center for Reading at the University of Illinois has carefully investigated the limitations of readability formulas as an assessment of text readability.[15]

However, readability formulas can be useful if intelligently interpreted. One fact of language is the high correlation between short words and words that are commonly used. Readability formulas, which reward a text for using short over long words, implicitly reward it for using common over uncommon words. In the writing of medical consent forms, there are ample opportunities to replace remote, forbidding wording with wording that is more common and colloquial. Thus, if the readability scores of an original and revised form are approximately similar, it may be an indication that the reviser has missed opportunities to make wordings simpler than they need be.

It is also a fact of language that the longer a sentence, the more risks that topical information will get buried in layers of coordination and subordination. Part of the skill of the consummate writer is the daring to take these risks—and succeed. A Norman Mailer or other skilled author can write sentences that are 30–300 words long and remain delightfully understandable. But the average writer does not have this skill and, for him or her, the tendency for a sentence structure to collapse as the sentence grows in length is real. Thus, if the readability scores of an original and revised form are approximately similar, it may be an indication that the reviser has missed opportunities to reduce not only sentence length but sentence convolution.

We ran a computer program that calculated four separate readability scores for our original and revised forms (Figure 3). The original was assessed, on average, at the 19th grade reading level, a reading level that would presumably tax Ph.Ds. The revised form was assessed, on average, at an 11th grade or high school reading level. Thus, the readability grades

```
readability grades:
        (Kincaid) 11.1 (auto) 11.5 (Coleman-Liau) 11.2 (Flesch) 11.7  (51.7)
sentence info:
        no. sent 14 no. wds 285
        av sent leng 20.4 av word leng 4.83
        no. questions 1 no. imperatives 0
        no. nonfunc wds 160 56.1%  av leng 6.54
        short sent (<15) 43% (6) long sent (>30) 21% (3)
        longest sent 41 wds at sent 2; shortest sent 7 wds at sent 1
sentence types:
        simple 43% (6) complex 36% (5)
        compound 7% (1) compound-complex 14% (2)
word usage:
        verb types as % of total verbs
        tobe 29% (11) aux 26% (10) inf 21% (8)
        passives as % of non-inf verbs 7% (2)
        types as % of total
        prep 7.7% (22) conj 3.2% (9) adv 4.9% (14)
        noun 23.2% (66) adj 17.2% (49) pron 9.1% (26)
        nominalizations 2% (5)
sentence beginnings:
        subject opener: noun (0) pron (5) pos (1) adj (5) art (2) tot 93%
        prep 0% (0) adv 0% (0)
        verb 0% (0) sub-conj 7% (1) conj 0% (0)
        expletives 0% (0)
```

FIGURE 3a. Computer test analysis of revised P-43.

```
readability grades:
        (Kincaid) 21.4 (auto) 23.7 (Coleman-Liau) 14.4 (Flesch) 17.0 (14.0)
sentence info:
        no. sent 5 no. wds 204
        av sent leng 40.8 av word leng 5.25
        no. questions 0 no. imperatives 0
        no. nonfunc wds 105 51.5% av leng 7.57
        short sent (<36) 40% (2) long sent (>49) 0% (0)
        longest sent 50 wds at sent 2; shortest sent 30 wds at sent 0
sentence types:
        simple 0% (0) complex 0% (0)
        compound 20% (1) compound-complex 80% (4)
word usage:
        verb types as % of total verbs
        tobe 48% (11) aux 35% (8) inf 9% (2)
        passives as % of non-inf verbs 24% (5)
        types as % of total
        prep 8.8% (18) conj 8.8% (18) adv 4.4% (9)
        noun 21.1% (43) adj 17.2% (35) pron 6.9% (14)
        nominalizations 5% (10)
sentence beginnings:
        subject opener: noun (0) pron (2) pos (0) adj (0) art (0) tot 40%
        prep 0% (0) adv 20% (1)
        verb 0% (0) sub-conj 0% (0) conj 0% (0)
        expletives 40% (2)
```

FIGURE 3b. Computer test analysis of original P-43.

seemed to show some sensitivity at reflecting differences between the original and revised forms. But we caution that readability indices should be used to evaluate revisions only with heavy doses of common sense mixed in. For example, breaking up a long sentence by laying it out on a page may make it easier to read, but it won't affect its readability score.

Computer-Based Text-Evaluation Programs

We shall limit our discussion to one component of the best software so far developed for analyzing text—Bell Lab's WRITER'S WORKBENCH. The STYLE component of WRITER'S WORKBENCH can, among other things, calculate sentence length and type (simple, compound, complex, compound-complex). It can keep records of initial sentence structures, passives, nominalizations, auxiliary verbs, and so on. It even computes, as we saw above, readability grades along four related indices.

Running the program STYLE on both the original and revised form (*see* Figure 3), we found that the length of sentences in the original was consistently long (an average of 41 words, with the shortest sentence 30 words). We also found that our revision had successfully introduced more variation in length—with 43 percent of the sentences being less than 15 words, 36 percent being between 15 and 30 words, and the remaining 21 percent being over 30 words. In addition, the computer analysis revealed a large number of compound-complex sentences in the original (80 percent) while only 14 percent of the revised form had compound-complex sentences. The revised form also fared better on variation of sentence type. Unlike the original, which had only compound-complex and compound (20 percent) sentences, the revised form had sentences which spanned all the major types (43 percent simple, 36 percent complex, 7 percent compound, and 14 percent compound-complex).

As for inactive "to be" verbs, which often inhibit readers from making quick connections between subjects and objects, 48 percent of the verbs on the original form were "be" verbs; only 29 percent of the verbs on the revised form were "be" verbs.

The final revealing measure was sentence beginnings or a sentence's capacity to come quickly to the main or most important information. On the original form, 40 percent of the sentence openings were expletives or empty "it's." Only 40 percent began with "important information" noun phrases. In the revised versions all beginning expletives were deleted and 93 percent of the sentence beginnings were substantive noun phrases.

Before completing our discussion of the computer analysis of forms, we should make clear that these results are best used as post hoc interpretations. A WRITER'S WORKBENCH analysis should probably not be used to *predict* what is wrong with a form. It should rather be used to help an evaluator confirm his or her worst suspicions.

User Tests

Clearly the most important and reliable technique for evaluating the worth of a revision is to test original and revised forms on real readers. If one is extremely fortunate, one will be able to test the forms on the clientele who must use them. If one can't do this, one is best advised to test them on a sample thought to be homogeneous with the population in which the clientele fall. We decided that undergraduate students (the easiest sample for us to obtain) might be expected to be more educated readers than the average person asked to sign a consent form. We took this assumption to mean that we could conclude a great deal about the deficiencies of a form if this population had trouble with them.

The question for any user test is, what should users be tested on? What do they need to get from a form such that, if they get it, we can judge the form to be a good one? For medical consent forms, we decided that the main provisions of the form should be *easy* to understand and should make it easy for a client to *report* his or her understanding.

To test for ease and quickness of understanding, we gave the original P-43 to 25 undergraduate students enrolled at a small university and the revised form to a different sample of 25, chosen from that same population. We gave each subject enough time to read the form until the subject felt he or she understood it—five minutes if necessary. We then removed the forms and administered a five-question short-answer test to measure understanding of the most important provisions (Figure 4). We tested not only the number of questions correctly answered, but the time it took subjects to answer all five questions. If our revision model is effective, more subjects reading the revised form should answer more questions correctly and in less time.

Our predictions were dramatically confirmed (Table 1). The 25 readers of the original answered an average of 2.36 questions correctly; the 25 readers of the revised form answered an average of 4.52 questions correctly. In the first group, only one person scored four correctly; but of the second group, seventeen answered all five questions and six scored four correctly. Figure 5 shows accuracy scores for all the subjects. The average response time for the first group was approximately 2½ minutes (159.16 seconds); the average response time for the second group was approximately 1½ minutes (98.64 seconds): Figure 6 shows response times for all the subjects.

Using a standard T-test, we found that accuracy was significantly better than for the original version ($p <$ 05.). We also found that subject responding to the revised form answered significantly more quickly than subjects responding to the original ($p <$ 05.).[16]

7.4 QUESTIONS ABOUT P-43 FOR COMPREHENSION TEST

1. You have given consent for and received a blood transfusion. Your doctor believes that you need yet another transfusion. Have you consented to a second transfusion?

2. In a routine situation, you give your consent for and receive a blood transfusion. However, you later discover that the blood given you does not match your blood type. Who is responsible?

3. Name two possible side effects of a transfusion.

4. In an emergency situation, you give your consent for and receive a blood transfusion. However, you later discover that the blood given you does not match your blood type. Who is responsible?

5. You give your consent for and receive a blood transfusion. However, you later discover that the blood given you was of poor quality. Who is responsible?

FIGURE 4. Questions about P-43 for Comprehension Test.

TABLE 1. Mean Correct Responses and Response Times.

	Correct Response (to 5 Questions)	Response Time (in Minutes)
Original	2.36	2.65
Revised	4.52	1.64

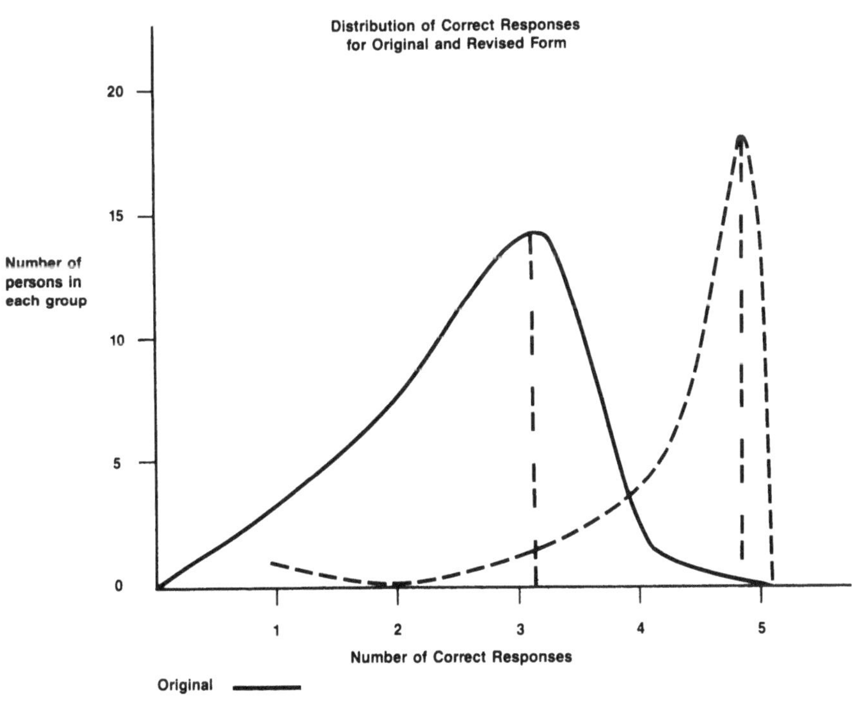

FIGURE 5. Distribution of correct responses for original and revised form.

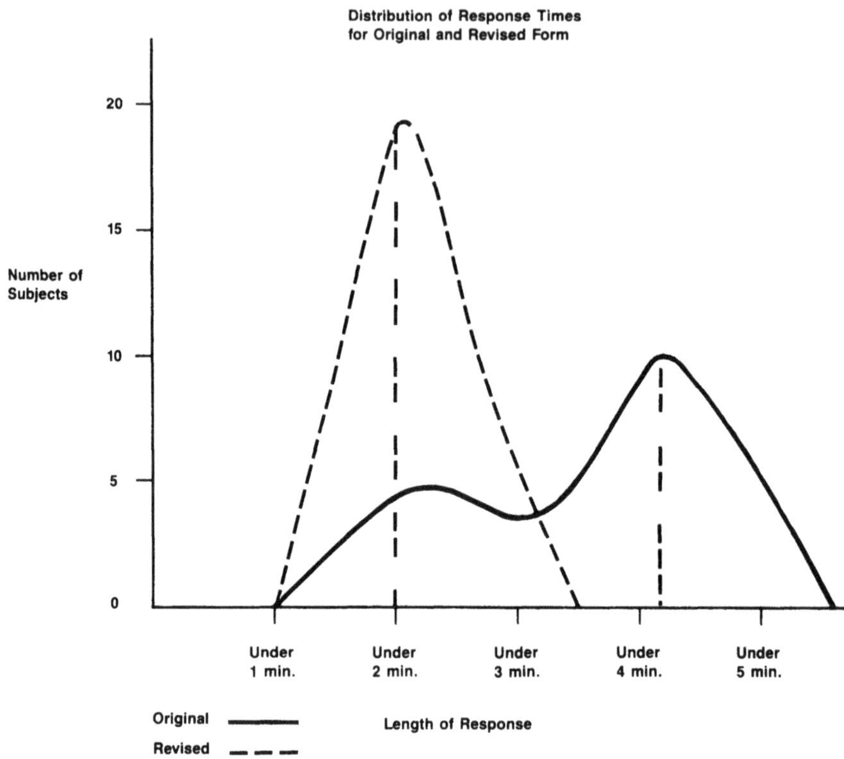

FIGURE 6. Distribution of response times for original and revised form.

The user test is the test that satisfies the skeptic who claims "the proof of the pudding is in the reading."

CONCLUSION

A comprehensible consent form is not, of course, a guarantee that physician and patient have communicated to either's satisfaction. It is, however, at least an indication of good faith and a reflection of the physician's sincere attempt not only to enable the patient to understand, but also to educate the patient. A physician who asks a patient to sign a consent form made up of long sentences clogged with technical medical terminology and stuffy legalisms that the patient cannot understand is asking for obedience, not consent. Indeed, courts have so held, in effect.

The consent form is a record of the discussion that has taken place between physician and patient. A well-written consent form (i.e., one that the patient can understand) protects medical personnel, the hospital, and the patient. It also reflects the patient's trust in the physician and the hospital. Thus, a consent form is a document which reflects a very basic and sensitive relationship. It should, therefore, be as simply and as sensitively written as possible.

Finally, should litigation occur, a consent form which is unclear or confusing, signed by the patient in ignorance, may well be rejected by a court. One which is written to be readily comprehensible, however, demonstrates a sincere and thoughtful attempt by the physician and the hospital to communicate adequately with the patient. Courts take notice of such intentions.

NOTES

1. Scott v. Bradford, 606 P. 2d 554 (Okla. 1974). For useful discussions of the history of informed consent, *see:* John F. Horty, "Consents," Chapter I, *Hospital Law* (Pittsburgh: Action Kit for Hospital Law, 1980); President's Commission for the Study of Ethical Problems in Medicine and Biomedical and Behavioral Research, *Making Health Care Decisions,* Vol. 1 (Washington, D.C.: Superintendent of Documents, 1982).
2. Schloendorff v. Society of New York Hospitals, 105 N.E. 92 (N.Y. 1914).
3. 28 Pa. Code 103.22 (adopted 1977), item (b) (8).
4. No physician or podiatrist shall be liable for failure to obtain an informed consent if it is established by a preponderance of the evidence that furnishing the information in question of the patient would have resulted in a seriously adverse effect on the patient or on the therapeutic process to the material detriment of the patient's health; 40 Pa. C.S.A. Section 1301.103 (Purdon's 1982-3 Supp.)
5. Harrison v. Brodmerkel, 127 Pgh.L.J. 151 (Pa.C.P., Allegheny County, 1979. *See also,* Pegram v. Sisco, 406 F.Supp. 776 (W.D.Arb. 1976).
6. President's Commission for the Study of Ethical Problems in Medicine and Biomedical and Behavioral Research, Minutes of Meeting XX, April 2–3, 1982. For a full discussion of these problems, see *Making Health Care Decisions.*
7. The specific phrase "in laymen's terms" does not appear in the American Hospital Association Patient Bill of Rights, approved in November of 1972. Item 3 of that document begins "The patient has the right to receive from his physician information necessary to give informed consent prior to the start of any procedure and/or treatment." That statement would seem to imply "in layman's terms," but does not say so explicitly. (*See* G.J. Annas, "Avoiding Malpractice Suits Through the Use of Informed Consent," Appendix B, *Current Problems in Pediatrics* 6 [1976] pp. 20–22.)
8. Gary R. Morrow, "How Readable Are Subject Consent Forms?" *Journal of the American Medical Association* 244 (July 4, 1980), p. 56.
9. *See,* for example: B.R. Cassileth, R.V. Zupkis, K. Sutton-Smith, and V. March, "Informed Consent—Why Are Its Goals Imperfectly Realized?", *New England Journal of Medicine* 302 (April 1980), 896–900; or T.M. Grundner, "On the

Readability of Surgical Consent Forms, *New England Journal of Medicine* 302 (April 1980), 900–902.

10. Over the last several years, for example, the staff of the Communication Design Center has revised a series of medical and surgical consent forms widely used in hospitals to make them more comprehensible. *See* John F. Horty, "Consents," Chapter 5, *Hospital Law* (Pittsburgh: Action Kit for Hospital Law, 1981).
11. Benjamin S. Bloom, J. Thomas Hastings, and George F. Madaus, *Handbook on Formative and Summative Evaluation of Student Learning* (New York: McGraw-Hill, 1971), p. 28.
12. Marshall Atlas, "The User Edit: Making Manuals Easier to Use," *IEEE Transactions on Professional Communication* PC-24, no. 1 (March 1981), 28.
13. John R. Hayes and Linda S. Flower, "Uncovering Cognitive Processes in Writing: An Introduction to Protocol Analysis," in P. Mosenthal, L. Tamor, and S. Walmsley (eds.) *Research in Writing: Principles and Methods* (New York: Longman, in press). [ERIC No. 202035]; Heidi Swarts, Linda S. Flower, and John R. Hayes, "Designing Protocol Studies of the Writing Process: An Introduction," in R. Beach and L. Bridwell (eds.) *New Directions in Composition Research* (New York: Guilford Press, in press).
14. Rudolph Flesch, *The Art of Readable Writing* (New York: Harper and Row, 1949.
15. A. Davidson, R. Kantor, J. Hannah, G. Hermon, R. Lutz, and R. Salzillo, "Limitations of Readability Formulas in Guiding Adaptations of Texts," Technical Report 162. Center for the Study of Reading, University of Illinois, Urbana, Illinois, 1981. *See also* Thomas M. Duffy and Paula Kabance, "Testing a Readable Writing Approach to Text Revision," *Journal of Educational Psychology* 74 (October 1982), 733–748.
16. We are indebted to Davida Charney for performing the statistical tests.

REFERENCES

Alfidi, R.J. "Informed consent: A study of patient reaction." *JAMA,* May 1971, 216(8), 1325–1329.

Annas, G.J. "Avoiding malpractice suits through the use of informed consent." *Current Problems in Pediatrics,* 1976, *6,* 3–48.

Barbour, G.L., & Blumenkrantz, M.J. "Videotape aids informed consent decision." *JAMA,* December 1978, *240(25),* 2741–2742.

Cassileth, B.R., Zupkis, R.V., Sutton-Smith, K., & March, V. "Informed consent—Why are its goals imperfectly realized?" *New England Journal of Medicine,* April 1980, *302(16),* 896–900.

Crile, G. "Breast cancer and informed consent." *Journal of Legal Medicine,* July/August 1973, *1,* 42–43.

Curran, William J. "The patient's Bill of Rights becomes law." *New England Journal of Medicine,* 1974, *290(1),* 32–33.

Denney, M.K., Williamson, D., & Penn, R. "Informed consent: Emotional responses of patients." *Postgraduate Medicine,* November 1975, *60(5),* 205–209.

(Editorial). "Documenting informed consent." *Journal of Legal Medicine,* July/August 1974, *2,* 6.

Faden, A.I., & Faden, R.R. "Informed consent in medical practice: With particular reference to neurology." *Archives of Neurology,* November 1978, *35,* 761-764.

Goldie, R.R. "The requirements of informed consent." *Hospitals,* May 16, 1972, *46,* 58-61, 126.

Goldsmith, L.S. "The myth about informed consent." *Journal of Legal Medicine,* September 1975, *3,* 9-12.

Grundner, T.M. "Two formulas for determining the readability of subject consent forms." *American Psychologist,* August 1978, *33,* 773-775.

Hassard, H. "Informed consent in focus." *California Medicine,* November 1973, *119(5),* 51-52.

Horty, John F. "Informed consent: Legal theories; Consents," Ch. 1. In *Hospital Law,* Pittsburgh, Pa.: John F. Horty, September 1980.

Horty, John F. "Specific requirements for informed consent; Consents," Ch. 2. In *Hospital Law,* Pittsburgh, Pa.: John F. Horty, November 1980.

Horty, John F. "Consent for imcompetent patients; Consents," Ch. 3. In *Hospital Law,* Pittsburgh, Pa.: John F. Horty, February 1981.

Horty, John F. "Statutes dealing with consent; Consents," Ch. 4. In *Hospital Law,* Pittsburgh, Pa.: John F. Horty, March 1981.

Horty, John F. "Consent forms; Consents," Ch. 5. In *Hospital Law,* Pittsburgh, Pa.: John F. Horty, May 1981.

Janik, C.J., Swaney, J.H., Bond, S.J., & Hayes, J.R. "Informed consent: Reality or illusion?" *Information Design Journal,* 1981, *2,* 197-207.

Laforet, E.G. "The fiction of informed consent." *JAMA,* April 12, 1976, *235(15),* 1579-1585.

Leeb, D., Bowers, D.G. Jr., & Lynch, J.B. "Observations on the myth of 'informed consent.'" *Plastic & Reconstructive Surgery,* September 1976, *58(3),* 580-582.

Lidz, C.W., & Roth, L.H. "The signed form—informed consent?" In Boruch, R.F., Ross, J. & Cecil, J.S. (Eds.), *Solutions to Legal and Ethical Problems in Applied Social Research,* New York: Academic Press, 1981.

Miller, Leslie J. "Informed consent: 1." *JAMA,* 1980, *244(18),* 2100-2103.

Miller, R., & Willner, H.S. "The two-part consent form: A suggestion for promoting free and informed consent." *New England Journal of Medicine,* 1974, *290(17),* 964-966.

Mills, D.H. "Whither informed consent?" *JAMA,* July 15, 1974, *229(3),* 305-310.

Moore, R.M. "Consent forms—how, or whether, they should be used." *Mayo Clinic Proceedings,* 1978, *53,* 393-396.

Morrow, Gary R. "How readable are subject consent forms?" *JAMA,* 1980, *244(1),* 56-58.

Morrow, G., Gootnick, J., & Schmale, A. "A simple technique for increasing cancer patients' knowledge of informed consent to treatment." *Cancer,* August 1978, *42,* 793-799.

Muss, H.B., White, D.R., Michielutte, R., et al. "Written informed consent in patients with breast cancer." *Cancer,* April 1979, *43,* 1549-1556.

Pasto, S. "Are cancer patients paying the price of chemotherapy?" *The Providence Eagle,* November 19, 1981, *2(10),* 1, 5.

Patten, B.M., & Stump, W. "Death related to informed consent." *Texas Medicine,* December 1978, *74,* 49–50.

Priluck, I.A., Robertson, D.M., & Buettner, H. "What patients recall of the preoperative discussion after retinal detachment surgery." *American Journal of Opthalmology,* 1979, *87,* 620–623.

Rennie, D. "Informed consent by 'well-nigh abject' adults." *New England Journal of Medicine,* April 1980, *302(16),* 917–918.

Robinson, G., & Merav, A. "Informed consent: Recall by patients tested postoperatively." *Annals of Thoracic Surgery,* September 1976, *22(3),* 209–212.

Rosenberg, S.H. "Informed consent: A reappraisal of patients' reactions." *California Medicine,* November 1973, *119(5),* 64–68.

Warren, S. "Informed consent in clinical investigation and practice." *Journal of Legal Medicine,* May/June 1973, *1,* 21–24.

Whitman, N. "A guide to clinical performance testing." Idea Paper No. 7, Center for Faculty Evaluation and Development, Kansas State University, February 1982.

Hospices: Medical and Legal Considerations

Marlene Scham, M.A., and Arnold Scham, M.D.

INTRODUCTION

Death awareness has become a major public concern of late. Threats of mass war, media exposure to monumentally tragic events, and technological advances which allow the prolongation of life, even diseased life, have aroused a new awareness of death in our society.

ATTITUDES TOWARD DEATH

"Our relationship to death is not purely cognitive. . . . We have both transient and relatively enduring attitudes that help define our position with respect to death—and these attitudes may be found at more than one level within our psyches."[1] Often, people are not consciously aware of their attitudes toward death. Individuals, for example, may deny being anxious about death because that anxiety exists on the unconscious level. Kalish cited a study by Feifel and Branscomb (1973) in which they said, "the deeper we probe into the unconscious, the more death fear and anxiety we find."[2]

On another level, people may simply be reluctant to admit their fear because they feel it is socially unacceptable to do so. And, there are some people who may not have given the matter much thought and are therefore unsure of what their attitudes actually are.

"The place of death [and attitudes toward it] are neither simple nor stable."[3] They can change and modify as one grows and experiences more of life and the world. At all psychic levels, thoughts and feelings surrounding death are related to one's background and upbringing, one's own methods of handling stress, and the environment in which one lives. Kastenbaum and

Aisenberg described the environmental influences which have helped to bring about a modern resurgence in death awareness.[4]

Until modern times, four conditions affected the way people viewed death. First, individuals had a severely limited life span. Infant mortality rates were enormous and average life spans were approximately half of what they are today. Second, exposure to death was a normal and a frequent occurrence. The realities of death and dying in animals and in humans were a part of each person's day-to-day existence. Third, there was a sense of powerlessness and mystery in the universe. One had no control over the forces of nature, and therefore had to accept whatever surprises or tragedies life had in store. Fourth, the status of the individual was less important than his role as part of the group. As a member of that group, he was part of the "Death System"—the rituals surrounding death. His actions, words, and gestures concerning burial, prayers, and mourning, were prescribed for him. He became an intrinsic part of the ritual process as a way of dealing with his feelings of powerlessness. The transition between life and death was a natural one. As a result, whatever personal anxiety was aroused by death was alleviated by participation in the ritual process.

In modern America, the death system has changed dramatically because of changing conditions. One of the most important changes has been the shift away from the immediacy of death for all but the very old. Infant mortality has decreased and life expectancies have increased to the point where we have begun to envision death as a function only of old age.

Another change has been our disassociation with the dying. For the most part, the dying are institutionalized out of our sight and out of our consciousness. Whatever exposure we do have is bound to be carefully orchestrated and cosmeticized so that the "unpleasantness" of death is kept to a minimum.

Technology has brought about many changes as well. We can now hope for and expect the moment when we can literally control the timing of death through our technological mastery of the world. At that point, we may no longer consider death inevitable.

Finally, we lack the ritual process to fall back on in times of crisis and death. Individualism is the concept of the day, and decisions concerning life and death are increasingly being left to the individual at the expense of the group. Kastenbaum and Aisenberg, in summarizing the conditions in which modern attitudes toward death have formed, state that death has been "transposed, insulated, technologized and decontextualized."[5]

What attitudes toward death result from the circumstances described? One is avoidance, the conscious action to keep from dealing with any unpleasant reality. As exposure to death and dying has decreased, death has become a taboo subject, either avoided completely or discussed in soft-sounding euphemisms such as "passed on" and "gone away." Further, we try to shield children from the reality of death by keeping them away from funerals and the sights and sounds and smells of dying people. This only serves to increase society's distance from, and negative reactions to, death.

Another attitude used to cope with death is denial, an unconscious defense mechanism to avoid threatening or painful thoughts. Our view of death as a function of old age is a form of denial of the possibility of death occurring at any time, to anyone.

Perhaps the most preponderant attitude toward death is fear. "*Fear* is the psychological state that is most often mentioned when clinicians or researchers discuss responses or attitudes toward death. It is possible that fear is the most typical or the most important psychological response to death."[6]

There are many variables which determine who is anxious and fearful about death and how each person deals with his anxiety or fear. These include age, previous experiences with illness or death, upbringing, religious orientation, personality style, and philosophical outlook. Fear of death is not a unitary concept: there are many types of death fears and there are many different kinds of thoughts about death that evoke anxiety.

One of the fears that many people have about death concerns the dying process itself: the fear of suffering and uncontrollable pain, and the fear of being alone. Another fear has to do with what comes after death: fear of the unknown. Uncertainty in any circumstance makes people uncomfortable and anxious. Anxiety is especially aroused when the uncertainty of life after death and the possibilities of eternal punishment are contemplated.

For many people, the fear of death is the fear of extinction. They view death as the cessation of feeling, thinking and being. For them, death is nothingness, annihilation and obliteration. Although psychologists insist that it is impossible to imagine such nothingness, it is the idea of extinction that is so terrifying to many.

The types of fears described may occur separately, all together, or in any combination. And they may occur when one contemplates his own death and dying, or the death and dying of others. The severity of the anxiety depends upon the interrelationship of all the factors of personality, culture and environment previously enumerated. Further, the level of death fear varies widely among individuals and also varies across time in any single individual.

Table 1 was constructed by Kastenbaum and Aisenberg to diagram death anxiety.[7]

There are other attitudes that people may express toward the thought of death. Sorrowing is feeling sad, either for the loss of others or for one's own loss. Overcoming is another way of coping with thoughts of death. "Religion is one of the highly organized cultural efforts to overcome or transcend death."[8] Or, one may participate in death, welcome it and treasure it as an

TABLE 1. Death-Related Fears: Self and Other

Fear	My death	Death of the other
Dying	Personal Suffering Personal Indignity	Vicarious Suffering (suffering along with the other) Vicarious Disintegration (vision of what is in store for me)
Afterlife	Punishment Rejection (by God)	Retaliation (by the dead in this life or the next) Loss of Relationship
Extinction	Basic Death Fear (ceasing to be) Attached Fears (other fears exacer- bated by death fear)	Abandonment Vulnerability (brought about by abandonment)

Note: Parenthetical comments ours.

end to suffering or a reunion with lost loved ones. Other attitudes may encompass awe, curiosity or dislike.

In the final analysis, death is the ultimate paradox, and how any individual views its contradictions determines that individual's measure of fear or anxiety associated with it.

With this new awareness has come the necessity of examining our feelings and attitudes toward death: the death of ourselves and the deaths of the people close to us. We have had to reexamine our attitudes toward the dying process, the prolongation of life at any cost, the definitions of life and death, and the terminally ill—those for whom medicine can offer no hope of cure.

For terminally ill patients, the emphasis has traditionally been on prolonging life as long as possible, despite the physical, financial and emotional costs to the patients and their families. Lately, the emphasis has started to shift from the total reliance on the measure of quantity of life to a consideration of the quality of life. There has been a reevaluation of the indiscriminate use of extraordinary procedures in an effort to determine what the patients and their families need and want.

Much of this examination has occurred under the aegis of the hospice movement. Hospice is a name used to designate a program which helps to provide for the needs of terminally ill patients and their families. This can be accomplished in an inpatient hospice facility, on an outpatient basis, in a general hospital, or in home care. The main concern in each of these facilities is to provide whatever comfort and support are needed and required to help patients live out their last days as they see fit.

This, of course, is a radical and timely departure from the standard solution of relegating terminal patients to a peripheral room in a hospital and condemning them to an isolated and often pain-filled dying experience. The value of the addition of a program like hospice to the array of medical treatments is unmistakable both in human terms and in terms of cost efficiency. Concrete evidence of this fact is the recent approval of Medicare funding for hospice care.[9]

HOSPICE: HISTORY AND DEFINITION

Hospice is a concept that has come of age in the last two decades. Many people have heard of hospice, and its goals and philosophy are becoming increasingly familiar to the general medical community and to the lay public. However, it is important to understand what hospice is and what it is not.

The history of the hospice concept can be traced to the earliest hospitals in ancient India and Egypt. The emphasis in those hospitals was not on the kind of treatment we know today, but rather on the "tender loving care" of the patient. The goal was to make each patient feel at home and as comfortable as possible.

This philosophy was expanded in ancient Greece and Rome. The Temples of Aescalapius, for example, provided medicine to the ill, and, in addition, welcomed sufferers to baths, gardens, libraries and visitors' facilities. Treatment consisted not merely of ministration to the injured part, but to the individual as a whole entity.

By the Middle Ages, the hospices, or Hospitia, had become travelers' rest stops and infirmaries. They were used as overnight stops for pilgrims and crusaders, and provided temporary food and shelter for all who stopped there. In addition to being rest stops, they were also hospitals which offered medical care, comfort and spiritual solace. For many, they were a place of last resort.

Although the modern hospice is no longer an overnight stop for crusaders, it is nevertheless a transitional place or program, a kind of rest stop for people on their final journey. The overall philosophy has not changed: hospice still offers medical, social, and spiritual comfort to terminally ill patients during their last days of life.

The quality of life of the dying patient is of paramount importance in hospice. It is hospice's guiding precept that individuals be able to die in a caring, familiar, comfortable and nonthreatening environment, whether that environment be at home, in a hospital or in a freestanding hospice facility. The emphasis is on care for the patient rather than treatment per se, when the disease is past the point where a cure is possible. Hospice tries to encourage "a *way of life* which seeks to meet the needs of dying patients and their families."[10]

Hospice is what Sandol Stoddard describes as "a caring community" at the center of which "is always one thing: a body coexisting with a belief. The body is the dying patient's and the belief is that the patient is something more than his body."[11]

The specific goals of hospice differ from those of the traditional hospital. When a patient enters the hospital, the staff endeavors to investigate the illness, make a diagnosis, carry out a treatment program, effect a cure, and thereby prolong the patient's life. In general, hospitals are ill-equipped to deal with those who have no hope of recovery or cure. Further, hospitals do not often have the resources to provide support for the families of terminally ill patients. As a result, dying patients and their families have needs that are not adequately met by the existing health care systems. Hospice tries to meet those needs. "Though there is 'no more to be done' for the cancer, much can still be done for the patient—and for his relatives."[12]

The emphasis in hospice programs is on the alleviation of pain and discomfort by dealing aggressively and effectively with its many facets. It is hoped that patients may spend their remaining time comfortably and meaningfully. To this end, they are offered the security of a caring environment and assured that they and their families will not be abandoned once all hope of cure is gone.

The specific goals of hospice include all of the following:

1. To provide palliative care, with emphasis on the multidisciplinary management of pain and other symptoms.
2. To make available medical, emotional, social, and spiritual support for patients and their families.
3. To promote the concept of the patients *and* their families as the treatment unit.
4. To provide continuing follow-up care for the bereaved.
5. To use trained volunteers to provide other than clinical services, to offer a diversity of skills and to promote contacts with the community.
6. To make available home care, hospital care or inpatient hospice care.
7. To provide staff support: the opportunity for staff members to deal with their concerns and receive professional and peer support.
8. To provide twenty-four-hour availability of services.
9. To make available services based on need.
10. To make available "educational opportunities for the wide variety of specialists who have contact with the dying."[13]

The modern hospice is obviously fulfilling a need, a gap in the modern health care system which has occurred because most health professionals have difficulty dealing with dying patients and their families. Health professionals react to their lack of experience with death by falling back on the time-honored maxims of treatment and preservation of life at any cost. For them, death represents failure and inadequacy because the whole thrust of medical education is aimed toward the fight against disease and death; any loss is considered a defeat.

Although these attitudes are changing and many health professionals are now considering the quality as well as quantity of life in their treatment decisions, the changes are coming about slowly. As a result, prior to the advent of hospice, counseling for terminal patients and their families had been provided, in large part, by nonprofessionals and clergy on an individual and haphazard basis. For the patients, medical treatment was often fragmented and intractable pain had become synonomous with terminal cancer.

What, specifically, does hospice do then, to improve these conditions and implement its goals? Perhaps the work of hospice can best be described by detailing how it treats the four components of pain.[14]

First is the social component of pain, the discomfort with interpersonal relationships that results from acknowledging a terminal illness. Patients must be helped to understand that their illness does not diminish their personal value, and they are helped to maintain their relationships throughout their remaining time. This gives them the opportunity to finish whatever unfinished business they have, gives them the opportunity to grieve with their loved ones, and prevents feelings of helplessness, loneliness and abandonment.

Second is treatment for the psychological component of the pain of terminal illness, which means simply helping the patients to cope. It means treatment of their fear, anxiety, depression, and anger with psychotherapy, or medication, or both.

The spiritual aspect is the third component of pain experienced by terminally ill patients. This component is different for each person and the form it takes and its severity are largely dependent upon the individual's background and past experiences. Counseling in this area is an intrinsic part of the hospice program.

The fourth pain component in terminal illness is the pain that originates from a somatic source. Most terminal patients experience somatic pain ranging from mild to unbearable, and from acute to chronic. Any somatic pain is exacerbated by the presence of the other three components. All are interwoven and all must be treated in order for any treatment to be effective.

Patients' pain and other symptoms are managed through the use of extensive drug therapy—what Dr. Cicely Saunders of St. Christopher's Hospice calls "polypharmacy." Drugs are administered in a regimen that attempts to prevent pain from occurring, rather than in controlling it or lessening it after it has occurred. The goal is to keep the patient symptom-free and as alert as possible, using an anticipatory timetable for the administration of drugs.

Proper drug management for the dying is definitely not the PRN (as the occasion arises, as needed) order for pain medication that is seen in the acute care hospital. The patient in a PRN regimen has to be in severe pain before getting relief, which causes a cycle of pain, anxiety, suffering, and depression, the anticipation of which triggers even more pain.[15]

Narcotics are the main ingredients in the pain control regimen. Addiction and toxic side effects are infrequent problems in terminal patients. In fact, "psychological dependence is created when the medication is *not* given in adequate doses on a regular basis."[16]

Experience has shown that drug dosages can often be lowered if narcotics and analgesics are given regularly. On such a timetable, anxiety and depression are relieved and patients do not constantly suffer through pain crises. They are then often able to tolerate lower doses of medication and are therefore most alert.

> With attention to detail and careful regulation of medication according to the patient's needs, it is possible to achieve, with few exceptions, a pain-free state without excessive sedation...and with the satisfactory control of other symptoms.[17]

Medication is also used freely to treat secondary symptoms which, though minor, may cause a great deal of discomfort and distress. These include nausea, loss of appetite, constipation, and depression, among others.

Types of Hospice Programs

One of the phrases most often repeated by those who work in hospice is "Hospice is not a place; it's a program." It is a program to enable patients to maintain control over and dignity in their lives for as long as possible. Its origins lie in inpatient programs, but over the years of its existence it has moved increasingly toward home care. The greater popularity of home care has happened both for financial and social reasons. This movement notwithstanding, hospice work can take place in many different settings, and in practice, several types of hospice arrangements have come into being.

The inpatient hospice is exemplified by St. Christopher's Hospice in England, the prototype of modern hospice care. St. Christopher's is a freestanding facility which opened in 1967, after 19 years of preparation by its founder, Dr. Cicely Saunders.

St. Christopher's is an inpatient facility to which 500–600 patients are admitted annually. Admission depends upon a review of the patient's medical history, the expected length of survival, and an indication of whether or not the patient and his family can benefit from hospice care.

In addition to its inpatient facility, St. Christopher's also has a home care program which is coordinated with the district nurse and the treating physician. At any one time, there are about 80 patients in the home care program. There is also an ambulatory patient clinic where patients who are well enough can receive outpatient care.

Volunteers are a large part of the St. Christopher's program, as they are at virtually all other hospice programs in existence. They assist in meal distribution, reading to patients, household chores and numerous other tasks which help to ease the burdens faced by families with a terminally ill member. There are also volunteer professionals—nurses, physicians, and therapists—who volunteer to take regular duty shifts in their professional capacities. The major goals of St. Christopher's have always been the alleviation of pain and the assurance that the patient will not die alone.

The first American hospice was Hospice, Inc. of New Haven, Connecticut. The initial emphasis at Hospice, Inc. was home care which enabled patients to remain at home as long as possible, if that was their desire. In order to be eligible for the program, patients have to have a diagnosis of cancer with a prognosis in weeks or months. The treating physicians' consent and cooperation are essential in this program because they continue to manage the patients' care.

One of the requirements of the Hospice, Inc. home care program is the presence of a primary caregiver in the home 24 hours a day. The caregiver receives help and support from visiting nurses who make house calls every day, from the hospice staff who visit twice a week, and from the hospice physician who visits once a week.

As with St. Christopher's, Hospice, Inc. depends in large measure upon its volunteers. Since its inception as a home care program, Hospice, Inc. has added a 44-bed inpatient facility, modeled on St. Christopher's.

Other hospices have sprung up around the United States since Hospice, Inc. was founded. In most of the programs, the patients' personal physicians continue to manage the patients' care, although that care is now coordinated with the hospice team. Most programs also emphasize home care and are often able to reduce patients' average hospital stays by two or more weeks. In addition to home care, some programs have units set aside in a general hospital which are specifically designated for hospice care. Others have hospice beds scattered throughout regular medical and surgical units. Whatever the arrangement, the goal is to promote an attitude of caring for the patients and their families according to their needs and wishes.

In any setting, the staff of the hospice team is a multidisciplinary one and usually includes the patient's personal physician working together with an oncologist, medical director, administrative and nursing coordinator, nurses, psychological support staff (psychiatrist, psychologist, and psychiatric social worker), clergy, volunteers and pharmacist consultants. The staff attempts to use its cumulative skills as a means to an end—the comfort of the patient—rather than as an end in itself. The members concentrate on what can be done to provide relief instead of assuming that a terminal diagnosis means there is nothing left to be done.

Hospice does not exist in opposition to regular hospital or medical care. Instead, it is an additional resource to be employed for the benefit of the patients and their families.

PAIN CONTROL

Inherent Problems

One of the most important aspects of hospice care is pain control. For many people, the prevailing attitude toward death is fear, and the most pervasive fear that individuals have about death concerns the dying process itself. Often dying is equated (in fact as well as fantasy) with suffering and somatic pain, debilitation and loss of control, and with dependency and abandonment. It is not surprising, then, that patients and families faced with a diagnosis of terminal cancer live with the fear that the remaining time for the patient will be spent in severe and uncontrollable pain.

While there is still much to be learned concerning pain control, it is nevertheless a fact that most patients can be maintained on a regimen which affords them excellent pain relief. If good pain control is indeed possible in terminal cancer, then why do so many patients experience intractable pain during the last stages of their illnesses? A clinical example will illustrate the problems involved.

A neighbor's father recently died as a result of prostatic cancer with bone metastases. He was described as having suffered terrible pain during the last few months of his illness.

A review and discussion of his case brought several facts to light. First, the dosage of narcotic which was prescribed for him was inadequate to control the type of pain associated with his type of cancer. Second, he had symptoms of marked depression, which went untreated and which exacerbated his pain. Further, the treating physician, who had taken an active and avuncular interest in the patient prior to the terminal prognosis, became distant and unresponsive once that prognosis was made.

This example is all too representative of the plight of the terminally ill patient and his family. The ineffective dosage of narcotic was used because of a pervasive fear—in both the medical and lay communities—of addiction, and because of the concern over the legal ramifications of using large doses of addictive drugs. Richard Lewis reported on a study done on narcotic administration at a large hospital. It was found that "Physicians prescribed narcotics at one-half to two-thirds the dose required to relieve severe pain and the nurses underadministered the drugs by another one-half to one-third," all because of the fear of using large amounts of narcotics, and particularly, of addiction.[18]

The missed diagnosis of depression, which is an easily and successfully treated disorder, is unfortunately common in patients such as the one described. Many professionals lack the knowledge of and the interest in the psychological and social aspects of terminal illness.

Finally, the emotional and physical withdrawal of the treating physician results from the difficulties that physicians face when confronted with terminal illness and death. As we mentioned earlier, medical training is life-oriented, and death represents defeat and failure. Consequently, health professionals, trained to cure, become confused, upset, angry and withdrawn when it becomes evident that no cure is possible. While this is not by any means a universal reaction, it is nevertheless a fairly common one.

It is vitally important, therefore, to educate both the health care professionals and the general public so that they are aware that something can be done for the terminally ill patient; care can be made available. Palliative care and symptom control are legitimate and imperative treatment goals for the patient. Support and symptom treatment are legitimate and imperative treatment goals for the family.

An example of symptom relief in the family is the treatment of sleep disorders, the successful resolution of which adds immeasurably to the family's comfort. The medical and emotional supports that the affected family members receive allow not only for the immediate symptom relief, but may also serve to obviate stress-induced illness, which often makes itself apparent at a time in the future when the "stress" is seemingly gone.

Some Issues in Pain Management

Pain is a perceptual experience combining a somatic source with a psychic response. The standard question of whether pain is mental or physical, or whether it is real or imagined, presents an absurd dichotomy.

All pain is real and the perception of it is the result of the interaction of two factors, the somatic and the psychic. Given the same somatic source, differing mental or emotional factors can cause the perception of the pain to range from ache to agony. Therefore, the successful treatment of pain necessitates the evaluation of both the somatic and the psychic components.

At this point, it might be useful to cite some brief examples of actual consultations for pain control on terminal patients.

Case 1

A female patient was reported by the staff to be in uncontrollable pain. On questioning, the patient stated that she had no physical pain, but was "in agony" because no one would tell her what was wrong with her. The subsequent honest exploration of her disease, its consequences, and the resulting "open awareness" brought tremendous relief to this patient.

Case 2

A male patient complained of a sudden and definite increase in pain. Careful questioning elicited reports of some respiratory difficulties. The patient was diagnosed as having pneumonia and was treated with antibiotics. The result was substantial pain reduction.

Case 3

A female patient complained of constant, incapacitating pain. She was diagnosed as experiencing severe depression and was treated with antidepressant medication. The result was a dramatic reduction in the level of her pain.

Case 4

A 35-year-old male patient with a rapidly growing brain tumor experienced severe uncontrollable pain and emotional problems. He was placed on a regimen which afforded excellent pain control and included daily brief psychotherapy and the following medications: Methadone—70 mg oral dose every 4 hours around the clock, Chlorpromazine—400 mg daily, Thiothixene—30 mg daily, and Amitriptyline—100 mg daily. This patient was able to return home and live with his family while remaining on this medication schedule.

It has been well-documented that pain intensity increases with the presence of anxiety, depression, emotional isolation, sleep disorders, loss of hope and the loss of one's control over life. Therefore, it follows that amelioration of any or all of these symptoms and situations contributes significantly to pain relief.

Incidence of Pain

Although intractable pain has become synonomous with cancer, in fact, not all cancer patients experience pain. Studies indicate that roughly 65 percent of cancer patients experience severe pain and about 35 percent range from no pain to moderate pain. Table 2 illustrates several different kinds of cancer and the percentage of patients who report severe pain.[19]

Causes of Pain

Pain associated with cancer can have more than one cause:

1. Direct Tumor Involvement: Bone Metasteses; Nerve Compression.
2. Cancer Therapy: Surgery; Chemotherapy; Radiotherapy.
3. Pain From Other Causes: Arthritis; Muscle Spasm; Stress.

Careful evaluation and diagnosis are necessary to determine the cause or causes of each patient's pain. It is also important to remember that patients often experience more than one type of pain.

Further, the meaning of the pain to the patient must be discussed with him. For example, a patient may interpret mild arthritis pain as an indication that a tumor has grown or spread. In this case, a discussion of the type and meaning of the particular pain can save the patient a tremendous amount of needless stress and anxiety.

The treatment of pain is, therefore, not simply the prescribing of nar-

TABLE 2. Types of Cancer and Percentage Patients Reporting Severe Pain

Type of cancer	Percent of patients experiencing severe pain
Bone and Prostate	85
Cervix	85
Breast	55–68
Kidney	55
Lung	50–70
Gastro-Intestinal	40–60
Lymphoma	20
Leukemia	5

cotics. Radiation and chemotherapy to shrink tumors and reduce pressure may be used for pain control as well. In addition, nerve blocks created by surgery or anesthesia are helpful in some cases. Steroids may also be used to reduce swelling and thereby relieve nerve compression. Finally, the treatment of pain involves the treatment of the social, psychological and spiritual aspects of the illness with all available means.

Principles of Pain Control

For the treatment of mild to moderate pain, the nonnarcotic analgesics should be tried first. These include aspirin, acetaminophen, and nonsteroidal antiinflammatory drugs. All of the aforementioned drugs are particularly useful in treating bone pain. When these medications fail to provide the necessary pain relief, they should be replaced by or supplemented with narcotics.

The following table (Table 3) lists the relative potencies of common narcotics in use, and the IM (injectable) to PO (oral) dosage ratio: This table illustrates several important concepts. First is the necessity of adjusting the narcotic dose to provide equivalent pain relief when switching from IM (injectable) to oral administration of the drug. It frequently occurs that patients who are in good pain control on IM morphine or another narcotic in the hospital are discharged and given the same milligram dose in oral form. Invariably, their pain increases, pain control is lost, and many experience narcotic withdrawal reactions.

Second, it is clear from the table that meperidine and codeine are relatively weak narcotics when compared with the others available.

The third consideration is that methadone has a longer half-life than the other listed drugs. This fact makes the home use of methadone easier for patients because they have to take it less often than they would any of the

TABLE 3. Relative Potencies of Common Narcotics, and IM (Injectable) to PO (Oral) Dosage Ratio

Narcotic	IM dose (mg)	PO dose (mg)	Length of action
Morphine	10 mg	30–60 mg	3–4 hours
Hydromorphone	1 mg	6 mg	3–4 hours
Meperidine	75 mg	300 mg	3–4 hours
Codeine	130 mg	200 mg	3–4 hours
Methadone	10 mg	20 mg	6–8 hours

other narcotics. However, the longer half-life of methadone means that the dosage must be increased more slowly than the other drugs because a rapid increase can result in respiratory depression.

As previously mentioned, chronic severe pain is best treated by the regular administration of drugs rather than the PRN system normally used in medical practice. A PRN regimen translates into a pain crisis, drug administration cycle during which the patient is either in severe pain or in a state of constant anxiety waiting for the next pain crisis to occur. On the other hand, patients on a regular regimen of narcotics given every three to four hours are almost invariably in better pain control, are clamer, and often require lower doses of medication. The old medical bugaboo of addiction is not relevant to these patients. Twycross, at the Fourth International Seminar on Terminal Care stated, "The use of [narcotics] should be dictated by the intensity of the pain, not the brevity of the prognosis. [Narcotics] exist to be given, not merely to be withheld." He further stated that "PRN in cancer patients [standardly] means 'pain relief negligable.'"[20]

As far as the route of drug administration is concerned, oral narcotics are just as effective as injectable medications provided two conditions are met: first, the drugs must be administered on a regular basis, and second, the dosage equivalencies shown in Table 3 must be taken into account.

Oral medications have the advantage of being easily administered at home, while the patient avoids the discomfort of constant injections. The major drawback to oral medications is the reluctance on the part of some physicians to prescribe what seems to them enormous amounts of narcotics, when in fact those dosages are adequate and necessary.

There are some side effects that occur when narcotics are used. For example, all patients receiving narcotics become constipated and some suffer from nausea in the beginning stages of this treatment. Therefore, all patients on narcotics should be routinely given stool softeners and mild laxatives. Needless to say, visiting nurses are most grateful to the physician who prescribes stool softeners regularly, rather than waiting for the inevitable fecal impaction to occur. Additionally, many patients need medication to reduce their nausea.

Pain is not a virtue and it does not, as some believe, build character. Uncontrolled pain causes only distress and suffering both for the patient and for the caregivers around him. Indeed, a patient's pain often drives these caregivers away. An example may serve to illustrate this point.

A consult was requested for a patient in the hospital who was demanding pain relief. He was diagnosed as having a brain tumor and his prognosis was terminal. His prescribed medication was inadequate to control his pain, and as a result of the constant discomfort, he was becoming increasingly unmanageable and agitated. The nurses on his unit, who had been very caring and supportive when the patient was cooperative and quiet, suddenly found themselves unable to handle the situation. They avoided the patient whenever possible and eventually requested that he be transferred to the psychiatric unit.

Pain that goes untreated or becomes uncontrollable affects not only the patients, but everyone around them as well. The pain inhibits the patients' ability to focus on anything outside of their own discomfort. It thereby displaces their relationships with the individuals around them and isolates them even more from the people who would otherwise share their final moments. Further, pain robs patients of the little control they retain over the remainder of their lives, and it reduces the quality of their remaining time to a level of fear and anxiety.

Addiction

At this point in the discussion of pain control, it becomes inevitable that the topic of addiction be discussed. Physicians are the first to question the use of large doses of narcotics in terminal patients for a number of reasons.

First, there are legal concerns that the Drug Enforcement Administration will step into a case where large amounts of narcotics are being prescribed. This fear is unfounded, since terminal illness with intractable pain is a valid indication for the large dosages. The DEA is much more concerned about the illicit use of drugs.

Second, physicians often try to postpone the use of narcotics as long as possible to "save them for the last moments when they will *really* be needed." In some instances the physicians are afraid that long-term use of a narcotic will reduce its effectiveness by increasing the patient's tolerance to the drug. In a study on the use of diamorphine over long periods of time, Twycross concluded that

> when used as part of a pattern of total care, diamorphine may be used for long periods without concern about tolerance. Moreover, although physical dependence

probably develops in most patients after several weeks of continuous treatment, this does not prevent the downward adjustment of dose if considered clinically feasible.[21]

These reasons aside, by far the most pressing concern among physicians is addiction. Nevertheless, experience with terminal patients has shown that those with no history of drug or alcohol addiction do not, by definition, become addicted when administered narcotics for pain relief.

At this point, we must define addiction. Addiction has three components and all must be present in order for an individual to be considered addicted to a particular substance.

Tolerance—the need for increasing doses of medication to get the same response. Some patients have virtually no limit to their tolerances to certain medications. Occasionally, very high doses of narcotics are required, but most often, dosages increase very slowly and may even be reduced when good pain control is achieved.

Physical Dependence—the need for the presence in the body of a particular drug in order to prevent an abstinence syndrome (withdrawal reaction). Sudden cessation of the drug causes this predictable withdrawal reaction. Patients who are on regular doses of narcotics over long intervals of time will experience an abstinence syndrome if the narcotic is *abruptly* discontinued. However, if the dosage is decreased gradually over a period of 7 to 14 days, no withdrawal reaction will take place. Any patient, therefore, can be tapered off a particular narcotic if that becomes necessary.

Psychological Dependence—the psychological desire to use a particular substance becomes so overwhelming that all goals and relationships are subordinated to the primary goal: obtaining the drug. The individual's time and energy, his life, in fact, are directed by the need to acquire the drug.

The real issue in addiction is neither tolerance nor physical dependence, but these two coupled with psychological dependence. This psychological dependence does *not* occur in patients who receive narcotics for pain control and who have no prior history of drug addiction.

Physicians who hear this lecture on pain control are dismayed and incredulous when told that, while patients may develop tolerance to, and physical dependence upon, a drug, those patients will not be truly addicted. They are then asked if they have had any patients with severe, uncontrollable cancer pain who have become drug addicts. Invariably, not one physician has seen any patients in this category.

We have been saying that pain patients who have no prior history of addiction do not become addicted. But there are some patients who do present a prior addictive history, and it is likely that these patients will become readdicted; moreover, they may require doses of narcotics that are higher than usual. Nevertheless, pain control in this circumstance is still a legitimate goal. Furthermore, detoxification from narcotics, even in these patients, is possible.

One of the questions that often arises from a discussion of narcotics and pain control is the place of such drugs as heroin, cocaine and marijuana. Heroin has no advantage over morphine in controlling pain, and it has a major disadvantage: it is illegal and it therefore requires close control and extremely tight security. Consequently, it is best to avoid its use altogether. In spite of its drawbacks, heroin's legalization for use in terminal patients was proposed by Senator Daniel Inouye of Hawaii. Most medical personnel, however, see no value in its legalization for pain control purposes.

Cocaine produces effects which are similar to those produced by potent amphetamines. Cocaine can cause agitation, confusion and paranoid reactions. It is a dangerous drug and has no place in pain control.

The use of marijuana is still in the experimental stage. Marijuana has the potential to cause hallucinations and psychoses. Much more research needs to be done before a determination of possible advantages can be made. In the meantime, it is recommended that the use of marijuana be avoided.

Treatment of Anxiety and Drepression

As mentioned previously, anxiety increases the perception of pain. The regular use of antianxiety agents in anxious patients can greatly enhance pain relief, and often reduces the dosage of narcotic needed for pain control.

Depression is common in seriously ill patients. These patients often evidence sleep disorders with early morning awakening, loss of interest and motivation, loss of appetite, poor self esteem, feelings of worthlessness, and multiple somatic symptoms that have no specific cause. Active use of antidepressant medication is extremely helpful in controlling the depression, with an attendant increase in the effectiveness of the pain control therapy.

Medically-oriented psychiatrists are the professionals who are most familiar with the use and effects of antidepressant and antianxiety drugs, particularly in combination with the various pain medications. It is vital, therefore, that hospice teams use psychiatric consultants in this area.

It is also extremely important that all of the people involved in patient care, including the doctors, nurses, family and the patients themselves, be educated in the correct use of medication for symptom control. Family members and patients, as well as professionals, labor under a great many misconceptions concerning the administration and effects of narcotic use. It is not uncommon to find the family withholding the narcotic prescribed by the physician because of fears of addiction. Education and continuing support, therefore, must be part of any comprehensive hospice program.

LEGAL AND ETHICAL ISSUES

The Right to Know

A major issue in hospice care is the right of patients to be told their diagnoses and prognoses in terms that they can reasonably be expected to understand.

Numerous research studies have shown that 90–95 percent of the people questioned would want to know the truth about their illnesses. It seems self-evident that the relationship between physician and patient should be based on nothing less than the truth and, in theory, this is the normally accepted standard of medical practice. In reality, however, this standard is often violated, particularly when the patient has a life-threatening or terminal illness. Unfortunately, a myriad of excuses is used by family members and physicians to conceal the truth from many terminally ill patients. These patients are thereby being deprived of their rights as living human beings.

One of the most frequently heard arguments against openness and honesty is based upon the supposed lack of will to know and the absence of medical sophistication of the patient. "He doesn't want to know, and anyway, he wouldn't understand even if it were explained to him."

The fact is that most people *do* want to know but are often initially ambivalent about asking for the truth. They are, in effect, postponing the time when they have to face the realities of the situation. This ambivalence is too often taken as a sign that patients never want to hear the truth, when all they really want is some time to adjust. Most people are able to grasp the salient facts of their illnesses if those facts are explained in language and style which are appropriate to their understanding. Furthermore, the patients alone can best comprehend the significance of their illnesses to themselves and their families.

The second argument against honesty speaks of the psychic trauma that will be suffered by patients who are told that they have a terminal illness. Some individuals, it is true, may not handle the truth well, and most will understandably react with depression, anger, denial and perhaps even suicide. Most of these patients, however, given time and understanding, will work through their feelings and eventually come to grips with them. Despite this, patients are not generally offered the opportunity or professional help to work through their feelings in order for them to reach some level of acceptance.

The explanation for the failure to be honest is obvious. The stated concern is the patient's feelings, but the true concern (albeit unconscious) is the emotional protection of the family members and the medical personnel involved. They are often the ones who are unable to handle the grief, feelings and emotions surrounding the illness as well as the honest communication with the terminally ill patient. If they "protect" the patient from the truth, they never have to face those uncomfortable feelings themselves.

The process of withholding the truth is a conspiracy of silence which develops between the physician and the family. The scenario goes something like this. The doctor, upon discovery of the nature of the diagnosis and prognosis, becomes uncomfortable about having to convey this information to the patient. He contacts the family and discusses the case with them before ever discussing it with the patient. The family, in turn, instructs the doctor not to divulge the truth to the patient, and while the physician feels that the family may not have the right to make this decision, he nonetheless feels obliged to honor their wishes.

None of this would take place if the normal pattern of physician-patient communication were followed. The truth would become an accomplished fact before any family involvement and a great deal of personal chaos would be avoided.

We have all heard the argument that it is cruel to remove all vestiges of hope from terminally ill patients by telling them the truth. But telling them the nature and seriousness of their illness is not the same as saying there is no hope. There is and should always be hope, however slim. Hope for a cure is only one type of hope. A person may also hope for extra time, for pain-free days, or for the opportunity to complete unfinished business. What is cruel is to allow a seriously ill individual to proceed with life as if nothing were wrong or different. It is crueler still to take away the preparations that the patient might make for death, preparations that include such practical matters as preparing a will and settling financial affairs, as well as the emotional preparations of settling familial accounts and saying good-byes.

Those who try to spare patients the agony of knowing they are going to die are creating for them an agony of another sort. Most terminally ill patients know, on some level, that they are dying. Often, because of others' reluctance to be honest, patients are put in the position of having to comfort their families and physicians when they should be receiving the comfort of others. They are being robbed of that solace to which they are entitled, and are left alone, dehumanized, and virtually untouchable.

No one is willing to talk to them about their illness or their feelings. The patients themselves will not initiate discussion of their feelings because they recognize the pain it causes in others. Ironically, patients wind up trying to protect their families and physicians from that pain. To add to their discomfort, some patients who have tried to discuss their feelings have experienced rejection by family members and friends who feel threatened by the situation. The patient who finds himself in this circumstance may then retreat from any honest exploration of feeling in order to avoid such rejection. For all of these reasons, many patients experience what Kalish describes as social death and are no longer accorded the legal and human rights of the living.[22]

For the terminal patient, the very act of dying makes him the loneliest person in the world. Even the most caring family member or health professional can never totally share or understand the patient's feelings. When, in addition to this isolation, there is an impenetrable barrier of lies or half-truths spoken in the name of kindness and love, the patient's loneliness and isolation are unbearably magnified.

Patients should, therefore, have the right to exercise control over medical decisions that affect them. In order to be able to participate in such decisions, patients need complete and accurate information, total honesty, and an atmosphere free of coercion. Patients should be encouraged to exercise these rights and to participate in medical decisions with the guidance, support and expertise of the medical community.

All patients have the right to know what is happening to their bodies. They should be told of their diagnoses and the way in which those diagnoses were determined. They should have access to their medical records and help in interpreting what is contained in them. They should be apprised of all the known and medically accepted forms of treatment, along with the risks and benefits of each. They should be free to seek as many other opinions as they wish. Above all, patients should have the right to participate in the medically accepted treatment of their choice, or to refuse to participate in a treatment regimen altogether.

We must also accept the fact that there are some patients who truly do not want to know about their illnesses and who wish to have all medical decisions taken out of their hands. These patients should have the right not to participate in their medical treatment decisions if that is their choice.

It should also be mentioned at this point that there are patients who express a desire to be fully informed and then use various forms and levels of denial about their illnesses. Physicians who try to be open with these patients may be confronted with anxiety, depression and anger, both from the patients and from their families.

The manner in which the information is transmitted, therefore, is extremely important, and involves a complex series of verbal and nonverbal clues from the patient. He usually sets the pace and sends out signals about how much he wants to know. This kind of give and take approach presupposes that the physician will spend some concentrated time with the patient in order to develop a personal and comfortable working relationship. It requires the medical staff members' willingness to tell the truth while respecting denial, to answer questions while not forcing the issue, and to be available when the patient is ready to face the truth. The patient must determine the level of openness and awareness.

This last concept is particularly important, as the following case example illustrates:

A psychiatric consult was ordered for Mrs. A., a middle-aged woman whose ovarian cancer had metastisized. She had had a colostomy, and had received radiation and chemotherapy. She had lost weight, had a poor appetite and was depressed.

When the psychiatrist introduced himself and asked her what was wrong with her, she replied that she was in the hospital because she was run-down and needed to gain weight. She denied any serious illness and even denied having had surgery.

The psychiatrist checked the chart to see if he had the correct patient. When he satisfied himself that this was indeed the patient on whom a consult had been requested, he questioned her once again about her hospitalization. She continued to deny all the facts of her illness, but did admit to having sleep difficulties and a poor appetite. She seemed eager to continue the psychiatric visits and stated that she was willing to take antidepressant medication when that course was suggested.

The psychiatrist visited each day and asked Mrs. A. how she was feeling, while encouraging her to discuss any concerns she might have. She continued to talk mostly of innocuous matters and still complained of a poor appetite. As she felt more comfortable with the psychiatric visits, she began to talk of wanting to go home.

Finally, on the sixth day, she said there was something she wanted to discuss. She stated, matter of factly, that she was dying of cancer, and knew that she had run the gamut of treatments including surgery, chemotherapy, and radiation. She knew, also, that her depressed appetite and weight loss were a result of her illness.

Mrs. A. went on to say that she had had a good life with her husband and now wanted to go home with him, to die in her own house. But, she said, her husband and her doctor could not accept that decision. Instead, they insisted that the only way she could go home would be to gain weight and "get well."

Her denial of her illness had been her attempt to prove that she was well enough to be allowed to go home to die. When Mrs. A.'s wishes were discussed with her husband and her physician, they were helped to work through their own denial, and they came to accept and respect Mrs. A.'s desire to die in familiar and comfortable surroundings.

This case illustrates the very complex issues surrounding the care of terminally ill patients and their families.

LEGAL QUESTIONS

Many legal questions, most of them as yet unanswered, have arisen in connection with hospice programs. Perhaps the most pervasive legal quandary concerns the cessation of medical treatment which, if allowed to continue, would prolong death rather than prolong life.

Harold Schmeck, in an article in *The New York Times,* stated that "the timing of death [has become] a matter of deliberate choice," a situation which has caused the "blurring [of] vital distinctions between natural death, euthanasia and suicide."[23]

These distinctions have not yet been codified into law in any rational and consistent manner, leaving medical personnel to make judgments based not necessarily on what is in the best interests of the patients, but on what actions are liable to civil and criminal prosecution.

> Prolonging the lives of certain terminally ill patients by [technological] means may at a certain point become incompatible with consideration of the quality of life remaining to them. Such prolongation may, in fact, considerably lessen the quality of the remaining period of life.[24]

Yet, "a good proportion of the medical profession and of hospital personnel are in the unfortunate position of not knowing the precise content of their legal duties" with respect to the cessation of treatment.[25]

Just as most people wish to be told the truth, most people also profess the wish not to be kept alive by artificial means when meaningful life has gone. In addition, most patients want to be part of the medical decision making process in order to assure that their wishes will be carried out. Therefore, patients should have the right to refuse treatment, and to demand that no extraordinary procedures be used to sustain their lives. They should have the right to die an "appropriate death," a term used by Avery Weisman to describe the death that each person would wish for himself, one in which he can retain his humanity and dignity.[26]

In terminal illness, doctors must deal daily with "what protocols must be followed if extraordinary treatments are not to be used or if ordinary treatments are to be discontinued. . . . There are no guidelines with the force of law that protect the physician. Technically, every time a physician decides not to resuscitate, not to treat pneumonia, or not to operate on a hopelessly ill patient, he could be charged with murder."[27]

And, indeed, two physicians in California were charged with and prosecuted for murder as a result of disconnecting a hopelessly comatose patient from life support systems. Although an appeals court dismissed the charges, the prosecution is planning to pursue the case through other avenues. At this moment, no clear-cut guideline has emerged from this case.

Even when a patient has signed a living will which specifies that he does not wish to be kept alive by extraordinary technical procedures, physicians who withhold those procedures may be liable for prosecution for neglect, and possibly, for murder. Fortunately, some states have passed or are in the process of writing legislation which makes provisions for a patient's wish to refuse extraordinary treatment measures. In addition, the Veterans Administration hospital system has adopted a new policy respecting patients' requests for "voluntary passive euthanasia." This means that a patient can ask that his life not be prolonged, and is similar in concept to the living will. These developments notwithstanding, social and legal policy is a quagmire of contradictions and has yet to catch up with science and technology in this area.

Another problem that comes out of the controversy over the cessation of treatment arises when the physicians feel that treatment should be terminated, but the family wants it to continue. This usually takes place with a patient who has never been competent or with a patient who was formerly competent and is now confused or comatose.

Ordinarily, the patients are the final decision makers and the choice to continue or discontinue treatment must be theirs. But, if patients are unable to make a decision, then the families must step in, assume guardianship, and decide whether or not to discontinue treatment based on either what they know the patients would want or what they feel is in the patients' best interests. If the doctors and family cannot agree on a course of treatment, or if the family members are in dispute over the decision, then the courts may have to assume the decision-making role.

Further upheavals will be felt in the not-too-distant future when choices of this kind may be made on the basis of the best and most judicious use of limited medical resources. It is possible to envision a time when, through the mechanism of funding, the government will intervene to make the determination of the cessation of treatment.

Lawmakers in this country need to write clear and specific requirements which govern the termination of life support, and the withholding of life sustaining treatment. They might be guided by the following recommendations from the Law Reform Commission of Canada concerning the cessation of treatment. These are valid and useful guidelines for those who treat terminally ill patients. The uniform adoption of these or similar precepts would go a long way in clarifying the roles and responsibilities of all those who are involved in patient care.

1. The law should recognize the competent patient's wishes and respect them as regards the cessation or non-initiation of treatment.
2. The law should clearly state that a physician acts legally when he decides to terminate or not initiate treatment which is useless or which no longer offers reasonable hope, unless the patient has expressed his wishes to the contrary.
3. The law should recognize that the prolonging of life is not an absolute value in itself and that therefore a physician does not act illegally when he fails to take measures to achieve this end, if these measures are useless or contrary to the patient's wishes or interests.
4. The law should recognize that a physician who continues to treat a patient against his wishes is subject to the provisions of the Criminal Code [Canada].
5. The law should recognize that the incapacity of a person to express his wishes is not sufficient a reason to oblige a physician to administer useless treatment for the purpose of prolonging his life.

6. The law should recognize that in the case of an unconscious or incompetent patient, a physician incurs no criminal responsibility by terminating treatment which has become useless.[28]

A second legal issue has arisen over the patient's right to knowledge concerning his diagnosis and prognosis. While we have previously described this as a human and moral right, we now approach it as a legal right. Although most medical practitioners and laymen alike would agree that openness and honesty are extremely important to the doctor-patient relationship, they would also agree that some patients, if told of a terminal illness, might act in an irrational and precipitous manner. Could a physician, for example, be held liable if a patient commits suicide upon learning the truth of his diagnosis?

The other side of the coin is the patient from whom the truth is withheld. An example of this situation is Mr. S., a successful businessman whose physician diagnosed cancer with an average life expectancy of six to twelve months. Mr. S.'s family insisted that he not be told the truth of his condition. His doctor told him that his condition was not serious and that it was treatable. Feeling like a man with a new lease on life, Mr. S. plunged into his work and, within a week, signed a million-dollar long-term business contract. Of course, he agreed to the deal in good faith, but he would never have accepted a financial obligation of that magnitude had he known the true nature of his illness. When he died shortly afterward, he left his business in debt and his family's finances in jeopardy.

The legal consequences of this type of situation, it would seem, are innumerable. If, for example, Mr. S. accidently found out about his condition, could he then hold the physician liable for not having been honest with him? And if he does not find out and acts upon the false information that he is given, can he or his survivors hold the physician responsible for the consequences of those actions? There are no consistent rules or laws to cover these contingencies. In the current climate of patients demanding their rights as medical consumers, it will probably not be long before test cases will be brought in these areas.

Another legal question arises in the area of pain control. In order to achieve pain relief in some patients with severe pain, the dosage of medications used may approach a level of lethal toxicity. In trying to achieve pain control, a physician may conceivably and unwittingly reduce a patient's life expectancy. Cancer patients, especially, react in unpredictable ways to certain drugs because, as a result of the disease process, their organs do not always function in expected ways. This can result in side effects which may diminish the patient's longevity, or it can result in a lethal overdose causing respiratory failure and death. Once again, civil and criminal liability in this instance are a matter of speculation rather than law.

A fourth question of liability has come about because of the new

Medicare regulations governing reimbursement for hospice care. One problem is that the regulations seem to treat hospice volunteers as employees, for purposes of determining the cost of hospice care. If, in fact, volunteers are considered employees, are the hospices for which they work liable for their actions? Will the hospices have to insure their volunteers or will the volunteers themselves have to carry some sort of liability or "malpractice" insurance?

Another problem is the Medicare requirement that the terminal patient choose between regular Medicare benefits and hospice care. If the patient opts for hospice care, expenses for certain treatments may not be covered, even though those treatments may be indicated for palliative therapy. In addition, the regulations do not presently provide for a mentally incompetent or unconscious patient to gain access to hospice care. These rules and regulations must be further refined to give all terminally ill patients the option of using hospice care should they so desire.

Finally, the issue of pronouncing death, while not necessarily a major concern in hospice care, is nevertheless a source of anguish and frustration to those families whose relative dies at home. It is no exaggeration to state that thousands of patients are now choosing home hospice care instead of institutional care. Most of these patients will die at home after prolonged illness. In most states, only a physician is permitted to certify death, and a funeral home cannot remove the body until that certification is made. Unfortunately, this process sometimes involves delays of hours while the family awaits the physician's visit to pronounce the patient dead.

New Jersey has recently adopted a rule which allows nurses to certify death so that the body may be removed from the house. This is a sensible and rational approach, since increasing numbers of terminal patients will undoubtedly choose to remain at home and be cared for under the supervision of those very same nurses. It is hoped that other states will follow New Jersey's lead in this area.

All of the legal questions that have arisen from the advent of hospice care have caused physicians to hesitate in their treatment decisions for terminal patients. These unsettled issues may, in the future, encourage less than ideal medical care because of the ambiguity of the legal response. Although this has by no means been an exhaustive review of the legal implications of hospice care, it has become clear that legal guidelines must be established which take into account the current state-of-the-art medical technology as well as the current social thinking regarding care for the terminally ill.

REFERENCES

1. Kastenbaum, Richard, and Ruth Aisenberg. 1976. *The Psychology of Death.* New York: Springer, 38.

2. Kalish, Richard. 1981. *Death, Grief, and Caring Relationships.* Monterey, California: Brooks/Cole, 87.
3. Kastenbaum, 395.
4. *Ibid.,* 144–159.
5. *Ibid.,* 160.
6. *Ibid.,* 40.
7. *Ibid.,* 44.
8. *Ibid.,* 94.
9. 1983. "Proposed Rules and Funding Requirements for Hospice Care." *Federal Register* 48 (August 22). Washington, D.C.: U.S. Government Printing Office, 38146–38175.
10. Anspaugh, David J. 1978. "Hospice: Advocate for the Dying." *Health Education* 9(Nov.-Dec.):3.
11. Stoddard, Sandol. 1978. *The Hospice Movement.* New York: Vintage, 219.
12. Luxton, R.W. 1979. "The Modern Hospice and Its Challenge to Medicine." *British Medical Journal* 2(Sept.):583.
13. Dubois, Paul M. 1980. *The Hospice Way of Death.* New York: Human Sciences Press, 65–66.
14. Cohen, Kenneth P. 1979. *Hospice, Prescription for Terminal Care.* Germantown, Maryland: Aspen Systems.
15. *Ibid.,* 93.
16. *Ibid.,* 97.
17. Ajenian, Ina, and Balfour M. Mount, eds. 1982. *The Royal Victoria Hospital Manual of Palliative Hospice Care.* Salem, New Hampshire: The Ayer Company, 20.
18. Lewis, Richard. 1983. "MDs Urged to Alter Prescribing Patterns for Dying Cancer Patients in Pain." *AMA News* 26(Feb. 18):1–2.
19. Bonica, John. 1982. "Cancer Pain." In *The Royal Victoria Hospital Manual on Palliative Hospice Care.* Salem, New Hampshire: The Ayer Company, 113–128.
20. Twycross, Robert G. 1982. "Principles and Practice of Pain Relief in Terminal Cancer." Presented at the Fourth International Seminar on Terminal Care, Montreal, October 4–6.
21. *Ibid.*
22. Kalish, *Death, Grief and Caring Relationships.*
23. Schmeck, Harold M. 1983. "Should Life Always Be Prolonged?" *New York Times* 28(June):C2.
24. Law Reform Commission of Canada. 1982. *Protection of Life: Euthanasia, Aiding Suicide and Cessation of Treatment.* Montreal: Minister of Supply and Services, 5.
25. *Ibid.,* 8.
26. Weisman, Avery. 1972. *On Dying and Denying.* New York: Behavioral Publications.
27. Breo, Dennis L., Doug Lefton, and Mark E. Rust. 1983. "For Terminating Treatment: MDs Face Unprecedented Murder Charge." *AMA News* 16(Sept.):20.
28. Law Reform Commission. *Protection of Life,* 65–66.

Physician in a Hospital Setting

Jerry Zaslow, M.D., J.D.

Most physicians and hospitals have a mutual need for each other. Since the common denominator is the care of patients, one needing a place to administer the care and the other supplying the facilities, it would appear that they would work in close harmony with each other and do what they could to enhance the efforts of both. Historically, this was true; each depended on the other to provide what each was best able to do. However, as time has passed and conditions have changed, various adversary relationships have developed among physicians themselves and between hospitals and physicians.

During the early part of the 1900s, the physicians and hospitals were autonomous in their separate spheres, each needing the other to exist and prosper. The hospital did not interfere in any way with the manner in which physicians practiced their profession, and the only question was whether or not the hospital would supply certain specific items that physicians desired. Since hospitals were protected by charitable immunity, acts of alleged negligence could not involve them financially and there was no need to monitor physicians' practices. The only conflicts that existed were between physicians themselves. This included keeping applicants to a hospital staff from becoming members of the staff, either because they were representative of a different approach to patient care (osteopathic versus allopathic) or for economic reasons. While the former was upheld by the courts,[1] the latter was never given as the true reason. Staff privileges were restricted because of insufficient facilities or other noncompetitive elements.[2]

In the 1950s, the Joint Commission of Accreditation was formed for the purpose of helping hospitals enhance the manner in which they delivered medical care. Among other things, it emphasized the importance of the bylaws of both the medical staff and the hospital in delineating the structure and duties of both. The landmark decision of Bing v. Thunig[3] proclaimed that a hospital was in the business of delivering health care and ruled that a hospital could be liable for the acts of its employees. Gradually over the next decade many jurisdictions judicially abolished hospital immunity, so that hospitals could be sued and be held liable in money damages for patients injured within their facilities. This naturally led to the hospital administration's taking an active part in monitoring the activities within it and instituting measures to decrease the incidence of those acts which could make it liable. When the Illinois Supreme Court, in its landmark decision in Darling v. Charleston Memorial Hospital[4] found that a hospital could be held directly liable for failing to follow its own bylaws in not reviewing the activities of its medical staff, impetus was given to the already developing attitude that the Governing Board of a hospital was not only to furnish the hospital facilities necessary to deliver medical care, but also to see that those rendering care within it, either employees or independent contractors, were doing so in a nonnegligent manner. More recently, judicial decisions utilizing the theory of ostensible or apparent authority have held hospitals liable for many of the negligent acts of independent contractors working within it.[5] All of the foregoing events have given the Governing Board of a hospital reason for it to exert its authority in whatever manner it feels would be helpful to the hospital, whether or not the medical staff necessarily agrees with the actions.

CONFLICTS BETWEEN PHYSICIANS

A principal area of conflict between physicians today, as was true in the past, concerns staff privileges. There is generally no problem when a physician in general practice, family practice, or the general practice of internal medicine applies to a hospital staff. This is welcomed both by physicians already on the medical staff and the hospital administrator. This is because both benefit from a large and active medical staff—the hospital benefits by maintaining a high patient census; the physicians, particularly specialists, by having patients referred to them for consultation. So long as the applicant's credentials indicate that he or she has graduated from an approved medical school, is properly licensed, and is apparently morally and ethically acceptable, no obstacle exists to the appointment.

The problem arises when various specialists, particularly in the surgical specialties, apply for hospital staff privileges. There is an extensive list of cases where judicial relief has been requested because of failure of a hospital to grant privileges. Generally, courts will not interfere with a decision by a hospital not to appoint a physician to its medical staff where the decision is neither arbitrary nor capricious, and is based upon reasonable grounds.[2] The reason usually relied upon has been that such appointments will interfere with the smooth and efficient delivery of medical care, and is supported by factual evidence that facilities are already fully employed and any additional burden upon them will prove detrimental. While this may be true in some circumstances, more often the true reason is that those on the medical staff wish to preserve what they already have. Most surgical (and some medical) specialists rely to a great degree on referred work from other members of the medical staff. When the number of specialists increases, it follows that the number of cases referred to each individual may decrease, since the feeding-pool is limited by a fixed number of patients in the hospital. While some have attempted to utilize either federal or state antitrust laws to gain hospital admission (or to seek damages), almost invariably they have failed. The evidence needed to prove a violation of antitrust laws must be convincing, is extremely difficult to collect, and is costly and time-consuming. Although a physician may prevail in gaining hospital staff privileges after a court battle, it may only be self-destructive to the physician, since, being granted such privileges, he or she may be looked upon as an outsider and interloper by other members of the staff, and referrals, being voluntary on the part of a physician, may not be given to the physician. Although the battle may be won, the war is lost.

Another conflict between physicians arises when a physician, already on the medical staff, is removed from the staff. The action usually arises because of the claim by one or more physicians that another is not meeting the acceptable medical standards of care or that he or she is a disruptive influence on the smooth and efficient operation of the hospital. The affected physician is entitled to all the rights afforded him or her by the bylaws of the medical staff and hospital, including appeals. Only after the physician has an adverse decision after all the proceedings have been completed can he or she avail himself or herself of recourse to the courts. The likelihood of prevailing in a court action is remote if the adverse decision is based upon reasonable grounds, and is neither capricious nor arbitrary.

All physicians who are either denied staff privileges or have them revoked or restricted in any way feel that they have a valid action in defamation against those who acted against their interests. It is readily appreciated why they should feel this way—physicians' training and experience lead them to believe that what they do is their right—a right to treat patients as they alone feel is in their patients' best interests. Any attack upon this premise should be grounds for a libel or slander action. However, such actions rarely prevail for the following reasons. In most jurisdictions, in the absence of actual malice, a qualified privilege does exist whereby even defamatory statements are not actionable when they are made for a proper purpose, in a proper manner, and under the proper circumstances. When a physician alleges that remarks made about him or her during a peer-review investigation are defamatory, in most jurisdictions the one making the remarks is further protected by statute, unless actual malice can be demonstrated. By definition, actual malice exists when one making a defamatory statement knows it is false or makes the statement with total disregard as to whether it is true or false. This is most difficult to prove.

CONFLICTS BETWEEN HOSPITAL AND PHYSICIAN

Since a hospital may be held both vicariously and directly liable for negligent acts which occur within it, it has taken an active part in preventing such acts from occurring. In order to ensure some system of actively controlling both the occurrence of tortious acts and their recurrence, hospitals have instituted various forms of "risk control." While these are designed only for the protection of patients, and should also benefit both the hospital and the physician, many physicians feel that this is only another step in the regulation of practice. Many aspects of risk control do oversee what the physician is doing and the manner in which it is done. Any deviation from an accepted protocol is brought to the attention of the physician, and generally all such incidents are kept on record in the physician's file. While the purpose of the program is meritorious, whenever any restrictive measures are placed upon physicians, and while they may acquiesce in observing them, their emotional reaction to them is generally negative. Since risk control programs are all-pervasive, every aspect of medical care being included—drugs ordered, drug dosage, frequency of studies when certain drugs are employed, various controls in the operating suites, among other things—the physicians inevitably feel that they no longer have the discretion in patient care that they once had. It is almost as if they are only small cogs in the wheel of medical care delivery. While an open confrontation between staff and hospital does not develop from such a rigid program, a feeling of antagonism does exist and grow within the physicians toward the hospital and the administrators who implement the regulations.

A more intense antagonism between the hospital and physicians arises as a result of alleged overutilization practices. A hospital, on its own initiative, does not order studies, admit patients to hospitals, or discharge them. All of these acts must be performed by physicians. In all hospitals an ongoing utilization review is operative, and it is concurrent with the patient's hospital stay. This is directly overviewed by Professional Standards Review Organization (PSRO) in hospitals which are not delegated to conduct their own reviews for patients whose hospital stay is covered by various government programs (Medicare, Medicaid, etc.) and by investigators of the various Blue Cross Plans for its own insureds. The purpose of the overview is to ensure that patients are admitted only for necessary medical care and that their hospital stay is no longer than necessary, as determined by medical standards. Custodial care is not covered under any insurance plan, and when a lesser medical care facility is indicated, hospitalization should be discontinued and transfer to the lesser care facility effected. When a denial of length of stay is made by the carrier or the insurer, it is the hospital who is asked to reimburse the insurer for payments already made to it. Therefore, it becomes a priority item for the hospital to monitor the hospital stay in such a way as to avoid having too many denials. At the present time, if a retrospective audit reveals a denial rate below a certain fixed number, the carrier for governmental programs does not monitor each case concurrently with the hospital stay. However, if the denial rate exceeds that number, the carrier will no longer automatically pay for all its insureds' admissions and then review the utilization pattern, but it will concurrently review each admission. When this occurs, it is likely that the denial rate will increase, resulting in a loss of revenue for the hospital. It must be recognized that it is to the economic benefit of the hospital to maintain a high census and for the physicians to keep their patients in the hospital as long as possible. While these would be compatible if the patient paid his own bills, when a third party pays the bills for hospitalization and denies any hospital day that is not medically necessary, a conflict may arise. This is due to the fact that the hospital must monitor the hospital stay and question the physician when it appears to whomever is reviewing the case that a transfer or discharge from the facility is in order. Once again the question of the physician's judgment as to the care rendered to the patient arises. A related issue exists when the patient is to be discharged, but is not prepared for care at home and must first go to a nursing home or convalescent facility. The problem should not arise if the physician considers this possibility during the hospital stay. Most hospitals have active social services departments whose function it is to make arrangements for transfer to lesser care facilities or for nursing care and other services at home. If the social service department is notified early during the hospital stay, by the time of discharge the necessary arrangements are completed. However, failure of the physician to keep others informed as to the need for such transfer, and as to the time of the transfer, frequently results in a patient's remaining in the hospital for many days when hospital care is no longer necessary, leading to a denial of payment by the third party payor. This, in turn, leads to a notification to the physician to be more concerned with length of hospital stay, to the annoyance of the physician.

An interesting question arises as to whether a hospital, being denied payment for hospital days, should seek reimbursement from either the physician or the patient. It would appear that if a hospital were to proceed against a patient, the latter's defense would be that he or she acted on the advice of the physician and that any recourse should be against the physician, and would probably join the physician if legal action is initiated. While the hospital may not desire to antagonize the physician by bringing an action directly against him, the end result would be the same—the physician is involved in a lawsuit asking for restitution to the hospital for the amount of the undenied hospital stay. This would undoubtedly further fan the fires of antagonism toward the hospital. A hospital depends upon its medical staff to maintain a reasonable hospital census, and if physicians leave the hospital and go to others, eventually the hospital will suffer.

There is truly no need for this situation to arise. The physicians must realize that, since we are in a third-party payor society, all must be alert to measures which will provide medical care only when it is necessary and not to be wasteful of limited resources. The hospital and physician must cooperate fully in this, lest both suffer.

A recent development in hospitals has been that of specialized services in the hospital where only a limited number of physicians may be active, excluding other members of the medical staff. This is exemplified by restricting the use of coronary care units and intensive care units to selected physicians on the medical staff. When a general practitioner or a family practice physician is caring for patients in the general areas of the hospital and an emergency arises, necessitating the transfer of the patient to the CCU or ICU, the family practitioner, no longer permitted to care for the patients in the unit, feels that the hospital is interfering with the physician-patient relationship. This leads to a feeling of antagonism toward the administration and those physicians now caring for the patient in the unit. The reason for the rule is that the hospital, in attempting to reduce its medical malpractice liability, is ensuring that the patient in its facility will get the best possible care by specialists in the field at issue. Many hospitals have attempted to resolve the problem by allowing the patient to remain on the family practitioner's service, but demanding that consultants be called in to oversee the patient's order and progress. This obviously increases the cost of medical care, with at least two physicians caring for the patient, instead of one. While increasing the cost, it has placated the family physician. However, this compromise may not last indefinitely when the third-party payor, if there is one, questions the need for multiple-physician care under the circumstances. The insurer will pay for one, not two, physicians. If payment is made only to the specialist, the family practitioner will again raise his voice in protest. While the only bargaining tool the family practitioner has is his ability to admit patients to the hospital, it is a powerful one, since the physician, dissatisfied with the rules in the hospital, may seek another one with less rigid rules. Of course, if there is no such recourse, legal action is the last resort. The likelihood of the family practitioner's prevailing is by no means guaranteed, in view of the arguments offered by the hospital—its desire to ensure the best possible medical care available.

A hospital has always had concession-type services in its facilities—x-ray diagnosis and treatment, laboratory facilities, and the like. More recently this has been expanded to include other services such as nephrology, cardiac angiography, insertion of pace-makers, insertion of cardiac catheters, and noninvasive vascular laboratories. Generally, these have not been contested by members of the medical staff, since their purpose has been to enhance medical care and have not interfered with the physician-patient relationship, since these services can, in fact, be performed only by those specially trained in their performance. The only problem that has arisen in these areas has been when a physician, trained and experienced in those techniques, wishes to perform them upon their own patients or patients referred to them in the Special Areas designated. An example of this situation was present in Adler v. Montefiore Hospital, wherein the Supreme Court of Pennsylvania found that the hospital could exclude all but one physician from doing cardiac catheterizations to promote efficiency of use of its facilities, to foster a good teaching program, and to render the best services to patients in the unit.[6] Similar rulings have involved other facilities in the past.[7]

One concession-type service which could produce problems is the emergency room. In the recent past, when staff physicians were on emergency room service on a rotating basis in a hospital, they frequently could admit patients to their own service if they were requested by the patient to do so, or if the patient was unassigned. However, more and more hospitals are utilizing the service of emergency room physicians who contract to use the unit on a fulltime basis, to the exclusion of any other individual working in the unit. If the contractual arrangement between the hospital and the physicians working in the emergency room permits them admitting privileges to the hospital, a real problem could, and would, arise. This became apparent at an early date, and when emergency-room physician groups now contract with a hospital, the physicians do become members of the staff and are subject to the bylaws and rules and regulations of the medical staff, but are denied admitting and treating privileges. All their activities must be confined to the emergency room. Fortunately, with the rapid development of the specialty of emergency medicine, those physicians are quite content to confine their activities to the emergency room, avoiding conflict with other members of the medical staff.

A very recent problem between medical staff and administration has arisen with the development of the Health Maintenance Organizations (HMOs). Physicians who are philosophically opposed to the HMO concept and endorse and practice on a fee-for-service basis have voiced strong opposition to the admission to the medical staff of those physicians practicing in HMOs. This raises a problem for the hospital administration. In order to ensure a high bed occupancy, and with the number of HMOs and other similar plans growing in number in many areas, hospitals are contracting with the HMOs, encouraging them to admit patients to their facilities.

Needless to say, the physicians practicing with the HMO are anxious to continue the physician-patient relationships previously developed when the patient is hospitalized, and therefore staff privileges are a necessity. Not willing to antagonize either side, administrators do what they can to convince the opposing members of the staff that the presence of the HMO physicians will not interfere with their own practices, but this is not always successful. Administrators can only rely on the medical staff bylaws to support their position, since all applicants to most hospitals, be they public or private, must be given a reason for their being denied a staff appointment, and the reason must not be capricious or arbitrary. While this may not satisfy the strong feelings of the anti-HMO physicians, and results in some becoming inactive and going to other hospitals, the likelihood that other hospitals will behave differently is small, since, as the HMO concept gains broader acceptance, particularly in the present economic climate, more and more hospitals will contract with HMOs in order to compete with other hospitals for the patient population.

A far more serious situation which is already with us and will continue to grow concerns the fact that hospitals, in greater numbers, are becoming actively involved in the practice of medicine, and not merely in supplying facilities for the use of independent-contractor physicians. The reason for this is economic. In order to augment the revenue of the hospital with additional income, the most direct means is to offer the medical care as well as the facilities. This is done by employing physicians on a fulltime basis. While this has been common in teaching hospitals, others are now engaging in the practice, and more physicians than ever before are willing to contract with them. Obviously, if all physicians were not receptive to the concept, the hospitals would be unable to attain their objective. However, many factors have helped the hospitals in their endeavors. Young graduates today are willing to work in and for a hospital and be relieved of the uncertainty of private practice with all the problems involved—paying for increasing and, in some cases, almost confiscatory malpractice insurance premiums, being concerned with all the regulations involved in current-day private practice, and being concerned with the business portion of private practice (maintaining an office, paying secretarial and professional help, and the other time-consuming activities of private practice). Instead, the physicians are assured a steady income and their only concern is patient care. When they become fulltime hospital employees, they do come into direct conflict with the independent-contractor physicians, since both are competing for the same patient population. While there is no conflict where employee-physicians are offering special services, there is when they offer the same service as all others. Since nonemployee family physicians will generally not refer patients to employees if they have a choice between the two, the hospital must get a patient population that will use the hospital-employed physicians. This can be accomplished by setting up clinics which are entirely staffed by hospital-employed family-practice physicians, who in turn then refer to the hospital-based physicians when a patient requires hospitalization. This is occurring more commonly, not only in inner-city hospitals of large urban areas, but also in hospitals out of the inner-city and in more rural areas. The conflict that arises from the hospital's engaging in the practice of medicine is enhanced by the fact that as this is occurring, in order for the hospital to succeed in its efforts, medical staff bylaw changes are being made wherein the structure of the Medical Executive Committee, by far the most important single committe of the medical staff, contains more and more hospital-employed physicians (in some instances, outnumbering the nonemployed ones). It is interesting to observe that, while changes in the bylaws may not occur without medical staff approval, and in spite of the fact that many among the staff indicate dissatisfaction, the changes do occur. This is only the result of the fact that, while a physician may not welcome the change, and even voice his displeasure, he either supports it grudgingly or fails to vote at all; and, as more physicians become hospital-employed or hospital-based, their aggregate vote becomes more effective. The fact must be accepted that this change is occurring and will have a decided effect on the way medicine will be practiced in the future.

To offset this development, many physicians have formed so-called voluntary staff associations consisting of those physicians who are not hospital-employed, but use the hospital facilities for the care of their patients. It is hoped that with a single objective and one voice they can exert pressure upon the hospital to ensure that their activities in the hospital will not be curtailed. Undoubtedly, if all nonemployed physicians would join such an association and actively support it in its dealings with the hospital administration, its efforts would be successful. However, the only ones who give total support to it are the specialists whose economic well-being is dependent upon referrals from generalists. The general, or family, practitioner is not dependent upon referrals from other physicians, and he is less inclined to become involved in the efforts of the voluntary association, since he believes he has nothing to gain from such an association and that his position and activities on the hospital staff are assured. This is obviously true, since the hospital welcomes those patients he admits to the hospitals and has nothing to gain by antagonizing the physicians who insure bed occupancy. The urgency of the situation is not apparent to the generalist, and he is too preoccupied caring for his patients both in and out of the hospital to exert his efforts and time in unprofitable endeavors. On the other hand, the specialist has much to lose. As more specialists become hospital-employed, the competition for cases becomes more acute. The patient pool from which such cases come is divided among a greater and greater number of specialists, to the economic detriment of those who are practicing independently. Fortunately for the independent specialists, the hospitals do need them at the present time. There are not, at this time, sufficient hospital-employed specialists to care for all of the patient population, and the position of the independents is secure. This is not to conclude that the situation will not change. As already discussed, more recent graduates are not reluctant to become hospital-employed, and, as time passes, more of the medical staff will consist of employed physicians. This must inevitably affect the way the independent practices—he no longer has a monopoly and he must be competitive to survive. What effect our national and local economic problems will have upon how rapidly this phenomenon develops no one can foretell with any degree of accuracy, but changes will occur because of the social revolution and the pressure put upon our social security system at the present time and in the foreseeable future. As long as Medicare and other third-party payors are with us, they will have an impact on the way medical care is delivered and how much will be paid for the medical care, directly affecting physicians and hospitals in their relationships with each other.

CONCLUSION

The many problems discussed will not abate unless they are recognized as existing and active measures are undertaken to resolve them. The state of the art of medical practice will continue to improve, but it does not follow that the practitioners of the art will fare well.

Physicians must recognize that once they have become members of a medical staff they should not actively try to keep others out in order to limit the size of the staff. It is to the benefit of all that every competent physician have the opportunity to develop himself in a hospital environment if he so chooses, or if the hospital is the only place where he can practice his specialty. In addition, freedom of choice by the physician should be paramount in the dealings with him. If he wishes to work independently or to be employed by a hospital, he should be encouraged to do so.

The independent and the physician employed by a hospital can work together. There is room for both in our complex hospital society, and each must realize the problems of others and attempt to accommodate them and help to resolve them.

Neither hospitals nor physicians can exist or operate without one another. Each plays a unique role in the health-delivery system. The hospitals do have problems in dealing with the third-party payors, and they must comply with the various regulations that have been promulgated. Physicians should be made aware of them and they will do all they can to aid the hospitals in following the regulations. Problems do arise when physicians are told what they must do without being told why. Much of the misunderstanding and antagonism that has arisen, and will continue to grow, is due to the manner in which hospitals communicate with physicians. Instead of relying on memoranda through the mail and direct communication only with department chairmen, direct communication with *all* active members of the staff must be instituted. When the problems confronting hospitals are presented to physicians, the latter will do what they can to aid the hospital, since the physicians are aware of the fact that the hospitals' well-being is in their, and their patients', best interests.

REFERENCES

1. Hayman v. City of Galveston, 273 U.S. 410, 47 S. Ct. 363.
2. Guerrero v. Burlington County Hospital, 36 A.2d. 334; Garrow v. Elizabeth General Hospital, 401 A.2d. 533; Silver v. Castle Memorial Hospital, 497 P.2d. 564.
3. Bing v. Thunig, 2 N.Y.2d. 656, 163 N.Y.S.2d. 3.
4. Darling v. Charleston Memorial Hospital, 211 N.E.2d. 253.
5. Adamski v. Tacoma General Hospital, 579 P.2d. 970; Capan v. Divine Providence Hospital, Pa. Super., 410 A.2d. 1282; Howard v. Park, 195 N.W.2d. 39; Beeck v. Tuscon General Hospital, 500 P.2d. 1153; Schagrin v. Wilmington Medical Center, 304 A.2d. 61; Mehlman v. Powell, 378 A.2d. 1121.
6. Adler v. Montefiore Hospital Association of West. Penna., 453 Pa. 60.
7. Benell v. City of Virginia, 104 N.W.2d. 633; Harron v. United Hospital Center, Inc., Clarksburg, W. Va., 522 F.2d. 1133.

The Sleeping Giant Awakens: The Physician and the Antitrust Laws

Harold L. Hirsh, M.D., J.D., F.C.L.M.

PART I: MEDICINE AS A BUSINESS

Since the 1940s it has been known that the medical profession is subject to antitrust laws.[1,2] Health care providers, physicians and hospitals, were protected by an economic philosophy which led to protective "laws" in the form of judicial precedents; only recently have they become subject to antitrust law. For years a variety of defenses limited application of federal antitrust law to health care services in general, and to physicians and hospitals in particular. But recent Supreme Court decisions,[3-8] some not related to health care, have greatly eroded, or eliminated, those defenses. Today it is clear that physicians and hospitals are subject to antitrust law.

The Supreme Court has recently decided several antitrust cases of major importance to the health care industry in general, and to the physician in particular. Taken together, these decisions demonstrate the increasing applicability of the antitrust laws to the health care sector, and substantially increase the vulnerability of physicians, hospitals and other health care institutions and insurers to serious antitrust challenge.

During its 1981–1982 term, the Supreme Court joined Congress and a number of state legislatures in a drive to create a more competitive environment in the health care industry. While state legislatures, such as California's and Arizona's, have attempted to create that environment by enacting competitive bidding practices and contracting systems into the Medicaid program, the Supreme Court has indicated that the judiciary will attempt to create that environment by exposing the health care delivery chain to antitrust review. This was accomplished primarily in three decisions—Arizona v.

Maricopa County Medical Society,[3] Blue Shield of Virginia v. McCready,[4] and Union Labor Life Insurance Co. v. Pireno[5]—sweeping away defenses to antitrust scrutiny based upon arguments that the health care industry was unique and entitled to special treatment under the antitrust laws, that the "business of insurance" exemption (McCarron–Ferguson Act) should be extended to peer review activities, and that consumers lacked standing to sue to challenge restrictive practices in the health care delivery chain. Taken together, the cases portend greater exposure to antitrust litigation and liability, not only for physicians and physician-controlled providers and agencies, but also for hospitals, nonphysician controlled providers and insurers.

INVOLVEMENT IN INTERSTATE COMMERCE

Learned Profession Defense

Antitrust law had not been applied to health care primarily because of four defenses against it. First, under the so-called learned profession exemption, it was argued that the practice of the learned professions was not trade or commerce and therefore not covered by antitrust law. That defense fell in Goldfarb v. Virginia State Bar,[6] a 1975 Supreme Court decision. The Court reaffirmed its rejection of the learned profession exemption three years later in National Society of Professional Engineers v. United States.[7] In the latter case, the Court found no reasonable basis, professional or other, for an ethical ban by the society on price bidding.

Local Versus Interstate Commerce Defense

The second traditional defense held that delivering health care services was local in character and that any effect on interstate commerce was incidental and remote. But, in 1976, one year after Goldfarb,[6] the Supreme Court, in Hospital Building Co. v. Trustees of the Rex Hospital,[8] found that the required effect on interstate commerce existed where the plaintiff hospital purchased out-of-state medicines and supplies, received revenues from out-of-state companies, and made payment to an out-of-state parent corporation. A similar philosophy was applied by several federal courts in cases involving physicians.[9,10]

A federal district court in Michigan held that the sending of claims and receipt of payments through the mails constituted interstate commerce.[9]

A federal district judge has held that coverage under Medicare, Medicaid and out-of-state carriers, plus hospital purchases of equipment from other states, gave the plaintiff physician the right to sue in federal court for antitrust violations by the defendant hospital.[10]

A pathologist in Utah contended that he was the victim of a conspiracy to bar him from fully practicing his specialty at a hospital. The result, he asserted, was limited competition, restrained trade, and the fixing of prices for pathology services at the institution. Despite a federal trial court's determination that the alleged restraint could have no substantial impact upon interstate commerce, the appeals court reversed the decision.[11] It was satisfied that enough impact upon commerce might be found because some pathology services were paid for by out-of-state insurance companies and federal programs; both the hospital and the pathologist purchased supplies moving in interstate commerce; and each served patients from outside of Utah. The pathologist thus earned the right to go to trial and try to prove that the alleged harmful results (limited competition and fixed prices) and the impact upon commerce actually occurred.

A Georgia doctor sued two hospitals and others for allegedly denying him privileges at the facilities where he might perform a quicker, less expensive urological procedure than is the conventional practice. Those opposing him, he contended, were trying to prevent the consequent reduction of their fees and income. The physician was allowed to maintain his suit because the complaint he had filed did assert interference by the hospital with the free flow of urological surgery supplies, possibly reducing purchases of out-of-state materials. He would have to prove these allegations during the trial, of course, but the opportunity to do so was achieved by this ruling.[12]

A radiologist was denied privileges by a number of hospitals in Texas. At each there was an agreement granting exclusive rights to perform radiology services. To the plaintiff, these were forbidden restraints of trade and attempts to monopolize the provision of radiology services. The defendants moved to dismiss the suit, but the Federal judge held that jurisdictional grounds had been asserted.[13] The Sherman Act has been held to apply to local restraints that substantially affect interstate commerce. In this case, it was the radiologist's purchase of supplies from other states. Also, the exclusive contracts between the hospitals and their radiology groups could have had a negative impact upon the radiologist's interstate transactions. Therefore, the plaintiff radiologist was entitled to get the trial stage and try to prove both the impact upon commerce and the restraint of trade that harmed her.

When a podiatrist was unable to obtain privileges at various hospitals, he sued on grounds of conspiracy to restrain trade in podiatry services. The first round was devoted to the jurisdictional issue: would a denial of privileges really affect interstate commerce sufficiently to allow application of federal antitrust laws? They would, the court found, and permitted the suit to continue.[14]

A change in a hospital's system for referring emergency room patients to medical staff members prompted a federal antitrust suit in Michigan.[15] The hospital decided to make referrals to specialists, thus reducing referrals to the plaintiff-generalists. There were both business and medical justifications for the new policy, hence any restraint involved was reasonable, the court held. In fact, the hospital could have awarded an exclusive contract for emergency room services without running afoul of antitrust laws, the court suggested.

State Action Defense

A third defense was the so-called state action defense. In deference to our federal-state system of government, that defense establishes that practices mandated or regulated by a state are immune from federal antitrust law. Since states, to varying degrees, regulate health care, such as the licensing of physicians, health care was presumed to be immune from federal antitrust law. But in 1976, again one year after Goldfarb,[6] the Supreme Court narrowed the "state action" defense, in Cantor v. Detroit Edison Co.[16] Mere acquiescence by the state in the conduct is not enough; rather, the state must mandate the conduct. Subsequent Supreme Court decisions further narrowed the "state action" exemption by requiring the state itself, not one of its political subdivisions such as a city or county, to mandate the conduct,[17] and requiring the state, when regulating conduct, to actively supervise that regulation.[18]

Business of Insurance Defense

Finally, since health care services often are paid for by one or more forms of insurance, the McCarran-Ferguson Act exemption for insurance had limited the application of antitrust law to the third-party payment system prevalent in health care. That act exempts from federal antitrust law the "business of insurance" to the extent such business is regulated by state law. But in 1979, in Group Life & Health Insurance Co. v. Royal Drug Co.,[19] the Supreme Court held that not all aspects of a provider agreement with Blue Shield were the "business of insurance" and therefore exempt from federal antitrust law. The business of insurance, the Court concluded, involves the relationship between insurer and insured and the spreading of risk. After applying that standard to the pharmacy provider agreement in question, the Court found that the agreement was merely a contract for the purchase of services. This has great implication, as will be shown later, for physicians dealing with Blue Cross-Blue Shield.

Per se Versus Rule of Reason Rationales

The decision of greatest import for physicians was the Supreme Court's 4–3 decision in Arizona v. Maricopa County Medical Society.[3] In this case, the Court rejected the argument that the health care industry should not be subject to stringent per se antitrust rules, and found that maximum price fixing agreements were per se violative of section 1 of the Sherman antitrust law.

Section 1 violations are determined under two standards of legality. One, the "per se" rule, is more stringent. It applies to restraints that are so inimical to competition that as a matter of law they are presumed to be unjustified. Generally, the per se rule had been applied to agreements between competitors, such as price-fixing or division of markets or customers. The second standard, which is more commonly applied, is the "rule of reason" standard. Under that standard the nature, purpose and effect of the restraint must be analyzed. If, given the totality of the facts in the case, the purpose or effect of the restraint is not to restrain competition, the restraint is lawful.

Maricopa involved maximum fee agreements established by two medical care foundations through majority vote of their member physicians. The state of Arizona sued, alleging that the agreements were a per se illegal price-fixing conspiracy under Section 1 of the Sherman Act. In response, the foundations contended that their fee agreements should not be subject to the harsh per se rule, and that they should instead be evaluated under the so-called rule of reason.

Traditional analysis of the maximum fee-setting by the physicians in Maricopa would apply the per se standard. At issue, however, was the question of whether, because the conduct involved physicians, the less stringent rule of reason should apply. The trial court and appellate court applied the rule of reason standard and did so, in part, because the conduct was by physicians. The Supreme Court reversed and held that the per se standard applied. The court rejected the argument that the medical profession's public service aspect required that the rule of reason, not the per se standard, be applied; public service, the Court noted, is not enhanced by setting fees, maximum or minimum. The Supreme Court held that the fee agreements were indeed per se illegal. In so doing, the Court rejected the arguments that the involvement of "professionals" (i.e., physicians) in the process required a rule of reason analysis, and that the judiciary's lack of experience in applying the antitrust laws to the health care industry likewise justified a more lenient rule. It also held that physicians who agree on maximum fees to be charged to subscribers of certain insurance plans violate per se the prohibition under Section 1 of the Sherman Act against agreements between competitors affecting price.

In addition, the Supreme Court ruled that the establishment of a maximum fee reimbursement schedule by majority vote of the membership of a physician-controlled foundation for medical care was also per se illegal price fixing. One significant aspect of the Court's decision was the implicit characterization of the actions of the membership as concerted activity and, therefore, subject to the antitrust laws. The real significance of the case, however, lies in the application of the per se rule to the health care industry. Application of the per se rule in Maricopa means that the Court believes that price competition is as important in the health care market as in other markets, and merits the same degree of protection. Thus, the Court rejected the argument that the peculiarities of the health care industry warrant special consideration. In so holding, the justices rejected the notion that the health care industry should not be subject to traditional, stringent per se antitrust rules because it is an industry with which courts have had little analytical experience and because traditional economic principles are not easily applied.

Maricopa, therefore, finally lays to rest the oft-repeated argument that the antitrust laws should not be applied with their full vigor to the health care industry—at least where price-fixing is at issue. The Court's refusal to consider any procompetitive justifications, while standard in per se cases, may for the first time bring home to the health care industry the significance of that small Latin term. Similarly, this opinion emphasizes once again that the fixing of maximum prices is just as objectionable under the antitrust laws as is the fixing of minimum prices, and that arguments based on "cost containment" or the special economics of health care are not likely to carry the day. As a practical matter, therefore, this decision highlights the potential antitrust risk for physicians, hospitals and others in participating in coalitions and other joint cost-containment activities. Thus, in turn, suggests the need for careful antitrust counseling in this area.

The Court, however, distinguished the facts of Maricopa from situations involving a joint venture in which capital as well as the risk of profit and loss are shared by the sponsors. While the extent of the risk which must be assumed to merit different treatment is unclear, arguably, providers such as health maintenance organizations (HMOs) could escape per se treatment. Nevertheless, because the scope of Maricopa is unclear, the per se approach could be applied to competing physicians who control pricing and other practices impacting directly on physicians even in joint venture organizations. Therefore, providers with any extent of physician control should carefully review their operating procedures in light of this decision.

One of the lessons to be learned as the result of the Maricopa decision is that practices typically found to be per se violations in other industries also will be found to be per se violations in the health care industry. Over the next several years, therefore, federal courts will be examining practices in health care delivery to determine whether they are boycotts, ties, forms of price fixing, or acts to divide markets—the traditional per se violations. Among those practices that already are subject to this type of inquiry are closed medical staffs, closed departments, exclusive contracts, and exclusions of nonphysician health professionals such as nurse anesthetists, podiatrists and nurse practitioners.

Other practices that will invite antitrust scrutiny will be direct progeny of language contained in the Maricopa decision. For example, the Supreme Court indicated that the foundation of medical care was not analogous to a partnership or other "joint arrangement" in which persons who would otherwise be competitors pool their capital and share the risks of loss, and that it therefore violated the antitrust laws. The question remains, therefore, to what extent federal courts will tolerate various "joint arrangements" among competitors if the competitors agree on some type of cooperative economic activity designed to provide "an integration of productive resources capable of yielding efficiencies beneficial to competition" (Solicitor General's Amicus Brief) with some risk spreading among them. This should be food for thought for physicians contemplating such ventures.

Maricopa also raises a number of unanswered questions. The most basic of these is whether the Maricopa analysis also will be applied to other traditional per se offenses, such as boycotts. For example, there is in practice considerable confusion about the scope of the per se rule in boycott cases such as hospital "exclusive" contracts and closed staffs, and it certainly is not clear from Maricopa what position the Supreme Court would take in a hospital privileges case. An alleged boycott involving the denial of hospital privileges could now, perhaps, be a per se violation, but would not have been under traditional analysis.

It should be noted, however, that in an earlier case,[20] a federal district court held that it was not an antitrust law violation for a specialty medical society to establish relative value fee guidelines for their members.

Arizona v. Maricopa County Medical Society is probably the most far-reaching case with respect to its implications for the health care industry. As the first case ever to be decided on the merits, it represents a logical culmination of past Supreme Court decisions that narrowed, and in some cases removed entirely, the jurisdictional hurdles and other exemptions that traditionally had shielded various sectors of the health care industry from antitrust scrutiny. It should be noted, however, that Maricopa was a 4–3 decision and, therefore, the scope of the decision and its future effect cannot be determined precisely. Significantly, although the facts of Maricopa are limited to price fixing, the Court's decision may signal the application of the per se rule to other cases involving traditional per se violations in the health care industry.

Reimbursement Problems

The ramifications of Maricopa, however, must be considered in conjunction with Blue Cross of Virginia v. McCready.[4] In McCready, the

Supreme Court held that a subscriber of a group health plan who was denied reimbursement for psychologist's services (as the result of an illegal boycott of psychologists) had standing under the federal antitrust laws to sue for damages. The Court's reasoning provides significant guidance for future cases, especially insofar as it identified the two main issues that limit the availability of redress—double recovery and the remoteness of the injury.

The McCready Court found that there would be no duplicative recovery because, although the boycotted psychologists could bring a class action for damages as a result of lost fees, any recovery in such cases could not include allowances for services that actually were rendered by the boycotted providers, and for which the boycotted providers received payment. The psychologist who treated McCready, therefore, would not be able to maintain an antitrust action for inability to treat McCready, because he was paid by the patient and consequently suffered no injury. He could, however, maintain an action for patients lost as a result of the boycott. A subscriber who paid for services that would have been reimbursed but for the boycott, however, is entitled to antitrust damages arising from direct and provable expenses. It is not clear from the decision whether patients who did not use (or pay for) psychologists' services would have a cause of action.

In applying this remoteness test, the Court looked to the "physical and economic nexus between the alleged violation and the harm to the plaintiff," and "to the relationship of the injury alleged and the core concerns of Congress in making the alleged conduct unlawful." The Court concluded that the goal of the boycott was to restrain the market for psychologist services and that the means chosen to accomplish the restraint was the refusal to reimburse subscribers for these services. Therefore, the Court held that McCready's injury was foreseeable and within the "target area" endangered by the anticompetitive conduct.

In McCready the Court held that health care plan subscribers who incurred costs for services rendered by clinical psychologists had standing to pursue an antitrust claim when Blue Shield would reimburse only for those services if rendered by a psychiatrist or if billed by a treating physician. In so holding, the Supreme Court held that the ability to pursue antitrust claims would not be limited to competitors of the providers rendering the service; instead, the Court found that the patient suffered an injury of sufficient proximity to allow patients to file their own independent private antitrust actions. Therefore, health care consumers and employers funding employee health plans, who believe that health care costs have been driven up by alleged anticompetitive practices, will be able to pursue those claims through antitrust challenges. Representative of such claims already disputed in this regard are cases including disputes involving anesthesiologists and anesthetists.[21,22]

In conclusion, the Supreme Court has invited a broad spectrum analysis of those features of the health care delivery system that restrain free competition. Those restraints that are based primarily upon economic relationships, as opposed to a desire for quality in the delivery of services to patients, now run a significant risk that they will be found to violate the antitrust laws. In McCready, a divided Supreme Court held that a subscriber has standing to sue a Blue Shield plan for damages caused due to the plan's refusal to reimburse for psychotherapy services rendered by clinical psychologists not acting under the supervision of a psychiatrist. McCready has expanded the list of potential plaintiffs in hospital antitrust cases to include patients. It may not open the floodgates, but it does add a new ingredient to be considered by a physician and hospital when reviewing the antitrust consequences and risks of a proposed action. Where McCready may lead is still uncharted; it is significant, however, because it lessens strictures on standing to bring suit, allowing patients or consumers to sue.

PART II

In the beginning physicians and the Blue Cross-Blue Shield plans were completely interlocked. Gradually, the marriage went bad; discontent is widespread, and cooperation is deteriorating.

In a recent case a federal district court, although it accepted the suit, did refuse to apply the per se rule. The case involved a physician antitrust challenge to third party reimbursement policies; instead of applying the rule of reason rationale, the Massachusetts federal district court, in Kartell v. Blue Shield of Massachusetts,[23] held that certain physician reimbursement policies of Blue Shield could be challenged under the federal antitrust laws. Four Massachusetts physicians and the Massachusetts Medical Society brought an antitrust action against Blue Shield of Massachusetts, Inc. and Blue Cross of Massachusetts, Inc. for alleged violations of Sections 1 and 2 of the Sherman Act (15 U.S.C. Sections 1 and 2). A federal trial court initially dismissed the action, but a federal appellate court reversed. Certain questions of state law were referred to the highest court of Massachusetts, which responded to them. The parties then moved for summary judgment.

Ruling on the motions, the trial court said that two of the practices were immune from federal antitrust statutes. Blue Shield's refusal to compensate nonparticipating physicians and Blue Cross's alleged conspiracy to stay out of the market of health insurance for treatment by physicians were both compelled by state law, "state action," and could not be the basis for an antitrust claim.

Blue Shield compensated participating physicians according to a schedule of customary and usual fees for treatment of Blue Shield subscribers. Participating physicians agreed to accept the payments in full satisfaction for their services and not to bill the patients for any additional amount. Blue Shield did not pay nonparticipating physicians for services rendered to subscribers. Blue Cross paid for hospital care and only paid for services rendered by physicians who were salaried members of institutions that were participating members.

Plaintiffs specifically had claimed that Blue Shield was engaged in illegal price fixing by refusing to reimburse physicians who had not signed participating physicians' agreements with Blue Shield for services rendered to Blue Shield subscribers, and by requiring that participating physicians accept Blue Shield's reimbursement as payment in full in most cases, and refrain from billing Blue Shield subscribers for any amount in excess of the amount which Blue Shield had agreed to pay participating physicians (ban on "balance billing"). Plaintiffs further alleged that Blue Cross had agreed with Blue Shield to refuse to provide benefits to Blue Cross subscribers for services rendered by physicians other than those rendered by the salaried staff of institutional providers, such as hospitals, and those rendered under Blue Cross' contract covering Massachusetts state employees. It was claimed that this had the effect of perpetuating Blue Shield's alleged market dominance.

The defendants first contended that the challenged practices were immune from federal antitrust scrutiny under the "state action" exemption (Parker v. Brown).[24] The court examined the challenged practices in light of the state action test as articulated in Community Communications Company, Inc. v. City of Boulder, Colorado,[25] (i.e., that the challenged restraint be one "clearly articulated and affirmatively expressed as state policy," and that the policy be "actively supervised" by the state itself).

With respect to the ban on balance billing, the court concluded that no clearly articulated and affirmatively expressed state policy compelled this practice, and hence it could not be protected from federal antitrust scrutiny under the state action exemption.

With respect to Blue Shield plan's alleged "lock-out" of nonparticipating physicians, the court found it clear from an examination of the applicable Massachusetts statute that the legislature intended to limit Blue Shield's system of reimbursement to participating physicians, except in those circumstances in which such services could not be reasonably obtained. Consequently, the subject practice was clearly articulated as state policy, satisfying the first part of the state action test. The court rejected plaintiff's argument that the second part of the state action test could not be satisfied because the challenged restraint was not "actively supervised" by the state itself. Since the first part of the test had been met, the court found that the second part was *a fortiori* satisfied.

The court found Blue Cross' general forebearance from providing benefits for physician's services to be immune under the state action doctrine.

Massachusetts state statutes clearly required Blue Cross to generally forebear from the insurance market covering physician's services.

Blue Shield then contended that the subject agreements constituted the "business of insurance" and thus were exempt from the antitrust laws under the McCarran-Ferguson Act. The court noted that the subject agreements were in substance the same as those found not to be the business of insurance in Group Life and Health Insurance Company v. Royal Drug Company,[19] with one significant difference represented by the "unit system."

Under the unit system, participating physicians agree to be compensated for their services rendered to Blue Shield subscribers on a *pro rate* basis if Blue Shield is unable at any time to compensate participating physicians in full because of a depletion of Blue Shield funds. Although this feature represented an element of risk, it was a risk to participating physicians and one which Blue Shield, not the subscribers, would have borne in the absence of participating physicians' agreement to do so. Under the decision reached in Royal Drug, only agreements which reduce the insured's risk fall within the "business of insurance." Thus, the subject agreements failed to qualify as the business of insurance and were not exempt under the McCarran-Ferguson Act.

Plaintiffs moved for partial summary judgment with respect to the ban on balance billing procedure, claiming it constituted a violation of Section 1 of the Sherman Act. The court denied the motion, finding that the subject agreements were not per se violative of Section 1, and that the facts were not sufficiently developed to allow a proper determination under the rule of reason analysis. In so finding, the court relied upon Medical Arts Pharmacy v. Blue Cross & Blue Shield of Connecticut,[26] which held that similar agreements did not amount to maximum price-fixing agreements.

The practice of prohibiting participating physicians from charging any amount higher than the scheduled amount paid by Blue Shield was not exempt from the antitrust laws. The practice was neither required by state law nor was it the business of insurance that was exempt under the McCarran-Ferguson Act, the court said. Although there was some sharing of risk by the participating physicians, only agreements that reduced the policyholder's or subscriber's risk fell within the business of insurance exemption. Agreements that reduced the insurer's risk were not included in the exemption. The court granted the Blue Cross-Blue Shield motions for summary judgment in part and denied them in part.

Kartell[23] reflects some of the issues that typically arise in antitrust cases involving challenges to third party reimbursement policies. However, a distinguishing aspect of this case was the Massachusetts plan's refusal to reimburse for nonemergency services rendered to subscribers in Massachusetts by nonparticipating physicians, a feature that the court found to be compelled by Massachusetts law and thus protected from federal antitrust scrutiny. The rules of law espoused in McCready and Maricopa did not apply when the alleged restraint of trade is incident to state action, as evidenced in Kartell.

Although the following case involves dentistry, it has obvious implications for physician-plaintiffs. A dental technician, two consumer groups, and one consumer of dentures sued the Kentucky Board of Dentistry, the Kentucky Dental Association, and individual defendant dentists for conspiracy to monopolize the denture market in Kentucky, restrain trade, and boycott the plaintiff dental technicians in violation of the Sherman Act.[27] Plaintiff's primary antitrust claim was that the defendant-dentists have refused to give denture prescriptions and dental laboratory work orders directly to patients so that they may thereafter seek the dental laboratory of their choice; instead, the dentists insist on sending denture orders directly to the laboratory of their choosing. Additionally, the complaint alleged that the Kentucky Board of Dentistry violated the dental technician's First Amendment right by effectively prohibiting his commercial speech and right to advertise, and that the Kentucky statute which governs the practice of dentistry in the state was unconstitutional.

The appeals court affirmed the lower court's action in dismissing the suit for failure to state a cause of action under the antitrust laws because the private actions complained of were commanded by state law and, hence, within the antitrust exception of Parker v. Brown.[24] The Court concluded that the Kentucky statute regulating the practice of dentistry plainly was a valid exercise of the police power of the state to protect the health and welfare of its citizens, and did not violate any constitutional rights of the plaintiffs under the Fourteenth Amendment. The court further held that the specific statutory restriction on the rights of the plaintiff dental technicians to advertise to the general public did not violate the First Amendment right of plaintiffs, because the statute permits the plaintiffs to sell their denture products and services only to licensed dentists, and not to the general public.

The McCready decision has already impacted on other interprofessional relationships. A group of podiatrists had filed four lawsuits at the district level against a number of prepaid health care provider plans, federal HMOs, and a federal IPA, in Hahn v. Oregon Physicians Service.[28] The podiatrists challenged on antitrust grounds and fair trade practice grounds three practices common to all of the defendants: (1) insureds were required to obtain certain foot care services exclusively from M.D.s; (2) insureds were not reimbursed for foot treatment rendered by a podiatrist unless they were referred by an M.D.; and (3) podiatrists were not allowed to be members of the defendant health care associations. The district court dismissed on summary judgment all the complaints, basing its decision on the McCarran-Ferguson Act, and failure to affect interstate commerce. The Ninth Circuit Court of Appeals reversed on both grounds.

To qualify under the McCarran-Ferguson exemption, the defendants had to show underwriting and risk-spreading functions to the exclusionary practices. The court found that there was no evidence to distinguish between the services of M.D.s and podiatrists, ". . . much less that such a distinction is at the core of what is commonly understood to be the business of insurance." The court was particularly suspicious of contractural arrangements arrived at outside the insurance industry, and suggested that insurance companies could not broaden the antitrust exemption by simply diversifying into areas not traditionally considered to be the business of insurance.

On the interstate commerce issue, the court remanded for identification of the relevant aspects of interstate commerce, and for a determination of whether defendants' relevant insurance activities, not simply their effect on the particular plaintiffs before the court, have, as a matter of practical economics, a substantial effect on interstate commerce.

The court's conclusions were that health care provider plans that allegedly boycotted podiatrists were not immune from antitrust laws under the McCarran-Ferguson Act as the "business of insurance." Furthermore, the podiatrists' insubstantial interstate contracts did not preclude Sherman Act jurisdiction. Excluding podiatric services from the plan's coverage was not part of the business of insurance. No risk-related reasons were found for an insurer to distinguish between physician and podiatric services. The court explained that the exclusionary practices were not limited to entities within the insurance industry, but had their impact on competition in the health care market. Such arrangements in noninsurance markets do not fall within the insurance exemption.

The court went on to say that jurisdiction under the Sherman Act extends not only to activities actually in interstate commerce, but also to activities wholly local in nature that substantially affect interstate commerce. On remand, the trial court was instructed to identify the relevant aspect of interstate commerce and determine whether the plans' insurance activities, taking into account the overall effect and not just their impact on the podiatrists, substantially affected interstate commerce.

Peer Review Activities

Recently, the Supreme Court held in Union Labor Life Insurance Co. v. Pireno[5] that peer review performed by chiropractors to advise an insurance company whether particular chiropractic treatments were "necessary and reasonable" was not the business of insurance because it did not involve the relationship between insurer and insured, did not spread risk, and involved parties outside the insurance industry. This has great significance for physicians who will be participating in the new Professional Review Organizations (PROs) programs (replacing PSROS).

The Court declined to apply the McCarran-Ferguson (business of insurance) exemption from the antitrust laws to nonbinding peer review conducted at the request of an insurance company. In making its decision, the Court examined the three factors identified in Group Life & Health Insurance Co. v. Royal Drug Co.[19] The first factor considered was whether the peer review agreement transferred risk. The Court reasoned that it did not, because the contract between the insurer and its subscribers required reimbursement only for reasonable charges for necessary services. Thus, the Court found that peer review agreement did not transfer risk because the risks of unreasonable charges or unnecessary services were never transferred to the insurer, but always remained with the insured.

The Court also found that the peer review agreement was not an integral part of the relationship between the insurer and its subscribers, noting that the peer review was a matter of indifference to the policyholder, whose only concern is whether his claim is paid, not why it is paid. The Court, therefore, rejected the argument that the private review function is essentially the same as claims adjustment; these activities could not be equated because the Peer Review Committee's opinion was not binding on the carrier.

Finally, the Court pointed out that, although the exemption was not denied solely for this reason, it was significant that the peer review agreement was between two insurers. Thus, because one party to the agreement was not an insurer, the Court found that the arrangement was not at the heart of the legislative concern for adoption of the McCarran-Ferguson exemption.

Although the Court's decision undoubtedly increases the potential exposure of peer review agreements to antitrust challenges, it does not mean that nonbinding peer review activities necessarily are illegal. First, it is important to remember that, nonwithstanding Pireno,[5] peer review mandated by federal or state law might be exempt from antitrust scrutiny under the "implied repeal" or "state action" doctrines. Moreover, many peer review arrangements should be permissible on the merits. For example, in an Advisory Opinion recently issued to the Iowa Dental Association, the Federal Trade Commission took the position that voluntary utilization and fee review are permissible under the antitrust laws as long as the power of the physician-controlled organization is limited to making recommendations, and ultimate authority to pay is elsewhere. For these reasons PRO arrangements will not be subject to antitrust provisions.

At issue in Pireno was whether the use of peer review committees to determine insurance company liability to pay "reasonable" charges for "necessary" medical care was a part of the business of insurance and, thereby, exempt from the application of the antitrust laws pursuant to the McCarran-Ferguson Act. The Court held that it was not the business of insurance, reasoning that peer review did not have the effect of transferring or spreading a policyholder's risk.

Pireno stands for the proposition that the peer review process used by many insurance companies in reviewing claims is not exempt from the antitrust laws. The effect of the Pireno decision is difficult to gauge. It does open up the insurance claims peer review process to antitrust scrutiny—an opening that the two dissenting Justices believe "will vastly curtail the peer review process." It is not likely that the peer review process will be vastly curtailed, but certain traditional elements of the process may be changed, because the process now clearly is subject to antitrust scrutiny. The probable changes (such as review by "peers" who are employed by an insurance company instead of "peers" who compete with the professional under review) may result in more restrictive claims decisions.

What can physicians who participate in peer review learn? It would appear that if noncompetitors of the provider under review are responsible for the review process, antitrust exposure is reduced. The problem, however, is that peer review committees by and large are made up of peers (i.e., specialists in the same discipline), who inevitably are competitors or potential competitors. Therefore, the decision actually left the entire issue of peer review up in the air, and its resolution probably will await additional court decisions determining whether the actual manner in which peer review was conducted was reasonable. Although the McCarran-Ferguson Act does not exempt peer review from antitrust challenge as part of the business of insurance in future cases, it is likely that properly structured peer review will not be found violative of the Sherman Act. Thus, it is possible that the Pireno decision can be disregarded.

Administrative Agency Jurisdiction

Increasingly, governmental administrative agencies are assuming jurisdiction over the activities of health care providers and their organizations. One example is the control of the National Labor Relation Board over hospital labor-management relations. Another example is the relationship of the Federal Trade Commission (FTC) to professional organizations like the American Medical Association (AMA). In the AMA case,[29] the Court in an equally divided vote sustained the FTC jurisdiction over the AMA, finding that certain of AMA's ethics provisions violated the FTC Act. The ruling is important not in itself, but because it has served as a catalyst for the AMA's effort to have Congress strip the FTC of jurisdiction over professions regulated by the states, including, of course, physicians. The jurisdictional issue in the case had nothing to do with whether the FTC should investigate the activities of physicians or other professionals as a matter of policy; rather, the issue was a technical one—whether the AMA itself was a not-for-profit entity as courts have defined that concept, and thus not subject to FTC jurisdiction. This issue would have been the same if the defendant had been a trade association of steel companies or grocery stores. In any event, the case has been at least partially responsible for a bill to curb the FTC's jurisdiction over professional associations, which so far has failed to be ratified.

PART III: EXCLUSIVE CONTRACTS

Exclusive contracts with specialty groups such as anesthesiology, radiology, pathology, psychiatry, cardiology and emergency room care have become an economic boon to physicians. Displeased physicians have complained and sued in vain. Except in one jury case,[30] considered to be a maverick, hospitals had been uniformly successful in defending antitrust challenges to privilege decisions involving exclusive contracts.

Typical is the case of an anesthesiologist, in the Don Santos case,[31] who challenged, under the antitrust laws, an exclusive dealing contract for the provision of anesthesia services at a medical center. The district court granted a preliminary injunction against the enforcement of the exclusive contract. The medical center appealed and the appeals court vacated the injunction. The court held that the anesthesiologist had not shown that she would suffer irreparable injury if the injunction were not granted. It found that her loss of income would be temporary and remedied by a treble damage award should she succeed on her claim. It also found that the hospital was not responsible for any injury to her reputation for denying her privilege. Furthermore, any loss of experience in the practice of anesthesiology did not constitute irreparable injury. The court further held that the balance of hardships did not favor issuance of an injunction. The injunction would have deprived the contracting anesthesiology group of its entire business and would have required it to terminate the employment of its nine physician-anesthesiologists and twelve nurse-anesthetists. The court found that hardship would also fall heavily on the medical center, which could no longer insure that needed anesthesia services would be available at all times. Therefore, the court reversed the grant of the preliminary injunction.

The court also established the direction of the inquiry which the lower court should follow in determining whether the exclusive contract violated the antitrust laws. The court held that the contract should be analyzed under rule of reason and that the court should question whether it is appropriate to regard the individual patient as the real purchaser of anesthesia services. The court said that it might be more appropriate for antitrust purposes to treat the hospital as the purchaser, in view of the hospital's responsibility for assuring the availability of anesthesia services for its patients, its incentive to maximize the use of its surgical facilities, and its potential liability for negligent rendition of anesthesia services in its operating rooms. The court found that if the hospital, rather than the individual patient, were to be regarded as the purchaser, the relevant market could be defined as the area in which the anesthesiology contracting group operated and in which the hospital (rather than the patient) could practicably turn for alternative provision of anesthesia services. Such a recharacterization of the economic relationships, the court found, could dramatically alter the definition of the relevant market, and with it the lawfulness of the exclusive contract. The appeals court said that the lower court should also examine whether the exclusive contract promoted competition among hospitals by creating efficiencies, and whether it stimulated competition among anesthesiologists to obtain such contracts. The Seventh Circuit Court of Appeals determined that the case involved a so-called vertical combination, rather than horizontal, to be analyzed therefore under the rule of reason and that the anesthesiologist was not entitled to injunctive relief to practice at the hospital.

That protection may have changed, however; a federal court of appeals recently held in the Hyde case[22] that a hospital's exclusive contract with an anesthesiology group was an illegal tying arrangement for which the antitrust per se rule should be applied. In this landmark decision, the Fifth Federal Appellate Circuit Court ruled that an exclusive contract between a hospital and an anesthesiology group violated the Sherman Antitrust Act. The court ruled that the closed-group policy was an illegal antitrust "tying" arrangement. Patients who wanted to be admitted to the hospital's operating room (the "tying" product) were compelled to purchase the hospital's chosen anesthesia service (the "tied" product).

Such tying arrangements are per se violations of the antitrust laws if certain conditions exist. The Sherman Act proscribes tying arrangements only if there is sufficient market power in the tying market to coerce purchase of the tied product, and if there are anticompetitive effects in the tied market. In determining the relevant geographic market, the Fifth Circuit held that since patients usually select their hospitals based more on location rather than on price or quality, the immediate geographical area that the hospital served should be the relevant market area considered. The Court did not look at competitive relations among the other hospitals in the region. In addition, the court held that, to show an antitrust violation in cases involving the health care industry, market domination was not required, and only a showing of an appreciable restraint on free competition within the immediate geographical area was necessary. These interpretations led the court to find a per se antitrust violation.

The defending hospital argued that business justifications, such as the possible improvement of the quality of patient care and around-the-clock staffing, could excuse the exclusive dealing contract from a per se violation of the antitrust laws. The court stated that an illegal tying arrangement could not be excused if a less restrictive way of accomplishing these business ends existed. The court believed that allowing the plaintiff one's anesthesiologist,

Hyde, to practice at the hospital would provide such a less restrictive alternative. In addition, the defendants argued that the exclusive dealing contract should be excused from application of the per se rule because it promoted competition among health care institutions. Citing Arizona v. Maricopa County Medical Society,[3] the court refused to depart from the per se rule. The Supreme Court held in Maricopa that, even if there are procompetitive justifications for a price-fixing arrangement, such an arrangement would violate federal antitrust laws because of its inherent, presumptively anticompetitive, ramifications.

The court ordered the hospital to appoint the plaintiff physician to its medical staff. The plaintiff was a board-certified anesthesiologist who brought the action to challenge his exclusion from the medical staff at the hospital. Although his application was approved in 1977 by both the credentials committee and the executive committee of the medical staff, it was rejected by the hospital board. The reason, said the court, was that the hospital had an exclusive contract with a group to provide anesthesia services. Under the terms of the contract, the four anesthesiologists in the group traveled between the hospital's 13 operating rooms to supervise the nurse anesthetists who routinely administered anesthesia. Although the group preferred not to have an "exclusive" contract arrangement, the closed-group policy persisted in the interest of quality patient care. The hospital officials said physicians employed by the group were familiar with the specialized equipment and knew how to supervise the nurses. Under the terms of the contract, the hospital officials said, the group provided 24-hour coverage. The closed-group policy facilitated the use of operating rooms, made one individual responsible for the development and management of the department, and permitted the hospital to monitor professional standards more closely.

The lower court ruled in favor of the hospital. The district court judge said the anticompetitive effects of the arrangement were few, and were far outweighed by the many benefits to patient care.

While reevaluating the possible anticompetitive effect of the closed-group policy, the appellate court considered the special nature of the practice of anesthesiology. An anesthesiologist normally is selected by the surgeon, rather than the patient. The surgeons who practice at the hospital, however, do not gain familiarity with any anesthesiologists other than those associated with the group. The plaintiff anesthesiologist argued that in his case, the exclusive arrangement was particularly unfair because he had a more personal relationship with his patients than many anesthesiologists did. The reason is that he specializes in obstetric anesthesiology and the administration of epidural anesthetics. If his patients were admitted to the hospital, he was unable to attend them.

The appellate court declared that the hospital's exclusive arrangement was based on its desire to increase profits by supplementing a small group of anesthesiologists with a much larger group of lower priced nurse anesthetists. The practice lacked candor, in that the patient was not informed that he would be billed for the services of an anesthesiologist who may have had very little contact with his case.

The court explained that to use the hospital's operating room, the patient also had to use the exclusive anesthesiology group chosen by the hospital, and thus competition between potentially competing anesthesiologists at the hospital was eliminated. Relying heavily on Maricopa, the court applied the per se rule.

If the rationale of this case, Hyde,[22] is adopted by other courts (there appears to be good arguments that it should and may), exclusives and hospitals that use them are in big trouble, regardless of the procompetitive effects that often result from this type of staffing arrangement. Maricopa and Hyde stir an already boiling cauldron of attacks on such contracts and hospital privileges decisions, not only on the legal theory accepted by the court in Hyde, but also on the theory that the exclusion amounts to a per se illegal group boycott. If Group A were to conspire with administrators at Hospital X to revoke the staff privileges of the members of Groups B and C, certainly a court would find an illegal group boycott.

Service allocation agreements—that is, agreements by which hospitals decide which will provide different services—also present a difficult question. Little doubt exists that, at least outside the health care sector, the per se rule applies to such agreements because they do no more than increase the market power of the sellers in the affected market. However, because of some peculiarities of health care economics—which Maricopa suggests are not relevant to the legal analysis—it is likely that many such arrangements between hospitals are "procompetitive" in the sense that cost savings and increased efficiencies outweigh any increased ability of the hospitals to exercise market power. This is the paradox of the Court's refusal to consider factors that are crucial in reaching a proper result. Such agreements may sometimes unreasonably restrain competition, but the question is sufficiently difficult to justify more than cursory treatment under the per se rule.

It is noteworthy that, in Dos Santos,[31] the Seventh Circuit relied on the district court opinion in Hyde, which the Fifth Circuit reversed in this case. This conflict between the circuits with respect to hospital exclusive dealing contracts may be resolved only with a clear Supreme Court decision.

An FTC spokesperson stated that the agency had received a number of inquiries about hospital exclusive dealing contracts and that, should the matter arise before the U.S. Supreme Court, the FTC plans to file an amicus brief stating that, under most circumstances, such contracts do not violate federal antitrust laws. Interestingly, the FTC has intervened when physicians have been excluded.[32]

In view of the conflicting federal appeal court decisions (compare Hyde v. Jefferson Parish Hospital District No. 2[22] with Dos Santos v. Columbus-Cuneo-Cabrini Medical Center[31]), a determination of whether a particular practice, such as the use of "exclusive" contracts, is one that will lead to a per se violation may not be agreed upon by various federal courts. For example, where the economic interests of a medical staff are paramount, with no legitimate interest of a hospital at stake, per se analysis of staff privileges denials may be appropriate. Where, however, staffing decisions are made in circumstances in which the economic interests of the medical staff are involved, but the hospital likewise has a quality or efficiency concern (for example, when an individual practitioner is denied staff privileges because of incompetence), a group boycott, per se analysis probably would not be applied. Once a determination is made that the practice in question does not fall under per se prohibitions, a traditional rule of reason analysis should be undertaken and a balance struck between the procompetitive and anticompetitive effects in the relevant market of the practice involved. This is exemplified in Robinson v. Magovern.[30] These are considerations to be employed by members of the medical staff:

- What is the relevant service and geographic market?
- Can a single hospital be a relevant market in a hospital privileges case?
- What are the procompetitive aspects of the practice in question?
- Is there an increase in efficiency from limitations in staff privileges and/or departments?

In a hospital privileges case, one might ask whether quality of care is a procompetitive result of the hospital privileges decision, or whether the decision was based upon a business determination; it should be noted that it can be both. To the extent that quality of care is part of the marketing strategy of the hospital, high quality medical staff contributes to that procompetitive strategy.

The anticompetitive aspects of limiting hospital privileges must be explored as well. To the extent that access to hospital privileges is necessary or desirable, competition by those denied privileges is severely limited or eliminated. If this becomes widespread in the area, or if the hospital facility is unique, some questions present themselves: Has the hospital become essential to the practice of the practitioner and the denial of privileges subsequently been challenged on the "essential facility" doctrine? Is the medical staff part of a "single entity" with the hospital in staff privileges cases? What is the effect of state Medicaid contracting legislation that requires an open staff except in specified departments, such as anesthesiology, pathology and radiology?

CONCLUSION

These decided cases are important, even critical, to the health care industry, particularly to physicians. Maricopa is probably the most important case because it dealt with the proper standard in determining whether specific conduct violated the antitrust laws, rather than with preliminary issues such as whether the conduct was exempt or whether the plaintiff had authority or standing to bring the case. The Court held that an agreement among physician-members of a foundation for medical care setting the maximum fee the physicians would charge insurers is conclusively presumed illegal, regardless of the physicians' purpose or the agreement's effect on competition; in antitrust jargon, the agreement was analyzed under the per se standard rather than the rule of reason.

The problem with the Maricopa decision is not that the Court found the agreement illegal, or even that the Justices prevented the defendant from introducing evidence to support its defenses. It is doubtful that the defenses, even if proven, would have shown that the agreement's procompetitive effects outweighed the anticompetitive effects. The troubling aspect of the opinion is that the Court's application of the per se rule prevented any defenses of procompetitive benefit regardless of their merit. The Court's critical holding was that, even if some health care sector industries fail to behave similarly to economics textbook models, the antitrust rules are certainly not uniformly anticompetitive.

Maricopa is not all bad news. The Court pointed out the different antitrust treatment of joint ventures where the joint venturers "pool their capital and share the risk of loss." This particular pigeonhole will shelter many joint activities, properly structured, of health care providers. In addition, despite its rejection of the learned professions defense, the Court seemingly reserved judjgment on anticompetitive conduct "premised on public service or ethical norms," or where it could be argued that the restraint actually enhanced the quality of service. While the Supreme Court decisions in Goldfarb v. Virginia State Bar and National Society of Professional Engineers v. United States would counsel caution in reading too much into this ambiguous language, the words at least keep alive the possibility of some more flexible treatment for professionals in some yet undefined cases.

In Union Labor Life Insurance Co. v. Pireno the Court held that peer review practices were not exempt from antitrust scrutiny under the McCarran-Ferguson Act exemption for the business of insurance, thereby subjecting peer review groups to antitrust challenge on the merits.

In Blue Shield of Virginia v. McCready the Court granted standing to sue under the antitrust laws to a health care consumer who concededly was not the target of an antitrust violation, thereby vastly increasing the potential liability of health care insurers and providers alike for violations of the antitrust laws—including, as was the case in McCready, exclusionary conduct aimed at "nontraditional" categories of health care personnel by their more traditional competitors. In a case not involving health care professionals, but still pertinent, American Society of Mechanical Engineers, Inc. v. Hydrolevel Corp.,[33] the Court decided that a voluntary, nonprofit, standard-setting association could be held liable for treble damages for the anticompetitive acts of its agents performed with apparent authority, even though the association never ratified its agents' acts, nor benefited from them, thereby substantially increasing the antitrust exposure of the many standard-setting organizations in the health care field.

In sum, the decisions of the Supreme Court underscore the Court's apparent continued determination to whittle down antitrust exemptions in the health care field—thereby forcing consideration of health/antitrust cases on their merits—and then to apply roughly the same antitrust rules to the health care industry as are applied to other sectors of the economy. That message seems clear, even if the scope of these rules remains uncertain.

After these Supreme Court decisions, the following points should be considered: Federal antitrust laws do apply to physicians and hospitals; although the learned profession exemption appears to exist no longer, other defenses remain, and their application should be reviewed.

Furthermore, the health care industry is not entitled to a special antitrust standard. Although the health care industry is not entitled to a special standard, that does not mean that the public service and professional aspects of health care are not relevant. Such considerations are appropriate when applying the rule of reason. Therefore, unless the conduct is per se unlawful, as was found in Maricopa, consideration of public interest, quality of care and professional aspects is appropriate and necessary under the rule of reason standard.

The cumulative effect of these decisions, then, is a significant increase in the exposure of health care providers to antitrust liability, both with regard to the legality of their actions, and to the number of possible plaintiffs who may institute an antitrust challenge. In particular, these cases suggest that government antitrust enforcement will increase, and that conduct in the health care marketplace will be analyzed increasingly in a purely commercial context.

REFERENCES

1. American Medical Association v. United States, 317 U.S. 519 (1943).
2. Group Health Cooperative of Puget Sound et al. v. King County Medical Society et al. 237 P.2d. 747 (Wash. 1951).
3. Arizona v. Maricopa County Medical Society, 102 S.Ct. 2466 (1982).
4. Blue Shield of Virginia v. McCready, 102 S.Ct. 2540 (1982).
5. Union Labor Life Insurance Co. v. Pireno, 102 S.Ct. 3002 (1982).

6. Goldfarb v. Virginia State Bar, 421 U.S. 773 (1975).
7. National Society of Professional Engineers v. United States, 435 U.S. 679 (1978).
8. Hospital Building Co. v. Trustees of the Rex Hospital, 425 U.S. 738 (1976).
9. Zamiri v. William Beaumont Hospital, 430 F.Supp. 875 (ED. Mich., 1970).
10. Robinson v. Magovern, 456 F.Supp. 1000 (D.C. W.D. Pa., 1978).
11. Crane v. Intermountain Health Care, Inc., 637 F.2d. 715 (C.A. 10, 1981).
12. McDonald v. St. Joseph's Hospital of Atlanta, Inc., 524 F.Supp. 122 (D.C.N.D. Ga., 1981).
13. Malini v. Singleton and Associates, 516 F.Supp. 440 (D.C.S.D. Tex., 1981).
14. Feldman v. Jackson Memorial Hospital, 509 F.Supp. 815 (D.C.S.D. Fla., 1981).
15. Smith v. Northern Michigan Hospitals, Inc., 518 F.Supp. 644 (D.C. Mich., 1981).
16. Cantor v. Detroit Edison Co., 428 U.S. 579 (1976).
17. Lafayette v. Louisiana Power & Light Co., 435 U.S. 389 (1978).
18. California Retail Dealers Association v. Midcal Aluminum, 445 U.S. 97 (1980).
19. Group Life & Health Insurance Co. v. Royal Drug Co., 440 U.S. 205 (1979).
20. United States v. American Society of Anesthesiologist, 473 F.Supp. 147 (D.C. N.Y. 1979).
21. Williams v. Kleaveland, 534 F.Supp. 912 (W.D. Mich., 1981).
22. Hyde v. Jefferson Parish Hospital District No. 2, 104 S.Ct. 1551 (1984).
23. Kartell v. Blue Shield of Massachusetts, 542 F.Supp. 782 (D.C., Mass., June 30, 1982; as amended, July 7, 1982).
24. Parker v. Brown (1943) 317 U.S. 341.
25. Community Communications Company Inc. v. City of Boulder, Colo. (1982).
26. Medical Arts Pharmacy v. Blue Cross & Blue Shield of Connecticut, 675 F.2d. 502 (C.A. 2, 1982).
27. Gambrel v. Kentucky Board of Dentistry, 689 F.2d. 692; cert. denied 459 U.S. 1208 (1983).
28. Hahn, et al. v. Oregon Physicians Service, et al., 689 F.2d. 840; cert. denied 103 S.Ct. 3115 (1983).
29. American Medical Association v. FTC, 638 F.2d. 443 (C.A. 2, 1980), *aff'd by an equally divided court,* 102 S.Ct. 1744 (1982).
30. Robinson v. Magovern, 521 F.Supp. 842 (W.D. Pa. 1981); *see also* Adler v. Montefiore Hospital Association of Western Pennsylvania, 311 A.2d. 634 (Pa. 1973) Cert. denied 94 S.Ct. 870 (1974); Harron v. United Hospital Center, Inc., 522 F.2d. 1133 (C.A. 10, 1975) Cert. denied 424 U.S. 916 (1976); Datillo v. Tucson General Hospital, 23 Ariz. App. 392, 533 P.2d. 700 (1975); Nankin v. Michigan Hospital Service, 361 F.Supp. 1199 (1977); Navato v. Sletten, 415 F.Supp. 312 (D.C. Mo. 1976); Cobb County-Kennestone Hospital Authority v. Prince, 249 S.E.2d. 581 (Ga., 1978); Balhuzin v. North Kansas City Memorial Hospital, (C.A. 8, 1978)—unpublished case; Radiology Professional Corp v. Trinidad Area Health Association, Inc., 565 P.2d. 952 (Colo. Sup. Ct. 1978).
31. Dos Santos v. Columbus-Cuneo-Cabrini Medical Center, C.A. 7, 1982.
32. In re Forbes Health Systems Medical Staff, FTC Rule No. 781-0009 Inherent Order, November 13, 1978.
33. American Society of Mechanical Engineers, Inc. v. Hydrolevel Corp., 102 S.Ct. 1935 (1982).

Problems Arising Between Physicians in Private Practice and Medicare

Jerry Zaslow, M.D., J.D.

This chapter is concerned with some problems that have arisen, and will continue to arise, for physicians who treat Medicare-eligible beneficiaries. The material herein is based upon a number of years of a practice involved with advising and guiding physicians in their dealings with Medicare, and is not theoretical, but practical. It is founded upon the author's own personal experiences gained from such involvement. Obviously, it does not cover all the problems that have been addressed, but does present the more common ones, and those that have given the physician the greatest concerns. It does not address the problems concerning payment by Medicare for physician's services when the physician is a fulltime hospital employee; it deals directly with the physician who is in the private practice of medicine and who works either for himself or with a group of other physicians.

The federal government has been involved with the payment for private physicians' services since 1965 when Medicare was enacted as an amendment to the Social Security Act. While organized medicine was initially opposed to having any governmental involvement in the physician-patient relationship, most physicians would likely not welcome any failure by the government to help pay for medical services to eligible beneficiaries within the system, although they would prefer that there be no governmental monitoring of the services for which payment is made. While a physician would like to be secure in the fact that he would be paid for services rendered, he abhors the fact that what he orders for his patients and how he practices is carefully scrutinized. However, if some controls were not operative, the cost of medical care would escalate far beyond what the government could safely pay without destroying the Trust Fund set up under the Medicare Act.

The Bennett Amendment in 1972 established the principle that payment would only be made for services medically necessary and that services rendered were within established and accepted standards of care. At no time has the government attempted to interfere with the methods or modalities a physician employs, or with how frequently he sees a patient. This statement may come as a surprise to many physicians who have been asked for reimbursement by Medicare because of alleged excessive utilization or because payment had been made for a nonapproved service. This is because most physicians do not understand the criteria used to determine whether a service falls within the scope for which payment is made. This is particularly true of physicians who have practiced only since Medicare has been in effect.

When Medicare first came into existence, physicians saw and treated their patients as they saw fit. Both patients and physicians believed that payment would be made for all services rendered, both being under the impression that this was implied in the Medicare Act. Payments were made upon receipt of services, but payments were not always what the physician billed. It soon became apparent that some criteria were selected to determine level of payment. This had been determined by Medicare by tabulating a list of all fees submitted by physicians for services and then allowing payments up to a certain level, originally established at the 90 percentile of fees submitted. Payment would not exceed this "prevailing fee," but could even be lower, if the physician's usual fee was below the highest in the "prevailing fee" schedule, since payment would be the lesser of the two. This alone led to much dissatisfaction, since one physician often received less than another for the same service rendered. Payment to him under the program was not a fault of the program, but was the result of his own fee schedule's being normally less than another's. While it would have been widely hailed by physicians receiving less than the prevailing fee to have been paid at the prevailing fee level, it was not the intent of the government to elevate his fee, but merely to guarantee his level of fee as it had been previously, except for those few whose fee was above the 90 percentile level. The level has since been lowered to the 70 percentile.

To ensure that a physician's fee is paid by Medicare the patient must subscribe to the program. However, such subscription will only pay 80 percent of either the usual or prevailing fee, less a deductible. A full payment of the prevailing or usual fee will be made only if the statutory deductible ($75 as of 1982) were paid and if the patient had also subscribed for payment of the remaining 20 percent.

A physician may or may not accept assignment for services rendered to an eligible beneficiary on a single service basis. In short, he may see a patient one day, accept assignment and be paid directly by Medicare. Subsequently, he may treat the same patient, refuse to accept assignment, and charge his patient directly. If he does accept assignment, he agrees to accept payment from Medicare as full payment, and may bill the patient only for the 20 percent not paid if the patient does not have the 65 Special coverage, and for any of the deductible not yet paid by the patient. However, if the entire 100 percent of his prevailing fee or usual fee (whichever is less) is paid to the physician, he may not bill the patient any additional amount. If he does, he is committing a misdemeanor, punishable by a fine of $2,000 or imprisonment for up to six months, or both, for each such violation.

If a physician does not accept assignment, the patient pays him directly, but then submits an invoice to Medicare for reimbursement. The patient is only reimbursed the amount the physician would have received, had he accepted assignment. This frequently disturbs the patient, since he expects to receive payment of the entire amount he has paid the physician. Patients do not, or are unwilling to, understand why the deductible is subtracted from the reasonable fee, why only 80 percent is paid (if coinsurance has not been purchased) or why the doctor's fee was more than the "reasonable" fee, and frequently conclude that if the physician's fee is greater than the "reasonable" one, that his fee is unreasonable. This arises because many patients believe that when they become eligible for Medicare full payment will be made for all services rendered. This leaves the patient dissatisfied with both the government and the physician. All of this can be avoided by carefully explaining to the patient what is paid for by the government, what the patient's responsibility is, and what the physician's obligation is under the Medicare Act. Neither the physician nor the government has generally taken the time or made the effort to clarify these issues with the patient.

There has been considerable confusion as to the deductible. The patient is responsible for payment of this for each calendar year that he is in the program. If the deductible amount has not been paid, and a physician, accepting assignment, submits an invoice for payment soon after the subscriber's year begins without collecting the deductible directly from the patient, this amount is deducted from the "reasonable" fee to be paid, and payment to the physician is made accordingly. As soon as the total deductible amount is deducted, further payments are made without deducting the deductible. This soon became obvious to many physicians, and, since an invoice may be submitted up to the end of the calendar year to receive payment, a physician frequently withheld submitting invoices as long as possible, so that no deductible would be subtracted from his invoice, leaving it to other physicians to get payment from the patient to satisfy the deductible.

The greater and more serious problem has concerned "overutilization." Physicians accepting assignment are paid reasonably promptly when invoices are received by the carrier for Medicare. Payment is based upon either the code number of the service or upon a description of the service, if a code number is not stated on the invoice, or if there is no code number for the service rendered. A record for each physician is kept of all payments made, whether to the physician or directly to the patient. When all of the profiles are put together it can easily be determined how frequently each procedure is performed on a single patient over a period of time, generally six months to a year. By scrutinizing the entire practice profile of all physicians it can be determined who does a single procedure most frequently, what the greater number of physicians do, and the like. When a physician's procedures on a given number of patients has exceeded the so-called norm he is so notified by the carrier, is interviewed by an investigator, and is given the opportunity to explain to a group of his peers his method of practice and give reasons for the apparently excessive utilization of the procedures under question. Generally this peer-group is selected by a state medical or osteopathic society. Following such review by his peers, a report is sent to the carrier and to the physician as to the conclusion reached. If there has been a finding of overutilization, the physician is notified as to the amount requested by the carrier for the excessive services. If the physician still questions the findings of overutilization or the amount, he may request a hearing before a hearing officer appointed by the Secretary of Health and Human Services or by the Secretary's designated appointee. At this hearing the physician has the opportunity to present evidence to support his claim that his services were within accepted medical standards, and he has the opportunity to bring witnesses and to cross-examine those testifying on behalf of Medicare. Following the hearing, the hearing officer files his report, together with all available evidence submitted, to the Secretary of Health and Human Services for a final decision. If the Secretary finds against the physician, no further review under the Medicare Act is available, since there is no statutory provision in the Medicare Act for judicial review of the Secretary's decision when the matter concerns the amount of payment under Part B of Medicare. Should the challenge to the amount of reimbursement be based upon a denial of due process, either that the method employed in the evaluation was beyond what the statute provided, or that the method employed was "unfair," then a federal district court would likely take the matter under its jurisdiction. While some federal courts have ruled that there is no judicial review of a final decision of the Secretary of Health and Human Services when the matter at issue is the amount of payment in a Medicare Part B dispute, other federal courts have referred the matter to the Court of Claims which has jurisdiction over claims by an individual against the U.S. Government. As of this date, no decision has come from the U.S. Court of Claims as to what disposition it has made of those cases referred to it.

When repayment for overutilization is made by a physician, it is generally done without any interest or penalties being added, and the government has been quite reasonable in allowing installment payments over a period of one or more years. Should the physician refuse to come to an agreement with Medicare, the government has several courses of action available: institute a civil action against the physician, withhold payment on future claims and use this to repay the debt, or suspend the physician from participation in the program. The latter alternative is usually employed when a physician is found guilty of fraud or flagrant overutilization, and not for the majority of cases under review. Of course, if a physician's payments on future claims are withheld, the physician then would counter the action by refusing to accept assignments and deal directly with the patient. Since the patient would be reimbursed by the government, it would not be able to recoup the debt, and could only satisfy the obligation by an action in court.

While a physician is always reluctant to repay the government for services he had rendered in good faith, and while reimbursement may seem to be a severe penalty, it is by no means an extreme one. When a physician has been found engaging in extreme overutilization, performing unnecessary procedures, a practice which may occur in various Medicare or Medicaid-mill type of practices (where a patient seeing a physician for a simple respiratory infection or skin lesion is subjected to a number of tests far beyond the scope of what the medical complaint would necessitate), the government may immediately suspend the physician from the program. When a physician is suspended, not only will he not be paid on assignment, but his patients will not be reimbursed for payments made directly by the patients to him, after a notice to them that the physician has been suspended. In addition, he is suspended from other governmentally-supported programs, the fact of suspension is advertised in a local newspaper, and notice is given to medical societies and other professional organizations, hospitals, skilled nursing facilities, home health agencies, Health Maintenance Organizations (HMOs) and the state's licensing agencies. While a suspended physician has recourse to the courts to challenge the action by the government, the summary suspension is likely not to be enjoined. This seems patently unfair to a physician who has not been given access to judicial relief prior to a suspension, but such action has been declared constitutional under the circumstances, without any deprivation of due process rights. The reason given by the courts has been that as long as the physician has the opportunity for a future hearing and subsequent judicial review, summary suspension is not unconstitutional and is necessary to preserve the integrity of the Trust Fund set up in the Medicare Act to pay for services rendered to eligible beneficiaries.

Physicians constantly state that the government has no right to deny payment to them for all services that they render in good faith to their patients. Obviously, patients express the same sentiments, being under the impression that when they become Medicare-eligible beneficiaries, the government will pay all bills, once the deductible has been paid, particularly when they also buy coinsurance to pay for the 20 percent not paid by the carrier. However, the statutory provision is that care is paid only for medically necessary services, and medical necessity is determined by the practice of the physician's peers, and not necessarily by that of any single physician. This is a concept many physicians do not accept and of which most patients are not aware.

After a physician has gone through an evaluation of his practice and has been asked to repay the government for overutilization, he feels frustrated as to what criteria he should use in the future to determine what studies to do on patients, or how often he should see patients. *There is only one answer.* Treat the patient according to standard medical practice. The frequency of visits and the number of studies to be done depend upon the medical condition and complaints of the patients. There must be a rational connection between a patient's complaint and what is done for and to him.

Physicians must be alerted to the fact that it is essential to keep proper records and to accurately prepare invoices for payment by Medicare. It is not sufficient only to keep an office record of a visit—the record must contain the reason for the visit, the findings, the recommendations made, and notation of any medication and laboratory studies ordered. In addition, the result of the studies should be permanently appended to the record, or at least kept in a separate file, so that access to the results are readily available to the physician and to any evaluation by Medicare agents. When a physician's practice is being evaluated for possible overutilization, the only material initially available to both Medicare and the physician are the invoices submitted and the physician's records. The office records must support statements made in the invoice, the basis for payments made. The records obviously must be truthful and contemporaneous with the patient's visit. Any falsifying of records either at the time of a patient's visit or subsequently can only lead to disaster—what may appear to be innocent overutilization at the outset can readily lead to an allegation of fraud with all its dire consequences.

Since the entire process of evaluation and establishing profiles begins with the invoices submitted for payment, it is essential that they be completed honestly and accurately. It is amazing how often physicians leave this entirely to some office aide who is untrained and submits forms haphazardly, occasionally inaccurately, and often falsely. Whether this is done out of ignorance on the part of the aide or with some ulterior motive is unimportant—it leads to annoyance and frequently grief. While payment is made promptly entirely on the basis of the facts in the invoice, the carrier does have the duty to check anything which would suggest either overutilization or fraud. If codes are used, they must be accurate; if no code is used, description of the services should be complete and truthful.

An investigation into a physician's practice frequently arises when a patient complains to Medicare about a payment that had been made by Medicare to the physician. This may be based upon the amount of payment or the date when the service was supposedly rendered. These alert the carrier to the fact that fraud may be involved—namely, that an invoice has been submitted for a service that was, in fact, not rendered at all. The first step in the investigation of either complaint is an interview with the complainant, followed by a review of the physician's assignments and then a visit to the physician's office for a personal interview with him and a review of specific patients' office records. The latter follows a notification to the physician to arrange such an appointment for the review of those records. It is clear that the records must be informative and accurate. It is not sufficient for the physician to attempt to fill in the blank spaces from his memory of why and what services were indicated and performed.

On occasion, investigations of invoices for services apparently rendered on a certain date reveal that the physician or the patient was not present on that date. While this may only be due to an error dated on the invoice, it raises the possibility of fraud, and leads to a more thorough investigation, which can only be time-consuming and frequently frustrating for the physician who attempts to explain discrepancies between billing and services performed to the investigator's satisfaction.

All of the foregoing has referred to office practice. However, since payments are also made for hospital services, the same applies to all situations, regardless of where the service is rendered.

PSRO AND THE PHYSICIAN

When the Bennett Amendment was enacted, the Professional Standards Review Organization (PSRO) was created. The function of the PSRO was to monitor care delivered to eligible beneficiaries to determine whether such care was within established standards of medical practice and medical necessity. The practice employed by physicians was to be evaluated by physicians only, unless the physicians in a particular PSRO geographic area abrogated that duty, in which case the Secretary of Health and Human Services could establish his own evaluating group. Rules and regulations were promulgated as to how the PSRO was to operate and what its statutory obligations were, whether at the local or state level.

When formed, the PSRO evaluated the care rendered in hospitals to beneficiaries under Medicare, Medicaid and other federally subsidized programs. This was done by an indepth review of patient's charts by physicians employed by the PSRO. The physicians selected were those practicing the same specialty of medicine in the same geographic area. When the reviewer finished his report, his findings as to necessity for hospitalization, length of hospitalization, and quality of care were submitted to the local PSRO. If any potential violations or actual violations were determined to exist by the PSRO, the physician whose charts were under review was given the opportunity to appear before the PSRO to explain the care rendered to his patients.

As a result of the foregoing, the physician may be given a warning, put on probation, or if in the PSRO's opinion there have been significant abuses, it may recommend a suspension from the physician's participation under the program. As a result of the Final Rules and Regulations promulgated in 1980, the physician has a further opportunity to appear before the local PSRO Board to present evidence as to why the decision of the PSRO was in error. The local PSRO Board may modify its decision, or it may affirm its previous decision and send it on to the Statewide PSRO, or if none exists, directly to the Health Care Financing Administrator (HCFA) for further proceedings. Prior to any final action by HCFA the physician is given a further opportunity to present evidence why he should not be subjected to any sanctions. If HCFA determines that a physician be suspended from the program, he is so notified, and at the same time he is told that he may appeal the ruling before a hearing officer. However, even prior to such hearing, the fact of suspension is published in a newspaper in the PSRO area in which the physician practices, he is also suspended from the Medicare Program and other federally subsidized ones, and notice is sent to the State Board of Licensure and hospitals and HMOs in the area. The physician does have a right to a hearing and then judicial review of the decision of the Secretary of Health and Human Services.

A suspension from participation in the program may be disastrous to a physician. While he may continue to practice medicine (unless his license is revoked or suspended after a hearing before the appropriate state licensure board), neither he nor any of his patients will be paid for medical services rendered by him, and, it is likely that many of his Medicare patients will seek services from a physician who, even if he does not accept assignment, could participate in the program, and his patients would at least be reimbursed for services for which they paid the physician directly. It is also likely that a suspended physician could not get employment with medical groups, hospitals or other medical facilities who depend upon Medicare eligible beneficiaries for much of their income. Even his staff appointments at hospitals come under review.

Should the physician prevail after a hearing or after judicial review, and he is reinstated to the program, damage resulting from the suspension order is difficult to overcome, and, for all practical purposes, he must start anew.

Fraud

If a physician engages in fraudulent practices and his activities are discovered, he must be suspended from the program. Within rapid succession, he loses his staff privileges, medical society memberships, licensure, and is subjected to criminal penalties (monetary fine, possible imprisonment, and a long probation period), and also must reimburse the government for the amount defrauded.

An obvious fraud occurs when a physician, knowing that he has not rendered services, submits invoices and receives payment. However, a physician may be suspected of fraud when he innocently submits inaccurate invoices. This is usually the result of careless bookkeeping, either by the physician himself or by his aides. Examples of this include improper codification, the date of service on the invoice not corresponding to when the service was actually rendered, submitting an invoice for daily hospital services when, in fact, the patient was not seen every day (such as over a weekend), having a patient sign a number of assignments in advance of when services are actually rendered and then submitting the invoices for services rendered when the physician is absent and could not possibly have rendered the service. Although there may be a reasonable explanation as to the fact that there was no intent to defraud, evidence of this type may lead to a fraud indictment with all the distressing events that accompany such a legal proceeding.

All efforts should be made to avoid such actions by accurate reporting and careful perusal of all forms that are sent to Medicare for payment for services rendered. In addition, adequate records should be made of all services rendered, whether they be in a hospital, office or at home.

Relationships between Physician, Hospital, and Medicare

A large proportion of the patient population in a hospital consists of Medicare beneficiaries. The PSRO has the responsibility to monitor the necessity and length of medical care delivered. Under the 1980 Rules and Regulations a provider who has been found to have overutilized medical services by the PSRO may be subjected to a penalty of either the cost of the overutilization or improper service, or of $5,000, whichever is less. While it is the physician who orders the services and admits the patient to the hospital, it may well be that the hospital will bear the burden of the penalty, since it is the one who bills for the hospital stay and for various services rendered. If the PSRO determined that the stay or studies were unnecessary, Medicare would ask for reimbursement of the amount it had paid to the hospital. This places the hospital and the physician in an adversary position, since while the physician believes that the stay and studies were indicated, it is the hospital that is being asked to bear the burden of the cost for these services. The end result is that the hospital must monitor necessity for admission, length of stay, and other aspects of medical care to be certain that they will satisfy criteria used for justification for payment by Medicare. The physician only sees this as an interference with his practice of medicine. Since the hospital and physician really have a common interest, namely, good patient care, the physician must understand the pressures put upon the hospital to see that such care is within reasonable limits of cost—and that facilities are utilized judiciously and reasonably. Laboratory studies should be an adjuvant to diagnosis and treatment, based upon sound clinical criteria, and not a primary modality for either diagnosis or treatment. The fact that facilities are readily available is no indication that they be used indiscriminately, or at the whim of an individual. Hospitalization should not be used for convenience of either physician or patient, or solely for economic improvement of a health care facility, but should be used when medically indicated. Resources to pay for these facilities are finite. Both hospital and physician must cooperate in efforts to use resources expeditiously. This is all that the Bennett Amendment requires.

While PSRO is the watchdog at the present time, and may no longer be operative in the near future, there is every reason to believe that some other agency will replace PSRO. It may well be that the carrier itself, which has been monitoring physicians' practices for many years, will take over the entire program, allowing the same review processes that are operative at the present time when physicians' services are monitored.

ADVICE TO PHYSICIANS

A question frequently posed to me by a physician is "What do I do when a patient wants to come in for a checkup? Do I submit a bill to Medicare?" The answer is quite simple. Explain to the patient that you would be only too glad to examine the patient and order all the tests you believe are necessary, but that Medicare does not pay for this service. The patient must pay you directly for the service and, while you will give the patient a receipted bill after payment, you will not falsify the bill by placing a diagnosis on it in order to help the patient receive reimbursement by Medicare.

Another question presented to me is "What if a patient wishes to see me in two weeks, when I indicate that I feel that the patient should not see me for six or eight weeks to follow the progress of the patient's condition?" Merely tell the patient you will see him as often as he wishes, but that Medicare will not pay for those additional visits, and that he must pay you directly for the service and not submit the bill to Medicare for reimbursement. Do not fall into the trap of doing the patient a favor and falsify an indication for a patient visit when it is not medically necessary. In the least, it is overutilization, and at the other extreme, it is fraudulent.

Finally, be honest with yourself and your patients. Tell them for which services Medicare will pay, and do not manufacture medical conditions which do not exist. This is true whether a patient is treated at your office or in a hospital.

The Disability Benefits Matrix: Medico-Legal Issues of Physician Participation

Mark E. Battista, M.D., J.D.

INTRODUCTION

Never have so many had such broad protection against income loss and medical costs associated with disability; never have so many filed claims to invoke the benefits of this protection. Important developments in the medical and legal aspects of disability determinations have paralleled the phenomenal growth of this industry.

First, the health care professions' ability to identify previously unrecognized impairments has escalated. Moreover, increased physician supply, malpractice concerns and other factors have heightened incentives to recognize impairments. Second, and integral to most disability claims, physicians have an enormous armamentarium of relatively noninvasive technology with which to document objectively the extent of many impairments. Third, hitherto undemonstrated cause-and-effect relationships have come to light. Similarly, as the pathophysiology of many occupational/environmental diseases is better understood, so is the correlation between exposure intensity/duration and the evolution of impairment.

Changes in "disability law" have been no less dramatic. With some exceptions recently, legislatures and courts have expanded steadily the parameters of coverage in many programs. The clear legal trend toward protecting individuals from arbitrary and capricious determinations is reflected both in the established process rules and in the aggressive and often successful stance taken by many whose claims initially were denied.

Overall, these and related developments have transformed conceptually simple, administratively expedient and relatively low-cost programs into a vast, expanding "three-dimensional" matrix characterized by an extensive medicine/law interface.

Along this interface lie a whole range of medico-legal issues physicians and attorneys must understand to participate effectively in disability determinations. Ironically, few physicians have specific training in this area, although increasingly there are calls for including "disability evaluation" in the curriculum of medical schools and residency programs[1] and in continuing medical education programs for the practicing physician.[2] Moreover, both physicians and attorneys must grasp the mechanics of the specific "programs" which comprise the matrix, for the role of the participants, as well as the resolution or even relevance of the various medico-legal issues, vary from program to program.

The purpose of this article, then, is to describe the disability benefits matrix and the nature of the medico-legal aspects of disability determinations.

THE MATRIX

Concepts of disability comprise one dimension, and an array of processes governing the allocation of benefits, a second. Hundreds of unique benefit packages, the third dimension, complete the framework of the matrix. Each component of the matrix, then, is a unique benefit package allocated according to a specific process applying a single disability concept.

Disability Concepts

Many taxonomies of "disability" exist.[3,4] Most attempt a distinction between impairment, disability and handicap, and for medico-legal purposes I think this distinction is necessary. Simply put, impairment is the loss of, or reduction of, function in a body part. A handicap exists when an impairment results in a barrier which the individual cannot or does not fully overcome, or which otherwise lessens the individual's ability to optimize his/her potential. The most important point to remember about disability, on the other hand, is that an individual is "disabled" only if a decision maker has determined that he/she has met all the requirements of a specific disability benefits program or policy.

Stated differently, there are many definitions of disability, and any one definition is relevant only to the program or policy which generated it.

Thus, the dimension of disability concepts reflects the range of program definitions, which, practically, fall into one of two categories: those which require a condition or impairment impacting on the claimant's capacity to work, and those which do not.

Work-referenced Disability

The requisite impact on work capacity varies across many parameters. First, some definitions reference not only a particular occupation, but also a particular job. Others use a broader yardstick, such as any related job. An even stricter reference is any job in the national economy.

Second, there is great variation in the degree of impact. Some programs require that the individual be unable to work at all. Others require only some reduction in capacity to work.

Third, timing is an important variable. Some programs exclude otherwise covered individuals if the inability to work is not expected to last the requisite time, which can range from days to years.

Non-work-referenced Disability

Further along the disability concepts dimension is non-work-referenced disability. These definitions specify the requisite functional or anatomic loss, or medical condition, but do not require any impact on work capacity, even though they might reference specific physical or mental demands. Thus, many programs provide disability benefits to individuals who have no concomitant limitation on their capacity to work, as well as to those for whom work is impossible.

In summary, traditional definitions of disability which require a work reference and exclude pure "impairment" benefits are underinclusive. The impact of an impairment may or may not be relevant; where it is considered its measurement varies, as does the effect of the result on the outcome of the claim. Moreover, not all who legitimately meet definitional requirements have an impairment—they might have a condition without functional or anatomic loss.

Thus, it is not only true that many who are "impaired" are not "disabled," but some who are disabled are not impaired. The range of disability concepts and their operational analogues leads inevitably to apparent, but not actual, inconsistencies in outcomes: disabled under one program but "denied" by another.

Clearly, then, "disability" means nothing more or less than what a specific program says it means, and "disabled" should be used only in this legalistic sense, and always modified by a reference to the relevant program or policy.

The Process Dimension

Whatever the process, it provides procedural rules for bringing and handling a claim and substantive rules for applying the relevant concept of disability to the facts of the case. The former relate to eligibility, time limitations on filing claims, the format for filing, the sequence and nature of interaction between the claimant and decision maker, the requirements for contesting denied claims, and similar matters. The latter rules involve and require two distinct formulations: does the claim allege a fact situation which, if proved, would result in a determination of disability? And, is the alleged fact situation "true"? Thus, the substantive rules reduce the general nature of the disability definition to concrete, and, where feasible, quantitative terms, prescribing how much functional compromise of what abilities to perform which tasks the claimant must demonstrate. They also establish what evidence is necessary to prove the existence of that compromise, and, where relevant, to prove a causal relationship or association between the impairment and a specific circumstance, like employment.

Practically, process rules are an integral part of any operational, as opposed to theoretical, definition of disability.

The Benefits Dimension

When the claimant gets to the intersection of the disability concepts dimension and the process dimension, he has won his case: the only remaining issue is how well he will be rewarded—where he'll land on the benefits dimension.

Benefits vary in nature, amount, duration, beneficiaries, onset of payment and other characteristics. While cash, either as a single award or periodic payments, is perhaps the most widely perceived type of benefit, reimbursement for medical care, physical and vocational rehabilitation, and other types of benefits are common. Even burial expenses are covered in some programs.

The extent of an award might depend on numerous factors, including the extent of functional compromise, the extent of adaptation, the needs of the claimant, the previous contributions of the claimant to the source fund, the effectiveness of the claimant's attorney, the skill and cooperation of examining physicians.

Duration of benefits also varies, both with the program and the facts of the case, including the quality and timeliness of medical care and both vocational and medical rehabilitation. Some policies and programs define maximum duration. In others, while benefits continue as long as the decision maker considers the claimant disabled, the frequency and thoroughness of periodic review of the individual's condition varies greatly, as does the quality and presentation of medical evidence.

When benefits "kick in" is yet another variable. Many benefits payable over the short term begin within a few days of the onset of work absence related to the alleged impairment. Other benefits begin only after a set waiting period, while the limiting factor for others is simply the length of the determination process.

To say that "disability benefits" is not a homogenous term, then, is a major understatement. Perhaps the most fundamental distinctions relate to their raison d'etre. Income for those who have never been able to work is different in kind from wage replacement or supplementation for lost earnings. Also unique is compensation for lost earnings potential, which differs yet again from compensation for the actual physical loss without regard to effect on earnings. Similarly, the frequently across-the-board (payment equals charges) reimbursement of all related medical care is not simply a liberal form of health insurance: it is intended to encourage prompt, competent treatment which, theoretically at least, might minimize both the extent and duration of the impairment. Provision of well-structured vocational rehabilitation benefits optimizes the likelihood that the impaired individual can return to some acceptable form of employment as quickly as possible. Obviously, some benefit packages encompass more than one of these goals.

SIZING UP THE MATRIX

As the process and benefits dimensions—if not the disability concepts dimension—grow, so does the matrix. To say that "just about everybody" has some sort of disability insurance is an exaggeration, but not a large one. And coverage is increasingly pervasive. The Health Insurance Institute of America reported that in 1980, 84 million employed persons were able to rely on disability income benefits from some form of accident and health insurance protection alone, nearly 9 out of 10 civilian workers. The vast majority of the approximately 30 million veterans can rely on varying amounts of disability "insurance" in the form of disabled veterans' benefits. Millions who have contributed sufficiently to FICA over the years are eligible for Social Security disability benefits, and millions more—in fact, virtually all of the truly impoverished can rely on Supplemental Security Income programs in the event of disability. A host of other sources, public and private, cover millions more. Obviously, many individuals have protection from more than one source, and some have better protection than others.

More prevalent among the employed, protection is also broader and deeper as one scales the income ladder. Many employed have coverage for work-related conditions under a Workers' Compensation law, for virtually any type of disability from a private insurance policy (often part of an employment benefit package), and are eligible for Social Security disability benefits simultaneously. Thus, the actual number of persons with at least some protection is less than it would appear; nonetheless, the matrix protects a good majority of our society to some extent.

More telling would be the number who actually receive benefits. Unfortunately, this number is not readily available. Indeed, one of the major obstacles to appropriate policy making at every level is the lack of standardized and universal statistics describing the matrix. No single agency or group perceives an incentive, apparently, to compile and integrate this information, despite the fact that most states keep program statistics on Workers' Compensation benefits, and many insurance companies and industrywide trade groups, federal agencies, and other interested observers, maintain record-keeping and reporting systems on various other components of the matrix. For example, the Bureau of Labor Statistics[5] and the Mine Safety and Health Administration, both of the U.S. Department of Labor, and the Federal Railroad Administration of the Department of Transportation, all measure occupational disease incidence and patterns in various private sector industries.

Too, even available statistics can be misleading. Overlapping coverage and the filing of multiple claims for different impairments are problematic; the concept of maximum monthly benefit is also difficult, because it represents only the outer limit available: average benefits are usually much lower. Occupational disease statistics are notoriously inconsistent because of the variations in definition.

While the exact number receiving benefits is elusive, it must exceed 20 million beneficiaries. In 1980, 2.3 million veterans received compensation for service-connected disability, and another 923,000 veterans received non-service-connected disability pensions.[6] Many of the 1.8 million surviving spouses, children and dependent parents receiving monthly survivor benefits[7] qualified because their related veteran died of a service-connected injury or disease. Many more veterans also receive benefits based on a favorable disability determination. There were more than 7 million workers' compensation awards in 1978,[8] and the trend is up. The Social Security Administration paid disability benefits to almost 4 million people in 1982, and Supplemental Security Income to more than 2 million needy blind or disabled.[9]

Private insurance companies send benefits within any one year to millions, and an untold number draw benefits from hundreds of other state, federal and municipal sources, to say nothing of the many private charitable organizations which provide benefits to certain categories of disabled persons on either a formal or informal basis.

It is no surprise, then, that the cost of providing protection is high. Moreover, a significant portion of every "premium dollar" goes to overhead, as the costs along the process dimension skyrocket. In addition, the commercial insurance companies also have a profit component. Thus, as one moves along the private-public spectrum, the benefit payload increases.

Again the exact cost is unknown, but clearly exceeds $100 billion per year. The VA spent more than 11 billion dollars in 1980 on disability-related benefits alone;[10] in addition, there are administrative costs. The Social Security Administration paid out more than $23 billion in 1982 for disability[11] and has significant overhead costs in addition. Workers' Compensation programs cost employers almost $16 billion in 1978[12] and yearly increases are large. Many more billions of dollars are paid out under private disability insurance policies and through the myriad of other sources of protection each year.

Moreover, there is another type of protection which is available to everyone, used by large and increasing numbers, and has an annual price tag in the billions: personal injury lawsuits. This protection does not lie within the disability benefits matrix per se, and is thus outside the scope of this discussion. Suffice it to say, by way of example, that many who find themselves ineligible for specific matrix benefits use this vehicle; thousands of asbestos claims not compensable under many Workers' Compensation programs are now pending in courts across the country and involve many billions of dollars. The cost and scope of this tenuous, but potentially rewarding, type of protection are of enormous magnitude, and affect the disability benefits matrix itself.

Note, too, that many who receive matrix benefits also sue a third party. One estimate suggests that even 10 years ago, 2 percent of Workers' Compensation claims also involved litigation against another party, often a product liability action; while the number involved was small, the suits generated $1.5 billion, almost 30 percent again of the compensation paid on all claims for that year (1974) under the Workers' Compensation program.[13] Moreover, since many jurisdictions are formulating more and more exceptions to the exclusive remedy doctrine, we can expect this extra-matrix disability compensation to expand.[14]

Actual cost, of course, exceeds the sum of all benefits and program cost; there are many non-recoupable personal costs for claimants.

WHO ARE THE DISABLED?

The precise answer to this question is difficult to come by, mostly because of the definitional problem. Knowing the characteristics of at least some of the matrix beneficiaries is useful, but less than definitive: some of them are free riders, and claimants unfairly denied benefits won't be represented. Moreover, many who might qualify do not apply for benefits. With this caveat in mind, though, one gets a flavor of the characteristics of disabled persons, or at least persons with a significant impairment, from a research summary published in late 1980 by the U.S. Department of Labor and a Social Security Administration report of the same vintage.[15] Depending on the definition of disability, from 12 to 15 percent of the noninstitutionalized population aged 20–64 were disabled. More men than women were disabled. Older people, the unmarried, blacks and Hispanics have a greater incidence of disability.

The reports also describe the functional limitations of the disabled: most of the severely disabled have limitations of movement, like walking or crouching. Almost 40 percent have limitations of vision, hearing or speech, while 1 in 17 are actually blind. Musculoskeletal and cardiovascular problems appeared most frequently, although lung, digestive and mental problems were also common. More than one-third of the disabled had conditions caused by accidental injury, the slight majority of which were job-related.

Given this description, one expects this population to be hospitalized more frequently, 25 percent of the severely disabled, but only 2 percent of the nondisabled, are hospitalized in an average year, and the average length of stay in hospital is longer for the disabled. It is not surprising that the disabled have a relatively lower income: one-fourth had a family income below the poverty line.

In addition to the population described, there are millions of other disabled persons; most of those who are institutionalized are disabled, for example, and many noninstitutionalized children and people over 65.

LOOKING INSIDE THE MATRIX

Seven major categories of benefits give rise to the bulk of all matrix benefits: the Social Security Administration's two major disability programs; disabled veterans' benefits; private nonprofit, charitable organizations; State and Federal Workers' Compensation programs; other federal benefits, like Railroad Disability Annuities; other state and municipal programs; and private disability insurance. Collectively, the Social Security programs, Workers' Compensation, VA benefits and private insurance protection provide nearly the entire spectrum of medico-legal issues regarding disability determinations, and a description of these programs will flesh out the matrix dimensions.

The Social Security Disability Programs

Supplemental Security Income (SSI)[16] is, pure and simple, a public assistance program for the needy aged, blind and disabled. Social Security Disability Insurance (SSDI),[17] the lesser known, but larger, of the two, is the prototypical social insurance program, through which employed individuals buy protection by "contributing" FICA.

With some exceptions, the Social Security Administration (SSA) delegates day-to-day operations to Disability Determination Services (DDS), one in each state, Puerto Rico and Guam. The workload of these agencies varies tremendously, from a 1981 estimate of 200 per year in Guam to 12,600 in Maine, 20,400 in Arizona, 110,300 in Florida and 306,100 in California.[18]

Each agency, 100 percent federally funded, must meet national DDS performance accuracy and processing time standards to ensure uniform operation of the programs.

Also known as Title XVI of the Social Security Act, SSI is financed through the general revenue at the federal level, with optional state supplementation. Eligibility depends, among other things, on need.

In contrast, SSDI (Title II) is funded through the Social Security Trust Fund via payroll deductions or quarterly contributions to FICA. To be eligible, the claimant must have contributed for a requisite number of quarters, which varies with age, the date of onset of disability, and other factors.

Some claimants are eligible for benefits under both programs simultaneously; thus, it is not surprising that both programs use essentially the same definition of disability, although the rules for determining if a claimant meets that definition vary to some extent depending on the category of the claimant: individuals who are statutorily blind, widows, widowers, and surviving divorced wives are subject to somewhat different rules.

As the SSA explains, the law defines disability as

> the inability to do any substantial gainful activity by reason of any medically determinable physical or mental impairment which can be expected to result in death or which has lasted or can be expected to last for a continuous period of not less than 12 months.[19]

Virtually every word has a program-specific meaning that has been the subject of judicial or administrative interpretation. The claimant must be unable to do his previous work or "any other substantial gainful activity which exists in the national economy," and to determine the latter activity, the decision maker looks at what the claimant can still do despite his limitations, taking into account his age, education, work experience and other factors. "Substantial gainful activity" refers to "significant and productive physical or mental duties done, or intended, for pay or profit."[20] The claimant must prove that his impairment results from an "anatomical, physiological or psychological abnormality which can be shown by medically acceptable clinical and laboratory diagnostic techniques."[21] In other words, concrete medical evidence is essential; moreover, a physician's certification that the claimant is disabled will not suffice without objective evidence to support that certification. Each claim is evaluated sequentially, so that if at the early stages of the review, the claimant is found to be doing "substantial gainful activity" his claim will be denied without further ado.

For those denied claims there is a well-marked path for contesting, and increasing numbers are taking it, indicating that claimants or their representatives perceive the validity of the initial determination as questionable.

Workers' Compensation

Workers' Compensation is probably the most widely known and least understood system of disability insurance. Its rapid expansion accounts for much of the growth rate of the matrix. It started out in the early part of this century (a European transplant) as a relatively simple substitution of the employee's right to sue his employer for damages with a guarantee of compensation for specific work-related injuries. This eased employees' difficulties tremendously; fault, for example, was no longer at issue, and the intimidating and expensive legal system could be avoided, although employees retained their right to sue in tort any third party who was not immune under the relevant Workers' Compensation law.

Its purpose was not to compensate the worker for all the costs of his injury, but simply to replace a sufficient amount of wages actually lost to allow him to get by during disability. Today, program objectives are much broader: to minimize the duration of disability extensive vocational rehabilitation benefits are frequently available. Too, some programs compensate the claimant for an impairment, regardless of its effect on ability to work. In other words, new objectives—compensation for the physical loss and replacement of lost earnings potential—were introduced.

Structure and administration of programs have also changed. At the state level, formal responsibility usually lies with a state agency, but financing and decision making follow one or more of three models. The simplest, permitted by almost all states, is self-insurance, where a company handles its own claims. A significant number of states also operate state funds. Private insurance, the prevailing model, accounts for the remainder. Where a dispute arises between the employee and employer, or between the claimant and the insurer, a hearing officer (a Workers' Compensation Commissioner, for example) or ultimately, a judge, adjudicates the case.

Federal Workers' Compensation laws have proliferated, primarily to cover those whom states could not cover. For example, the Federal Employees Compensation Act (FECA)[22] covers federal civilian employees. One notable exception to this primary objective of federal programs is the Black Lung Benefits program[23] for coal miners, established by Congress in 1969 in response to a widespread belief that coverage of coal workers' lung diseases under existing state laws was inadequate—coverage the states could have provided, but did not. Another important federal law is the Longshoremen's and Harbor Workers' Compensation Act.[24]

Altogether, these state and federal laws cover about 90 percent of U.S. workers.[25] The remainder are primarily self-employed persons, employees of small firms, agricultural, domestic and casual workers, and certain state and municipal government workers.

The Nature of Workers' Compensation Claims

The vast majority of claims are for "injury," although this includes "cumulative" injuries, conditions due to repetitive trauma or stresses. Claims involving occupational disease—as opposed to injury—account for a small minority of claims in many states, but are on the increase. They often involve heart, lung and mental disorders, as well as diseases of the skin and other conditions.

The unique and common denominator of Workers' Compensation programs is that an eligible worker must prove that his condition is work-related. Standards for determining work-relatedness vary. Most strict is the requirement that employment conditions or stresses actually caused the condition. A more liberal standard requires only a showing that employment, while not the sole cause, was a significant contributing factor, or simply aggravated an existing condition. Whatever the standard, though, this issue is primary in 20 percent of contested injury claims, and more than 50 percent of contested occupational disease claims.[26]

Another aspect of Workers' Compensation is the concept of partial disability, which is not harbored by the Social Security programs. Thus, claimants who can still work to some degree frequently receive benefits. The amount of benefits often depends on the extent, or percentage, of disability. This determination is often vexsome, arbitrary and subjective, and as frustrating to the physicians who are asked to come up with an opinion as it is to the decision maker. Indeed, the extent of disability is the most commonly litigated issue in contested injury claims,[27] and is commonly at issue in occupational disease claims.

In contrast, "impairment benefits" are relatively straightforward. FECA, for example, pays 46 weeks of benefits for the loss of the "first finger," 75 weeks worth for the loss of a thumb, and so on, to compensate the claimant for these permanent losses.[28] If the impairment also results in temporary disability, additional benefits are paid.

Expansion of the Workers' Compensation System

An important stimulus to the expansion and rising costs of the system came from the National Commission on State Workers Compensation Laws, which in 1972 made 19 essential recommendations for improvements in state laws, backed up by the threat of federal involvement. Many have been implemented by a majority of states. For example, the commission recommended that there be no statutory limits of time or dollar amount for medical care or physical rehabilitation services for any work-related impairment.[29] All 52 states now comply with this recommendation, and, not surprisingly, the majority of all awards (but not of all benefits paid) are made as direct medical payments.[30] While not every state has complied with all recommendations, virtually all legislatures are continually amending the law.

Nor has the expansion occurred only at the state level. The evolution of the Black Lung program, which covers more than 200,000 miners, has been marked by frequent changes which have broadened eligibility requirements and eased coverage restrictions, so that as of 1981 more than half a million miners and survivors had filed claims, and almost $10 billion had been paid to 365,000 beneficiaries.[31] Similarly, in 1974, Congress increased the benefit levels under FECA.

Courts have further hastened the expansion of relief available to claimants with very broad statutory interpretations. The cost of this expansion, of course, is high. Typically, both the number of claims and total amount of benefits paid have increased following liberalization. After the series of liberalizing amendments to the act governing the Black Lung Program, annual cost had reached $800 million, and the special trust fund, established in 1977 and financed by a tax on coal sold by producers, was $1.5 billion in debt.[32] Similarly, after the expansion of FECA benefits, the number of lost-time claims involving traumatic injury increased dramatically in the next five years, even though the workforce did not increase significantly. State Workers' Compensation costs more than doubled from 1975 to 1979.[33]

One of the most controversial issues in many programs is the extent of occupational disease coverage. All states now have an occupational disease law, but few are comprehensive. For the most part, these laws limit compensation through a variety of presumptions, filing limitations and other vehicles. Many exclude entire categories of diseases, like "ordinary diseases of life," all infectious diseases, and illnesses which do not result from unexpected exposures. Some states deny coverage if any non-work-related factor contributed to the condition in any way.

Yet, occupational diseases claims have the potential to reshape the Workers' Compensation system, and to some extent the entire disability benefits matrix. First, there are many more occupational disease victims than there are claims. A recent Rand Institute report states that by most accounts "only a tiny fraction of occupationally related disease cases enter the Workers' Compensation system."[34] The U.S. Department of Labor's estimate of 3 percent[35] supports this statement. Most state legislatures are under intense pressure to broaden their occupational disease law, yet any liberalizing amendment would significantly increase claims volume and benefits paid.

The potential cost is obvious: one observer calculated that if occupational disease coverage were expanded to include even 1 percent of all U.S. deaths from cardiovascular problems, death claims awards would triple; if 2 percent of all cancer deaths were included, awards would double.[36] While the number of deaths resulting in awards is very small, these awards consume an important fraction of benefits. Adding to this the tremendous increase in the number of awards that would be made for permanent disability due to similar causes, one begins to understand the resistance to expansion from industry and many legislatures: awards for death and permanent disability account for well over one-half of all benefits paid, even though they constitute only a small fraction of the number of awards.[37] In addition, occupational disease claims are associated with very high administrative costs.

The concept of permanent partial disability is also the focus of much debate. PPD benefits account for the majority of all cash benefits and, like occupational disease claims, consume an inordinate portion of administrative funds. Moreover, some authorities believe it represents the strongest disincentive to rehabilitation.[38] Needless to say, others disagree, and the concept, generally, is still deeply ingrained in the system.

Overall, then, the complex and highly variable Workers' Compensation programs have crowded the dimensions of the matrix and constitute a major determinant of its evolution.

VA Benefits for Disabled Veterans

The VA provides eligible disabled veterans an array of benefits. A monthly income benefit, for example, is paid to veterans (who left the service under other than dishonorable conditions) with service-connected disabilities.[39] The actual amount depends on the "disability rating," the equivalent of "percentage disability" in other programs. Beneficiaries who have at least 30 percent disability also receive an additional allowance for dependents.[40] An annual clothing allowance is available to those who use appliances, like a wheelchair, which increase wear and tear on clothing. Comprehensive medical care is also available at VA facilities, as well as nursing home care. Their dependents or survivors are frequently eligible for coverage of at least some of their medical costs. Home care, too, is available under certain conditions.

A full range of vocational rehabilitation is available, and in addition to tuition, books, fees and supplies, the benefit frequently includes a monthly subsistence allowance which varies with the type and intensity of training, and increases from this basic range according to the number of dependents. This allowance is in addition to disability compensation. Many other disabled veterans receive further training under the GI bill instead of the vocational rehabilitation benefit.

Benefits are not by any means limited to those with service-connected disabilities. Disability pensions, for example, are available to a large number of veterans for disabilities not traceable to service (or to "willful misconduct or vicious habits").[41]

Several factors in the VA system of benefits for disabled veterans make it unique. First, compensation for service-connected disability is "scheduled" according to the extent of disability.[42] Unlike many Workers' Compensation programs, then, the amount of the compensation does not vary with the previous wage level of the claimant; everyone who is 80 percent disabled, for example, receives the same basic benefit. Second, unlike the Social Security programs, the VA, like most Workers' Compensation programs, recognizes the concept of partial disability in its compensation program for service-connected disabilities; however, it requires a finding of permanent and total disability in its pension program for non-service-connected disabilities.[43] On paper, permanent and total disability is a much tougher standard than the Social Security programs' standard; in fact, it is nearly at one end of the disability concepts dimension. The process used to determine disability, however, may be considerably more liberal. For example, veterans over 65 who are not working are presumed to be permanently and totally disabled,[44] and the lack of any time limitation for filing a claim for disability compensation contrasts starkly with the restrictions in many Workers' Compensation programs.

Third, the system attempts to provide much more comprehensive benefits for disabled persons than many other programs. Some veterans, for example, are eligible for adaptive equipment for their vehicle.[45]

Fourth, there is comparatively little of the adversarial element characteristic of other programs.

Private Disability Insurance

This massive industry provides benefits to millions, and in many cases supplements benefits they receive from other programs. Like health and life insurance, disability insurance is available to both groups and individuals. Group disability income plans are aimed, primarily, at replacing part of a totally disabled employee's lost wages. The majority of plans, unlike Workers' Compensation, are etiology-blind, covering disability whether or not it is job-related. However, if a disability is job-related and Workers' Compensation benefits are also available, the private plan benefits are reduced in many cases.

Both short- and long-term coverage are available, the dividing line being two years. The Health Insurance Institute has indicated that in 1979 of all employees with a short-term plan, almost three out of four could rely on up to 26 weeks of income coverage if they became disabled, and benefits usually begin within a few days after disability onsets. Long-term benefits range from two years to death, or as long as disability lasts. They often do not "kick in" for six months after the onset of disability, although many individuals with long-term protection also have some short-term coverage to tide them over.

A large number, however, do not have group coverage, and many purchase an individual policy tailored to their needs. A self-employed surgeon, for example, might want a policy that provides benefits for the duration of disability, with a waiting period of one month. He might choose a policy which defines disability, for him, an inability to do surgery. If he loses a hand in an accident, he will be covered because he would not be able to operate, even though he might still be able to do general practice or psychiatry, or sell real estate, for that matter.

The ability to narrowly define disability is one of the major advantages of private insurance. There is less likelihood of litigation, for example: the surgeon simply has to show he cannot operate with one hand, and does not have to worry about many of the other issues complicating the matrix. Similarly, the insurer can underwrite such defined risks with much greater certainty and precision.

Other disability options are also available. The surgeon might choose to add an overhead protection option. Obviously, office costs continue over a short-term disability, and this option allows the surgeon to rely on a set amount per month to cover these costs. His premium will be a function of how much protection he wants, among other things.

Private insurance is fundamentally different from other programs in several respects. Many policies set a ceiling on the dollar amount of benefits, thus both limiting and defining liability. Many provide an agreed-upon schedule of benefits. Many avoid or limit the issue of work-relatedness. And the amount of protection, like life insurance protection, can usually be increased or decreased simply by adjusting the premium. Beneficiaries can be specified. For the most part the rules for processing and adjudicating claims are set out in the terms of the policies.

Private insurance, then, probably has contributed the most variables to the disability concepts dimension, and perhaps to the other dimensions as well.

MEDICO-LEGAL ASPECTS OF THE MATRIX

Given the enormous complexity of the matrix, it is not surprising that the medicine-law interface is both vast and growing. Two major categories of medico-legal issues are presented. The first relates to the intrinsically medical nature of identifying and describing impairments. What is meant by "the extent of the impairment?" What is the prognosis? When does the healing period terminate? What impact does the impairment have on the individual's capacity to meet specific physical or mental demands? What caused the impairment? Is the individual a candidate for rehabilitation?

The second category of issues springs from the impact of the physician's role as an evaluator on the physician's legal duties to the patient, insurers and others. What duty exists to perform a "disability evaluation" on an established patient? What duty exists to submit adequate and timely reports? What duty, if any, does the physician owe to payers when he/she encounters an obvious malingerer, and what limitations on patient confidentiality are relevant here? What relationship exists when a physician sees a patient once for the express purpose of "disability evaluation?" What duty has this physician to disclose to the patient any abnormal findings? What duty exists to report any reportable diseases to the state? What duty exists to disclose to the claimant the discovery of previous negligent and injurious acts on the part of other providers? What malpractice risks are inherent in return-to-work recommendations? Does the physician have a duty to report an occupational hazard? What role does informed consent have in disability evaluations?

Finally, other related medico-legal issues are raised, and the need for awareness and analysis is highlighted.

Medico-Legal Issues Related to Identifying and Describing Impairments

Most questions appearing on requests for information regarding a patient's impairment—for example, an "attending physician's statement"—require either documentation of data, or an opinion.[45] While many questions appear straightforward, the medico-legal implications of the range of possible responses are less than clear-cut.

The Extent of the Impairment

Theoretically, physicians should be able to assess the extent of any impairment objectively at any time. Practically, of course, objective measurements are frequently elusive, and the subjective substitutes are not standardized, thus lacking both reliability and validity in many cases. Many guides to evaluating impairments and disability are available.[46-49] Most clearly distinguish between impairment and disability. Some individuals have attempted to demonstrate the reliability and validity of certain guides.[50] Generally, though, "guide" is the operative word. Since the extent of the impairment, as determined by the decision maker, frequently dictates or at least impacts on the outcome of the claim, it is predictable that the "extent of the impairment" is frequently the focus of litigation. Physicians are drawn into this arena both as expert and ordinary witnesses.

Thus, it behooves examining physicians to use standardized, objective measurements to the extent feasible. When a subjective measurement is necessary, it should, at least, be based on a thorough history and physical examination, and it should follow logically, and be consistent with, coexisting objective data.[51]

Impact of Impairment on Capacity to Perform

It is clear that labels like "moderate" or "mild" have no place in describing the extent of impairments. They are, in fact, misleading in many cases. Similarly, to suggest that an impairment has a "great" impact or "minimal" impact on the individual's "ability to work" simply begs the question and frequently reflects the physician's philosophy and lack of competence in "disability evaluation" more than it does the impact itself. While it is often stated that disability is an administrative determination, not a medical one, the physician's well-reasoned and articulated opinion regarding the impact on ability to work frequently carries great weight. Since this determination might shape the outcome and is often based on subjective evidence, it too is frequently contested.

Most important for an acceptable response to this question is knowledge of the threshold demands of the patient's activities, often the patient's job. The physician can acquire this knowledge from the patient, the employer and other sources, including the *Dictionary of Occupational Titles.*[52] Moreover, an appendix[53] to that document broadly categorizes and describes physical demands and working conditions. For example, physical demands express "both the physical requirements of the job and the physical capacities (specific physical traits) a worker must have to meet the requirements."[54] Strength factors (lifting, carrying, pushing and/or pulling) are defined and categorized in five degrees, ranging from "sedentary work" to "very heavy work," the latter involving "lifting objects in excess of 100 pounds with frequent lifting and/or carrying of objects weighing 50 pounds or more."[55] Working conditions, the "physical surroundings of a worker in a specific job," are also described. For example, a job is considered "outside" if the worker spends at least 75 percent of working time without "effective protection from the weather." Extremes of ambient temperature, humidity, noise, vibration, and fumes are among the other factors set out in this appendix. While hardly definitive or comprehensive, these factors are both a starting point and a reference standard for the physician.

In addition, the physician must consider mental demands, where relevant. These include cognitive requirements, social interaction, responsibility for others, deadlines, and other factors.

Armed with this knowledge of work requirements, the physician can specify the impact of various aspects of the functional impairment on the individual's capacity to meet these requirements. While this is difficult for many physicians, it is well within their potential competence in many cases, and is an integral component of adequate physician participation in many disability determinations.

Where work requirements are not relevant, the physician can estimate the impairment's impact on activities of daily living.

Perhaps most important, the physician must recognize his/her limitations if confronted with a question about the claimant's capacity to perform a specific function, when it is clear that existing available data shed no light on that capacity.

Prognosis

Some programs require that the impairment—and its impact on capacity to meet specific requirements—last for at least a specified number of months in order for the individual to receive benefits. Thus, prognosis sometimes is critical to outcome of a claim. While an opinion regarding prognosis is usually well within the physician's bailiwick, the evolution or resolution of any impairment is notoriously variable. The promptness, and competence, of medical care, the attitude of the patient (and the patient's family), financial incentives to return to work, the availability of adequate rehabilitation and the inherent nature of the condition superimposed on the patient's overall health status all affect prognosis. Thus, the physician's opinion must be based on a thorough evaluation of the patient and thorough familiarity with the category of impairment.

Termination of the Healing Period

The concept of a discrete "healing period" ending when there is no reasonable expectation of further recovery is basic to many programs. Either recovery is complete, or maximal, though incomplete, recovery has occurred. While this is related to prognosis, it serves a fundamentally distinct objective. Prognosis might determine if one of the criteria for disability is met and/or might be required to set reserves; termination of the healing period, however, can trigger termination of temporary benefits and a final determination as to whether permanent impairment exists. This legalistic concept of a healing period is not consistent with the slow but steady and long-term improvement many patients exhibit, particularly those with chronic back pain syndromes.[56]

Thus, the physician statement that the patient has reached maximum medical improvement ("MMI") will often come earlier than the actual date of MMI and would reflect the physician's belief that very little measurable progress toward further recovery is ongoing.

Causation

Some programs, notably Workers' Compensation, require, for a claim to be compensable, that the condition arise out of or in the course of employment. Too, some VA benefits hinge on whether the impairment was "service connected." Standards for determining work-relatedness vary, although in most jurisdictions a showing that employment was a significant contributing factor or aggravated an existing condition will satisfy the condition. Once again, the physician's opinion is often determinative, yet often subjective, and, as noted earlier, the issue is frequently litigated.

While causation—or, at least, work-relatedness—is frequently obvious, it is sometimes obscure. First, of course, there are conditions, resulting in impairments, for which etiology has yet to be established. Coronary artery disease is a case in point. Some jurisdictions handle this by creating certain statutory presumptions regarding compensability of impairing coronary artery disease in certain categories of workers. Generally, though, while one can identify the patient's risk factors, and allocate them according to their work-relatedness, it is difficult to state with reasonable certainty that this condition arose "out of employment."[57]

Perhaps more troublesome for physicians is the concept of cumulative injury and disease, wherein repetitive job-related physical or mental trauma results in a compensable impairment. In California, for example, back conditions and heart/vascular conditions were primary in more than 50 percent of all cumulative injury claims in 1978,[58] even though cumulative injury claims comprise only a small percentage of all claims.

Neuropsychiatric illness is particularly difficult for physicians to deal with.[59] Stresses frequently are cumulative and multiple, and many stressors are job-related. Many jurisdictions now consider job-related psychic injuries compensable[60] whether they result from cumulative stress or a single occurrence. Moreover, a preexisting mental impairment is not usually an absolute bar to recovery,[61] although a stricter standard of proof may be required. Again, the physician's opinion must rest on a full evaluation performed with an understanding of the relevant program requirements. In general, the physician's opinion regarding work-relatedness carries greater weight when known determinants are specified and reasonably labelled as work-related or not.

Apportionment

Physicians who do venture an opinion on the work-relatedness of cumulative injuries or diseases must be sensitive to apportionment of liability. Basically, apportionment issues arise only after the decision maker has determined the claim is compensable, although generically apportionment is related to causation. For example, where both work-related and non-work-related factors caused the condition, the decision maker might apportion liability according to the contribution of work-related factors. A patient with a low back pain syndrome who lifts heavy objects on the job and lifts weights for exercise might present this problem. Similarly, when separate impairing accidents occurred during different jobs, liability might be apportioned to each employer according to the effect of each accident; this might also occur when the patient was exposed to toxins or dusts on successive jobs. Finally, liability of a particular employer, though not compensability, might depend on the extent a preexisting disease contributed to the ultimate impairment.

Many jurisdictions do not attempt apportionment when an injury aggravates a preexisting condition. Instead, some apply the "full responsibility" rule, based on the so-called eggshell theory, the rationale being that "the employer takes his employees as the employer finds them." [62,63] Many observers feel this rule places an extra burden on the ultimate employer and might deter employers who are subject to it from hiring individuals with a preexisting impairment. Establishment of a "second injury fund" is considered a nice compromise.[64]

Regardless of the jurisdiction's stand, though, the physician's approach to causation in general should reflect an awareness of the role of multiple and successive contributing factors in the patient's impairment.

Rehabilitation

The need for rehabilitation, both medical and vocational, varies with the observer; yet a physician's recommendation for or against rehabilitation can seriously impact the outcome of the claims. Thus, this recommendation should be made only after a competent and thorough evaluation based on accepted medical standards.[65]

Obviously, only some of these issues will arise in any one case, but the physician must be aware of them, and of the implications of inadequate participation.

Medico-Legal Issues Relating to the Physician-Claimant Relationship

An individual applying for disability benefits wears several hats. As a patient, his/her incentive to obtain optimal and prompt medical care is strong. As a claimant, though, the primary goal is to obtain from the physician optimal and prompt medico-legal reports. Finally, as an attorney's client, the objective is to cooperate fully with the attorney to optimize the claim's potential. Suffice it to say that sometimes these objectives are not consistent. Similarly, physicians may have different though entirely acceptable incentives in evaluating a disability claimant.

Duty to Perform Disability Evaluations

When the treating physician also is the evaluating physician, there exist two separate relationships, physician-patient and physician-claimant. Does the physician owe the patient a duty to perform the evaluation, assuming the physician is qualified to do it? While in most jurisdictions it is clear that the treating physician must comply with a duly authorized request or statutory requirement for release of medical information relative to the disability claim, whether the physician has a legal obligation to perform an evaluation solely for the purpose of participating further in the disability determination process is unclear. Some primary care physicians might well argue that such an obligation has the potential to interfere with the primary therapeutic relationship, even though a competently performed evaluation practically is a clinical opportunity to validate and monitor the diagnostic and therapeutic approaches.[66] Even if there is not a legal obligation to do the evaluation, however, the physician probably has a duty to notify the patient promptly of his/her intention not to participate, beyond otherwise required medical information releases.

Duty to Participate Competently in the Disability Evaluation Process

Once the physician agrees to perform the evaluation, other legal duties arise. At the very least, the physician has a duty to perform the evaluation objectively, comprehensively and promptly, and in a manner responsive to the specific medical evidence requirements. Theoretically, at least, a physician who negligently performs in this arena might be liable in a malpractice suit should the negligent participation proximately cause an outcome less favorable to the claimant then would have occurred with competent performance.

Duty to Notify Payer of Claimant Misrepresentation

What duty does the examining physician have to notify the payer that the patient-claimant is a malingerer? First, on basic principles, the physician who deliberately misrepresents (overstates) the patient's impairment, or its impact, leading to a spuriously successful outcome, might be liable should the payer sue for fraud. Criminal prosecution is a theoretical, though less likely, possibility, and carries the risk not only of the usual penalties but also of professional sanction. Similarly, a physician who knows the patient is a malingerer and does not notify the payer of the specific contradicting facts might be liable. The common example is the patient, who, trusting that he/she and the physician are on good terms and on the same side against the large insurance company, confides that the back injury actually occurred while playing racquetball rather than on the job as he/she had alleged. Even if the physician remains silent on the job-relatedness question there is a likelihood that knowing silence would not remove liability. On the other hand, disclosure in this situation would impact enormously on the physician-patient relationship, to say the least.

Return to Work Recommendations

Another medico-legal issue arises when the physician recommends "return to work," with or without job modification or activity restrictions. In some cases, recommending return to work without a graduated activity program and suggestions for job modifications or initial activity restrictions can result in unnecessary further injury. Theoretically, the physician's performance here must meet the requisite standard of care to avoid liability in a malpractice suit, another good reason for the physician to know a lot about the patient and work requirements before formulating recommendations. Various types of stress testing prior to return to work are now available, and, while outside the scope of this article, their use generates another set of medico-legal issues.

Disclosure of Abnormal Findings

When the treating physician identifies a previously undetected, potentially reversible abnormality, it is clear that his/her duty requires, at the very least, whatever is necessary to completely diagnose and treat the problem. The consultative or examining physician who has no specific involvement in the claimant's medical case, though, arguably has a duty to assure, at the very least, that the claimant promptly receives the benefit of this finding, and this requires some sort of notification. Some physicians disclose directly to the patient. Others disclose to the payer. In the latter case, the physician might request that the payer notify the physician, within a reasonable time, that it has disclosed the information to the appropriate individual and/or made reasonable recommendations regarding follow-up. The physician might add that failure to notify, as requested, will trigger his/her direct intervention. Ideally, this mechanism is established as a ground rule for physician-payer interaction, prior to consultation.

Disclosure of Previously Negligent, Injurious Acts

When the examining physician discovers a clearly negligent act which has resulted in injury, and which itself might be reversible or not, is there a duty to disclose? The answer varies with the jurisdiction, the facts of the case, and other factors. Increasingly, though, courts have expanded treating physicians' duty to disclose information of this sort,[67] and arguably this duty would extend to the pure physician-claimant relationship. Thus, evaluating physicians should be aware of this issue and its status in their jurisdiction.

Informed Consent in Disability Evaluations

While therapeutic interventions are not a part of evaluations, diagnostic tests are common. Theoretically, informed consent requirements would apply in disability evaluations when they would apply in a therapeutic physician-patient relationship. While some might argue that the claimant waives these requirements by submitting to an evaluation, a waiver argument might seem a thin defense for the evaluating cardiologist who did not properly inform the claimant about an exercise test and obtain consent, after the claimant suffers serious injury during the otherwise competently performed stress test and sues the physician for damages, alleging a breach of duty to obtain informed consent. In addition to reducing medico-legal risks, the proper use of informed consent as a clinical test probably increases the likelihood of a better evaluation.[68]

Reporting Occupational Hazards and Reportable Diseases

When an evaluating physician who is also the treating physician incidently detects a reportable disease or condition, it seems clear that his/her duty to report is not diluted simply because of the context of the examination. The nontreating evaluator is in a somewhat different position, once again, and even where that evaluator's duty is not clearly covered by statute the physician arguably would be violating the reporting statute if he/she made no attempt to have the condition reported. Moreover, theoretically this physician might be liable to third parties who suffered preventable injury because of the nondisclosure.

Reporting "reportable" occupational hazards identified in the course of an evaluation raises similar considerations. In general, before the physician decides not to report, he/she should investigate the legal status of these issues in the relevant jurisdiction.

Other Medico-Legal Issues in Disability Evaluation

The above discussion is by no means comprehensive or exhaustive, and is intended to acquaint participants in disability evaluations with some of the medico-legal issues that arise, rather than to describe the resolution of those issues. Other medico-legal issues requiring at least an awareness, and further analysis, follow.

Competence of the Evaluator

The evaluating physician arguably has at least as great a duty to perform a competent clinical assessment as the treating physician. This global duty includes the duty to take a full, relevant history, perform a targeted, competent physical examination, and employ whatever diagnostic modalities are indicated, including referral to the appropriate specialist. To the extent system or other constraints limit the evaluation, the opinion should be qualified by documenting the limitations. Increasingly it is recognized that competence in disability evaluation requires special knowledge, training and experience. Arguably, a physician whose qualifications and ability to participate competently in this arena are minimal would nevertheless be held to the standard of a physician with the requisite competence, in any suit alleging negligent performance of a disability evaluation. While no widely accepted measure of competence in "disability evaluation," nor generally recognized certifying body, exists, the creation and early success of the National Association of Disability Evaluating Physicians[69] is just one of many indications of a trend in that direction.

Physician's Liability for Employees' Negligent Errors

In general a physician-employer is liable for negligent errors on the part of secretarial staff and paramedical staff, including physician-assistants and nurse-practitioners, when the errors proximately cause injury to patients. One would expect the same principle of *respondeat superior* to apply in disability evaluations.

Other Issues

To what extent does the medico-legal report become part of the medical record? May the physician release a report, prepared and submitted to the plaintiff's attorney, to the defendant? What is the role of the evaluating physician as ordinary witness and expert witness? What disclosure by the treating physician/evaluating physician might violate the patient's right to confidentiality? What authorization for release will suffice when substance abuse or mental impairment is referred to in the record or the report? Must the physician allow an attorney to be present during an evaluation if the claimant consents?

CONCLUSION

The disability benefits matrix, albeit complex, is definable. Each component derives its three major characteristics from the matrix dimensions: disability concepts, processes and benefit packages. The vast medicine-law interface generates at least two major categories of issues. The first relates to identifying, describing and explaining impairments and their impact on functional capacity. The second arises from the physician-claimant relationship.

For physicians, in particular, participation in disability evaluation is a frustrating, tedious task, mostly because they lack fundamental knowledge and expertise in this area. In part this lack of competence stems from the scarcity of objective, valid and standardized approaches to medical evaluations in disability determinations. Moreover, if the art/science of assessing impairments is in its infancy, the status of many of the troubling medico-legal issues is gestational.

Nonetheless, tolerance of inadequate physician participation is fading as the implications of these inadequacies become more apparent. Comfortable, effective participation at the minimal legal risk requires a detailed and operational knowledge of the matrix and the attendant medico-legal issues.

REFERENCES

1. Battista, M.E. 1983. "Disability Assessment and the Family Physician." *J Fam Pract* 16:835.
2. Ziporyn, T. 1983. "Disability Evaluation: A Fledgling Science?" *JAMA* 250:873–880.
3. Singleton, W.T., and L.M. Debney. *Occupational Disability: The Approaches of Government, Industry and the Universities.* George A. Bogden and Son. 11–34.
4. U.S. Department of Health and Human Services (formerly HEW). 1977. *Defining Disability: A Cross Country Study.* HEW Pub. No. (SSA) 77-11853.
5. Bureau of Labor Statistics. July, 1980. *Major Programs.* Report No. 552, 32.
6. Veteran's Administration, Reports and Statistics Service. 1981. *Selected Compensation and Pension Data, by State of Residence* (hereinafter VA Report).
7. *Ibid.*
8. Darling-Hammond, L., and T.J. Kniesner. 1980. *The Law and Economics of Workers' Compensation.* The Institute for Civil Justice: The Rand Corporation, 4.
9. Ziporyn, 874.
10. VA Report.
11. Ziporyn, 874. This figure includes state supplementation for SSI as well as federal payments under SSI and SSDI.
12. Darling-Hammond, X.

13. *Ibid.*
14. Stander, I. 1982. "Current Trends in Workers' Compensation." *Law, Medicine and Health Care* (April), 70.
15. "Work Disability In The United States." U.S. DHHS, SSA Publication No. SSA 13-11978.
16. Title XVI of the Social Security Act.
17. Title II of the Social Security Act.
18. 1982. Request for Proposal Number SSA-RFP-82-0089. "Disability Determination Services (DDS) Cost Effectiveness Measurement," Attachment A, Appendix A, and Appendix B.
19. 1981. *Social Security Regulations: Rules for Determining Disability and Blindness.* U.S. DHHS, SSA Pub. No. 64-014 (June), 2.
20. *Ibid.*, 3.
21. *Ibid.*
22. 5 USC §8101 et seq.
23. Title IV of Federal Coal Mine Health and Safety Act, 30 USC 801.
24. 33 USC §901 et seq.
25. Darling-Hammond, 4.
26. *Ibid.*, 33.
27. *Ibid.*
28. U.S. Department of Labor. 1980. *Federal Injury Compensation.* Pamphlet CA-550, 17.
29. 1972. "Essential Recommendation R4.2 of the National Commission on State Workers' Compensation Laws." Report, U.S. Government Printing Office.
30. Darling-Hammond, X.
31. 1982. *Legislation Authorized Benefits without Adequate Evidence of Black Lung or Disability.* Report to the Congress by the Comptroller General, 1.
32. Request For Proposal (RFP) L/A 82-10. "Study of Medical Methods Used in Diagnosing Coal Workers' Pneumoconiosis," 3.
33. Darling-Hammond, 5.
34. *Ibid.*, xi.
35. *Ibid.*, from U.S. Department of Labor, Interim Report to Congress on Occupational Diseases, 67.
36. *Ibid.*, xii.
37. *Ibid.*, 5.
38. Stander, 69.
39. Veterans Administration. 1982. *Federal Benefits for Veterans and Dependents.* IS-1 Fact Sheet.
40. *Ibid.*
41. *Ibid.*
42. *Ibid.*
43. *Ibid.*
44. *Ibid.*
45. Battista, M.E. 1982. "How to Keep Disability Forms From Wasting Your Time." *Medical Economics* (August 23):128.

46. American Medical Association. *Guides to the Evaluation of Permanent Impairment.*
47. Department of Health and Human Services. *Disability Evaluation Under Social Security.*
48. Veterans Administration. *Physician's Guide to Disability Evaluation Examination.*
49. American Thoracic Society. *Evaluation of Impairment/Disability Secondary to Respiratory Disease.*
50. Gloss, D.S., and M.G. Wardle. 1982. "Reliability and Validity of American Medical Association: Guide to Ratings of Permanent Impairment." *JAMA* 248:2292–96.
51. Battista, M.E. "Responding to Administrative Requests for Your Opinion." *Physician's Management.*
52. U.S. Department of Labor. *Dictionary of Occupational Titles.* Washington, D.C.: Government Printing Office.
53. *Ibid.,* Appendix, "Physical Demands and Working Conditions."
54. *Ibid.*
55. *Ibid.*
56. Lehmann, T.R., and R.A. Brand. 1982. "Disability in the Patient with Low Back Pain." *Orthopedic Clinics of North America* 13:559–568.
57. LaDou, J., et al. "Cumulative Injury or Disease Claims: An Attempt to Define Employer's Liability for Workers' Compensation." *American Journal of Law and Medicine* 6(1):1–28.
58. *Ibid.,* 9.
59. *Ibid.,* 17.
60. Miller, C.N. 1981. "Recovery for Psychic Injuries under Workers' Compensation." *Law, Medicine and Health Care* (December):25.
61. *Ibid.,* 27.
62. *Ibid.,* 27.
63. For a discussion of apportionment, *see* LaDou, 25.
64. *See* Stander for a discussion of the mechanics of second injury funds.
65. Battista, M.E. 1983. "Optimizing the Role of the Primary Care Physician in the Rehabilitation Process." *Rehabilitation Forum* (Spring):1–8.
66. Battista, "Disability Assessment and the Family Physician."
67. LeBlang, T.R. 1981. "Disclosure of Injury and Illness: Responsibilities in Physician-Patient Relationship." *Law, Medicine and Health Care* (Sept.):4–7.
68. Battista, M.E. "Making 'Informed Consent' Work for You—And Your Practice." *Physician's Management.*
69. National Association of Disability Evaluating Physicians, chartered 1982, Ann Arbor, Michigan. The organization states its basic purpose as follows: "To provide for the enhancement and protection of professional standards in medical disability evaluation, and to provide a vehicle for obtaining information on, training for, and credentialling in scientifically-sound methods of *measuring* work capacity in relation to physical impairment."

Index

About the Editor

Dr. Wecht received his B.S. at the University of Pittsburgh, his M.D. at the University of Pittsburgh School of Medicine, his LL.B. at the University of Maryland School of Law, and his J.D. at the University of Pittsburgh School of Law. He is a Clinical Associate Professor of Pathology at the University of Pittsburgh Schools of Medicine and Dental Medicine. He is both a physician and an attorney, and is well-versed in medico-legal issues. In addition to his position as Adjunct Professor of Law at Duquesne University School of Law, he is the President and Director of the Pittsburgh Institute of Legal Medicine and a Charter Diplomate of the American Board of Law in Medicine. A Past President of the American College of Legal Medicine and the American Academy of Forensic Sciences, Dr. Wecht is the author or editor of over 230 publications, including a well-known three volume work entitled *Forensic Sciences.*

www.ingramcontent.com/pod-product-compliance
Ingram Content Group UK Ltd.
Pitfield, Milton Keynes, MK11 3LW, UK
UKHW020219041026
15470UKWH00012B/464

9 780275 901820